"the only true people"

"the only true people"

Linking Maya Identities Past and Present

EDITED BY

Bethany J. Beyyette AND Lisa J. LeCount

UNIVERSITY PRESS OF COLORADO

Boulder

© 2017 by University Press of Colorado

Published by University Press of Colorado
5589 Arapahoe Avenue, Suite 206C
Boulder, Colorado 80303

⁄⁄▲⊔⊐ The University Press of Colorado is a proud member of
The Association of American University Presses.

The University Press of Colorado is a cooperative publishing enterprise supported, in part, by
Adams State University, Colorado State University, Fort Lewis College, Metropolitan State
University of Denver, Regis University, University of Colorado, University of Northern Colorado,
Utah State University, and Western State Colorado University.

ISBN: 978-1-60732-566-6 (cloth)
ISBN: 978-1-60732-567-3 (ebook)

Library of Congress Cataloging-in-Publication Data

Names: Beyyette, Bethany J., editor. | LeCount, Lisa J. (Lisa Jeanne), 1955– editor.
Title: "The only true people" : linking Maya identities past and present / edited by Bethany J. Beyyette,
    Lisa J. LeCount.
Description: Boulder : University Press of Colorado, [2017]
Identifiers: LCCN 2016040704| ISBN 9781607325666 (cloth) | ISBN 9781607325673 (ebook)
Subjects: LCSH: Mayas—Ethnic identity.
Classification: LCC F1435.3.E72 O55 2017 | DDC 305.89742—dc23
LC record available at https://lccn.loc.gov/2016040704

KU An electronic version of this book is freely available, thanks to the support of libraries
working with Knowledge Unlatched. KU is a collaborative initiative designed to make
high-quality books open access for the public good. The open access ISBN for this book is
978-1-60732-699-1. More information about the initiative and links to the open-access version can be
found at www.knowledgeunlatched.org.

Front cover illustrations, top to bottom: Motul Dictionary (courtesy of the John Carter Brown
Library); Mount Maloney type bowl from Actuncan (photo by Lisa LeCount); Caste War defense
work in Iturbide (photo by Ute Schüren); Creation Tablet from Palenque (rubbing by Merle Greene
Robertson); Caste War fortifications in Bacalar (photo by Ute Schüren); Talking Cross in Felipe
Carrillo Puerto (photo by Wolfgang Gabbert)

Contents

List of Figures   vii

List of Maps   ix

List of Tables   xi

Foreword
     Jonathan D. Hill   xiii

Chapter 1. INTRODUCTION: ON CONSTRUCTING A SHARED
     UNDERSTANDING OF HISTORICAL PASTS AND NEARING FUTURES
     Bethany J. Beyyette   3

Part I: MAYA IDENTITIES OF THE PRESENT
AND THE ETHNOGRAPHIC PAST

Chapter 2. REIMAGING THE WORLD: MAYA RELIGIOUS PRACTICES
     AND THE CONSTRUCTION OF ETHNICITY IN A MESOAMERICAN FRAME
     C. Mathews Samson   27

Chapter 3. ETHNOEXODUS: ESCAPING MAYALAND
     Juan Castillo Cocom, Timoteo Rodriguez, and McCale Ashenbrener   47

Chapter 4. ITZAJ AND MOPAN IDENTITIES IN PETÉN, GUATEMALA
   Charles Andrew Hofling   73

Chapter 5. MAYA ETHNOGENESIS AND GROUP IDENTITY IN YUCATÁN,
1500–1900
   Matthew Restall and Wolfgang Gabbert   91

Chapter 6. DIFFERENTIATION AMONG MAYAN SPEAKERS: EVIDENCE
   FROM COMPARATIVE LINGUISTICS AND HIEROGLYPHIC TEXTS
   Martha J. Macri   131

Part II: ARCHAEOLOGICAL EXPLORATIONS OF
   IDENTITY CONSTRUCTION

Chapter 7. ESTABLISHING THE PRECONDITIONS FOR ETHNOGENESIS
   AMONG THE CLASSIC MAYA OF THE UPPER BELIZE RIVER VALLEY
   Lisa J. LeCount   157

Chapter 8. HE'S MAYA, BUT HE'S NOT MY BROTHER: EXPLORING THE
   PLACE OF ETHNICITY IN CLASSIC MAYA SOCIAL ORGANIZATION
   Damien B. Marken, Stanley P. Guenter, and David A. Freidel   187

Chapter 9. CONSIDERING THE EDGE EFFECT: ETHNOGENESIS AND
   CLASSIC PERIOD SOCIETY IN THE SOUTHEASTERN MAYA AREA
   Marcello A. Canuto and Ellen E. Bell   219

Chapter 10. COPÁN, HONDURAS: A MULTIETHNIC MELTING POT
   DURING THE LATE CLASSIC?
   Rebecca Storey   243

Chapter 11. CONCLUSION: IDENTITY, NETWORKS, AND ETHNICITY
   Edward Schortman   265

   List of Contributors   279
   Index   281

Figures

2.1   Mural painted by Marcello Jiménez, plaza of Felipe Carrillo
Puerto, Quintana Roo   29

3.1.   The Quincunx   54

4.1.   Yukatekan branch of the Mayan language family   74

5.1.   Motul Dictionary   95

5.2.   Chilam Balam of Chumayel   96

5.3.   Caste War defense work in Iturbide   114

5.4.   Caste War fortifications in Bacalar   115

5.5.   Talking Cross in Felipe Carrillo Puerto   117

6.1.   Mayan languages of the Yukatekan and Greater Tzeltalan
subfamilies   133

6.2.   a–b. Four spellings of yotoch 'house'; glyphs for 'fire'   140

6.3.   Creation Tablet from Palenque   141

6.4.   a–b. Glyphs for Calakmul with AA1 ka; Kan B'ahlam's name
with AA1 ka   142

6.5.   a–b. Glyphs ba'-ka-b'a spelling the title b'akab'; glyphs te-ku-yu
spelling the title tekuy(u)   143

6.6.	a–c. Graphemes for ti: 3M2.1, 3M2.2, BV3; d–j. Graphemes for ta: 3M3, 1B1.2, 1B1.1, 1B1.3, XQB, YM2, ZS1	145
6.7.	Naranjo, Stele 24, front	148
6.8.	Naranjo, Stela 24, back, D4–D7	149
6.9.	Chichén Itzá, Las Monjas, Lintel 2aA C1	151
7.1.	Mount Maloney Type bowl from Actuncan	173
7.2.	Upper Belize River valley burial practices at Actuncan Group 1	174
8.1.	Schematic of vertical and horizontal interaction networks operating across the Maya region	191
8.2.	Temple plans at Palenque through time: Temple Olvidado, Temple V, Temple XVII, Temple XII, Temple XXI	196
8.3.	Perspective cross-section of Temple of the Sun, Palenque, showing interior symbolic sweatbath	197
8.4.	Early attestation of the –wan suffix from Palenque's Temple of the Inscriptions East Tablet, in a passage relating the accession of K'inich Janaab' Pakal I	199
8.5.	Early attestation of –wan suffix from Dos Pilas Stela 8	200
8.6.	Two Palenque emblem glyphs from the Palace Tablet	201
10.1.	Dental measures taken on Maya skeletal samples	249

Maps

4.1.	Lowland Mayan languages, AD 1500	75
4.2.	Mayan languages after 1700	76
7.1.	Upper Belize River valley and sites mentioned in the text	168
7.2.	Site of Actuncan	171
9.1.	Southeast Maya area	224
9.2.	Settlement in the El Paraíso Valley, western Honduras	226
9.3.	El Paraíso site map	227
9.4.	El Cafetal site map	229

Tables

4.1. Contact with Q'eqchi'   81

4.2. Contact with Eastern Ch'olan   81

4.3. Reconstructable for Proto-Yukatekan   82

4.4. Southern versus Northern Yukatekan   82

4.5. Lexicon only in Mopan and Itzaj   83

4.6. Lexicon unique to Mopan   84

5.1. Uses of the term *Maya* in Colonial Mayan–language sources   93

5.2. Maya terms of self-description containing possible ethnic implications   103

5.3. Ethnic diversity of Mesoamericans brought into Yucatán in the 1540s   107

6.1. Person markers of Greater Tzeltalan and Yukatekan languages   134

6.2. Person markers grouped person markers according to similar source
      patterns   137

8.1. Common archaeological measures to distinguish class   193

10.1. Copán 9N-8 Compound skeletal sample polar teeth measures   252

10.2. Copán rural skeletal sample polar teeth measures   253

10.3. K'axob skeletal sample polar teeth measures   254

10.4. Comparison of mortuary treatment in Late Classic Copán   259

Foreword

JONATHAN D. HILL

In *"The Only True People": Linking Maya Identities Past and Present*, Bethany Beyyette and Lisa LeCount have assembled the works of ethnologists, linguists, and archaeologists to critically rethink the complex interrelations between contemporary Maya identities and those known through archaeological studies of ancient Mayan sites. In the waning years of the twentieth century and the first decades of the twenty-first century, indigenous Mayan peoples have shown a remarkable ability to embrace new technologies and create new forms of political organization for representing their interests among themselves and at state, regional, national, and global levels. These indigenous forms of political and cultural creativity are unfolding today in contexts of the globalizing nation-states of Latin America and across the long-term historical processes of Colonial and national state expansion as well as associated traumatic losses of life, autonomy, land, and other resources.

Rapid intergenerational shifts are unfolding in villages, towns, and cities across Mesoamerica and the rest of Latin America as indigenous peoples move from oral traditions to literacy and from word of mouth to the Internet in a matter of years. Researching these contemporary transformations and the emergence of new forms of identity politics has become a rich field of study for ethnologists and historians (see, e.g., Warren and Jackson 2002; Ramos 1998). Because of their concern for documenting ethnogenesis and other long-term historical processes, including not only socio-cultural and historical but also linguistic and archaeological lines of inquiry, the essays that make up *"The Only True People"* are directly relevant to the rapidly

DOI: 10.5876/9781607325673.c000

changing cultural politics of indigeneity in Mesoamerica. The past lives on in the present in a diversity of ways, and the struggles of today's Mayan peoples to create new political and cultural spaces for persisting within the globalizing nation-states of Mesoamerica are both shaped by and give new form and meaning to cultural transformations that have been under way in the region for at least two millennia.

As wrong as it would be to ignore the momentous historical events and forces of Colonial and national state expansions in Latin America while trying to understand contemporary indigenous forms of creativity and identity, it would be just as incorrect to assert that these contemporary practices have little or no relevance for understanding long-term processes that have been unfolding in Mesoamerica for at least two millennia and that "pre-contact" Mayan peoples lived in some pristine, "prehistoric" state of nature. The concept of ethnogenesis, first used in a Latin American context by Norman Whitten (1976) and later developed in *History, Power, and Identity* (Hill 1996) and other works (Anderson 1999; Galloway 1995; Restall 2004; Hornborg 2005; Fennell 2007; Hornborg and Hill 2011), offers a way out of the essentializing of "peoples without history," whether in past or present times. This approach is rooted in Fredrik Barth's (1969) pioneering approach to social differentiation as a process of ethnic boundary marking and also builds upon Edward and Rosamond Spicer's (1992) concept of "persistent identity systems" that have endured across centuries of Colonial domination.

More recently, James Clifford (2004:20) has drawn upon ethnogenesis and related concepts to argue that emerging indigenous American identities are better understood as a creative process of "authentically remaking" rather than "a wholly new genesis, a made-up identity, a postmodernist 'simulacrum,' or the rather narrowly political 'invention of tradition' analyzed by Hobsbawm and Ranger..., with its contrast of lived custom and artificial tradition." *"The Only True People"* expands upon Clifford's characterization of ethnogenesis as a process of authentically remaking new social identities through creatively rediscovering and refashioning components of "tradition," such as oral narratives, written texts, and material artifacts. We can see this ethnogenetic process of authentically remaking identities at work not only in the efforts of contemporary Mayan peoples struggling to refashion identities through ancestral languages, attachments to specific geographic places, and shared senses of history but also in material artifacts from Late and Terminal Classic Maya society that demonstrate an escalation in the use of diacritics and boundary-marking practices (see LeCount, this volume).

Ethnogenesis, when defined in broad terms as "a concept encompassing peoples' simultaneously cultural and political struggles to create enduring identities in general contexts of radical change and discontinuity" (Hill 1996:1) as well as peoples' historical consciousness of these struggles, allows for an integrated historical, linguistic, and archaeological approach to studies of pre- and post-contact transformations of indigenous Mayan social identities and cultural landscapes. While acknowledging the profound changes brought about by European colonization and the rise of independent nation-states, the chapters of *"The Only True People"* also avoid essentializing approaches that categorize pre-contact Mayans as "peoples without history" or post-contact indigenous identities as merely artificial "reinventions" of past cultures.

"The Only True People" addresses these theoretical issues and makes a strong case for the value of integrating ethnology, linguistics, and archaeology as a means for generating new knowledge and lines of inquiry that are inaccessible to scholars working in any one of these specializations in isolation from the others. The kinds of material artifacts Mayan peoples use in creating distinct ethnic identities are often the most likely to perish rather than preserve in the archaeological record. The goal of establishing a clear-cut ethnic habitus, whether for contemporary Mayan peoples or in the archaeological remains of past Mayan communities, remains elusive or worse, since different groups wear similar clothing, have similar work habits, eat the same foods, and construct identically shaped houses. Ethnic identities are instead more likely to be defined through markers far less likely to show up in the archaeological record: "cultural elements such as language, place of residence, and a sense of common history" (see Marken, Guenter, and Friedel, this volume). This heightens the need for collaboration with ethnographers who can explore what kinds of artifacts are most likely to indicate ethnic differences and how they are made, exchanged, and used in public contexts.

The cross-disciplinary collaboration found in *"The Only True People"* also contributes to the growing awareness in anthropology that material things and associated ideologies of materiality are often radically different in indigenous American societies than in societies with capitalist regimes of value. The objects and artifacts unearthed by archaeologists are likely to have had a plethora of different meanings and degrees of agency for the people who made and used them. Although many of these differences of subjectivity and agentivity are irretrievable from the archaeological record, ethnographic studies of the different ways of being a thing in contemporary Mayan communities can provide guidelines for hypothesizing about which kinds of things are most likely to become subjectified and to be regarded as having agentive powers (Santos-Granero 2009a). Researchers working on similar issues in Amazonian South America (Basso 1985; Santos-Granero 2009b) have found that artifacts associated with communicative powers, such as sacred wind instruments or shamanic stones, are usually regarded as the most agentive. For the Mayan communities discussed in *"The Only True People,"* perhaps the increased importance of diacritics indicating attachments to specific geographic locales (see LeCount, this volume) provides an example of artifacts having heightened communicative and agentive powers.

The chapters in *"The Only True People"* also demonstrate that collaborative efforts among ethnologists, linguists, and archaeologists can identify possible correlations between linguistic affiliations and socio-cultural practices in ways that avoid the essentializing and spatializing of such correlations and that rigorously embrace both reflexive awareness of power relations inherent in the construction of scientific knowledge and the central importance of studying and comparing language histories (Hill and Santos-Granero 2002). Adherences among material cultures, language families, and other markers of ethnicity can be discerned in archaeological, linguistic, ethnological, and historical records, but it cannot be assumed that such correlations are inevitable or unchanging. A more nuanced, historically dynamic perspective "suggests that language affiliation and material culture tend to stick together, not because there is any sticky glue involved but because both are transmitted over similar channels. Depending on circumstances, this 'null' condition may be reinforced, actively resisted, or casually ignored" (DeBoer 2011:95). As anthropologists, we need to study these processes of convergence and divergence among languages, material cultures, and ethnic identities.

Finally, *"The Only True People"* contributes to a growing recognition of the need for anthropologists to understand how they identify themselves both within and beyond academia, how they "divide up the continuum of human cultural variation into analytical units," and how "power plays a large part in determining in what ways and by whom cultural variation is compartmentalized" (see Schortman, this volume). The problem here is a specific example of the more general need for cultivating a critical reflexive awareness of the historical roots of such Western scientific concepts as "language family," the use of which historically coincided with the political subjugation of New World and other non-European peoples and with the Enlightenment project of rationalist social theories. The very notion of "family" is based on a metaphor of biological relatedness that tends to place emphasis on exclusivity, fixity, and boundedness and to shift attention away from inclusivity, fluidity, and historical engagement across language differences. The role of language documentation and classification as tools for political subjugation during Colonial history cannot be overestimated, and they have continued in that historical role throughout the modern period of nation-state expansion in Latin America. With its focus on the Mayan peoples of Mesoamerica, *"The Only True People"* makes important substantive, methodological, and theoretical contributions to these challenging issues.

REFERENCES CITED

Anderson, Gary. 1999. *The Indian Southwest, 1580–1830: Ethnogenesis and Reinvention*. Norman: University of Oklahoma Press.

Barth, Fredrik, ed. 1969. *Ethnic Groups and Boundaries: The Social Organization of Cultural Difference*. Boston: Little, Brown.

Basso, Ellen B. 1985. *A Musical View of the Universe: Kalapalo Myth and Ritual Performances*. Philadelphia: University of Pennsylvania Press.

Clifford, James. 2004. "Looking Several Ways: Anthropology and Native Heritage in Alaska." *Current Anthropology* 45 (1): 5–30. http://dx.doi.org/10.1086/379634.

DeBoer, Warren. 2011. "Deep Time, Big Space: An Archaeologist Skirts the Topic at Hand." In *Ethnicity in Ancient Amazonia: Reconstructing Past Identities from Archaeology, Linguistics, and Ethnohistory*, ed. Alf Hornborg and Jonathan D. Hill, 75–98. Boulder: University Press of Colorado.

Fennell, Christopher. 2007. *Crossroads and Cosmologies: Diasporas and Ethnogenesis in the New World*. Gainesville: University Press of Florida.

Galloway, Patricia. 1995. *Seventeenth Century Overtures to Contact: Choctaw Genesis 1500–1700*. Lincoln: University of Nebraska Press.

Hill, Jonathan D. 1996. "Introduction: Ethnogenesis in the Americas, 1492–1992." In *History, Power, and Identity: Ethnogenesis in the Americas, 1492–1992*, ed. Jonathan D. Hill, 1–19. Iowa City: University of Iowa Press.

Hill, Jonathan D., and Fernando Santos-Granero, eds. 2002. *Comparative Arawakan Histories: Rethinking Language Family and Culture Area in Amazonia*. Urbana: University of Illinois Press.

Hornborg, Alf. 2005. "Ethnogenesis, Regional Integration, and Ecology in Prehistoric Amazonia." *Current Anthropology* 46 (4): 589–620. http://dx.doi.org/10.1086/431530.

Hornborg, Alf, and Jonathan D. Hill, eds. 2011. *Ethnicity in Ancient Amazonia: Reconstructing Past Identities from Archaeology, Linguistics, and Ethnohistory*. Boulder: University Press of Colorado.

Ramos, Alcida. 1998. *Indigenism: Ethnic Politics in Brazil*. Madison: University of Wisconsin Press.

Restall, Matthew. 2004. "Maya Ethnogenesis." *Journal of Latin American Anthropology* 9 (1): 64–89. http://dx.doi.org/10.1525/jlca.2004.9.1.64.

Santos-Granero, Fernando. 2009a. "Introduction: Amerindian Constructional Views of the World." In *The Occult Life of Things: Native Amazonian Theories of Materiality and Personhood*, ed. Fernando Santos-Granero, 1–29. Tucson: University of Arizona Press.

Santos-Granero, Fernando, ed. 2009b. *The Occult Life of Things: Native Amazonian Theories of Materiality and Personhood*. Tucson: University of Arizona Press.

Spicer, Edward, and Rosamond B. Spicer. 1992. "The Nations of a State." *Boundary 2* 19 (3): 26–48. http://dx.doi.org/10.2307/303547.

Warren, Kay, and Jean Jackson, eds. 2002. *Indigenous Movements, Self-Representation, and the State in Latin America*. Austin: University of Texas Press.

Whitten, Norman E., Jr. 1976. *Sacha Runa: Ethnicity and Adaptation of Ecuadorian Jungle Quichua*. Urbana: University of Illinois Press.

"the only true people"

1

Introduction

On Constructing a Shared Understanding of Historical Pasts and Nearing Futures

BETHANY J. BEYYETTE

The invention of the Maya' could be attributed to Maya scholarship: the archaeologists, anthropologists, etc. who started to use this label for cultural horizons and continuities that interested them. Some of their numbers implicitly ascribe to these continuities an imagined Mayan essence transcending history. (Schackt 2001:11)

This goal of this volume is to evaluate views of Maya history and prehistory and more accurately characterize the uniqueness of the people called Mayas by exploring the construction of their identities, past and present. This volume brings together scholars representing a wide variety of Maya studies, including archaeologists, linguists, ethnographers, ethnohistorians, historians, epigraphers, and sociologists. Each author evaluates the distinctiveness of identifiable socio-cultural units, which we collectively refer to as "ethnicities." Together the contributors investigate ethnicity at a number of Maya places from the northern reaches of Yucatán to the Southern Periphery, from modern day to the Classic period. Each author challenges the notion of ethnically homogeneous "Maya peoples" for his or her region and chronology and has been asked to define how his or her work contributes to the definition of "ethnicity" for ancient Maya society. By addressing the social constructs and conditions behind Maya ethnicity, past and present, the volume contributes to our understanding of ethnicity as a complex set of relationships among people who live in real and imagined communities, as well as between people separated by cultural and physical boundaries.

How do we explore the histories that have contributed to ethnic formations of Maya peoples? We propose that the best way to understand and identify different

DOI: 10.5876/9781607325673.c001

identities is through the study of diachronic cultural processes in a regional perspective that acknowledge identities through the use of language, community, history, myth, and politics, as well as the material reflections of these, such as dress, pottery styles, political emblems, scripts, and architecture. Contributions in the volume go beyond issues of materialization and create a two-way discussion that applies ethnographic conceptualizations of ethnicity to the archaeological record, as well as identifies the contributions of archaeological research for a better understanding of contemporary Maya identities.

Archaeologists and anthropologists currently raise two major issues with the conceptualization and utilization of ethnicity. The first problem concerns the simple definition of *ethnicity*. How do different ethnic groups define themselves? To what scale, scope, and manner must they differentiate themselves from others to be members? How does expression change in the time-space continuum? How do these expressions alter anthropologists' external analytical explorations of ethnicity? There is no clear understanding of what ethnicity is for all of human society, and many authors err in not clearly defining what they mean by the term when discussing the topic. The second problem focuses attention directly on identifying ethnic differences. Even if we can define what ethnicity means and meant for present and past society, when and how is it expressed? When is ethnicity marked by overt expressions of group membership, and, conversely, when is it hidden from view? What are the processes that transform ethnic identities and their expressions?

It is not the intended goal of this volume to reach an overarching single definition of what contributes to Maya ethnic identities and how they are expressed, as these varied according to history and place. The goal is to conceptualize the processes behind ethnogenesis and ethnoexodus, as suggested by Cocom and Rodriguez (this volume). The chapters in this volume are written by ethnographers, historians, ethnohistorians, sociologists, linguists, epigraphers, and archaeologists from a variety of different anthropological and *ethnic* backgrounds, including European, American, Cherokee, Mexicano, and Yukateko. No two authors share identical views of Maya identity and ethnogenesis; nor do they rely on the same approaches and literature. Yet each shares the aim of better understanding human behavior and the forces that have shaped the history and future of Maya peoples. This volume is a multidisciplinary investigation into the possibilities of a multilingual and multiethnic landscape, past and present.

DEFINITIONS

It is common in anthropological discussions to use the term *ethnicity* to describe social identity. Kunstadter (1979) defines an "ethnic group" as a set of individuals with mutual interests based on shared understandings and cultural values. Ethnic identity is described as a permanent and fundamental aspect of human identity (Banks 1996:185), as well as a strategic conscious construct used to manipulate groups for social, political, and economic ends. Characteristics that unify groups under a common ethnic identity include common descent (van den Berghe 1986), shared experiences and social practices (Geertz 1973:109), and shared cultural attributes such as dress, bodily adornment, architecture, and language.

Most ethnographers, linguists, and ethnohistorians consider cultural differences, the maintenance of these divisions, and the functional role in both social and political landscapes as evidence of ethnic formation. Yet from an archaeological standpoint, "ethnicity" is not commonly used in reference to material culture and the people who produced it; nor is it given much explanation in theoretical discussions of the organization and complexity of ancient societies. Most anthropologists would agree that *ethnicity* expresses a shift to multicultural, multiethnic interactive contexts where attention is focused on group dynamics marked to some degree by social and cultural commonality. Cohen (1978) defined ethnicity as a series of nesting dichotomizations of inclusiveness and exclusiveness, similar to a social distance scale. In Cohen's model, ethnic boundaries are not stable and enduring. Although each group continually strives to maintain distinctiveness, identity remains fluid and shifting.

Knapp (2001) divides anthropological approaches to ethnicity into three categories: primordialist, instrumental, and situational. The primordialist view holds that ethnicity is a permanent and essential condition of human nature. As such, the members of the group have a deep-rooted sense of identity. The instrumental approach states that ethnicity is a construct created to bring people together for a common (political or economic) purpose. It is motivated, goal-driven. Situational ethnicity is one in which members essentially choose their group affiliation, based on need or want.

The deep-seated differences in these theoretical approaches are numerous. Among those discussed in this volume is the distinction between groups rooted and tied to specific geographic locations (Barth 1969) and those that are not spatially bounded (Appadurai 1991; Brettell 2006). While older models position ethnicities in their homelands, later approaches consider people living outside their homelands. In the modern era, these are most often transnational groups and diaspora. However, the application of diaspora is relevant to historical approaches as well, as these are communities of people displaced from their homelands as a result of economic, social, and political forces. Gupta and Ferguson (1992) caution against conceiving "communities" as distinct entities or places, as these are often the result of cultural misunderstanding.

Another theoretical difference is the application of goal-oriented identity expression. When is ethnic display socially, politically, economically, or otherwise beneficial? Bucholtz and Hall (2005) discuss identity as encompassing both macro-level demographic categories and local cultural positions. They explore how people position themselves in opposition to certain others and evaluate the identity positions that are available. From this, they question which identities are chosen, note the active participation, and indicate for what reasons. These are referred to as relational identities. Knapp's (2001) instrumental approach also posits ethnic identity as an active construction aimed at a certain goal.

This is closely tied to situational ethnicity, which is also geared at specific needs or wants of the community but is perhaps more fluid and changing. Investigating situational constructs of ethnicity is different than goal-oriented approaches, as these approaches also take into consideration the times and circumstances when either outside or state-level governance removes the ability to construct distinct identities. Here it is not merely a question of when it is beneficial to display ethnicity or, as is often the case, multiple ethnicities but also when the right and ability to do so has been denied.

No single approach has sufficient explanatory power to account for the complexities of ethnicity and ethnic group formation (Hostettler 2004). Is ethnicity deep-rooted or goal-oriented? Is it controlled by elites, or do members situationally place themselves into groups? To polarize approaches to ethnicity and identity oversimplifies the issue. To understand group membership, we must understand basic principles of group membership, why groups expand or contract, and when membership is exclusive or inclusive (Cohen 1978).

DEFINING BOUNDARIES

A problem faced by those studying ethnicity is the issue of "unit." Ancient ethnic groups tend to be thought of in terms of majorities, yet contradictorily they are tied in modern times to notions of minorities, especially remote tribes, and indigenous peoples of the Third World. There is a problem not only with scale but also of the components of group composition in time and space.

Groups, be they political, social, economic, religious, or ethnic, are neither isolated nor self-contained; they are created and sustained through interaction and shared markers of affiliation (Barth 1969). All form a kind of supra-ordinate, multidimensional entity. The difference between these types of group affiliation is more an issue of scale than of different kinds of formation processes.

Ethnicities are anchored to geographic locations (Dietler 1994), as one of the markers for ethnic membership is claiming a shared ancestral homeland. Yet they may be found dispersed away from this homeland. Although they may be deeply rooted geographically (and even socially), they are not timeless (Carrier 1992), and evidence of shared belonging may be visible in multiple geographic locales. Researchers must continually remind themselves they are studying *these* people in *this* time and not inaccurately impose named ethnicities on particular groups (ibid.; Cohen 1978).

As with many things anthropological, the key to understanding identity is *context*. The understanding of context must begin with first discerning and apprehending local culture histories, mythic histories, power relations, and the politics of historical construction (Cohen 1978; Friedman 1992; Santos-Granero 1986; Staats 1996). There is a Western tendency to divide myth, history, and political discourse (Warren and Jackson 2003), but if we are to understand the formation, growth, and disintegration of specific identities, this tendency must be abandoned.

Context determines the type of in-group markers, overt or covert, that are displayed or made visible. If the context is framed in terms of situational advantage of differences, more overt markers may be expected. If context is framed in terms of dominance and discrimination, covert identity markers are more likely to be enacted, posing a problem for some anthropologists who may not be able to as readily identify covert markers. Overt markers are such things as dress, language, action, and style. Covert markers include blood, heritage, and history. Both types of markers, although not equally identifiable, are equally important. Behavior, ideas, material culture, and values must first be understood in their own contexts before we can deconstruct their significance (Cohen 1978).

ANTHROPOLOGICAL STUDIES OF MAYA ETHNICITIES

In this section, I discuss contributions to ethnic studies by ethnohistorians and ethnographers, followed by a detailed discussion of ethnic studies in archaeology. Archaeology is the most contested sub-discipline of anthropology in which to examine topics of ethnic identity. The heavy focus here on archaeological formation of ethnic affiliation and attribution results from the controversy of ethnic studies as a viable topic of research for archaeologists. This volume is framed by cultural approaches to ethnicity, which are in themselves complex and at times problematic, and their application to investigations of ancient ethnicities.

Ethnohistoric and Ethnographic Studies of Maya Ethnicities

Ethnohistoric and ethnographic accounts indicate that the historic Maya area was composed of multiple competing ethnic and political groups with distinctive senses of social identity. While there are examples of groups that shared superordinate identities across different Maya polities, there is no evidence that people held an explicit identity as "Maya" (Restall 2004). What evidence is there for group and individual identity? Restall states that one is the community, or *cah*. Another is patronym group. Although not specifically addressed in Restall's paper, language is another strong indicator of shared identity. Language is particularly powerful because it unites people beyond locality and creates feelings of shared belonging across different Maya communities. Further, Gabbert (2004) notes that while there are not different names for competing ethnic groups, there are different Mayan language terms for commoner and foreigner (*macehual* and *dzul*, respectively). The term for foreigner alludes to differences in lifestyle and status, particularly expressing the social distance to the speaker. This distinction can be recognized in a variety of ways, including dress, surname, and language.

Farriss (1984) addresses the effects of Spanish Colonial rule from the perspective of the Yukatek Maya. She explores the ways Yukatek Maya were able to sustain their traditional cultural lifeways longer than other Maya groups prior to the eighteenth century. This is an important piece because it recognizes important cultural differences between Maya groups. It also distinguishes different Maya practices and gives a glimpse of the diversity of Maya traditions in historic times.

Wasserstrom (1983), in contrast, cautions against being overly rigorous in defining cultural boundaries. He argues that the cultural diversity in Chiapas is far overestimated and frankly a-historical. He is criticized for his "obliviousness to native peoples' own interpretation of their historical circumstances" (Gossen 1985:576) and what I would argue is naïveté about the very real cultural boundaries that result from differential access to wealth. That said, he is right in his criticism of overreliance on Colonial records, which are not unbiased documents, and he makes the case for the use of regional analysis when clear boundaries have yet to be drawn by scholars.

While most ethnographies contribute to the discussion of identities, some specifically address the complexities of Maya identities. Watanabe (1992) explores the Mam-speaking Maya of Western Highland Guatemala. He describes how Chimlatecos locally define themselves in contrast to other Maya in the region and explores contexts that led to cultural change. Wilson's (1995) work with the Q'eqchi'-speaking Maya of Alta Verapas contributes to the discussion of post-Colonial cultural change, and explores ethnogenesis in an effort to create a pan-Q'eqchi' ethnic identity in the modern era. Finally, Montejo (2005) examines identity politics among the Maya in Guatemala and presents different forms of "resistance leadership" that have arisen in an attempt to maintain cultural traditions. He provides an excellent discussion of Maya diversity in terms of ideology and approach to identity construction.

Although ethnic groups can arise independently through phylogenetic processes involving parallel descent of genes, language, and culture (Kirch and Green 2001; Ortman 2012; Shennan 2002), in multicultural landscapes they arise through the cultural interactions that result in the combining of bits and pieces of preexisting practices into novel arrangements (Moore 1996:30). Hill's (1996) volume on ethnogenesis in the Americas provides an in-depth study of Arawak peoples. This volume was the inspiration for the present book, as it brought together scholars from various fields and addressed ways of being Arawak from modern, ethnohistoric, and archaeological perspectives. It also provides an excellent overview of ethnogenesis, the building of cultural and ethnic identities by colonized or otherwise oppressed people. The volume provides a synthesis of struggles to exist and shared experiences of powerlessness and marginalization of cultural minorities. It also highlights the regaining of self-determination of indigenous peoples and the contexts that present opportunities for change. Voss (2008) continues the discussion of ethnogenesis, applying it archaeologically to the people who lived and worked at El Presidio de San Francisco. She presents ethnogenesis as not only a useful concept for archaeologists but a recognizable pattern to be observed in the archaeological record through the investigation of landscape, architecture, and material culture. Hu's (2013) more recent work nicely summarizes past and present archaeological approaches to ethnogenesis, providing an excellent overview of the contributions of scholars who have attempted to apply this difficult concept to the archaeological record.

What has been lacking in Maya studies is a proper contextualization of ongoing overt political struggles of modern and pre-modern Maya groups (Castañeda 2004). Modern peoples of southern Mesoamerica have different pre-Conquest histories and geographies. They also have different histories of conquest, colonization, independence, and incorporation into larger nation-states (see, for example, ibid.). Yet archaeologists, linguists, and some social anthropologists have used the general term *Maya* to lump together members of more than thirty related but distinct language groups (Grofe 2005:1) distributed over a wide area and a variety of different environments. Embracing the encompassing and distorting label of *Maya* imposes a unified ethnic history on people who have not necessarily thought of themselves as "Maya," neither in the past nor in the present (Hostettler 2004:193). As a result, both Western and non-Western people have assigned and taken for granted a single identity to a heterogeneous population (ibid.:189). Assuming an essential unity of ethnic, cultural, and social identity among all Mayas is a Western construction. While not denying a pan-Maya movement that has been in the works for several decades, we must realize that this movement is a new kind of cultural politics (Castañeda 2004). Maya identities have been and continue to be politically, not historically, rooted (Restall 2004).

ARCHAEOLOGICAL STUDIES OF MAYA ETHNICITIES

In literature concerning Maya archaeology, the ancient people of southern Mesoamerica are frequently and inappropriately viewed as a single ethnic identity. Ethnic continuity is often left unquestioned across vastly different highland and lowland landscapes and three millennia of prehistory, which archaeologists characterize as socio-political dynamic. In contrast, the "Maya" are compared with a variety of different yet competing "Mexican" groups of the north, be they Olmec, Zapotecan, Teotihuacano, Toltec, or Mexica. This distinction alone confuses concepts of pre-Columbian identities and ethnicity with modern-day nation-states. After over a century of research in the Maya area, the Maya remain "mysterious" and living outside of time (Castañeda 2004).

Understanding the multiethnic fabric of Classic period Maya societies has not been an area of intense interest in archaeological research. Some archaeologists are beginning to realize that regional variations indicate a multiethnic environment, despite similarities in elite material culture. While there were many similarities among sites, contexts, and the built environment, there were also significant regional variations in architecture, ceramic assemblages, iconographic styles, and hieroglyphic writing (see, for example, Sabloff and Henderson 1993; Morris 2004:9). These variations existed not only during later Maya prehistory but throughout the Preclassic, Classic, and Postclassic periods as well.

Greater familiarity with Jones's (1997) work on the archaeology of ethnicity would greatly facilitate more open conversations about identity research in archaeology. As argued here, Jones (ibid.) points out that the first issue in archaeological explorations of ethnicity is often definition. There is no single concept of ethnicity, and Jones explores subjectivist versus objectivist approaches as well as primordialist versus instrumentalist approaches, citing lack of consensus by socio-cultural anthropologists as a primary source of contention. Yet Jones emphasizes the importance of observable patterns as socially and culturally meaningful and therefore accessible as spheres of investigation. We attempt to address this problem in this volume by having each author explicitly contextualize ethnicity for his or her own examples to provide a more clear understanding of how identities can be constructed and reconstructed from archaeological data.

Volumes such as *The Kowoj* by Rice and Rice (2009) are invaluable contributions to the archaeological study of identity, as the contributors use archaeological, bioarchaeological, historic, linguistic, and ethnographic data to reconstruct the Kowoj. This volume is broadly integrative and provides a clear image of Kowoj people and society, and it should be a model for scholars in all regions. Similarly, Sachse's (2006) volume on Maya ethnicities explores ethnic identity construction from the

Preclassic to the modern era. Graham's (2006) chapter is especially pertinent to this discussion, as she investigates how the concept of ethnicity can be useful to archaeologists. While she maintains that finding ethnic groups archaeologically may remain elusive, the archaeologists in this volume have striven to provide data that do allow for the recognition of ethnic groups in the archaeological record.

Archaeological investigations can be expected to contribute to our understandings of ethnicity. First, ethnicity studies in archaeology can contribute to studies of the structural relationships that exist between elites and commoners, centers and their supporting communities, dominant and subordinate regional polities, and intra-regional populations. It is important to define the ways structures of power and control can be identified archaeologically, both in terms of primary power brokers and those whom they control. At the smallest scale of analysis, elites can be defined in contrast to commoners, since they are generally considered influential agents concerned with power and control (G. Marcus 1983), but they existed in larger dynamic networks with other subordinate, dominant, and foreign elites for which they must have displayed or hidden conflicting identities. Examining the function ethnicity may have played in the past will better define the relationship that existed between groups within their sphere of influence. Previous downplaying of diversity by scholars, attributing ethnicity only to political and ecological factors, is unproductive and overlooks the dominant and subordinate relations in the formation of ethnicity.

Archaeology can also contribute to studies of ethnogenesis, a term used to describe the historical, not just contemporary, emergence of a people who define themselves in relation to a socio-cultural and linguistic heritage and the process of building new ethnic identities (Hill 1996; Voss 2008; Hu 2013). Ethnogenesis is also an analytical tool for developing critical historical approaches to culture as an ongoing process of conflict and the struggle of existence and people's positioning within and against a general history of domination. Though there is little disagreement about hierarchical ranking of settlements (in modern or pre-Colonial contexts), the degree of community autonomy versus centralization is still in question. While kinship-based segmentary structure (McAnany 1995; Carmack 1966; Fox 1988; Fox, Cook, and Demarest 1996; Hayden 1994; Southall 1956; Vogt 1969) and centralized, non–kinship-based structures (Chase and Chase 1996; Farriss 1984; Hassig 1985) seem to be competing models, in fact both may be correct (even complementary) when geographic heterogeneity and chronological depth are taken into consideration (Demarest 1996; J. Marcus 1993).

The role of political economy and the degree of polity centralization in Mesoamerica continues to be a principal research focus, requiring broad regional surveys such as those conducted by Sanders (Sanders and Price 1968; Sanders, Parsons, and Santley 1979), Blanton and colleagues (1993), Flannery and Marcus (1983), and

Culbert and Rice (1990). A more recent approach to political economy highlights the concept of social heterarchy, examining the interdependencies that manifest within and between members of a group (Crumley 1995; Scarborough, Valdez, and Dunning 2003; Tourtellot et al. 2003; King and Shaw 2003; Hageman and Lohse 2003). Heterarchy can exist within preexisting hierarchies (see, for example, Feinman, Lightfoot, and Upham 2000 for an example outside Mesoamerica). Taking ethnic diversity under consideration can heighten our understanding of the variability and complexity that existed amid a society in which technology was fundamentally limited and environmental settings are diverse.

Finally, studies in ethnicity will also contribute to small site and commoner studies, especially in frontier or border regions. Trends in small site/community studies include agency and activities of commoners, understanding social and economic diversity among households, households in articulation with the broader social universe, and domestic versus prestige economies at the local level (Robin 2003). Community studies are critical to contemporary archaeological approaches to understanding political economy and development. Related to this, there has been a recent shift away from elite members of the culture (which have been the subject of most academic inquiry) to the lives of the non-elite Maya (see, for example, edited volumes by Scarborough, Valdez, and Dunning [2003] and Lohse and Valdez [2004]). Studies of commoners have focused on how material goods, daily activities, family structure, and rituals provide important information about commoner life, organization, and variability (Arroyo 2004; Robin 2016; Vogt 2004). The effect of community life, *group affiliation*, population size, and mobility on elites' ability to control the commoner population is also of central importance (Inomata 2004; Yaeger and Robin 2004). This, of course, is directly tied to how elites acquired the ability to extract labor and goods from commoners (Costin 1991; Lucero 2003). Models that account for salient identity networks tell us not only about commoner lives and the ways they impacted and articulated with the political economy but also how they formed communities of practice.

The problems facing studies of the ethnic past are not unique to Maya studies. Berdan and colleagues (2008) contributed a volume on the multidisciplinary survey of Nahua in Mexico. Similar to this volume, the authors approached ethnic identity using archaeological, ethnohistorical, and contemporary ethnographic data. On the subject of the archaeology of Amazonia, anthropologist Alf Hornborg (2005) strongly criticized archaeologists for studying what was commonly referred to as "Arawak peoples." He asked archaeologists to "abandon notions of essentialized, bounded 'peoples' as coherent, persistent entities to be identified in the archaeological record" (ibid.:596). Like the term *Mayan*, the term *Arawak* actually refers to sets of related languages that (among Arawak speakers) have diffused throughout prehistory along the waterways of the Amazon. As Hornborg points out, there are many languages in the Arawakan language family, and it is misleading to imagine that *anyone* who speaks an Arawakan language is a member of a defined set of "peoples."

Jonathan Hill, whose primary research interest also lies in Amazonia, reminds us that anthropology is only one of many competing ways of representing culture and history and that by broadening our theoretical approaches, we open new avenues of historically informed research and action (Hill 1992). It is important to consider both present and past identity construction and abandon using a-historical models that reify indigenous peoples as passive and without interests and as defined by the modern post-Colonial landscape. As anthropologists, we all strive to create accurate syntheses of peoples' cultural, political, and historical struggles to exist (Hill 1996). Instead of denying peoples' past because it is difficult to research or subject to more open-ended questions, it is our responsibility to construct a shared understanding of the historical past that enables indigenous peoples to better understand their present conditions.

QUESTIONS TO BE EXAMINED

This volume is the result of the 106th Annual Meeting of the American Anthropological Association (AAA) in Washington, DC, which took place in 2007. When organizing this volume, we asked that each contributor consider one or more of three overarching topics we wished to address, as outlined below. Most important, all authors were asked to be explicit in their descriptions, clearly stating their own definition of ethnicity or identity in the context of each unique personal study.

The first topic was definitions, scales, and dimensions. Almost any cultural-social unit, indeed, any term describing social structures and relations, can be referred to as an ethnic group. This situation still holds today, as many participants in the 2007 AAA symposium tacked back and forth among identity, social networks, and ethnicity with few qualifiers. Others looked for new ways to address ethnicity in an attempt to frame the discussion of ethnicity beyond cultural units and social boundaries. In this edited volume, we asked the cultural anthropologists to take the lead and discuss some of the essential, instrumental, and situational parameters of ethnicity they encounter in their own work.

The second topic addressed the identification of critical points in time and place in which ethnogenesis likely occurred in the past through contextual studies. Archaeologists, linguists, and ethnohistorians are in a unique position to question the common assumption that ethnogenesis is a contemporary phenomenon, essentially an outcome of modern, Western nation building. Certainly, Maya groups as we know them today emerged during the sixteenth and seventeenth centuries in response to Spanish political and social strategies. Nonetheless, incorporation of structurally dissimilar groups into a single political economy is not limited to the modern era. On the contrary, ancient Maya populations experienced multiple cycles of statecraft and subsequent balkanization. Can all of us—ethnographers, linguists, ethnohistorians, and archaeologists alike—comment on formation of ethnic groups in situations of interaction as opposed to situations of isolation, as has often been previously assumed?

The final topic directly involves the identification of archaeological contexts that are valuable for investigating ethnicity. Material styles play an active role in expressing ethnic membership, but the relationship between material culture and ethnicity is not straightforward (DeBoer 1984, 1990; Dietler and Herbich 1998; Hayden and Cannon 1983; Hodder 1982; Janusek 2004; Stark, Heller, and Ohnersorgen 1998). We recommend a cautious approach to object-based studies in which styles are placed in their contexts of production, consumption, and significance. Style is not simply decorative techniques and motifs but also a result of specific bio-mechanical, technical, and ritual processes. Here, the contexts of identification are critical for identifying diacritics. Without a focus on significant context, material styles may not be very informative for the archaeologist interested in ethnicity and ethnogenesis. Archaeologists are faced with the difficult challenge of sorting out which contexts are beneficial in reconstructing the social past. They draw on mythologies, artwork, cultural traditions (usually in the production of certain types of artifacts), language, and historical and contemporary correlates. But most important, they must focus on contexts of identification: specifically, those contexts where there can be identification.

What is the value of identity? What unit of identity is being examined? What contexts are favorable for identification? What approaches will we as archaeologists use for identifying differing identities? We must take into account the meanings of identity, geographic variation, historical and political instabilities, and sociocultural diversity. In doing so, we accept and affirm the heterogeneity and cultural diversity of Maya peoples.

Once we find ways of detecting this heterogeneity, we have not completed our inquiry but rather just begun it. No single theoretical approach can sufficiently explain the complexity we see in ethnic group formation and maintenance. The most promising approach for this kind of research is multidisciplinary (Hostettler 2004). We must form multiple working hypotheses and continue to question accepted interpretations of archaeological data.

Part I of this volume contains chapters written by sociologists, ethnographers, ethnohistorians, linguists, and epigraphers. In looking at modern and post-Colonial

Maya populations, this section is designed to outline the variety of theoretical and methodological techniques useful in examining ethnic differences and provide suggestions for archaeologists who have far greater impediments to study this complex topic. First, Samson explores the use of the term *Maya* in relation to Guatemala's Maya Movement. He evaluates the differential appropriation of the ethnic term *Maya* by indigenous peoples in Mexico and Guatemala, suggesting that differences result from the relationship of the state to those populations. Samson then examines ways of framing pan-Mayanism in local, national, and transnational contexts. In chapter 3, Castillo Cocom, Rodriguez, and Ashenbrener explore "ethnoexodus," the removal of oneself from a particular construction of identity, and how social agents move fluidly between identities. They critically assess racial and ethnic categorization and related social terminology (habitus, ethnos, genesis) as inextricably tied to Western narratives. They reflect instead on the concept of *iknal,* where one is physically/habitually present but not actively engaged in games of social status, a concept they argue is at the core of Maya thinking.

Hofling's chapter examines the evolution of Itzaj and Mopan identities in Petén Guatemala. Both Itzaj and Mopan are members of the Yukatekan branch of the Mayan language family. He evaluates linguistic evidence of ethnic differences and periodic contact between the two groups. Hofling also revisits the meaning and use of the term *Maya* and examines the relationships of toponyms to ethnic or linguistic groups.

The chapter by Restall and Gabbert begins to bridge present with past constructions of ethnicity. The authors explore the genesis of the term *Maya* and the effects of early Spanish ethnoracial concepts on social order. They review the history and usage of the term *Maya* in Yucatán, then explore the nature of Maya identities during the Conquest and Colonial periods.

The final chapter in Part I completes the bridge to Part II, which is dedicated to archaeological explorations of identity construction. In this chapter Macri questions how languages found in written hieroglyphic records can provide insights into various forms of social organization. She examines linguistic variations reflected in Classic period Maya texts, in both their chronological and geographic contexts. Macri provides evidence from several linguistic features for the development of regional social/ethnic groups and suggests that data such as those presented in this chapter should be matched with parallel developments in portable objects, architecture, burial customs, and demography.

Part II of this volume is dedicated to archaeological works that analyze data in the context of identity formation and identification and includes chapters by archaeologists, biological anthropologists, and epigraphers. While frontiers or borderlands are especially productive areas of research on the topic of identity, not all chapters in Part II are from areas considered ancient frontiers. My reason for highlighting this distinction is to show that almost any region in the Maya area can be a good location for investigations into the anthropology or archaeology of identity, if the right contexts are analyzed. LeCount's chapter serves both as an introduction to the archaeological study of Maya ethnicities and a case example. Her research in the upper Belize River valley suggests a frontier between the Petén and the polities of the coastal plain of Belize. In this chapter she identifies the micro- and macro-processes significant for the formation of ethnic groups and suggests means of identifying their archaeological signatures. She argues for the emergence of distinct regional populations that were disconnected from the broadly recognized international elite culture during the Late and Terminal Classic periods.

The chapter by Marken, Guenter, and Freidel concerns work in Chiapas, a region not strongly associated as a Maya frontier. They begin by explaining how current models of ancient Maya social organization can be enhanced by evaluating input from approaches to ethnic group formation and maintenance. The authors then begin an inquiry into the interplay between ethnic identity and class identity during the Classic period at the site of Palenque. They draw heavily on the analysis of ancient written texts and suggest ways epigraphic, iconographic, and ritual symbols could have been used to highlight class and ethnic differences.

The final two chapters in this section are from the Southeast Periphery, an important frontier at the southern reaches of the Maya realm. Unlike the chapters by Marken and colleagues and LeCount, the ethnic differences in this region are not simply inter-Maya ethnic divisions but a complex interplay among local Maya, intrusive elite Maya cultural assemblages, and local non-Maya. Canuto and Bell investigate how identities were formed, tolerated, and maintained in the El Paraíso Valley in western Honduras. They compare two sites located between Quiriguá and Copán over time and suggest that the Late Classic "Mayanization" of the Copán region was related more to political fission between these two centers than to enculturation of local non-Maya peoples. Finally, Storey examines how archaeological approaches to ethnic identity can be based on both cultural and biological traits. Bioarchaeology, she argues, contributes to studies of identity and ethnicity through biological relatedness and archaeological context. Using them both, she analyzes burials from Classic and Late Classic Copán to investigate whether Mayas can be identified separately from non-Mayas.

These studies indicate that it difficult to elicit evidence of ethnicity in the archaeological record, but this does not mean it *cannot* be found. Hodder, following Cohen (1978), states that social identity and ethnicity are best evidenced in the archaeological record when investigated as "the mechanism by which *interest groups* use culture to symbolize their *within-group* organization in *opposition* to and in competition with *other interest groups*" (Hodder 1979:452, emphasis added). Archaeologists may never be able to identify specific ethnic groups in the archaeological record for same reasons that ethnographers have criticized static concepts of ethnicity. But what we can identify is change and material characteristics of change in the material record. We can observe shifts in how people view themselves, their neighbors, and others.

It is clear, as Restall and Gabbert (this volume) point out, that the image of a timeless Maya ethnic community is an illusion. This brief outline and chronological overview of approaches to ethnicity and past directions of research in Maya studies only touches on the complexity of the topic. As there is no agreement on the definition and usage of the term *ethnicity* in Maya studies, specific contextualized definitions are necessary. The interpretive benefits of different approaches must be explored and empirically tested to progress ethnic studies. The need for the interdisciplinary perspective pursued in this volume has, I hope, been demonstrated. The real contribution of this volume is not that there are different Maya ethnic groups but rather that it *is possible to explore* ethnicity in the past (including the archaeological past) as well as the present by approaching ethnicity from an interdisciplinary perspective and to provide a number of methodologies for understanding the multiplicity of Maya identities.

REFERENCES CITED

Appadurai, Arjun. 1991. "Global Ethnoscapes: Notes and Queries for a Transnational Anthropology." In *Recapturing Anthropology Working in the Present*, ed. Richard G. Fox, 191–210. Santa Fe: School of American Research Press.

Arroyo, Barbara. 2004. "Of Salt and Water: Ancient Commoners on the Pacific Coast of Guatemala." In *Ancient Maya Commoners*, ed. Jon C. Lohse and Fred Valdez Jr., 73–94. Austin: University of Texas Press.

Banks, Marcus. 1996. *Ethnicity: Anthropological Constructions*. New York: Routledge. http://dx.doi.org/10.4324/9780203417935.

Barth, Fredrik. 1969. *Ethnic Groups and Boundaries: The Social Organization of Cultural Difference*. Boston: Little, Brown.

Berdan, Francis F., John K. Chance, Alan R. Sandstrom, Barbara L. Stark, James M. Taggart, and Emily Umberger. 2008. *Ethnic Identity in Nahua Mesoamerica: The View from Archaeology, Art History, Ethnohistory, and Contemporary Ethnography*. Salt Lake City: University of Utah Press.

Blanton, Richard E., Stephen A. Kowalewski, Gary M. Feinman, and Laura M. Finsten. 1993. *Ancient Mesoamerica: A Comparison of Change in Three Regions*, 2nd ed. Cambridge: Cambridge University Press.

Brettell, Caroline B. 2006. "Introduction: Global Spaces/Local Places: Transnationalism, Diaspora, and the Meaning of Home. Identities Global Studies." *Culture and Power* 13 (3): 327–34.

Bucholtz, Mary, and Kira Hall. 2005. "Identity and Interaction: A Sociocultural Linguistic Approach." *Discourse Studies* 7 (4–5): 585–614. http://dx.doi.org/10.1177/1461445605 054407.

Carmack, Robert. 1966. "La perpetuación del clan patrilineal en Totonicapan." *Antropología y Historia de Guatemala* 18 (2): 43–60.

Carrier, James G. 1992. "Occidentalism: The World Turned Upside-Down." *American Ethnologist* 19 (2): 195–212. http://dx.doi.org/10.1525/ae.1992.19.2.02a00010.

Castañeda, Quetzil E. 2004. "'We Are Not Indigenous!' An Introduction to the Maya Identity of Yucatán." *Journal of Latin American Anthropology* 9 (1): 36–63. http://dx.doi .org/10.1525/jlca.2004.9.1.36.

Chase, Arlen, and Diane Chase. 1996. "More than Kin and King: Centralized Political Organization among the Late Classic Maya." *Current Anthropology* 37 (5): 803–10. http://dx.doi.org/10.1086/204564.

Cohen, Ronald. 1978. "Ethnicity: Problem and Focus in Anthropology." *Annual Review of Anthropology* 7 (1): 379–403. http://dx.doi.org/10.1146/annurev.an.07.100178.002115.

Costin, Cathy Lynne. 1991. "Craft Specialization: Issues in Defining, Documenting, and Explaining the Organization of Production." In *Archaeological Method and Theory*, vol. 3, ed. Michael Schiffer, 1–56. Tucson: University of Arizona Press.

Crumley, Carol L. 1995. "Heterarchy and the Analysis of Complex Societies." In *Heterarchy and the Analysis of Complex Societies*, ed. Robert R. Ehrenreich, Carole L. Crumley, and Janet E. Levy, 1–5. Archaeological Papers of the American Anthropological Association 6. Washington, DC: American Anthropological Association. http://dx.doi.org/10.1525 /ap3a.1995.6.1.1.

Culbert, T. Patrick, and Don S. Rice, eds. 1990. *Precolumbian Population History in the Maya Lowlands*. Albuquerque: University of New Mexico Press.

DeBoer, Warren. 1984. "The Last Pottery Show: System and Sense in Ceramic Studies." In *The Many Dimensions of Pottery: Ceramics in Archaeology and Anthropology*, ed. S. E. van der Leeuw and A. C. Pritchard, 527–68. Amsterdam: Institute for Pre- and Proto-History, University of Amsterdam.

DeBoer, Warren. 1990. "Interaction, Imitation, and Communication as Expressed in Style: The Ucayali Experience." In *Uses of Style in Archaeology*, ed. M. Conkey and C. Hastorf, 82–104. Cambridge: Cambridge University Press.

Demarest, Arthur. 1996. "Closing Comment." *Current Anthropology* 37 (5): 821–24.

Dietler, Michael. 1994. "'Our Ancestors the Gauls': Archaeology, Ethnic Nationalism, and the Manipulation of Celtic Identity in Modern Europe." *American Anthropologist* 96 (3): 584–605. http://dx.doi.org/10.1525/aa.1994.96.3.02a00090.

Dietler, Michael, and Ingrid Herbich. 1998. "Habitus, Techniques, Style: An Integrated Approach to the Social Understanding of Material Culture and Boundaries." In *The Archaeology of Social Boundaries*, ed. Miriam Stark, 232–63. Washington, DC: Smithsonian Institution Scholarly Press.

Farriss, Nancy. 1984. *Maya Society under Colonial Rule: The Collective Enterprises of Survival*. Princeton: Princeton University Press.

Feinman, Gary M., Kent G. Lightfoot, and Stedman Upham. 2000. "Political Hierarchies and Organizational Strategies in the Puebloan Southwest." *American Antiquity* 65 (3): 449–70. http://dx.doi.org/10.2307/2694530.

Flannery, Kent V., and Joyce Marcus. 1983. *Cloud People: Divergent Evolution of the Zapotec and Mixtec Civilizations*. New York: Academic.

Fox, John W. 1988. *Maya Postclassic State Formation: Segmentary Lineage Migration in Advancing Frontiers*. Cambridge: Cambridge University Press.

Fox, John W., Garrett W. Cook, and Arthur A. Demarest. 1996. "Constructing Maya Communities: Ethnography for Archaeology." *Current Anthropology* 37 (5): 811–30. http://dx.doi.org/10.1086/204565.

Friedman, Jonathan. 1992. "The Past in the Future: History and the Politics of Identity." *American Anthropologist* 94 (4): 837–59. http://dx.doi.org/10.1525/aa.1992.94.4.02a00040.

Gabbert, Wolfgang. 2004. "Of Friends and Foes: The Caste War and Ethnicity in Yucatan." *Journal of Latin American Anthropology* 9 (1): 90–118. http://dx.doi.org/10.1525/jlca.2004.9.1.90.

Geertz, Clifford. 1973. *The Interpretation of Cultures: Selected Essays*, vol. 5019. New York: Basic Books.

Gossen, Gary. 1985. "Review of Class and Society in Central Chiapas by Robert Wasserstrom." *Hispanic American Historical Review* 65 (3): 575–77. http://dx.doi.org/10.2307/2514852.

Graham, Elizabeth. 2006. "An Ethnicity to Know." In *Maya Ethnicity—the Construction of Ethnic Identity from Preclassic to Modern Times*, ed. Frauke Sachse, 109–24. Verlag Anton Saurwein, Germany: Markt Schwaben.

Grofe, Michael J. 2005. "The Construction of Maya Identity." *Current Anthropology* 46 (1): 1–2.

Gupta, Akhil, and James Ferguson. 1992. "'Beyond Culture': Space, Identity, and the Politics of Difference." *Cultural Anthropology* 7 (1): 6–23. http://dx.doi.org/10.1525/can.1992.7.1.02a00020.

Hageman, Jon B., and Jon C. Lohse. 2003. "Heterarchy, Corporate Groups, and Late Classic Resource Management in Northwestern Belize." In *Heterarchy, Political Economy, and the Ancient Maya*, ed. Vernon L. Scarborough, Fred Valdez Jr., and Nicholas Dunning, 109–21. Tucson: University of Arizona Press.

Hassig, Ross. 1985. *Trade, Tribute, and Transportation: The Sixteenth Century Political Economy of the Valley of Mexico*. Civilizations of the American Indian Series, 171. Norman: University of Oklahoma Press.

Hayden, Brian. 1994. "Village Approaches to Complex Societies." In *Archaeological Views from the Countryside: Village Communities in Early Complex Societies*, ed. G. Schwarz and S. Falconer, 198–206. Washington, DC: Smithsonian Institution Press.

Hayden, Brian, and Aubrey Cannon. 1983. "Where the Garbage Goes: Refuse Disposal in the Maya Highlands." *Journal of Anthropological Archaeology* 2 (2): 117–163. http://dx .doi.org/10.1016/0278-4165(83)90010-7.

Hill, Jonathan. 1992. "Overview: 'Contested Pasts and the Practice of Anthropology.'" *Contemporary Issues Forum, American Anthropologist* 94 (4): 809–859. http://dx.doi .org/10.1525/aa.1992.94.4.02a00020.

Hill, Jonathan. 1996. "Introduction." In *History, Power, and Identity: Ethnogenesis in the Americas, 1492–1992*, ed. Jonathan Hill, 1–19. Iowa City: University of Iowa Press. http://dx.doi.org/10.1111/j.1749-6632.1996.tb32464.x.

Hodder, Ian. 1979. "Economic and Social Stress and Material Culture Patterning." *American Antiquity* 44 (3): 446–54. http://dx.doi.org/10.2307/279544.

Hodder, Ian. 1982. *Symbols in Action: Ethnoarchaeological Studies of Material Culture*. Cambridge: Cambridge University Press.

Hornborg, Alf. 2005. "Ethnogenesis, Regional Integration, and Ecology in Prehistoric Amazonia: Toward a System Perspective." *Current Anthropology* 46 (4): 589–620. http://dx.doi.org/10.1086/431530.

Hostettler, Ueli. 2004. "Rethinking Maya Identity in Yucatan, 1500–1940." *Journal of Latin American Anthropology* 9 (1): 187–98. http://dx.doi.org/10.1525/jlca.2004.9.1.187.

Hu, Di. 2013. "Approaches to the Archaeology of Ethnogenesis: Past and Emergent Perspectives." *Journal of Archaeological Research* 21 (4): 371–402. http://dx.doi.org /10.1007/s10814-013-9066-0.

Inomata, Takeshi. 2004. "The Spatial Mobility of Non-Elite Populations in Classic Maya Society and Its Political Implications." In *Ancient Maya Commoners*, ed. Jon C. Lohse and Fred Valdez Jr., 175–196. Austin: University of Texas Press.

Janusek, John Wayne. 2004. *Identity and Power in the Ancient Andes: Tiwanaku Cities through Time*. New York: Routledge. http://dx.doi.org/10.4324/9780203324615.

Jones, Sian. 1997. *The Archaeology of Ethnicity: Constructing Identities in the Past and Present*. London: Routledge. http://dx.doi.org/10.4324/9780203438732.

King, Eleanor M., and Leslie C. Shaw. 2003. "A Heterarchical Approach to Site Variability." In *Heterarchy, Political Economy, and the Ancient Maya*, ed. Vernon L. Scarborough, Fred Valdez Jr., and Nicholas Dunning, 64–76. Tucson: University of Arizona Press.

Kirch, Patrick Vinton, and Roger C. Green. 2001. *Hawaik, Ancestral Polynesia: An Essay in Historical Anthropology*. Cambridge: Cambridge University Press. http://dx.doi.org /10.1017/CBO9780511613678.

Knapp, Bernard. 2001. "Archaeology and Ethnicity: A Dangerous Liaison." *Archaeologia Cypria* 4: 29–36.

Kunstadter, Peter. 1979. "Ethnic Group, Category, and Identity: Karen in Northern Thailand." In *Ethnic Adaptation and Identity: The Karen on the Thai Frontier with Burma*, ed. Charles F. Keyes, 119–163. Philadelphia: Institute for the Study of Human Issues.

Lohse, Jon C., and Fred Valdez Jr., eds. 2004. *Ancient Maya Commoners*. Austin: University of Texas Press.

Lucero, Lisa J. 2003. "The Politics of Ritual: The Emergence of Classic Maya Rulers." *Current Anthropology* 44 (4): 523–58. http://dx.doi.org/10.1086/375870.

Marcus, George. 1983. "'Elite,' as a Concept, Theory, and Research Tradition." In *Elites: Ethnographic Issues*, ed. George E. Marcus, 7–27. Albuquerque: University of New Mexico Press.

Marcus, Joyce. 1993. "Ancient Maya Political Organization." In *Lowland Maya Civilization in the Eighth Century AD*, ed. Jeremy A. Sabloff and John Stanley Henderson, 111–84. Washington, DC: Dumbarton Oaks.

McAnany, Patricia A. 1995. *Living with the Ancestors: Kinship and Kingship in Ancient Maya Society*. Austin: University of Texas Press.

Montejo, Victor. 2005. *Maya Intellectual Renaissance: Identity, Representation, and Leadership*. Austin: University of Texas Press.

Moore, John H. 1996. *The Cheyenne*. Oxford: Blackwell.

Morris, John M. 2004. "Archaeological Research at the Mountain Cow Sites: The Archaeology of Sociocultural Diversity, Ethnicity, and Identity Formation." PhD dissertation, Department of Anthropology, University of California at Los Angeles.

Ortman, Scott G. 2012. *Winds from the North: Tewa Origins and Historical Anthropology*. Salt Lake City: University of Utah Press.

Restall, Matthew. 2004. "Maya Ethnogenesis." *Journal of Latin American Anthropology* 9 (1): 64–89. http://dx.doi.org/10.1525/jlca.2004.9.1.64.

Rice, Prudence, and Don S. Rice. 2009. *The Kowoj: Identity, Migration, and Geopolitics in Late Postclassic Peten, Guatemala*. Boulder: University Press of Colorado.

Robin, Cynthia. 2003. "New Directions in Classic Maya Household Archaeology." *Journal of Archaeological Research* 11 (4): 307–56. http://dx.doi.org/10.1023/A:1026327105877.

Robin, Cynthia. 2016. *Everyday Life Matter: Maya Farmers at Chan*. Gainesville: University Press of Florida.

Sabloff, Jeremy, and John Henderson, eds. 1993. *Lowland Maya Civilization in the Eighth Century AD*. Washington, DC: Dumbarton Oaks.

Sachse, Frauke, ed. 2006. "Maya Ethnicity: The Construction of Ethnic Identity from Preclassic to Modern Times." Ninth European Maya Conference, University of Bonn, December 7–12, 2004. Acta Mesoamericana 19. Markt Schwaben, Germany: Saurwein.

Sanders, William T., Jeffrey R. Parsons, and Robert S. Santley. 1979. *Basin of Mexico: Ecological Processes in the Evolution of a Civilization*, vol. 2. New York: Academic.

Sanders, William T., and Barbara J. Price. 1968. *Mesoamerica: The Evolution of a Civilization*. Studies in Anthropology, AS9. New York: Random House.

Santos-Granero, Fernando. 1986. "Power, Ideology, and the Ritual of Production in Lowland South America." *New Series* 21 (4): 657–79.

Scarborough, Vernon L., Fred Valdez, and Nicholas Dunning, eds. 2003. *Heterarchy, Political Economy, and the Ancient Maya*. Tucson: University of Arizona Press.

Schackt, Jon. 2001. "The Emerging Maya: A Case of Ethnogenesis." In *Maya Survivalism*, ed. Ueli Hostettler and Matthew Restall, 3–14. Markt Schwaben, Germany: Verlag Anton Saurwein.

Shennan, Stephen. 2002. *Genes, Memes and Human History: Darwinian Archaeology and Cultural Evolution*. London: Thames and Hudson.

Southall, Aiden. 1956. *Alur Society: A Study in Process and Types of Domination*. Cambridge: Heffer.

Staats, Susan K. 1996. "Fighting in a Different Way: Indigenous Resistance through the Alleluia Religion of Guyana." In *History, Power, and Identity: Ethnogenesis in the Americas, 1492–1992*, ed. Jonathan D. Hill, 161–79. Iowa City: University of Iowa Press.

Stark, Barbara L., Lynette Heller, and Michael A. Ohnersorgen. 1998. "People with Cloth: Mesoamerican Economic Change from the Perspective of Cotton in South-Central Veracruz." *Latin American Antiquity* 9 (1): 7–36. http://dx.doi.org/10.2307/972126.

Tourtellot, Gair, Francisco Estrada Belli, John J. Rose, and Norman Hammond. 2003. "Late Classic Maya Heterarchy, Hierarchy, and Landscape at La Milpa, Belize." In *Heterarchy, Political Economy, and the Ancient Maya*, ed. Vernon L. Scarborough, Fred Valdez Jr., and Nicholas Dunning, 37–51. Tucson: University of Arizona Press.

van den Berghe, P. L. 1986. "Ethnicity and the Sociobiology Debate." In *Theories of Race and Ethnic Relations*, ed. John Rex and David Mason, 246–263. Cambridge: Cambridge University Press. http://dx.doi.org/10.1017/CBO9780511557828.013.

Vogt, Evon Z. 1969. *Zinacantan: A Maya Community in the Highlands of Chaipas*. Cambridge, MA: Harvard University Press. http://dx.doi.org/10.4159/harvard.97806 74436886.

Vogt, Evon C. 2004. "Daily Life in the Highland Maya Community: Zinacantan in Mid-Twentieth Century." In *Ancient Maya Commoners*, ed. Jon C. Lohse and Fred Valdez Jr., 23–48. Austin: University of Texas Press.

Voss, Barbara L. 2008. *The Archaeology of Ethnogenesis: Race and Sexuality in Colonial San Francisco*. Berkeley: University of California Press.

Warren, Kay, and Jean Jackson, eds. 2003. *Indigenous Movements, Self-Representation, and the State in Latin America*. Austin: University of Texas Press.

Wasserstrom, Robert. 1983. *Class and Society in Central Chiapas*. Berkeley: University of California Press.

Watanabe, John M. 1992. *Maya Saints and Souls in a Changing World*. Austin: University of Texas Press.

Wilson, Richard. 1995. *Maya Resurgence in Guatemala: Q'eqchi' Experiences*. Norman: University of Oklahoma Press.

Yaeger, Jason, and Cynthia Robin. 2004. "Heterogeneous Hinterlands: The Social and Political Organization of Commoner Settlements Near Xunantunich, Belize." In *Ancient Maya Commoners*, ed. Jon C. Lohse and Fred Valdez Jr., 147–173. Austin: University of Texas Press.

Part I

*Maya Identities of the Present and
the Ethnographic Past*

2

Reimaging the World

Maya Religious Practices and the Construction of Ethnicity in a Mesoamerican Frame

C. MATHEWS SAMSON

I visited the Yucatán Peninsula during the summer of 2007 for the first time in over two decades and for the first time since I began doing formal ethnographic work in highland Guatemala in the mid-1990s. I was there mostly as a tourist, hoping to meet my daughter for a few days as she ended an environmental course on the peninsula, and then I stayed for two weeks trying to get a better sense of how people are dealing with cultural and economic changes in the region, as well as a sense of what it means to be Maya among the lowland Yukatek population whose language and culture are often referred to simply as "Maya." This was not formal research, but some of the cursory differences from Guatemala, where I have been working for the past twenty years, were startling. The sense of openness in movement was a relief after my experience in an increasingly gated Guatemala City, where the population continues to struggle with the increase in violence nearly two decades after the end of the civil conflict there. At the same time, this apparent openness also took other forms—women in shorts, for example, driving motorcycles as the preferred mode of transportation in places like Ticul on the edge of the Puuc region south of Mérida. Although I sometimes found evidence of political or social organizations among the local Maya population—and near the Loltun Caverns I even picked up a self-published book by a local scholar, *apellido* Xiu, on Maya views of death—the closest I came to an obvious public political statement directed toward indigenous concerns was on a mural outside the Casa de la Cultura in the plaza of Felipe Carrillo Puerto (see figure 2.1).[1] Depicting a Maya

DOI: 10.5876/9781607325673.c002

person emerging from an ear of corn with a pyramid in the background and with various Maya glyphs and numbers setting the iconographic context for this emergence, the mural bore the words "La Zona Maya No Es Un Museo Etnográfico Es Un Pueblo En Marcha" (The Maya Zone Is Not an Ethnographic Museum; It Is a People on the Move).

Reflecting on those words now, from the perspective of visual and symbolic ethnography, they clearly resonate with my field experiences observing ethnic organizing in the context of the Maya Movement in Guatemala. Often referenced outside of Guatemala as a *pan*-Maya movement driven by the impetus of uniting all Maya peoples (*pueblos*) within a common sense of Maya identity, the movement begins by "reappropriating (from Western academia) and reinterpreting (from an indigenous perspective) research on the ancient and modern Maya" (Fischer 1996:64). Nevertheless, in practice, some tension remains between this overarching *Maya* identity and the local identities affirmed by people who continue to claim affiliation with their language group or community (*municipio*) of residence.

Moreover, while at its broadest extent a pan-Maya identity would indeed cross national boundaries to include all Mayan speakers in Mesoamerica, I suspect that the sentiment of "this" people on the move, like identity more generally, is more rooted in place. Place here is circumscribed by the local context of the Caribbean coast of the Mexican state of Quintana Roo, a place that is also home to the sanctuary of the Talking Cross and a site of ethnic resistance and independence during the Caste War—with both the symbol and the resistance enduring from the mid-nineteenth century. Although the reference to the "Zona Maya" could refer to the larger Mesoamerican region where the Maya live and the Ruta Maya has developed in fits and starts to foment economic, cultural, and tourist interaction in the region, it can probably best be interpreted as an embracing of the independent spirit of the Maya—Yukatek—ancestors who participated in the Caste War. The resistance to exoticization, as if the Maya were pieces in a museum, is surely a statement in response to the sheer volume of tourism in the area—both in the beach resort corridor in Quintana Roo and in the appropriation of the archaeological sites throughout the peninsula in the context of the Mexican government's policy of indigenismo, which focused on giving attention to Mexico's prehistoric indigenous heritage while continuing to promote the assimilation of indigenous peoples into mestizo Mexico.[2] Such resistance is far from the only narrative of engagement with the rapid social change on the peninsula since the 1980s, but it provides a frame of reference and a point of comparison with the cultural emphasis on Maya identity in the Guatemalan highlands.

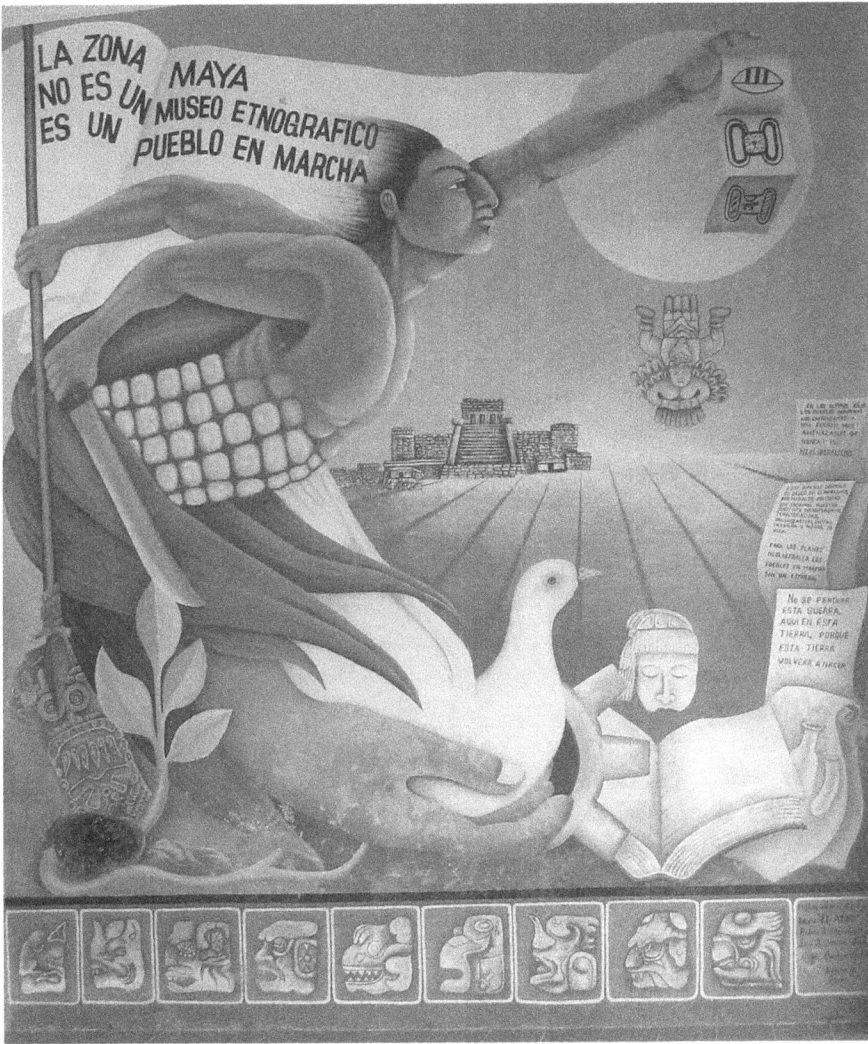

FIGURE 2.1. Mural, painted by Marcello Jiménez, in the plaza of Felipe Carrillo Puerto, Quintana Roo. Photo by the author.

MAYA NATIONALISM AFTER THE WAR

I begin with this extended vignette because there has been some call for more comparative study of indigenous culture across national boundaries in Mesoamerica (Watanabe and Fischer 2004), and because the multidisciplinary perspective in which this volume is grounded can benefit from consideration of ethnic organizing in Guatemala, as it has become more trenchant in the post-conflict years. As noted, in various contexts, the ethnogenesis of "the Maya" in Guatemala has been referred to as a movement for Maya nationalism and as a pan-Maya movement that crosses boundaries and seeks to unite in a broad historical and cultural framework perhaps as many as 6 million to 8 million people who continue to speak twenty-eight different languages and who share a cultural tradition rooted in common language origins, cosmology, and lifeways in southern Mexico, Guatemala, and parts of Belize and Honduras.[3] As one attempt describes the nature of the movement, "To look for *the unity of the Maya People* has been one of the principal ideals of the Maya Movement in Guatemala. A political and ideological mobilization has been established around this ideal that has appealed to ties of common cultural experience among the indigenous population—a shared past and a collective destiny" (Cumes 2007:86, original emphasis).

The movement burst onto the Guatemalan political scene in the late 1980s and early 1990s as the thirty-year civil conflict wound down, and the trappings of formal democracy were restored on the way to a peace accord that definitively ended the war in 1996. One of the earliest published articles on the movement (Smith 1991) was written for the North American Council on Latin America (NACLA); by the time the Kaqchikel Presbyterian executive of the Hermandad de Presbiterios Mayas wrote for the same publication in 1996, it was claimed that there were over 300 organizations with Maya constituencies (Otzoy 1996). By the end of the conflict, the movement seemed well poised to push for a "multiethnic, pluricultural, and multilingual" state that was the articulated goal of a number of organizations within the movement. This momentum, along with the awarding of the Nobel Peace Prize to Rigoberta Menchú in 1992, was emblematic of the rise of Maya identity and the confluence of social movements directed toward the fomenting of ethnic identity and culture as well as toward pushing for the realization of a peace that would end Guatemala's conflict. The Maya also had an intelligentsia that promoted its agenda both within Guatemalan social and political arenas and among academics in an international context, as well as sometimes through elements of the global human rights community that took an interest in Guatemalan affairs. The most visible spokesperson in articulating the Maya nationalist agenda has been Demetrio Cojtí Cuxil, who served as vice minister of education during the administration of Alfonso Portillo (2000–2004) and whose latest book is titled *New Perspectives for the Construction of the Multinational State: Proposals to Overcome the Non-Fulfillment of the Accord on the Identity and Rights of the Indigenous Peoples* (Waqi' Q'anil Demetrio Cojtí, Son Chonay, and Guaján 2007). The title references the side agreement on indigenous affairs that was negotiated as part of the peace process and finally concluded by the negotiating parties in 1995, but the proposal continues to push for the creation of a truly multiethnic state.

In many ways, the title of the latter work illustrates the force of the Maya Movement in strictly political terms. Although some have argued that Menchú has never been totally accepted by the Maya community as a whole, her seventh-place showing as the presidential candidate for the Encuentro por Guatemala coalition during the 2007 campaign with a total of 101,316 votes (3.09%) puts an exclamation point on the political force of Maya organizing in the national electoral arena at the present time. These results should not overshadow the historic fact of an indigenous woman running for president of Guatemala. At the same time, the comments of the report of the European Union observer commission for the 2007 elections in regard to Menchú's candidacy raise skepticism regarding the possibility of a Maya voting bloc (or perhaps even a Maya political party) in the near future: "The electoral failure of her candidature, which is obviously due to several different factors, seems to underline the fact that at the moment in Guatemala, the conscious indigenous vote is far from being a relevant force" (European Union 2007:48).[4]

Nevertheless, some of the salient issues of ethnogenesis and ethnic identity are brought to the fore in a brief comparison of the context of Maya organizing in Guatemala and in Mexico. In commentary on a series of articles dealing with Maya identity in the Yucatán Peninsula in the *Journal of Latin American Anthropology*, Ueli Hostettler makes these observations regarding Maya identity on the peninsula when refracted in the light of Guatemala's Maya Movement:

> By problematizing the "Maya" label, these articles reject an essential approach to ethnicity in the peninsula . . . On the other hand, while they concur in problematizing the history of Maya identity . . . the authors only indirectly address the fact that in the larger Maya area, especially in Guatemala, the term "Maya" and related issues of "Mayaness" have gone "public" and left the academic setting to become one of the mainstays of the Pan-Maya Movement. All political implications of anti-essentialism aside (Warren 1998), it seems that over the last decades a new Maya identity was born in Guatemala which makes deliberate use of the symbolic capital related to the complex and controversial image of the "Maya." (Hostettler 2004:193)

Two issues stand out in Hostettler's commentary. First, there is a differential appropriation of Maya identity in Mexico and Guatemala. While somewhat outside the scope of this chapter, I suggest that some of the difference can be attributed to the relationship of the state to indigenous populations. For a host of reasons, the Maya population in Mexico did not experience the kind of genocidal war experienced by the Maya in Guatemala. Both the legacy of the Mexican Revolution in constituting the state and the character of Mexican *indigenismo* in relation to the state are relevant to this issue, as is the manner in which the state dealt with agrarian concerns in the post-revolutionary period. In the Mexican highlands (in contrast to the Yucatán Peninsula), the Zapatista uprising coincided with the formal implementation of the North American Free Trade Agreement (NAFTA) in 1994, and this was on the heels of the Salinas administration's attack on the foundations of historical agrarian policy when it amended Article 27 of the constitution in 1992, thus privatizing *ejido* land in the context of other changes. While Zapatismo continues to receive scrutiny from a number of directions, including attention drawn to local-level democratization in the context of pluralistic ethnic communities, the movement has not translated into the same kind of engagement with the Mexican state by the Maya population—as Maya—that has been the case in Guatemala. The success of engagement with the state seems open to question in both highland Chiapas and Guatemala, and the issue of autonomy will figure to some degree in how one might gauge the success of the Maya or a more broadly construed indigenous agenda in the context of either nation.[5] June Nash, in one of the few comparative articles dealing with Maya organizing and the issue of autonomy, argues that so far "Maya have not strengthened their ties with their Maya neighbors across the border. We do not see the fertile exchanges possibly because the governments on both sides have precluded this possibility" (Nash 2004:196).[6]

Second, although issues of indigenous and collective rights require more scrutiny from a number of angles, in the particular case of Guatemala, Richard Adams's early commentary on the Guatemala context situates the Maya movement squarely within a framework of ethnogenesis:

> The Maya *intelligentsia* in Guatemala has been very successful in the promotion of the use of the term "Maya" for all of the indigenous people of Guatemala. The objective is to provide a stronger group solidarity to those that before were known as "*indios*" or "*indígenas*." The term "Maya" is, in fact, constantly arising as a general term for the Guatemalan indigenous population. The consequence of this is that the Mayas of Guatemala triumphed in the invention of a new ethnic group: the Maya, who did not exist in 1950 but who many acknowledge exist in the present, which should be considered a happening of evolutionary significance. (Adams 1995:410, my translation)

Matthew Restall's article on Maya ethnogenesis puts an exclamation point on Adams's interpretation of the historical significance of the "invention" of the Maya. With a particular focus on the lack of a Maya identity in the Colonial period, he writes of an "invented ancient Maya identity (hence the current Maya 'revival,' 'renaissance,' and 'resurgence')" and of "three or four centuries of 'Maya' history during which Maya peoples refused to accept categories of identity assigned to them, be it indio or Maya. In a sense, then, the Maya struggled for centuries in the face of steady opposition *against* their own ethnogenesis" (Restall 2004:82, original emphasis).[7]

The recognition of a pan-Maya identity that crosses national and linguistic boundaries contrasts with perceptions of identity-in-place bound to kinship or village groups with shared lifeways and worldviews in both pre-contact and Colonial Mesoamerica. Such recognition clearly entails a constructivist perspective, although it does not address activist essentialism that has become much discussed in terms of the way the larger movement has appropriated cultural traits and the cosmovision of the "ancient Maya" and projected them into the public sphere in support of its pan-Maya agenda. Essentialism is fairly well-trodden ground at this juncture, but it is useful to note the dialectical way the term can be used depending upon who is doing the essentializing. Jon Schackt notes that "'the invention of the Maya' could be attributed to Maya scholarship: the archaeologists, anthropologists, etc. who started to use this label for cultural horizons and continuities that interested them. Some of their numbers implicitly ascribe to these continuities an imagined Mayan essence transcending history" (Schackt 2001:11).[8]

BEYOND ETHNOGENESIS

The argument underlying this chapter is that issues of ethnogenesis are probably less important at this point in time than is continued consideration of how indigenous peoples negotiate their multiple identities within the framework of personal experience while in some cases projecting a unified identity in the political arena. Although I ran across at least two references to multiple identities in recent literature on ethnicity in Mesoamerica, I first remember hearing the term in a conversation with Kaqchikel Maya anthropologist Alberto Esquit Choy when we were graduate school colleagues several years ago. Alberto's family had been affected by *la violencia* in Patzicía during the war, and he had coauthored a book on the Maya Movement (Gálvez Borrell and Esquit Choy 1997). I was working on a project dealing with evangelical participation (or not) in the process of consolidating democracy in Guatemala around the turn of the millennium. A larger issue for me at the time was how to frame pan-Mayanism, on the one hand, while asking how it is possible to be both Maya and Protestant on the other.

What struck me in the field, beginning in 1997 and in some ways continuing to the present, was the frequent disjuncture between the passion surrounding Maya activism in the capital in certain forums designed to foment Maya identity and how little in some ways the Maya Movement seemed to have permeated the fabric of the municipio and the local historical Protestant community where I had done my work in the western part of the department of Quetzaltenango. There were a number of Maya organizations as well as non-government organizations (NGOs) active in the region, so it was not a case of total disassociation unless I asked a question, for example, about Maya priests or spiritual guides. Among evangelicals I received the almost inevitable response, "Oh, you mean *brujos*." While the tone sounds dismissive, further investigation revealed considerable certainty that indeed the shamans had power that was counterposed to new power encountered in the person of Jesus, brought initially by the Protestant missionaries. Beyond the immediate issues of conversion and the implications of conversation for identity formation, national political (and therefore cultural) agendas did not loom as large on the horizon of the people with whom I worked. Moreover, even among those who did dedicate themselves to social concerns in terms of pro-community activities or the informal investigation of their indigenous identity and *costumbre,* there was wariness about the new openness immediately after the signing of the peace accord. "Things can change," one person told me on several occasions.

Some of this wariness has to do with the rural-urban split in Guatemala that frequently shapes social and political perspectives in profound ways. One example can be seen in terms of access to information in rural communities. San Juan Ostuncalco, the municipio where I conducted the majority of my field research, is only seven miles from Guatemala's second city, Quetzaltenango, but in the late 1990s one could rarely buy a newspaper after noon on a weekday. Even so, in terms of what the media offered during those times of social ferment, supplements to the regular paper were published on a rotating basis in Mam, Kaqchikel, and K'iche'. The offerings reflected the momentum, if not the actual power, of the Maya Movement at that time, and the situation with the print media in the far western highlands today appears less bilingual in many ways than it was at the end of the 1990s.[9]

My own areas of research are grounded in the shifting religious landscape of Guatemala and how that shifting panorama articulates with religion writ large in Latin America and with the political landscape in social and ethnic renewal movements. The nexus, then, is one of religion, ethnicity, politics, and social change in a post-conflict situation. The processes of identity formation in the parallel frames of religion and ethnicity raise the issue of how the ethnography of religion contributes to contemporary understandings of Mayaness—in place and in transnational contexts. Immigrants to the United States, for example, provide satellite video of a patron saint's fiesta in Florida for the consumption of the home community in the department of Huehuetenango (Steigenga 2006).

Being neither an archaeologist nor an ethnohistorian, I have tended to focus my attention on processes of ethnic renewal, which take into account both individual and collective sense(s) of identity formation and the constraining and adaptive aspects of culture perhaps best articulated in Sherry Ortner's (2006) version of practice theory. Renewal here entails an emphasis on the processual nature of identity construction when a movement defines its identity in relation to other groups. Joane Nagel's emphasis on ethnic renewal is rooted in a constructivist view of culture and is a reflection of how "cultural constructions assist in the construction of community when they act to define the boundaries of collective identity, establish membership criteria, generate a shared symbolic vocabulary, and define a common purpose. Cultural constructions promote collective mobilization when they serve as a basis for group solidarity, combine into symbolic systems for defining grievances and setting agendas for collective action, and provide a blueprint or repertoire of tactics" (Nagel 1994:163; cf. Nagel 1996). Ultimately, this perspective provides a more complete framework for considering ethnicity and the possibility of ethnogenesis in Mesoamerica than does the essentialist-constructivist terminology we have been using most recently or the substantist-instrumental terminology Clifford Geertz (1973) and others were using forty years ago.

In describing her own engagement with practice coming out of a concern with feminism, Ortner found the theory compelling in that it "provid[ed] a dialectical synthesis of the opposition between 'structure' (or the social world as constituted) and 'agency' (or the interested practices of real people) that had not previously been achieved. Moreover, the idea that the world is 'made'—in a very extended and complex sense, of course—through the actions of ordinary people also meant that it could be unmade and remade" (Ortner 2006:16–17). This space of practice is the place where both Maya Movement activists and individuals trying to make sense of their own identity in place engage the *costumbre* handed down by the ancestors and may find themselves differentially engaged in processes directed toward the *reivindicación* of Maya identity. In terms of agency, the issue here is the scale at which people are engaged with political processes involving such *reivindicación*.[10] Are they focused more on the local context and the quotidian activities surrounding community life and subsistence, or do they begin with the more expansive national or transnational context, where the frame of activity involves dialogue even with those who today might insist that they maintain a cosmopolitan perspective on place and identity?

RELIGIOUS PRACTICE, PLURALISM, AND IDENTITY

In certain regards, religion as such received rather less attention than I envisioned when I first became involved with the panel out of which this volume has come. Because much of my work is done with evangelicals, I have reflected for several years on Alan Sandstrom's comment about how Protestantism in Mexico (and by extension in Mesoamerica) can be conceived of as a "third ethnicity." Protestantism in these contexts surely fits the framework of ethnogenesis:

With people's choices defined by the Indian-Mestizo divide, there was little room for radical change in ethnic identity. The Protestant missionaries probably unknowingly provided a third alternative for people experiencing the collapse of the old colonial arrangements and growing influence of the new economic order. Instead of choosing between Indian and Mestizo, they could now become *hermanos*. Converts to Protestantism are neither Indians nor Mestizos but instead form a third ethnic group that sidesteps the traditional social hierarchy with its roots in the colonial past. Members of this new group see themselves as dynamic, progressive, and closely affiliated with the prestige of the United States and its perceived technological and economic superiority. (Sandstrom 2001:277–78)

If Sandstrom is correct, the argument can be made that we have actually witnessed not one but two ethnic movements in Mesoamerica over the past three decades. Moreover, both pan-Mayanism and the advent of Protestantism can be situated within the context of rapid social change indexed in Latin America by post-Colonial global movements of indigenous activism and the oft-noted shift in the center of gravity of Christianity to the global South.[11] Nevertheless, given the pluralism of Protestantisms in Latin America, I suspect that Sandstrom's observation holds true more at the community level than at larger scales of analysis.

In framing the issue at the community level, I am suggesting that practice approaches linking structure and agency are more useful in examining the interplay of religious and ethnic identity than are more rigid notions of ethnogenesis, although both optics are useful for understanding identity construction in place and across borders in the Americas. While identity in pre-contact and Colonial Mesoamerica is typically understood to be rooted in particular places and communities, indigenous or Maya Protestant "ethnicity" itself fragments into disparate groups that have differential valences with Mayaness, the larger evangelical community, and the nation-state. Maya evangelicals continue to identify with their language and cultural communities even as they also identify with particular denominations or more broadly conceived religious currents such as Pentecostalism. In this view, in Guatemala and probably in Chiapas and the Yucatán region across the border as well, it is not a coincidence that evangelical religions gained traction and began significant growth only in the 1960s. Henri Gooren reports that in 1960 Guatemala was 5 percent Protestant; that number had grown to 7 percent by 1976 (Gooren 2001:183) and to at least 25 percent by 2001 (Grossman 2002:128).[12]

From another perspective, conversion viewed from the local rather than the aggregate level can be seen as a process that simultaneously involves identity formation and the segmenting of identity.[13] Geoffrey Braswell attributes the historical evidence for the Nahualization of K'iche' elite culture in the decades prior to contact in Guatemala to a "pragmatic adaptive strategy" related in part to the development of classes within K'iche' society and in part to instrumental concerns about the presence of Nahua speakers in close vicinity in the Xoconochco (Soconusco) region along the Pacific Coast (Braswell 2003:303). To be sure, Maya Protestantism represents a different kind of adaptation embodying simultaneously identification with *lo maya* and the potential for the fragmentation of what it means to be Maya within both the individual person and the community as a whole. These dual potentialities are both in evidence when the Biblical Society of Guatemala releases a new translation of the Bible in the Q'eqchi' language or when a Pentecostal congregation in an *aldea* of Ostuncalco with 9,000 inhabitants has 800 adherents.

This aldea is also one in which local shamans are said to have burned the house of Presbyterian missionaries in the 1930s, yet the Mam language predominates in the community and the women, at least, have not given up their distinctive dress as a marker of identity. Such Pentecostal congregations also sometimes provide room for women prophets and pastors, even if they do not address social development issues within local communities. I suggest that this points to a process of the reconstruction of identity at the community level, and it remains to be seen how this reconstruction will be projected into larger spatial frameworks such as that of the municipio, which in its entirely is over 80 percent Mam speaking. It is worth noting that the *alcalde* between 2004 and 2008 was a Catholic from the same aldea.

One might even argue that in the long term, conversion also represents a process wherein costumbre is traded for a new costumbre, the shape of which projects a Maya identity of unknown character into the precarious future that is Guatemala's destiny. Such a new costumbre may well incorporate new content in terms of both cosmovision and practice, but it will also reflect continuity with lifeways associated with Maya communities and local ways of adapting to outside influence evident in the Maya cultural tradition for at least two millennia.[14] As in the past, this mode of adaptation will articulate multiple agendas in other frames of reference that remain under negotiation. The nature of Maya identity in the congregation mentioned above surely contrasts with the sense of identity articulated in June 1996, when Presbyterians in the Kaqchikel Presbytery of the National Evangelical Presbyterian Church memorialized Manuel Saquic, their assassinated colleague and director of the presbytery's human rights office, as a triple martyr—a Maya and a Christian (in the ecumenical sense) dedicated to human rights (Samson 2007:104–7).[15]

The ambiguity of these identity struggles in light of larger processes of identity formation can be seen in this excerpt from an interview with a Maya Presbyterian minister. He is literate, with almost a high school education, and he has a long history of activism as a catechist and a member of pro–community service committees in the largely Mam municipio of San Juan Ostuncalco. My question had to do with what being Maya or even Mam meant to him:

> Well if we speak [of] Mam, we understand that we are a group or tribe of the Maya people, descendants of the Maya . . . Some say that we don't come from the Maya, as if we came with the Maya. Now they say we are descendants of the Maya. So there isn't a version or exact information. But as Mams we feel that, yes, we are Maya, we are descendants of the Maya people, and we are from the Mam tribe . . . We feel that, yes, we are an authentic and native (*genuino y natural*) people from Guatemala, a Maya people.

> And also, we feel that [our culture] is a treasure. We are not ashamed of being Mams; on the contrary, we are proud to speak in our . . . own language; and now our women dress in their own style of clothes. [It's] not like before when there was shame in front of the Ladinos, because they say we are *indios*, compared us to pigs—dirty, useless. Because the word *indio* means useless, he doesn't know anything. But on the contrary, I am not ashamed to speak my language before the Ladinos. It is my mother language; it is an inheritance from our ancestors. But I am Mam as well; I am proud to be Mam, to be authentic and native from Guatemala.

CONCLUSION

This returns us to the image of the Maya as a *pueblo en marcha*. Responding to pluralism in the arena of the continuing construction of ethnic identity—and in the somewhat more restricted frame of religious practice—demands a move beyond conceptualizations of ethnicity solely defined by the practice of a unified costumbre that shapes personal and collective identity through the generations. Even so, contemporary formulations of pluralism begin for many in a sense of participation growing out of an enduring identity in continuity with the past. In Mesoamerica, such formulations of ethnicity have the potential to articulate profound political and social challenges to the legitimacy of nation-states founded on constructs of *mestizaje* or *indigenismo* that continue to marginalize indigenous peoples in discourses about the nature of citizenship and the state. More sophisticated affirmations of pluralism move us into the realm of embracing difference within the context of common projects; when it comes to nation building and reconciliation in post-conflict Guatemala, the character of the state itself is brought under scrutiny by the process of Maya ethnic renewal.

Maya religious practices will continue to be a key aspect of the definition of Mayaness and the construction of ethnicity on the Guatemalan national stage. I attended a book presentation in a downtown hotel in Guatemala City during the summer field season of 2007. Admittedly, it was held in Zone 1 and not in the swank hotels of Zones 9 and 10 of the city's "Zona Viva." Nevertheless, it was attended by 75 to 100 people, mostly Maya, as the book dealt with political parties in the national elections and their stance in regard to Maya issues, specifically Maya women (Ochoa and Garoz 2007). It was also an educational event, with a lively presentation on the book, commentary from two critics, and questions from the audience. I was handed a program as I entered the room where the event was held, and I saw that the assembled were turning in the four directions as a Maya spiritual guide (a priestess in this case) lit candles and opened the event. The invocation was listed as part of the program, and after nearly an hour and a half of presentations, with everyone ready for food, the "closing of the invocation" took place. It was rather hurried but surprisingly ecumenical in nature and tone, much like a hasty benediction when the 11:00 Sunday church service has gone ten minutes too long.

As I left, I wondered about North American battles over the separation of church and state and how the pluralism of religious practices in Guatemala will shape the march of Maya identity and Guatemalan-ness in both time and transnational space in the years to come. It seems clear that governments in Mesoamerica will continue to resist agendas related to the autonomy and collective rights of indigenous peoples even as activists pursue a variety of agendas that will span the spectrum from the ostensibly cultural to the overtly political. The invocation at the book signing demonstrates the increased focus on religion or cosmology as a central aspect of ethnic identity and points to culture as a point of contestation as the Maya deal with multiple or multifaceted identities (LeCount, this volume) tied to local, national, and transnational spaces into the future. For the past, ethnohistorical and archaeological evidence reveals instances of pan-regional identity undergirding the legitimation of elite power in various contexts throughout Mesoamerica (cf. Carmack 1968; Ringle 2004).[16] Although interpreting the record remains an ongoing process, the legitimizing forces of mythology and cosmology strengthen identity construction in the present.

The Maya Movement itself often has a different valence depending on whether the reference is to Maya nationalism in a multi- or pluricultural society or to Maya identity at the local level. In fact, defining Maya culture or identity is complicated at the community level, where purity of "Maya" practice might be less of a problem than at the level of those involved in the creation of a national ideology rooted to some degree in opposition to the culture of "the Other."[17] In pragmatic and political terms, what takes place beyond the community, such as transnational migration or the shaping of government policy in regard to cultural issues like bilingual education or respect for sacred places on the landscape as facets of collective or cultural rights, will also have a bearing on whether identity is reinforced or contested in various spatial frames. Meanwhile, ethnographers and archaeologists alike will gain a better understanding of the shape of identity in Mesoamerica in the past precisely to the extent that we dedicate ourselves to a clearer reading of the movements of Maya peoples in the present.

ACKNOWLEDGMENTS

I thank Grant Jones for reading and making comments on the version of this chapter that was presented at the 2006 meeting of the American Anthropological Association, as well as for ceding me the opportunity to make a presentation on the panel in the first instance. I am also grateful to Bill Ringle for his continuing efforts in helping me think through some of the ways contemporary social and political activity in Mesoamerica is reflected in the past. Kate O'Connor, a recent Davidson College graduate, helped with some of the final edits.

NOTES

1. Xiu was the name of the dominant lineage near Mani at the time of the Spanish incursion (Clendinnen 1987:25).

2. As a colleague notes, the east coast of the peninsula is known as the Maya Riviera in tourist circles.

3. On the use of "cultural tradition" for Mesoamerica, see Carmack, Gasco, and Gossen (2007:5–6). I also continue to be informed by conceptualizations such as that of a Maya cultural region for the place inhabited by contemporary Maya populations in both lowland and highland areas. This perspective is not meant to deny differences between different regions, differences that can also be indexed by the lowland-highland dichotomy and that are reflected in cosmology as well.

4. It is significant that the rural and indigenous population carried center-left candidate Álvaro Colom to victory in the runoff election with Otto Pérez Molina, a retired army general. Colom won in twenty of Guatemala's twenty-two departments, the first time a candidate won the presidency without carrying Guatemala City since the formal return to democracy in the mid-1980s. This is also pertinent to differential ethnic organizing in rural and urban areas, mentioned below. See the analysis in European Union Election Observation Mission, Guatemala (European Union 2007:59) and the transcript of the interview with Guatemalan author Francisco Goldman on the Democracy Now website (http://www.democracynow.org/2007/11/6/guatemalas_indigenous_countryside_drives_election_victory; accessed October 27, 2009). According to Guatemala's Supreme Electoral Commission, Menchú, who ran on a left-wing coalition ticket, received 145,080 votes in the 2001 presidential election; that was 2.87 percent of the vote (TSE 2012:156).

None of my commentary here should be taken as ignoring the fragmentation of Guatemalan party politics or the difficulties of forming leftist coalitions in Guatemala and much of Latin America (see Samson 2012).

5. In Guatemala, the Accord on the Right and Identity of Indigenous Peoples has never been ratified by the congress, despite having been approved by the government and guerrilla negotiators in 1995. Likewise, the San Andrés Accords negotiated between the Mexican government and the Zapatista National Liberation Party (EZLN) in late 1995 and 1996 represented a push for both autonomy and Indian rights, but it has also not been acted upon by the Mexican congress (Womack 1999:304–15; Aubrey 2003; Esteva 2003).

6. Other reasons for the divergent trajectories include the geography and the multiplicity of languages spoken in the region. The Maya on the peninsula in Mexico are also separated by long distances from the central power of the Federal District and by their own history of separatism and resistance. In addition, the more diverse indigenous population in Mexico complicates efforts at pan-indigenous organizing in a way not experienced in Guatemala, despite the insistence that the government acknowledge the rights of the Maya, Garífuna, and Xinca peoples (Bill Ringle, personal communication, 2008).

7. While I agree with the general idea here, I am less comfortable with the notion of the invention of an ancient identity. The process seems more dialectical to me, although that is surely a space for debate among ethnohistorians, archaeologists, and ethnographers. This is one of the reasons I emphasize the notion of ethnic renewal (cf. chapter 5, this volume).

8. Schackt's take on the issue of authenticity is that "a person's ethnic identity is authentic to the extent that it is really felt and taken for granted by him/herself and his or her social surroundings" (2001:10). On the essentialism issue, see the relevant sections in Warren (1998) and Fischer (2001).

9. The issue of communications media as a whole requires more formal investigation in terms of how it influences identity and organizing in both urban and rural areas. I suspect that radio and recording media present different stories in terms of bilingualism. From the standpoint of religion in Maya communities, both Catholics and Protestants have access to the airwaves. Moreover, the Protestant traffic in cassette and CD technology with music in Mayan languages as well as Spanish is ubiquitous in the weekly market context.

10. Cojtí and others use this Spanish term frequently in discussing the process of projecting Maya culture into the public sphere. It has not been examined closely enough, although while revising my dissertation for publication I came across a helpful definition of revendicate in the context of Louisiana civil law: "to bring an action to enforce rights in (specific property) esp. for the recognition of ownership and the recovery of possession from one wrongfully in possession." See the entry at www.merriam-webster.com/legal/revendicate, accessed October 14, 2016. This provides a powerful interpretive framework in light of the attempt to reclaim culture and identity from the Mestizo state while simultaneously pushing for the creation of a multiethnic state.

11. On indigenous activism, see Brysk (2000) and Cleary and Steigenga (2004). Jenkins (2002) provides a useful introduction to recent changes affecting the character of the global Christian movement.

12. Figures of 30 percent and higher are routinely cited, and occasionally a number as high as 40 percent is given. The 25 percent figure is likely applicable to Chiapas and the states of Yucatán, Campeche, and Quintana Roo as well. In the Guatemalan case (and in Latin America as a whole), 70 percent of Protestants are Pentecostal. To give some time depth, historical Protestants were invited into the country in the early 1880s in the context of efforts by the liberal government to promote modernization and secularization in the face of the Catholic Church. The actual growth rate of evangelicalism appears to have leveled off in the early 1990s, perhaps in part because of the end of the war.

13. The nature of conversion itself is receiving increasing attention in the literature on religion in various disciplines. The notion of conversion as a process makes generalization about the significance of the increasing number of Protestant adherents in various parts of Latin America hazardous at best. See Steigenga and Cleary (2007) for articles that address these issues both theoretically and in various places in Latin America. Humberto Ruz and Garma Navarro (2005) provide a window into the meaning of religious pluralism in contemporary Mesoamerica.

14. See the discussion of "conventions of community" in Watanabe (1992); cf. the sense of communal adaptation discussed in Cook (2001). MacKenzie's (2010) work examining networks and hierarchy in Maya ethnic activism adds another important dimension for consideration both in Guatemala and in the cross-cultural analysis of ethnic organizing.

15. For more on this kind of inculturated indigenous Protestantism, see also Garrard-Burnett (2004).

16. The references to Tulan as a place of origin in the ethnohistorical record and the spread of the cult of the Feathered Serpent in the archaeological record highlight the historical influence emanating from the core region of central Mexico.

17. In making these comments, I am drawing largely from some of the conclusions of Bastos (2007:373–78), who analyzes the Maya Movement as a process of "Mayanization" within the frame of a multicultural ideology.

REFERENCES CITED

Adams, Richard N. 1995. "Evolución y etnía en la Guatemala contemporánea." In *Etnías en evolución social: Estudios de Guatemala y Centroamérica*, ed. Richard N. Adams, 395–413. Mexico City: Universidad Autónoma Metropolitana.

Aubrey, Andrés. 2003. "Autonomy in the San Andrés Accords: Expression and Fulfillment of a New Federal Pact." In *Mayan Lives, Mayan Utopias: The Indigenous Peoples of*

Chiapas and the Zapatista Rebellion, ed. Jan Rus, Aída Hernández Castillo Rosalva, and Shannan L. Mattiace, 219–41. Lanham, MD: Rowman and Littlefield.

Bastos, Santiago. 2007. "La ideología multicultural en la Guatemala del cambio del milenio." In *Mayanizacion y vida cotidiana: La ideolgía multicultural en la sociedad guatemalateca,* vol. 1, ed. Santiago Basos and Aura Cumes, 209–378. Guatemala City: FLACSO, CIRMA, Cholsamaj.

Braswell, Geoffery E. 2003. "K'iche'an Origins, Symbolic Emulation, and Ethonogenesis in the Maya Highlands, AD 1450–1524." In *The Postclassic Mesomerican World*, ed. Michael E. Smith and Francis F. Berdan, 297–303. Salt Lake City: University of Utah Press.

Brysk, Alison. 2000. *From Tribal Village to Global Village: Indian Rights and International Relations in Latin America*. Stanford, CA: Stanford University Press.

Carmack, Robert M. 1968. "Toltec Influences on the Postclassic Culture History of Highland Guatemala." In *Archaeological Studies of Middle America*, 49–92. Middle American Research Institute 26. New Orleans: Tulane University.

Carmack, Robert M., Janine L. Gasco, and Gary H. Gossen, eds. 2007. *The Legacy of Mesoamerica: History and Culture of a Native American Civilization*, 2nd ed. Upper Saddle River, NJ: Prentice-Hall.

Cleary, Edward L., and Timothy Steigenga, eds. 2004. *Resurgent Voices in Latin America: Indigenous Peoples, Political Mobilization, and Religious Change*. New Brunswick, NJ: Rutgers University Press.

Clendinnen, Inga. 1987. *Ambivalent Conquests: Maya and Spaniard in Yucatan, 1517–1570*. New York: Cambridge University Press.

Cook, Garrett W. 2001. "The Maya Pentecost." In *Holy Saints and Fiery Preachers: The Anthropology of Protestantism in Mexico and Central America*, ed. James W. Dow and Alan R. Sandstrom, 147–68. Westport, CT: Praeger.

Cumes, Aura. 2007. "Mayanización y el sueño de la emancipación indígena en Guatemala." In *Mayanizacion y vida cotidiana: La ideolgía multicultural en la sociedad guatema-lateca,* vol. 1, ed. Santiago Basos and Aura Cumes, 79–208. Guatemala City: FLACSO, CIRMA, Cholsamaj.

Esteva, Gustavo. 2003. "The Meaning and Scope of the Struggle for Autonomy." In *Mayan Lives, Mayan Utopias: The Indigenous Peoples of Chiapas and the Zapatista Rebellion*, ed. Jan Rus, Aída Hernández Castillo Rosalva, and Shannan L. Mattiace, 243–69. Lanham, MD: Rowman and Littlefield.

European Union Election Observation Mission, Guatemala. 2007. Final Report on the General Elections. Accessed October 10, 2016. http://aceproject.org/regions-en/countries-and-territories/GT/reports/guatemala-general-elections-2007-final-report-by.

Fischer, Edward F. 1996. "Induced Culture Change as a Strategy for Socioeconomic Development: The Pan-Maya Movment in Guatemala." In *Maya Cultural Activism in Guatemala*, ed. Edward F. Fischer and R. McKenna Brown, 51–73. Austin: University of Texas Press.

Fischer, Edward F. 2001. *Cultural Logics and Global Economics: Maya Identity in Thought and Practice*. Austin: University of Texas Press.

Gálvez Borrell, Victor, and Alberto Esquit Choy. 1997. *The Mayan Movement Today: Issues of Indigenous Culture and Development in Guatemala*. Trans. Matthew Creelman. Guatemala City: FLACSO.

Garrard-Burnett, Virginia. 2004. "God Was Already Here When Columbus Arrived: Inculturation Theology and the Mayan Movement in Guatemala." In *Resurgent Voices in Latin America: Indigenous Peoples, Political Mobilization, and Religious Change*, ed. Edward L. Cleary and Timothy Steigenga, 125–53. New Brunswick, NJ: Rutgers University Press.

Geertz, Clifford. 1973. "The Integrative Revolution: Primordial Sentiments and Civil Politics in the New States." In *The Interpretation of Cultures*, ed. Clifford Geertz, 255–310. New York: Basic Books.

Gooren, Henri. 2001. "Reconsidering Protestant Growth in Guatemala, 1900–1995." In *Holy Saints and Fiery Preachers: The Anthropology of Protestantism in Mexico and Central America*, ed. James W. Dow and Alan R. Sandstrom, 169–203. Westport, CT: Praeger.

Grossman, Roger. 2002. "Interpreting the Development of the Evangelical Church in Guatemala, 2002." DMin dissertation, Southeastern Baptist Theological Seminary, Wake Forest, NC.

Hostettler, Ueli. 2004. "Rethinking Maya Identity in Yucatan, 1500–1940." *Journal of Latin American and Caribbean Anthropology* 9 (1): 187–98. http://dx.doi.org/10.1525 /jlat.2004.9.1.187.

Humberto Ruz, Mario, and Carlos Garma Navarro, eds. 2005. *Protestantismo en el mundo Maya contemporáneo*. Mexico City: Universidad Nacional Autónoma de México, Instituto de Investigaciones Filológicas, and Universidad Autónoma Metropolitana, Unidad Iztapalapa.

Jenkins, Philip. 2002. *The Next Christendom: The Coming of Global Christianity*. New York: Oxford University Press. http://dx.doi.org/10.1093/0195146166.001.0001.

MacKenzie, C. James. 2010. "Of Networks and Hierarchies: Pan-Mayanism and Ethnic Ambivalence in Guatemala." *Latin American and Caribbean Ethnic Studies* 5 (1): 27–52. http://dx.doi.org/10.1080/17442220903506891.

Nagel, Joane. 1994. "Constructing Ethnicity: Creating and Recreating Ethnic Identity and Culture." *Social Problems* 41 (1): 152–76. http://dx.doi.org/10.2307/3096847.

Nagel, Joane. 1996. *American Indian Ethnic Renewal: Red Power and the Resurgence of Identity and Culture*. New York: Oxford University Press.

Nash, June. 2004. "Beyond Resistance and Protest: The Maya Quest for Autonomy." In *Pluralizing Ethnography: Comparison and Representation in Maya Cultures, Histories, and Identities*, ed. John M. Watanabe and Edward F. Fischer, 163–98. Santa Fe, NM: School for American Research.

Ochoa, Luis Rodolfo, and Byron Garoz. 2007. *Sistematización del origen, ideología y propuesta de los partidos políticos inscritos en el TSE, 2007*. Guatemala City: Asociación Política de Mujeres Mayas MOLOJ.

Ortner, Sherry B. 2006. "Updating Practice Theory." In *Anthropology and Social Theory: Culture, Power, and the Acting Subject*, ed. Sherry B. Ortner, 1–18. Durham, NC: Duke University Press. http://dx.doi.org/10.1215/9780822388456-001.

Otzoy, Antonio. 1996. "Guatemala: The Struggle for Maya Unity." *Report on the Americas* 29 (5): 33–35. http://dx.doi.org/10.1080/10714839.1996.11725758.

Restall, Matthew. 2004. "Maya Ethnogenesis." *Journal of Latin American and Caribbean Anthropology* 9 (1): 64–89. http://dx.doi.org/10.1525/jlat.2004.9.1.64.

Ringle, William M. 2004. "On the Political Organization of Chichen Itza." *Ancient Mesoamerica* 15 (2): 167–218. http://dx.doi.org/10.1017/S0956536104040131.

Samson, C. Mathews. 2007. *Re-enchanting the World: Maya Protestantism in the Guatemalan Highlands*. Tuscaloosa: University of Alabama Press.

Samson, C. Mathews. 2012. "Interrogating Human Security and Religion in Guatemala." In *Religion and Human Security: A Global Perspective*, ed. James K. Wellman Jr. and Clark B. Lombardi, 150–71. New York: Oxford University Press. http://dx.doi.org/10.1093/acprof:oso/9780199827732.003.0009.

Sandstrom, Alan R. 2001. "Conclusion: Anthropological Perspectives on Protestant Conversion in Mesoamerica." In *Holy Saints and Fiery Preachers: The Anthropology of Protestantism in Mexico and Central America*, ed. James W. Dow and Alan R. Sandstrom, 263–89. Westport, CT: Praeger.

Schackt, Jon. 2001. "Emerging Maya: A Case of Ethnogenesis." In *Maya Survivalism*, ed. Ueli Hostettler and Matthew Restall, 3–14. Acta Mesoamericana, vol. 12. Markt Schwaben, Germany: A. Saurwein.

Smith, Carol A. 1991. "Maya Nationalism." *Report on the Americas* 25 (3): 29–33. http://dx.doi.org/10.1080/10714839.1991.11723136.

Steigenga, Timothy J. 2006. "Transnationalism and Collective Mobilization among the Maya of Jupiter: Ambiguities of Transnational Identity and Lived Religion." Paper presented at the symposium Transnational Religion in Contemporary Latin America and the United States, Teresa Lozano Long Institute of Latin American Studies, University of Texas, Austin, January 26–27.

Steigenga, Timothy J., and Edward L. Cleary, eds. 2007. *Conversion of a Continent: Contemporary Religious Change in Latin America*. New Brunswick, NJ: Rutgers University Press.

TSE (Tribunal Supremo Electoral). 2012. *La memoria de elecciones generales y al parlamento centroamericano 20011*. Guatemala City: TSE.

Waqi' Q'anil Demetrio Cojtí, Ixtz'ulu', Elsa Son Chonay, and Raxche' Rodriguez Guaján. 2007. *Ri K'ak'a' runuk'ik ri Saqamaq', Nuevas perspectivas para la construcción del estado multinacional: Propuestas para superar el incumplimiento del Acuerdo sobre Identidad y Derechos de los Pueblos Indígenas*. Guatemala City: CHOLSAMAJ.

Warren, Kay. 1998. *Indigenous Movements and Their Critics: Pan-Mayanism and Ethnic Resurgence in Guatemala*. Princeton, NJ: Princeton University Press.

Watanabe, John M. 1992. *Maya Saints and Souls in a Changing World*. Austin: University of Texas Press.

Watanabe, John M., and Edward F. Fischer. 2004. "Introduction: Emergent Anthropologies and Pluricultural Ethnography in Two Postcolonial Nations." In *Pluralizing Ethnography: Comparison and Representation in Maya Cultures, Histories, and Identities*, ed. John M. Watanabe and Edward F. Fischer, 3–33. Santa Fe, NM: School for American Research.

Womack, John, Jr. 1999. *Rebellion in Chiapas: An Historical Reader*. New York: Free Press.

3

Ethnoexodus

Escaping Mayaland

Juan Castillo Cocom, Timoteo Rodriguez, and McCale Ashenbrener

Some commentators have deemed me either "too black" or "not black" enough.

BARACK OBAMA, *A More Perfect Union* SPEECH

Eager to establish a dialogue with Mayanist thinkers in a session on the ethnogenesis of the Maya, I accepted an invitation to engage on a panel with distinct uneasiness, perhaps because I cannot really conceive of a notion of "the birth of an ethnos" either as event or process per se (Anderson 1999; Fennell 2007; Hill 1996; Roosens 1989; Smoak 2006). Or perhaps I was unsettled by the arbitrariness by which academics split time into recognizable points of reference, as to where exactly forms of Maya Yucatec identity took place—such as the Spanish Conquest (and its subsequent imposition of the race concept), the Caste War of the nineteenth century, and the emergence of ethnic politics in the twentieth century (Restall 2004).

Ethnogenesis uses historical markers in a constructivist manner in which non-essentialist social "artifacts" are used to determine spatial and temporal "ethno-topographies." It is not a coincidence that these moments and places are signaled in economic, political, and military conflicts—contexts that conveniently lend themselves to constituted identifications. As such, ethnogenesis exercises epistemic control over "politically correct" discourses about inequality and justice or civil rights for humans and cultural practices, effectively creating a modern form of peonage by not allowing the people I belong to a way to exist apart from reductive and politically constructed identities.

DOI: 10.5876/9781607325673.c003

JUAN AND TIMOTEO IN A TAXI FROM SAN FRANCISCO
INTERNATIONAL AIRPORT, JANUARY 2008, JUAN CASTILLO COCOM

The plane landed in the eye of a storm. A sense of terror was still present as other passengers and I stepped on the ground of the San Francisco Airport. Timo (Timoteo Rodriguez) picked me up at the terminal and asked, "So what is your Berkeley graduate seminar 'Ethnoexodus' about?" As I launched into the notion of ethnoexodus, a presence clear in my mind, I could notice from his expression that he had no idea what I was talking about. "The seminar, my friend, is a little experiment aimed at unraveling the limits of ethnogenesis." Timo told me he had invited some colleagues to participate in this little experiment, and on the first day of the seminar there were five of us: Linda Barrera, Diana Negrín, María Cruz, Timo, and me. The title posted on the website of Berkeley's anthropology department read "Anthropology 230–3: Special Topics in Archaeology: Ethnoexodus: Maya Yucatec Topographic Ruptures."

Up until that first day of the seminar, my soul was filled with pedagogical terror at the thought of teaching at UC Berkeley. I called my friend Quetzil Castañeda: "I don't know how to structure, systematize, and present the fundamental ideas of the course 'Ethnoexodus: Maya Yucatec Topographic Ruptures' to a public that is already expert on the topography of the imaginaries of Baudrillard, Bourdieu, Foucault, and Jameson."

He said, "Don't worry; simply share your experiences with them."

KROEBER HALL, ROOM 151, ANTHROPOLOGY 179, "HISTORY AND
ETHNOGRAPHY OF THE MAYA," DECEMBER 2008, TIMOTEO RODRIGUEZ

My lecture, titled "Technologies of History," required that the undergraduates bring questions from their reading of the Kroeber Anthropological Society Papers Special Edition, Mayab Bejlae: Yucatan Today (Reyes-Cortés and Rodriguez 2007). The students were initially very excited to read Dr. Juan Castillo Cocom's (2007) article for, after all, he is a Cocom. Earlier in the semester they had read the history of the Cocom lineage in Sharer's (1994) massive textbook.

They learned about the Cocoms' relationship to the fall of Chichén Itzá and the establishing of the great city of Mayapan (Màayapáan in Maya T'aan and Mayapán en español), where the Cocoms were massacred by the Xiu in the 1440s. Then in the 1530s, after the Xiu allied with the Spanish, they studied the infamous Cocom revenge massacre during a pilgrimage to the Sacred Cenote in the ruins of Chichén Itzá. And the students knew about the great Cocom warrior Nachi Cocom, Lord of Sotuta, who never surrendered to the invading Spanish forces (de Landa 1959).

There was mixed engagement with and understanding of Castillo Cocom's article. One student loved the disruptions in the text—that *his* writing was "in and out" of the normative of the anthropological canon. Another student wondered why Castillo Cocom's writing was so confusing and segmented. Why does he continually interrupt the flow of the paper with different dates, times, places, and narratives? The student wanted an introduction with three points and evidence of support throughout the chapter, topped off with a concise conclusion. The discussion was fruitful: it stirred debate among the seventy undergraduates.

I explained that Castillo Cocom (who at the time was both *there* and *not there*; unable to attend because the idea of him was, in light of people's responses, obviously *elsewhere*) had selected this writing style and structure carefully in writing this article. His pedagogical movement was more an epistemic rupture in the anthropological understanding. I pointed out that in practice, "understanding" was conceptual, political, ethical, and aesthetic (Rabinow 2003); Castillo Cocom did not necessarily prescribe to that particular anthropological understanding in his own writing.

IKNAL: ESCAPING FROM *STATUS* BUT NEVER FROM PRESENCE, JUAN CASTILLO COCOM

Speakers of Maya T'aan or Yucatec Mayan have a commonsense reference to this quality of "being present," known as one's *iknal*. In Maya T'aan, iknal is at the same time the *context* and *product* of relationships. It is both a shared and an individuated mobile field of sensory awareness or action (Hanks 1999:91). Iknal entails understanding one's bodily space in relation to one's perception, opinion, and attitude. Thus, epistemically, iknal is at the core of Maya thinking, the core of this chapter.

As a text, this is our iknal for right here, right now; we take up a space in both your hands and your head, for we inhabit with these words. The argument we put forth is captured with this Maya notion of "perpetual presence" as both *context* and *product* in an "ethnoexodus," simultaneously a critique of the idea of ethnogenesis as a way of understanding "Maya" identity and of identity formation in general.

As a conceptual tool, ethnoexodus focuses on how a social actor may "exit" at a temporal "point" in an identity suture without having necessarily ever been "in" that particular construct of identity. Simultaneously, ethnoexodus conveys how a social agent "enters" the territories of fictional identities, multiplying his or her already numerous imagined identity formations in the name of the apparent "genesis of the ethnos." This fantastic *mobility between "identities"* constitutes what we dare to term an "ethnoexodus," a more viable analytical alternative to ethnogenesis as identity politic in the Colonial matrix of power constructs (Mignolo 2001).

Iknal is roughly translated as an extension of social agency, of *perspective, presence, action*, and *attitude*. Both ethnoexodus and iknal should help situate Bourdieu's (1990) concept of "habitus" in geopolitical terms relating to identity formation, but though both iknal and habitus require a generative, habituated presence—that is, a disposition of where you can be both physically and habitually—iknal references a key quality that habitus cannot. It can be a spatial marker disembodied from the individual that indexes the presence of a specific person (Hanks 1990). Thus, one's iknal can be present in a location even when an individual is not physically in that locality. Our fundamental proposal is that ethnoexodus is associated with identity formation by escaping from *status*, from how one fits into social structures, but never from presence.

Intuitively, everybody may embody, possess, or acquire both a habitus and an iknal. Still, the two notions are not the same; neither are they in competition. Yet in the geopolitics of knowledge, habitus is considered a more "universal theory" of embodied action and a means to consider identity formation in *practice*. Furthermore, for Bourdieu, habitus is necessarily connected to social power relations as conceptualized within a "field" of symbolic capital and thus embedded in the interplay of *status* through the accumulation of social capital in a given field. As such, one may never escape one's habitus; one may just learn to turn it "off and on" within a field of relations or slowly develop new habituations or dispositions. Thus, identity formation as understood through habitus, field, and capital is the condition that never escapes the game of status. In other words, you are always in your body regardless of the symbolic capital you acquire. In this regard, social status through symbolic capital is never guaranteed, especially when the "body" one embodies counts as a symbolic deficit, such as one's accent, cultural bodily mannerisms and taste, stature or physique, and phenotypical features like skin, eye, or hair color. Thus, as Aihwa Ong (1999:92) puts it, "There is a mismatch, from the hegemonic standpoint, between the symbolic capital and its embodiment."

For Timoteo and me, ethnoexodus is a means to conceptualize identity formation by putting aside the necessity of status and understanding the role of iknal beyond Maya T'aan (Yucatec Maya language) speech acts, as well as subsuming its analysis into an academic framework that broadens social phenomena and human experience to realms that are necessarily in and out of Maya context (Castillo Cocom 2007). Certain questions arise here: How is it possible to consider power relations and identity formations *not* linked to status? And why is it important to not consider status in identity formation in the first place?

UNIVERSIDAD INTERCULTURAL MAYA DE QUINTANA ROO, ROOM 201, SEPTEMBER–DECEMBER 2014, MCCALE ASHENBRENER

I took Castillo Cocom's Derechos Humanos Indígenas y Organización Étnica (Indigenous Human Rights and Ethnic Organization) class in the fall of 2014 during my stay at the Universidad Intercultural Maya de Quintana Roo for my Fulbright Distinguished Awards in Teaching Program. As he entered the room the students, about fifteen men and five women, started dragging the chairs into a circle, already trained for the informality of his lectures. Castillo Cocom asked the class to define Maya. As we unsuccessfully attempted to use historical, cultural, and sociopolitical ideation to encapsulate Maya identity, he meticulously unraveled each conception, exposing it as separate, carefully constructed narratives created by anthropologists, the tourism industry, and colonizers.

It was fascinating to see him destroy and break down everything the students thought to be true in order to have them rebuild their ideas from the rubble. These were primarily Maya (in terms of the quincunx) students at an intercultural Maya university, and Castillo Cocom was telling them that "Maya" was a recently made-up construct. The term *Maya* was first designated to describe architectural remnants of the ancient civilization in the mid-1800s, and it was not until the end of the nineteenth century that Maya was used to refer also to the people who spoke Yucatec Maya or other Maya-related languages (Schackt 2001).

The students—including me—were struggling to keep up. It felt as if we had all boarded the same train to cross Mayaland, but Castillo Cocom was soon moving fluidly in and out of contexts, and we were forced out of our comfortable seats to observe the train from various perspectives in the field. Crouched in the corn, we watched ourselves pass by and questioned if what we saw was really a train after all. We were *there* not as discrete imagery but as people who were dialoguing *here* as subjects who see and are seen, who evade and probe back, echo, and reverberate with each other in the *everywhere*.

Castillo Cocom uses iknal in his classes, requiring his students to reflect on their own physical and intellectual perceptions, their attitudes toward and opinions of what they are told is Maya, to decipher a new, imagined identity less tethered by ideas of status and physical limitations of space.

SITTING AT AN OUTDOOR TABLE AT STRADA CAFÉ ACROSS THE STREET FROM KROEBER HALL, UC BERKELEY, FEBRUARY 2008, JUAN CASTILLO COCOM AND TIMOTEO RODRIGUEZ

Timo and I talk about the idea of ethnogenesis and ethnoexodus. It is cold. Very cold. I miss the warmth of the Yucatán sun.

JCC.   So, ethnogenesis is about attempting to encapsulate what will always escape to the "encapsulators."

TR.   If escape is the mode for the exodus, how does this relate to doing research and producing knowledge? Is it like a diffusion of knowledge?

JCC.   Let me explain it like this . . . what courses did you take before starting your first ethnographic research in Yucatán?

TR.   Well, in the spring of 2001 I took three UC Berkeley undergraduate courses on the Maya—Maya Cosmovisions, History and Ethnography of the Maya, and Mesoamerican Archeology. These classes equipped me with a solid knowledge base to conduct ethnographic fieldwork at ancient Maya archaeology sites.

JCC.   Was it the summer when we met in Merida?

TR.   Yes, and if you remember, my initial research question was simple: how do local Maya farmers in Chunchucmil and Kochol feel about foreign academics working on their communal farmland, hiring locals as laborers, and essentially telling locals how to work their land (Rodriguez 2001)? It was an ethnography of archaeologists. I worked as an archaeological apprentice for a graduate student; it was an ideal situation . . .

JCC.   Okay, but how did you understand the Maya from all your readings?

TR.   Well, the Maya I had in mind were the ones from ethnographies by Villa Rojas (1978), Redfield (1941, 1950), Redfield and Villa Rojas (1934), and Castañeda (1996). In terms of linguistics, the studies of Hanks (1990, 1999, 2003) of deixis (spatial referencing) and indexicality in Maya T'aan and the Chicago audio recordings of spoken Yucatec Maya (Blair and Vermont Salas 1967) helped me grasp the Yucatec Maya language. Historically, Sullivan (1989) painted a picture of the contradiction between Maya rebels and archaeologists; from the archeological perspective, my images of the ancient Maya were shaped by the massive book *The Ancient Maya* by Morley, Brainerd, and Sharer (1983), *Mesoamerican Elites* by Chase and Chase (1994), and works on the site of Chunchucmil in Yucatán by Dahlin (2000), Ardren (2002), and Ardren, Hutson, and Magnoni (2000). My academic vision of Maya culture and the archaeological site of Chunchucmil was shaped by these discourses.

JCC.   These readings were your introduction to the ethnogenesis of the Maya.[1]

TR.   I see what you mean. Already in my first field season I began to understand the dynamics, in practice, of how archaeologists produce knowledge on the ancient Maya. This reality became ethnographically transparent when the pueblo of Kochol did not allow the archaeological project to conduct research on its *ejido* for a few months (Rodriguez 2006).

Field Journal, May 2001, Timoteo Rodriguez

Lunch break at the archaeological dig site on the ejido of Kochol.

The five archaeologists sit together, and about fifteen Kocholeños (people of Kochol) sit in three groups. I climb the 10-meter mound adjacent to the household structure we are excavating; a few of the farmers join me.

One is the town's evangelical minister. He had been very kind to me as we worked together, so I thought I would make my first steps in ethnographic fieldwork with him. I ask, "Who do you think built these ancient pyramids?"

He pauses, then looks me directly in the eyes and says, "¡*Los Aztecas*!"

I had anticipated a different answer. It should have been "my glorious Maya ancestors. The archaeologists are helping us remember and discover our lost history." But that was not the case. My academic visions start to crumble with his answer.

ETHNOGENESIS IS A HUGE QUINCUNX, JUAN CASTILLO COCOM.

Ethnogenesis has great appeal. Some scholars are in love with the term. Others fall in and out of love with it. What we mean by love is *philos*, love of knowledge. It is this love of new information, new terms, that gives continuous birth and rebirth to the idea of ethnos or belonging. Those obsessed with ethnos think it it possible to build their philos through the concept of ethnogenesis.

Ethnogenesis explains the historical creation and recreation of identity through time and space. In particular, the "cultures" that are most inculcated to being "born" are in fact the peoples who survived conquest and colonialization. In the maintenance of Colonial social order, these obsessives can arrange and constitute their explanations still further by *structuring structures*, responding, as they see it, to the already established needs of a generative epistemic order. Lovers become pregnant with explanation, and what is born is not new life but a huge and unwieldy "ethnos quincunx."

In the Chilam Balam de Chumayel, the earth is described geometrically as a rectangular plane—an enormous *Ceiba* tree grows at its center (Bricker 1990; Roys 1933).[2] The tree supports the skies along with the other four mythical trees rooted at each corner of the plane (Montoliu Villar 1987). This is the quincunx (fig. 3.1).

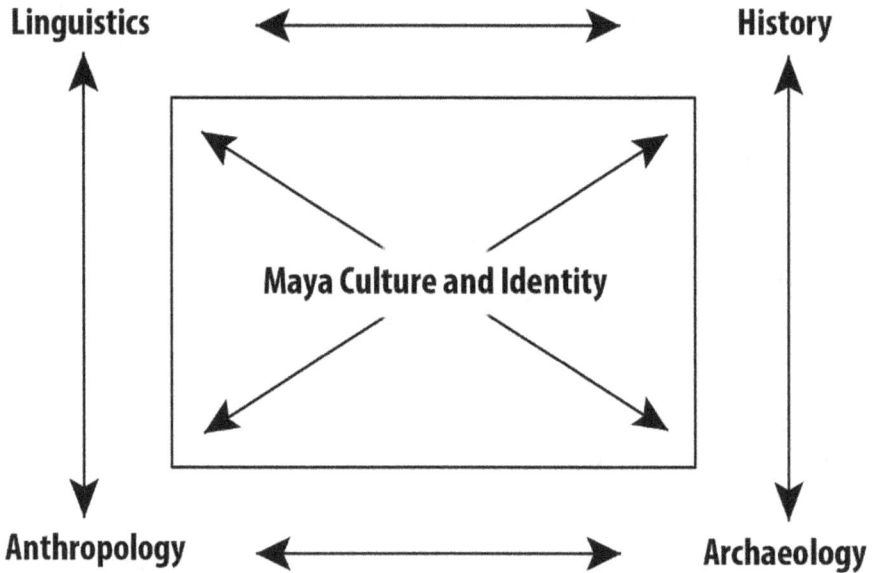

FIGURE 3.1. The quincunx

The Zinacantecos named it "Balamil." In their world, the center of the upper sur-face—the navel—is a low, rounded mound of earth located at the ceremonial center of Zinacantán. This place is a vortex from which the world extends from inside out and vice versa (Vogt 1990).

Touring the quincunx means traversing with the objectivist samples of knowing. According to what we have read of the Maya, the original quincunx explains how earth and humans were created, but for ethnogenisists the quincunx functions as more of a decoder that can disentangle and define the parameters of Maya identity. This model is composed of five dominions. The first four are history, linguistics, anthropology, and archaeology. The fifth emerges at the intersection of the other four: Maya culture and identity, the holy center, the *Ceiba*. Each dominion is a sacred tree of Westernizing knowledge.

SITTING IN A COLE'S COFFEEHOUSE ACROSS THE STREET FROM SAFEWAY, OAKLAND, CA. THE COFFEE HERE IS BETTER. MARCH 2008, JUAN CASTILLO COCOM AND TIMOTEO RODRIGUEZ

TR.   What do you mean by ethnoexodus?

JCC.   My point is that ethnoexodus is about interpellating the socially consti-tuted status. You escape one frame by slipping into another.

TR.   Okay, and in Bourdieu's theory of practice, one's habitus operates in different fields of power relations with symbolic capital. Look here, in *The Logic of Practice* he defines *habitus* as follows:

The conditioning associated with a particular class of conditions of existence produce[s] *habitus*, systems of durable, transposable dispositions, structured structures predisposed to function as structuring structures, that is, as principles which generate and organize practices and representations that can be objectively adapted to their outcomes without presupposing a conscious aiming at ends or an express mastery of the operations necessary in order to attain them. Objectively "regulated" and "regular" without in any way being the product of obedience to rules, they can be collectively orchestrated without being the product of the orchestrating action of a conductor. (Bourdieu 1990:181–90)

JCC.   I like how Bourdieu writes tautologically. But Timo, why do we have to explain everything with Bourdieu or Foucault? What these thinkers say is no doubt very important, but there are other ways of thinking. In anthropology, you are trained to think of things in a Westernized knowledge framework.

TR.   Of course, I agree that there are other ways of being that are distinct ways of knowing. In anthropology a baseline epistemic violence is done when Westernizing conceptual frames absorb indigenous ways of thinking into the "taboo effect"—that is, when an indigenous concept like "taboo" loses its meaning in translation and then comes to mean many things. The key here is that in modes of translation, it is important not to colonize meaning by attempting to create the conditions of possibility for what should be knowable and thinkable.

JCC.   Taboo effect . . . I'll have to think about that. Translation is about moving "in and out of context." It is about deepening the human experience. And Timo, you wrote in the KAS [Kroeber Anthropological Society] article (Rodriguez 2007) that habitus is useful for thinking through generative accumulative ways of being, right?

TR.   Yes, and Juan, you cannot pretend that you are not in the academy. You are always in a Western frame on a very fundamental level.

JCC.   That is exactly the problem! Anthropology always leaves little space to allow indigenous people, in fact all people, the opportunity to produce their own knowledge . . . That's "the Ishi effect," and thus we are forced to explain our notions in their Eurocentric framings. So, with ethnoexodus it's about interpellating social status in epistemic framings. You escape one frame by slipping into another. And surprisingly, we end up in the same frame of ethnogenesis. Thus, escape is just an illusionary act.

TR.   Well, that is exactly why I say that ethnoexodus is still Eurocentric from an epistemic position.

JCC.   Uh huh, experts on us, *los Indios*, came to us, studied us, and explained how the act of becoming Maya is performed through ethno-topographies that are epochal events and historical processes. So, ethnogenesis is an act of faith because it is completely constructed, and for it to exist someone needs to believe in it; ethnoexodus is the act of living, NOT surviving.

TR.   This calls for the necessity to de-colonialize the act of living in an epistemic way. For example, Barack Obama's election to the White House may correctly be considered a de-colonializing political defeat of "Jim Crow."[3] But it is not necessarily a counter to epistemic racism (Grosfoguel 2007). Ethnogenesis, as an epistemic act of faith, is like Bourdieu's idea of the *doxa*, which is about "practical faith" as an inherent part of belonging to an academic "field" of knowledge production.

JCC.   And for Maya identity politics or identity formation in general, this kind of academic doxa is an assuming imposition of a disposition (a performing ethnos) in the "structured structures predisposed to function as structuring structures" of identification. This is ethnogenesis.

TR.   Yes, and for Bourdieu, doxa is "the precondition and the product of function of the field . . . constituting the collective enterprise of creating symbolic capital" [Bourdieu 1990:68]. As such, doxa establishes the relationship between habitus and the field it engages. In the practice trichotomy (capital, field, and habitus), what is at stake, or rather the bare unit of analysis the entire theory rests on, is the notion of status.

JCC.   When considering status in relation to identity formation, there is a distinction between "identity" and "identification," where identification is about an assuming imposition of a position in a "generative field" embedded in power relations. Identity is something else.

TR.   So the question for me becomes: if capital, field, and habitus are about identity formation and what is at stake in practice is status, and given the "incorporated" and "objectified" historical power relations that constitute identification, how does one's durable, transposable race expose the limits to the notion of acquired dispositions? In other words, identity formation is acquired in a field through gaining more symbolic value or capital. This is in fact not at all symbolic. Rather, it is a lived experience through your body. The trichotomy of practice is related to your culture, class, and embodiment of habitus. The materiality and features of a person's body exist prior to its habitus, which constitutes the schematic dispositions accumulated through symbolic capital in a social field of power relationships.

JCC.   Yeah, so this is simply about how you look. It is about your phenotypical features, your racial construction. Your habitus is always in your racialized body regardless of all the capital you gain and status you believe you have or the multiple fields you enter and exit.

TR.   And, of course, the salience of racialization will vary across context. It depends upon the gaze. How you "view" yourself and how you internalize "views" of yourself. In a phenomenological sense, a person is "looked at" more during a typical day than he or she looks at himself or herself.

JCC.   True . . . And have you seen the speech on *race* Obama just gave called "A More Perfect Union" (Obama 2008)?

TR.   It was fantastic!

JCC.   The movement in Obama's speech exemplifies what I mean by ethnoexodus. He conveyed an entry into territories of identities that multiply his already numerous identity formations. He said something like "[mine is] a story that has seared into my genetic makeup the idea that this nation is more than the sum of its parts—that out of many, we are truly one." Then he said, "Some commentators have deemed me either 'too black' or 'not black enough.'" His perpetual exiting and entering of identity is completely embedded in an "incorporated" and "objectified" historical power relation of identification. With ease, he slips in and out through his own identity politics.

TR.   So going beyond the imaginary and the symbolic by connecting one's presences to an epistemic form, that is a decolonizing epistemology and thus doesn't necessarily rely on Westernizing frameworks of status, when status translates to more hierarchies.

JCC.   Yes, and what I am doing with ethnoexodus is what I like to call the "Indian Casino Effect." I am conceptually cashing in on the reservation of notions the gringos imposed. I am flipping *La Tiendas de Raya*.

LINDA, A FORMER STUDENT, AND TIMOTEO HAVING CAPPUCCINOS AND CONVERSATION ABOUT MAYA PEOPLE IN CALIFORNIA AT AN ITALIAN RESTAURANT IN SAN FRANCISCO'S NORTH BEACH NEIGHBORHOOD, FEBRUARY 2008, TIMOTEO RODRIGUEZ AND LINDA BARRERA

TR.   Well, critically understanding the usage of the term *Maya* as a concept requires grappling with the ways different people speak *about* the Maya, *to* the Maya, *for* the Maya, and *as* the Maya.

LB.   Oh, like how Juan Castillo Cocom decides to be Maya depending on the situation. (Laughs.)

TR.   By critically rethinking *who* is Maya, *how,* and *when* is his point. Thus, to be Maya today has different meanings for a Yucateco maize farmer, a North American anthropologist, an activist involved in the pan-Maya movement, or for Juan Castillo Cocom.

LB.   Or the dishwasher in this restaurant.

TR.   Yes.

LB.   That busboy from Merida thinks differently about being Maya than the dishwasher who is from a *pueblito*.

TR.   Yeah, so there is an ethnoracial signifier that associates as part of the ethnos category: for instances, dress or attire and certainly pheno-types as biological features categorize as racial markers.

LB.   But race is a social construct.

TR.   Yes, and as a social construct, ethnoracial categories affect social attitudes, emotional dispositions, and political-economic rationales in a legacy of colonial power relations, also called the colonial matrix of power.

KROEBER HALL, ROOM 151, ANTHROPOLOGY 179, HISTORY AND ETHNOGRAPHY OF THE MAYA, *"TECHNOLOGIES OF HISTORY,"* DECEMBER 2008, TIMOTEO RODRIGUEZ

If we consider the proposition *what could be more important than the truth* or, put another way, who has the capacity, force, and access to certain kinds of power relations that facilitate or inculcate individuals with a practical sense, belief, or faith in prescribed parameters of what can be thought of as truth and falsehood, then the question becomes: how are status and identity politics related to the claims of truth in history?

As such, through an "event" in history and the "process" of re-collecting the *socio-genic* (Fanon 1967) historical fragments of past contexts in a "continuous contextu-alizing" present, we find that human conditions rotate through a series of embed-ded power struggles. To tell history is to interpret the present, and William Hanks (1996:269) writes: "The telling of history is filtered through the genres in which it occurs." So, an understanding of this human condition is considered one and the same, a bodily human object of existence in symbiotic relation to a human epis-temic subject of knowledge.

Given this, the question becomes: how are status and identity related to a bio-logical hierarchy?

In Yucatán, Mexico, the ethnos of the Maya is in many ways a consequence of what Walter Mignolo (2001) schematized as the modern/Colonial world system. During the initial conquest, native people were legally referred to and racially categorized as Indio, Indians. In this early Colonial period, other racial-legal con-figurations such as Mestizo, Mulatto, and Negro were developed and invented. In the Spanish colony, the people who embodied these categories operated in a social order of apartheid. The most segregated were the Indios, who lived in their own physical and social sphere—La República de Indios.

The colonizing European "man"—Peninsular or Criollo—positioned himself at the top of this racial hierarchy. These were self-identified *gente de razón* (rational people) (Lockhart and Schwartz 1999). This position linked an epistemic configu-ration to biological structures.

As the Bourbon reforms and then hacienda plantations gained more prominence, Yucatec native identification moved away from Maya T'aan terms such as Almehen or Chembal Uinic through the Franciscan missionary notion of Indio reducido and into lunero, a native who worked on a Hispanic estate on Mondays. These luneros then became full-fledge debt peonage peasants, *campesinos*, or *henequeneros*. My point with this Yucatec genealogy of identity politics is that each historical form of identification perpetuated a racial-legal and socioeconomic norm of the colonial-ized subject.

In the early 1800s, as Spanish American colonies declared independence, New Spain and La República de Indios collapsed, yet the emergences of Criollo nation-alist identity maintained internal Colonial structures and identity markers (Bonfil Batalla 1994; Lockhart and Schwartz 1999). Even though Colonial administrations had been dismantled, Colonial relations with identification continued, as exem-plified by terms from the social categories of the Colonial period for Maya peo-ple, such as *Indio, Lunero, Hidalgo, J-Wíit, Masewal, Almehen, Mehen,* and *Uinic* (Hervik 2003; Restall 2004).

In Yucatán today, identifiers and social categories are terms like Indio, Mestizo, *X-éek' pik* (*justán sucio*), *Wiro, Naco*, Totonaco, Indígena, and Maya. As Güemez Pineda writes:

> The urban discrimination toward Maya Yucateco speakers and/or "mestizos" is manifested in the use of pejorative terms and expressions like *wiro*, "*mestiza*" (or "*wirito*" or "*mesticita*" . . .). "*Gente ignorante*" (ignorant people); "*Gente pobre*" (poor people); "*indio*" (Indian), even "*Naco*." These terms are usually used to refer to the Maya-campesino population. Thus, one can hear in the popular jargon expressions like: "*Pareces mestiza de pueblo*" (You seem racially a mestiza of a pueblo); "*es un wiro*" (he is wiro'); "*es más naco*" (he is very naco). Even "*ser de pueblo*" (to come from a pueblo) still constitutes a social stigma. (Güémez Pineda n.d.)

The next paragraph is an example of the use of these offensive terms. Conrado Roche Reyes (2007), a journalist and respected writer who confesses that he is a racist and who in the quincunx is a *Catrín, Ts'ul*, or *Blanco*, was struck in his knee by a bus of the urban transport service of Mérida, Yucatán. In telling his story he writes:

> I felt a great pain. First thing that came to my mind was to tell to him: "*chinga tu madre indio de mierda*." Like *hunouaye* [*sic*],[4] he step[ped] down from his bus and came on me to hit me . . . Forgive me *indigenistas* for my enormous racism, but I have noticed that nothing is more offensive to an Indio than to be called Indio. I affirm it. (Roche Reyes 2007:4)

> Lo primero que se me ocurrió fue decirle: "chinga tu madre indio de mierda." Como *hunouaye* [*sic*], se bajó de su "unidad" y se me fue encima. Y es que, perdónenme los indigenistas, en mi enorme racismo, me he dado cuenta que nada ofende más a un indio, que le llamen indio. Yo . . . lo afirmo. (Roche Reyes 2007:4)

Since colonialism is imbricated in the formation of the modern nation-state, many Colonial forms of domination and normative hierarchies of labor, spirituality, aesthetics, gender, sexuality, epistemology, and ethno-racial identity persist. Anibal Quijano (2000) refers to these relations as *coloniality*. Thus, enlightened nationalism brought civil liberties for some and subjugation to the "coloniality of power" for others. Ramón Grosfoguel (2003:4) concisely defines coloniality of power as referring to "a crucial structuring process in the modern/Colonial capitalist world-system that articulates peripheral locations in the international division of labor, subaltern group political strategies, and Third World migrant's [*sic*] inscription in the racial/ethnic hierarchy of metropolitan global cities."

How the coloniality of power takes shape in identity formation through the second nationalist movement after the 1910 Mexican Revolution is particularly important to contemporary epistemic framings. The post-revolutionary nationalism, Mexican archaeology, and ethnography provided the state with fresh pre-Columbian *cultural capital* to affirm nationalist roots (Rus 2004; Watanabe and Fischer 2004) yet simultaneously relegated indigenous people to an idyllic past, as such quintessentially pre-modern.

Robert Redfield's "urban-folk continuum" (1941) operates in this coloniality matrix, and Mel Gibson's (2006) *Apocalypto* film further exemplifies its legacy. Hence, the notion of the Maya in the framework of coloniality emerged in the twentieth century as an *anthropos* in the ethnos—as a non-European "man" in the colonialized identification subject position (subjectivity)—to be investigated from the nationalist side of the coloniality of power (as opposed to the side of de-colonializing epistemic difference).

In broadening the scope to Guatemala, Chiapas, and the pan-Maya Movement, the challenges posed by Maya intellectuals not only emphasize coloniality in anthropological inquiry but also stress its configuration of research agendas toward identity formation (Cojtí Cuxil 1991; Montejo 1999; Zapeta 1997). Epistemically, what takes shape is an anastrophe-like effect on the ethnos. This movement is an affect practice that traverses the topography of reasoned anthropological discourse toward a trans-ethnos attitude (Rodriguez 2007). The "traditional" normalized social order of the anthropos (the third-person ontological unit) in the ethnos (the exotic bounded unit of analysis) is epistemically transfigured, or rather de-colonialized, by subsuming and turning back to the rationale of Westernizing constructs that positioned the colonizing European man as gente de razón. Further, this trans-ethnos attitude is a contemporary body politics of knowledge that escapes the game of status by not falling into anticipation of historically produced conditions of possibility that tell you and me "who we are" and "how we should be." As such, the legacy of the Colonial matrix of power, which linked an epistemic configuration to phenotype and biological structures, is thus inverted but not as an essentialist or reductionist form of identity politics—rather, as a contemporary inquiry that critically pushes beyond the limits imposed through the normalized technologies of history.

ETHNOS: A GENESIS OF THE WESTERN CIVILIZATION IMAGINARY, TIMOTEO RODRIGUEZ

The term *ethnos* (ἔθνος) is rooted in ancient Greece, the birthplace of the Western civilization imaginary. The concept of ethnos had the connotation of an oppositional category of identification for ancient Greeks. Originally meaning "a number of people living together, host of men, of a particular tribe or caste," ethnos further referred to "non-Athenian athletes during the Olympics." Later, in the Roman period, the term signified a "province" or colony of the empire. In general, ethnos meant "nation or people." But it also came to mean "foreign, barbarous nation or people" (Liddell and Scott 1948). As such, ethnos indexes more than a convenience for early anthropologists in their study of the "savage" (ethnology) and the writing of colonized people (ethnography). An anthropology without an ethnos is unthinkable. Thus, the thinkable or politically correct anthropologist activates a technology of history in a specific locus and within a framing of a particular epistemic position. A trichotomy of time, space, and an episteme are the elements that constitute an ethnogenesis.

Whereas the ancient Greeks are the genesis of democracy, civility, morality, and philosophy in a macro-narrative of Western civilization, the ethnos is the diametric identity marker for this Westernizing imaginary. As such, this macro-narrative is tied to a celebratory historiography that first occurred during the Renaissance. Iberian colonialism of the Americas and Africa is the "darker side of the Renaissance" (Mignolo 1999). This darker side in the sixteenth century is the coloniality embedded in the modernity of the twenty-first century. Further, for Quijano (2000), coloniality of power is a principle and strategy of control and domination that can be conceived of as a configuration of modernity.

It follows that European imperialist arrangements of materials, events, processes, and people took a hierarchical order, distinguishing primary sources of thought in the pristine development of a birthplace for Western civilization in its land of origin: Greece (Mignolo 2001). The consolidation of a Western civilization imaginary occurs with northwestern European imperialist ambitions, the French Enlightenment, German Romantic philosophy, and the British Industrial Revolution (all nations and ideas that are part of Mexico's convoluted history). The emergence and epistemic framing of the social sciences in the nineteenth century are inseparable from this Westernizing macro-narrative (Mignolo 2000, 2001). The principles of Western epistemology developed out of an invented set of values that started in Greece.

The European imperial difference draws out a time/space matrix that creates a Western civilization imaginary, which first flourished with the Spanish Conquest of the indigenous people and places of the Americas. The conquest marked the distinction between imperial and Colonial difference at one level and simultaneously produced clear hierarchies that were ethnoracialized categories, a specific set of sexual/gender relations, a Christo-spiritual qualification, forced labor, and a Eurocentric episteme.

Those hierarchies were not static and did not produce strict lines of brown and white or a clear mestizaje. Hence, there is no real contemporary dichotomy between the Maya and non-Maya. For example, *h meen* (roughly translated as "shaman") epitomize something that is/is not Spanish, is/is not Maya, and certainly is/is not Mestizo or any "mathematical" combination of those identity tags. In diasporic times and places of the 40,000 Mayas living in California, a *h meen* in this context might be a Chicano, a Cholo, a Mara Salvatrucha, a Latino, a cook, a busser, a day laborer, a heroin user, an *evangélico*, and so on. This is *Nepantla* (Anzaldúa 1999), which references living at the *crossroads*, in the *borderlands* of identity formation. Its analytical traction is a way to think through embodied in-betweenness and multiplicity through identity. As such, Nepantla is the movement in and out of ethnogenesis boxes.

The writers of the Books of Chilam Balam, or contemporary *h meen*, interpellated the Colonial framing of knowledge production. They subsumed the epistemology and the spiritualization of knowledge from the locus of the so-called ethnos. The Franciscan missionaries in their "peaceful conquest" and with the project of *reducción* attempted to produce *indios reducidos* through *policía cristiana* by coordinating space, conduct, and language (Hanks 2010), with the hope of "structurating" the conditions of possibility for predictable anticipations of identification. Centuries later, a consequence of imposed identification from reducción is the epistemic emergence of anthropologists (like Morley, Redfield, and Villa Rojas) believed to have unearthed an ethnos at Chichén Itzá or in Chan Kom and X-cacal, respectively. This ethnogenesis identification, rooted in the Western civilization imaginary, maintains a pristine narrative that sustains a prosperous academic paradigm and Yucatán's tourist industries but leaves Mayas like Castillo Cocom trapped in a quincunx of air conditioning and stuffed, painted iguanas.

ESCAPING THE QUINCUNX: THE INDIVIDUAL INTERPLAY OF IKNAL AND THE CURRENT OF SELF-GENERATED IDENTIFICATIONS, JUAN CASTILLO COCOM

Ethnoexodus moves in and out of imposed limits of epistemic frameworks in a Westernizing legacy. It migrates, uses, and draws upon one's disposition in a given social environment, corporal field, or neglect situation. Perhaps we could think of this movement as one's habitus because at one level, habitus is exactly that: a disposition in a field of power that brings out one's capacities to act in a particular social setting. That is also what ethnoexodus does because it is "who you are" and "how you are" identified that creates an embodied cultural, social, or academic capital.

As habitus is transposable, it goes with you wherever you are; in one context you will act one way, and in another you draw upon a different disposition. This depends on what is at stake in a particular social field of power relations; thus, the social actor will access dispositions that are bodily. Ethnoexodus could be described in this way, too. The problem with habitus, if we are thinking from the perspective of a Colonial difference, and the problem with ethnoexodus, if we are thinking of the epistemic rupture of the Colonial difference, is that like genesis, "habitus," "ethnos," and "exodus" all draw upon a lexicon and a conceptualization that do not necessarily break with an epistemic narrative of the Western civilization imaginary.

Ethnoexodus disrupts the idea of ethnogenesis by interpellating it; it still hangs on to the Westernizing epistemic framing, though, as does habitus. Nevertheless, there are crucial distinctions between habitus and ethnoexodus. Habitus has a universal or neutral connotation of identity formation that falls on either side of the dichotomy that is the Colonial or imperial epistemic difference. Ethnoexodus or ethnogenesis, in contrast, seems to always fall on the side of the Colonial difference because ethnos cannot be neutral or universal. It always refers to non-dominant people through discourses and practices. This is why epistemically there is history and then there is ethnohistory; there is botany and ethnobotany, musicology and ethnomusicology, anthropology and ethnic studies. What is needed is a notion that does not necessarily draw its conceptual tradition from a Westernizing imaginary but rather subsumes it. This would be something like a trans-ethnos movement (Rodriguez 2007), but it would not actually need to move in and then beyond a Eurocentricizing knowledge base. It does not need to be a *trans* or an *ethnos*. We propose the concept of iknal.

Iknal is not necessarily related to status as its most basic unit of analysis in the way habitus necessitates status. Iknal has most of the characteristics of habitus but also conceptualizes other situations, frames of reference, and indexical fields that are not possible to conceptualize with habitus. One's habitus is always with that individual, whereas one's iknal can reside in a locality without the person's physical presence and yet still index that person's *place*. Iknal has been defined as "in front of, with, before, *presence*" (Bricker, Po'ot Yah, and Dzul de Po'ot 1998:11, emphasis added). So one could say in Maya T'aan *ko'oten t'inwiknal* San Francisco, which translates as "come to my place in San Francisco." According to the Cordemex Maya Dictionary, iknal is defined as "con/with, en compañía/in the company of, *en poder/in charge of or in control of*, en casa/at home, o donde alguno está/ or where someone is" (Barrera Vásquez et al. 1980, emphasis added). With a focus on *presence* and *en poder*, one's iknal is the embodied *context* and *product* of social relations. Thus, iknal has to do with where a person is physically and habitually present but is not caught in the power game of status.

Another distinction is expressed by the phrase *tinwiknal*, which means "*at* (or *to*) my place" in association with space transformed by labor or inhabitance (Hanks 1990:436–40). It becomes a kind of *place*holder as long as that person habitually frequents that locality through his or her presence. A person's iknal could reside at the side of the kitchen in the fine restaurant at which he or she works or on the step a person sits on in front of his or her apartment in San Francisco's Mission District, on a bicycle ride, or at the place I stand in a crowded metro train (Rodriguez 2007).

Epistemically, iknal is at the core of Maya thinking. In Maya T'aan one's iknal is the embodied and disembodied quality of "being present" as the *context* and *product* of relationships. It is both a shared and an individuated transposable field of sensory awareness and action. It is "presence" and "en poder." The iknal is an understanding of one's bodily space and one's perceptive opinion and attitude. Iknal is the potential of omnipresence: the state of being present in all places at all times. Wherever you are at any moment, your iknal is there with you. Iknal is a human experience, experienced by experiencing Maya philosophy. Ethnoexodus is the movement in and out of the context of power relations through identity formations without status. Although what is familiar is not the same, iknal is an example of a universal human performance that exceeds status. Iknal through ethnoexodus is the complexity of human experience—always existing in the dynamism of past, present, and imagined spaces informed by the fluidity of multiple identifications and experiences.

On another level, ethnoexodus embodies and breaks the limits of "epistemic double-consciousness." It subsumes what is believed to be generative to knowledge that produces tradition—the genesis of the ethnos—and then perverts ethnogenesis by forcing it into the box it pretends to never be a part of, which is "essentialism." Ethnoexodus does not mean there is no Maya; rather, it means that what is Maya is the individual interplay of iknal and the current of self-generated identifications, removed from the quincunx.

In the same way colonialism is constitutive of modernity, the concept of ethnogenesis emphasizes the study of the ethnos. As such, the ethnos is not necessarily the most productive unit of analysis of the construction of a Maya identity (or identity formation in general). Thus, the ethnos simply maintains the status of Westernizing science and the identity structures that hold that science to be true.

ANOTHER FANCY RESTAURANT IN JOSÉ MARÍA MORELOS, QUINTANA ROO, MEXICO, DRINKING UNFILTERED AGUA DE CHAYA CON PIÑA, SEPTEMBER–DECEMBER 2014, MCCALE ASHENBRENER

Castillo Cocom's course Derechos Humanos Indígenas y Organización Étnica (Human Rights and Ethnic Indigenous Organization) was enlightening, fascinating, and frustrating. I was intrigued by ethnoexodus but often confused by his segmented and ruptured delivery. Over the course of many long lunches, I was able to tease out my understanding of ethnoexodus. This concept focuses on the movement between and among identities, reflecting on the situational variables that cause one to highlight or hide indigeneities to escape from discriminatory processes of socio-cultural marginalization. Essentially, Castillo Cocom is tired of having to define himself within a Western imaginary paradigm, which uses static ideas of time, space, and "objective" knowledge. He proposes iknal as a new lens with which to view identity construction that is more fluid and dynamic and that can encompass the almost ineffable complexity of interplay between competing identifications. Just as all of what we are cannot exist in a box of unidentifiable remains, our presence is not constricted purely to our physical location or status; therefore, it is worth exploring another perspective on what it means to be.

In the end, I believe Castillo Cocom wants to transcend ethnogenesis, which uses the quincunx as a decoder of sorts where you plug in certain variables and out pops a formulaic and fictitious identification of "Maya." Perhaps through ethnoexodus, Castillo Cocom would like to focus less on what Maya *is* than on what it is *not*; instead, exploring the temporal sutures in which we choose to escape the identity social constructs inevitably provide to us and which we find inadequate. Castillo Cocom has a unique perspective in that he has traversed the gleaming halls of academia at Florida International University, the University of Maryland, and the University of California, Berkeley, but he exists primarily in the haunted ground of his ancestors (whoever they were). He feels the enormous weight of the quincunx, like Ishi, trapped in a museum of words in which the ethnogenesist delineation of "Maya" is rooted in a fictitious and constructed past. In a very real way, for him as Maya it is imperative to escape the concrete galoshes of the quincunx to re-conceptualize the long fetishized Maya identity through the ubiquity of iknal and the mobility of ethnoexodus that interpellates the inherent rules to the network of discursive and non-discursive relations that has been defining who, what, when, where, and why is Maya since the late nineteenth century.

ACKNOWLEDGMENTS, JUAN CASTILLO COCOM

I express my gratitude to William Hanks. His studies of iknal as deixis, or spatial referencing, and indexicality in Maya T'aan are at the core of this chapter. Understanding Iknal as a spatial marker disembodied from the individual indexing presence of a specific person marked the path to ethnoexodus.

I owe special thanks to Patricia Baquedano López for inviting me to participate in the 2007 Center for Latino Policy Research Seminar series at UC Berkeley. Many of the ideas on ethnoexodus started spinning in my head in that seminar, and she helped me shape them. Without her, this chapter would never have found its way.

Special thanks to Beatriz Reyes-Foster for her significant contributions to this chapter.

Thanks to Robert Brocklehurst for his encouragement and refining commentary in finalizing my text.

Finally, I want to recognize Selmi Salomé, Mark Aleksi, and Juan Ariel for their unconditional support during the many years this chapter has been churning inside my head and heart until it made its way out of my hands and onto paper.

NOTES

1. My studies at Berkeley covered what Castillo Cocom refers to as the "quincunx." But finally I was going to take my first stab at producing knowledge about not just the Maya but the producers of the production of the Maya.

2. *Ceiba pentandra*, or Ya'axché in Yucatec Maya.

3. The Jim Crow laws created segregated public facilities, which designated "separate but equal" status for black Americans and other non-white racial groups between 1876 and 1965 in the United States.

4. Roche Reyes (2007) uses this term as a combination of two quincunxs (Hun and Uaye') to imply that an Indio is a savage, brute, beast, wild man/woman, ruffian, vandal, troglodyte. Huns: Savage and barbaric people who invaded Europe in the fourth century. Uaye' (*waye'*): in Maya T'aan that means "here" (aquí, acá). *Tene' uayileen* (*tene' wayile'en*) [yo soy de aquí o acá].

REFERENCES CITED

Anderson, Gary C. 1999. *The Indian Southwest, 1580–1830: Ethnogenesis and Reinvention*. Norman: University of Oklahoma Press.

Anzaldúa, Gloria. 1999. *Borderlands = La Frontera*. San Francisco: Aunt Lute Books.

Ardren, Traci, ed. 2002. *Ancient Maya Women*. Walnut Creek, CA: Altamira.

Ardren, Traci, Scott Hutson, and Aline Magnoni. 2000. "In and Out of Place: Regionalization, Circulation, and the Social Production of Space at Prehispanic Chunchucmil, Yucatan, Mexico." Paper presented at the 99th Annual Meeting of the American Anthropological Association, San Francisco, CA, November 15–19.

Barrera Vásquez, Alfredo, Juan Ramón Bastarrachea Manzano, William Brito Sansores, Vermont Salas Refugio, and David Dzul Góngora. 1980. *Diccionario Maya Cordemex*. Mérida, Yucatán, Mexico: Ediciones Cordemex.

Blair, Robert, and Refugio Vermont Salas. 1967. *Spoken (Yucatec) Maya*. Chicago: Department of Anthropology, University of Chicago.

Bonfil Batalla, Guillermo. 1994. *México Profundo: Una Civilización Negada*. Mexico City: Editorial Grijalbo.

Bourdieu, Pierre. 1990. *The Logic of Practice*. Oxford: Basil Blackwell.

Bricker, Victoria R. 1990. *A Morpheme Concordance of the Book of Chilam Balam of Chumayel*. New Orleans: Middle American Research Institute.

Bricker, Victoria R., Eleuterio Po'ot Yah, and Ofelia Dzul de Po'ot, eds. 1998. *A Dictionary of the Maya Language as Spoken in Hocabá, Yucatán*. Salt Lake City: University of Utah Press.

Castañeda, Quetzil E. 1996. *In the Museum of Maya Culture: Touring Chichén Itzá*. Minneapolis: University of Minnesota Press.

Castillo Cocom, Juan A. 2007. "Maya Scenarios: Indian Stories In and Out of Contexts." *Kroeber Anthropological Society* 96: 13–35.

Chase, Diane, and Arlen Chase. 1994. *Mesoamerican Elites: An Archaeological Assessment*. Norman: University of Oklahoma Press.

Cojtí Cuxil, Demetrio. 1991. *Configuración del pensamiento político del pueblo maya*. Quetzaltenango: Asociación de Escritores Mayances de Guatemala.

Dahlin, Bruce H. 2000. "The Barricade and Abandonment of Chunchucmil: Implications for Northern Maya Warfare." *Latin American Antiquity* 11 (3): 283–98. http://dx.doi .org/10.2307/972179.

de Landa, Diego. 1959. *Relación de las Cosas de Yucatán*. Mexico City: Editorial Porrúa.

Fanon, Frantz. 1967. *Black Skin, White Masks*. New York: Grove.

Fennell, Christopher C. 2007. *Crossroads and Cosmologies: Diasporas and Ethnogenesis in the New World*. Gainesville: University Press of Florida.

Gibson, Mel. 2006. *Apocalypto*. Burbank, CA: Touchstone Pictures.

Grosfoguel, Ramón. 2003. *Colonial Subjects: Puerto Ricans in a Global Perspective*. Berkeley: University of California Press.

Grosfoguel, Ramón. 2007. "The Epistemic Decolonial Turn: Beyond Political-Economy Paradigms." *Cultural Studies* 21 (2–3): 211–23. http://dx.doi.org/10.1080/0950238060 1162514.

Güémez Pineda, Miguel. n.d. "Mujer 'Maya': Identidad y Cambio Cultural en el Sur de Yucatán." Accessed October 14, 2016. http://www.mayas.uady.mx/articulos/mujer.html.

Hanks, William F. 1990. *Referential Practice: Language and Lived Space among the Maya*. Chicago: University of Chicago Press.

Hanks, William F. 1996. *Language and Communicative Practices: Critical Essays in Anthropology*. Boulder: Westview.

Hanks, William F. 1999. *Intertexts: Writing on Language, Utterance, and Context*. Denver: Rowman and Littlefield.

Hanks, William F. 2003. " 'Reducción' and the Remaking of the Social Landscape in Colonial Yucatán." In *Espacios Mayas: Representaciones, Usos, Creencias*, ed. Alain Breton, Aurore Monod Becquelin, and Mario Humberto Ruz, 161–80. Mexico City: Universidad Nacional Autónoma de México.

Hanks, William F. 2010. *Converting Words: Maya in the Age of the Cross*. Berkeley: University of California Press. http://dx.doi.org/10.1525/california/9780520257702 .001.0001.

Hervik, Peter. 2003. *Mayan People within and beyond Boundaries: Social Categories and Lived Identity in Yucatán*. New York: Routledge.

Hill, Jonathan D., ed. 1996. *History, Power, and Identity: Ethnogenesis in the Americas, 1492–1992*. Iowa City: University of Iowa Press.

Liddell, Henry George, and Robert Scott, eds. 1948. *Greek-English Lexicon*, vol. 1. London: Oxford University Press.

Lockhart, James, and Stuart B. Schwartz. 1999. *Early Latin America: A History of Colonial Spanish and Brazil*. Cambridge: Cambridge University Press.

Mignolo, Walter. 1999. *The Darker Side of the Renaissance: Literacy, Territoriality, and Colonialization*. Ann Arbor: University of Michigan Press.

Mignolo, Walter. 2000. *Local Histories/Global Designs: Coloniality, Subaltern Knowledges, and Border Thinking*. Princeton, NJ: Princeton University Press.

Mignolo, Walter. 2001. "The Geopolitics of Knowledge and the Colonial Difference." *South Atlantic Quarterly* (Winter) 100 (1): 57–96.

Montejo, Víctor. 1999. *Voices from Exile: Violence and Survival in Modern Maya History*. Norman: University of Oklahoma Press.

Montoliu Villar, María. 1987. "Conceptos Sobre la Forma de los Cielos entre los Mayas." In *Historia de la Religión en Mesoamérica y Áreas Afines: I Coloquio*, ed. Barbro Dahlgren de Jordán, 139–44. Mexico City: Universidad Nacional Autónoma de México.

Morley, Sylvanus, George Brainerd, and Robert Sharer. 1983. *The Ancient Maya*, 4th ed. Stanford, CA: Stanford University Press.

Obama, Barack. 2008. "Barack Obama: 'A More Perfect Union' (Full Speech)." Accessed March 18, 2008. https://www.youtube.com/watch?v=zrp-v2tHaDo.

Ong, Aihwa. 1999. *Flexible Citizenship: The Cultural Logics of Transnationality*. Durham, NC: Duke University Press.

Quijano, Anibal. 2000. "Colonality of Power, Eurocentrism and Latin America." *Nepantla* 1 (2): 221–44.

Rabinow, Paul. 2003. *Anthropos Today: Reflections on the Modern Equipment*. Princeton, NJ: Princeton University Press.

Redfield, Robert. 1941. *The Folk Culture of Yucatan*. Chicago: University of Chicago Press.

Redfield, Robert. 1950. *A Village That Chose Progress: Chan Kom Revisited*. Chicago: University of Chicago Press.

Redfield, Robert, and Alfonso Villa Rojas. 1934. *Chan Kom: A Maya Village*. Washington, DC: Carnegie Institution of Washington.

Restall, Matthew. 2004. "Etnogénesis Maya." In *Estrategias Identitarias: Educación y la Antropología Histórica en Yucatán*, ed. Juan A. Castillo Cocom and Quetzil E. Castañeda, 33–60. Mexico City: OSEA-CITE/UPN/SE.

Reyes-Cortés, Beatriz, and Timoteo Rodriguez. 2007. *Mayab Bejlae: Yucatan Today*. Kroeber Anthropological Society Papers 96. Berkeley: Kroeber Anthropological Society, University of California.

Roche Reyes, Conrado. 2007. "Ciudadanos (Allons Enfants de la Patrie)." *Por Esto!* Accessed December 27, 2007. http://www.poresto.net/content/view/442/56/.

Rodriguez, Timoteo. 2001. "Maya Perceptions of Ancestral Remains: Multiple Places in a Local Space." *McNair Scholars* (9): 21–46.

Rodriguez, Timoteo. 2006. "Conjunctures in the Making of a Maya Archaeological Site." In *Ethnographies of Archaeology*, ed. Matt Edgeworth, 161–72. Walnut Creek, CA: Altamira.

Rodriguez, Timoteo. 2007. "Contextualizing Mayab Bejlae: Ethos, Transethnos, and Iknal." *Kroeber Anthropological Society Papers* (96): 1–12.

Roosens, Eugeen. 1989. *Creating Ethnicity: The Process of Ethnogenesis*. Newbury Park, CA: Sage.

Roys, Ralph. 1933. *The Book of Chilam Balam of Chumayel*. Washington, DC: Carnegie Institution of Washington.

Rus, Jan. 2004. "Rereading Tzotzil Ethnography: Recent Scholarship from Chiapas, Mexico." In *Pluralizing Ethnography: Comparison and Representation in Maya Cultures, Histories, and Identities*, ed. John Watanabe and Edward Fischer, 199–230. Santa Fe: School of American Research Press.

Schackt, Jon. 2001. "The Emerging Maya: A Case of Ethnogenesis." In *Maya Survivalism*, ed. Ueli Hostettler and Matthew Restall, vol. 12: 3–14. Acta Mesoamericana. Markt Schwaben, Germany: Verlag Anton Saurwien, Markt Schwaben.

Sharer, Robert. 1994. *The Ancient Maya*. Stanford, CA: Stanford University Press.

Smoak, Gregory E. 2006. *Ghost Dances and Identity: Prophetic Religion and American Indian Ethnogenesis in Nineteenth Century Berkeley*. Berkeley: University of California Press.

Sullivan, Paul. 1989. *Unfinished Conversations: Mayas and Foreigners between Two Wars*. New York: Alfred A. Knopf.

Villa Rojas, Alfonso. 1978. *Los Elegidos de Dios: Etnografía de los Mayas de Quintana Roo*. Mexico City: Instituto Nacional Indigenista.

Vogt, Evon Z. 1990. *The Zinacantecos of Mexico: A Modern Maya Way of Life*. New York: Holt, Rinehart, and Winston.

Watanabe, John M., and Edward F. Fischer. 2004. *Pluralizing Ethnography: Comparison and Representation in Maya Cultures, Histories, and Identities*. Santa Fe: School of American Research Press.

Zapeta, Estuardo. 1997. *Maya Cultural Activism in Guatemala*. Mexico City: Siglo 21.

4

Itzaj and Mopan Identities in Petén, Guatemala

Charles Andrew Hofling

INTRODUCTION

Itzaj and Mopan are members of the Yukatekan branch of the Mayan language family. Itzaj is spoken around Lake Petén–Itzá in Petén, Guatemala.[1] Mopan is spoken in southern Petén and the neighboring Maya Mountains region of Belize. The Yukatekan branch of the Mayan language family is diagramed in figure 4.1. Language differences index differences in group identity. People who communicate more with one another tend to speak more like one another; over time, these differences in communicative interaction and identity lead to dialect and language differences. References to the Itza as an ethnic group, with a distinct culture history and identity, begin in the Classic period (AD 250–900) in the Lake Petén Itzá region of Petén and in northern Yucatán and continue in ethnohistorical and historical documents to the present. Boot has extensively documented hieroglyphic references to the Itza and their ruler Kan Ek' at Petén sites and at Chichén Itzá in Yucatán (Boot 2005:36–193). The Yukatekan Books of Chilam Balam also refer to the Itza as foreigners who came to Yucatán from the south. A group of Itzas later migrated back south to Petén from the northern Yucatán during an 8 Ajaw k'atun period, perhaps AD 1185–1204 (ibid.:145–64).[2] The Kowojs were another Yukatekan group that migrated south from Mayapan during an 8 Ajaw k'atun in the fifteenth century or earlier (Pugh 2001) and settled in the region to the north and east of Lake Petén–Itzá (Jones 1998; Rice and Rice 2009). The linguistic differences between the Kowojs and Itzas were minor, but they clearly had separate identities and were

DOI: 10.5876/9781607325673.c004

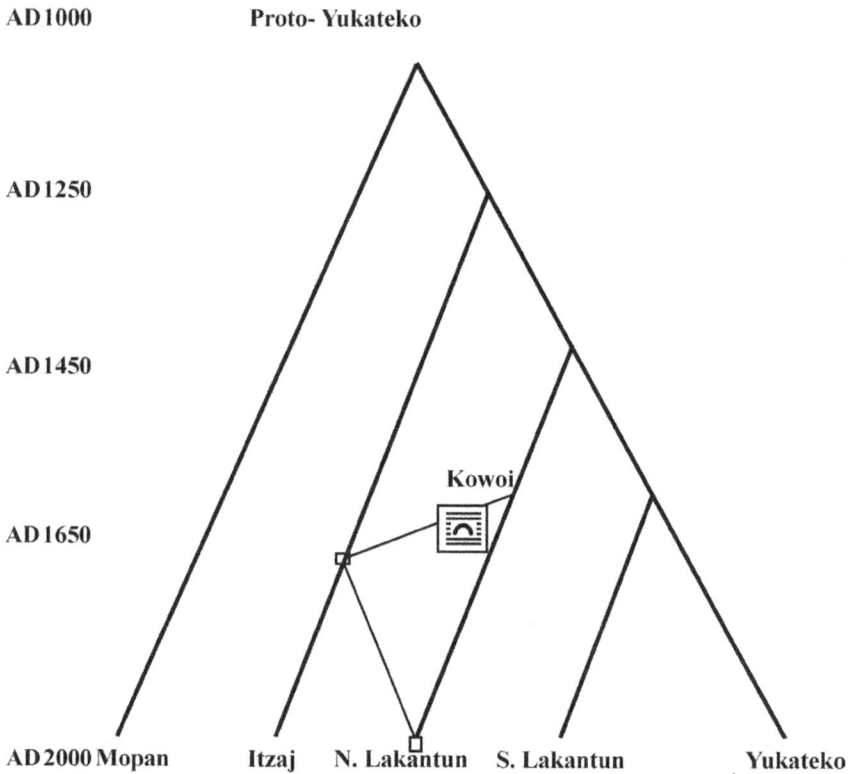

FIGURE 4.1. Yukatekan branch of the Mayan language family

hostile toward one another (Jones 1998, 2009; Rice and Rice 2009; Hofling 2009).

The approximate distribution of lowland Mayan languages at the time of contact is shown on map 4.1. According to Spanish accounts in the sixteenth and seventeenth centuries, the Itzajs dominated the Petén lakes region southward, including the Mopan area. Mopan is mentioned hieroglyphically as a toponym at Naj Tunich, a cave in the southern Petén region that Mopans currently occupy. The Petén has been an ethnically and linguistically heterogeneous region since the Classic period (see Macri, this volume). A group named the Kejaches occupied the area north of the lake (Jones 1998), and the Ikaiches were north of them. The Ikaiches were a powerful rebel group during the Caste War of the mid-nineteenth century (Reed 1964), and Tozzer (1907:2) reports that the Ikaiches formed a "practically independent Indian state" at the turn of the twentieth century. During the seventeenth century, the Spanish removed Ch'olan populations from the lowland Lacandon forest region of Chiapas and resettled them in the highlands.

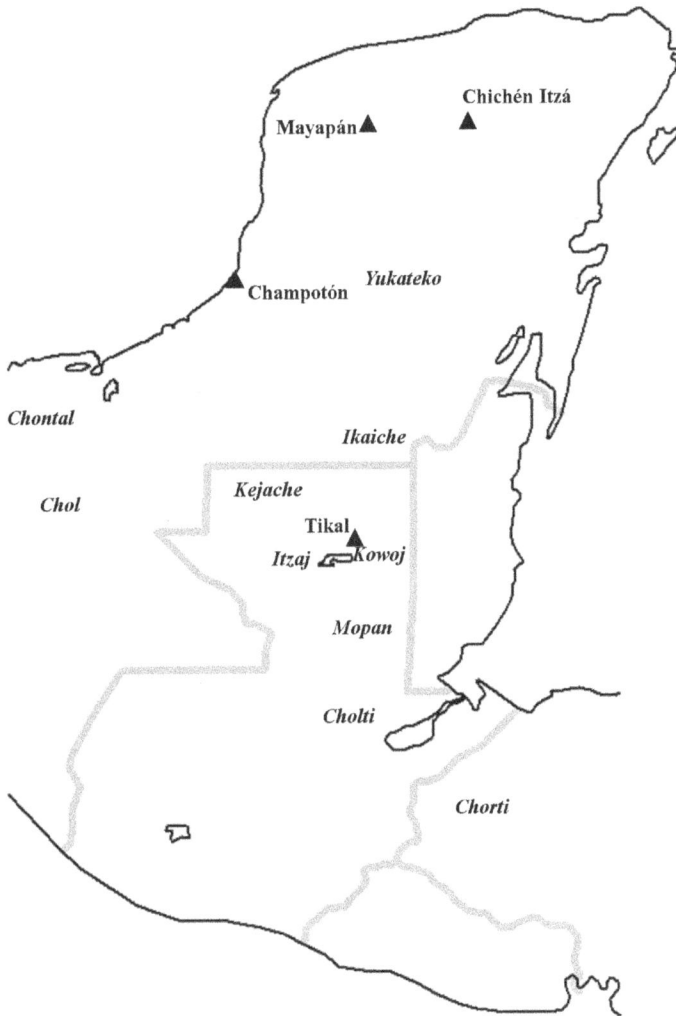

MAP 4.1. Lowland Mayan languages, AD 1500

Following the Itza conquest in 1697, the indigenous groups of the region were gathered into *congregaciones*, where previously distinct groups were forced to live together in mission towns. Many of them resisted and fled into the forest, including the Lacandon forest. The demography of the region altered dramatically (map 4.2), with a major decrease in indigenous populations. In looking at the use of terms such as *Maya*, *Yukatan*, *Itzaj*, *Mopan*, and *Lakantun*, it becomes clear that their meanings change over time, involving shifts from toponymic emphasis to language name and

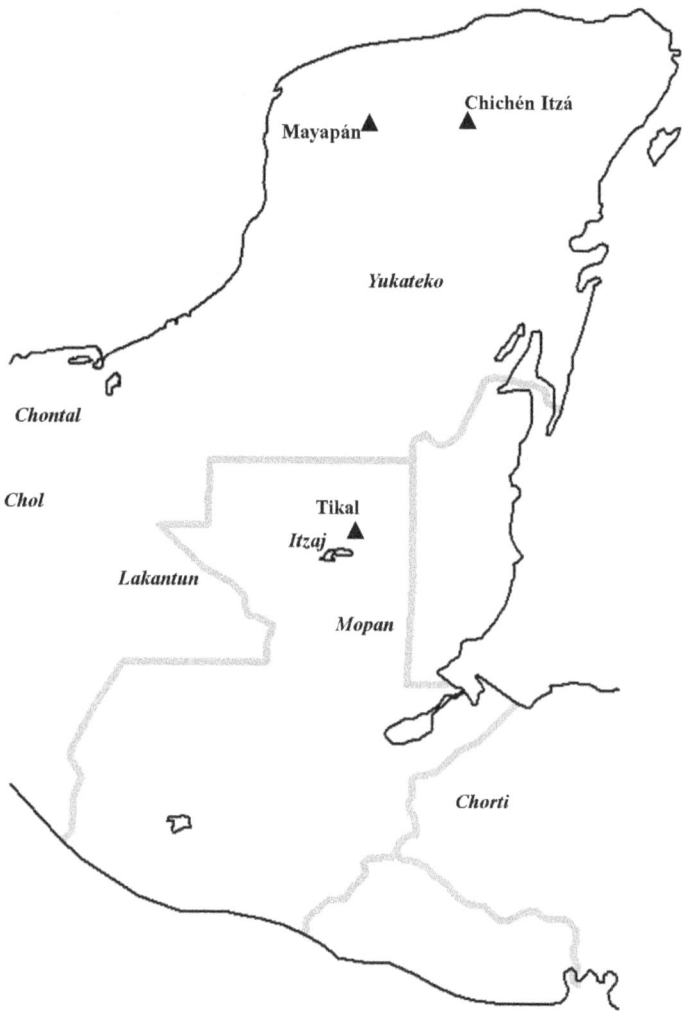

MAP 4.2. Mayan languages after 1700

social or ethnic group name. It is also clear that there are differences between terms used as self-references by these groups and labels outsiders use to refer to them.

MAYA

Recently, there has been considerable discussion of the meaning and use of the term *Maya* in Colonial Yukateko and elsewhere. In Colonial Yukateko, *Maya* appears to have been used primarily as the name of the language spoken in the region of Mayapan (Voss N. 2002; Restall 2004; Restall and Gabbert, this volume), but it was adopted by the Spanish as both a language name and an ethnic label applied widely to Yukatekan peoples.

Edmonson (1986:100) observes that in the Books of Chilam Balam of Chumayel, written from the perspective of people in the western half of the Yucatán Peninsula, *Maya* is used to name the language and ethnic groups of western Yucatán and the capital of Mayapan, while *Itza* refers to eastern groups and their center at Chichén Itzá. In the Chilam Balam of Tizimin, the Itzas use the term *Xiu* to refer to the western groups (Hofling 2009). Restall (2004) and Restall and Gabbert (this volume) similarly argue that the term *Maya* had different meanings to different groups, including both language and social groups. It is clear that there were differences in language and identity among groups in Yucatán, with differences between eastern and western groups, as well as between northern and southern groups. Social identity was largely focused on the community (*kaj*) and exogamous patronymic groups or lineages (*ch'ib'al*) for Colonial Yukatekos (Restall 2004:73). Considering that Yukatekos had arrived in the region by 1000 BC (Kaufman 1976), it is hardly surprising that dialectal differences arose, and they exist to this day. The Academia de la Lengua Maya de Yucatán (2002) identifies five dialects of modern Yukateko. Similar findings on dialect variation are reported by Blaha Pfeiler and Hofling (2006).

A number of scholars, especially in Mexico and Guatemala (e.g., Litzinger and Bruce 1998:5–6; Schumann Gálvez 2000), stress that in modern times all Yukatekan groups speak the same language, which they call *Maayaj*; they claim that the linguistic labels Mopan and Itzá are very recent, largely the result of interactions with linguists, anthropologists, and cultural activists (Schumann Gálvez 1997, 2000). Since the 1980s, *Maya* has been used by Maya cultural activists and others interested in language revitalization to refer to all languages of the Mayan language family and the peoples who speak them (Fischer 2001). The Academia de Lenguas Mayas de Guatemala (ALMG) has reinforced the labels *Mopan* and *Itza'* and has offices in San José and San Luís that encourage pride in Mayan identity within the respective groups. Similarly, interactions with linguists, anthropologists, and non-government organizations (NGOs) involved with conservation have encouraged a sense of distinct ethnic identity of San Joseños as Itzajs and San Luiseños as Mopans (Hofling 1996).

Lakantun

Lakantun was originally a toponym that came to refer to Ch'olan-speaking groups who lived in the Chiapas lowlands (Palka 2005). The Ch'olan speakers had been largely removed by the Spanish by 1700 (Schwartz 1990:34). Previously, I have argued that the label *Lakandon* or *Lakantun* does not refer to a single ethnic or linguistic group but rather to a variety of groups descended primarily from various Yukatekan-speaking groups that took refuge in the Lacandon forest (Hofling 2004, 2006a). The Northern Lakantun seem to have especially strong ties to the Itzaj and Kowoj (Pugh 2001; Hofling 2004, 2006a), which is reflected in patronyms and language. The Southern Lakantun have closer ties to northern Yukatekans, also reflected in dialect differences (Hofling 2013, 2014). As Schwartz (1990), Borremanse (1998), and Palka (2005), among others, have shown, the Lakantuns were not and are not a culturally homogeneous group, and there has been a constant process of ethnogenesis (cf. Hill 1996) in this refuge area from about 1700 to the present. Northen Lakantuns call themselves *jach winik*, or "true people," and their language *jach t'an*, "true language." Southern Lakantuns similarly use the terms *jach wïinik* and *jach t'aan*, and both groups are aware of differences between them (Bruce 1968:36; Hofling 2014).

Itzajs and Mopans

Today, the Itzajs and Mopans are both ethnic and linguistic groups. However, they are very different groups than those described prior to the conquest of the Itzas in 1697, at which time the two groups were enemies but had been in contact with one another for a long time. The Itzas dominated the region in an ever-changing system of alliances among Itza groups and others (Jones 1998). After the conquest the Spanish forced diverse ethnic groups, often enemies, to be resettled in mission towns around Lake Petén–Itzá, including San Andrés and San José on the north shore, and in congregaciones to the south, including San Luís, the Mopan capital (Schwartz 1990). Many indigenous groups refused to settle in the congregaciones and fled into the forest (ibid.; Palka 2005). After 1700 the Mopans in southern Petén had limited contact with the Itzas around Lake Petén–Itzá. In modern times, *Itzá* and *Maya* have been Spanish ethnic labels for indigenous people living in the Central Lakes towns, especially San José and San Andrés, on the north shore of Lake Petén–Itzá. Schwartz (1990:60) notes the possibility that San Andrés was founded on the site of a Kowoj village and that a sense of Kowoj ancestry exists to this day. Similarly, in San José there is a sense of Itzaj ancestry, among both San Joseños and outsiders.

The ethnic identity differences so prominent before the conquest have largely faded, and Kejaches, Mopans, and Kowojs have been absorbed. In the nineteenth and twentieth centuries, Yukatekos continued to migrate into Petén. The nineteenth-century Caste War in Yucatán had a major impact on Petén, as Yukatekan groups arrived from the north, with some raiding Petén communities. The Itzajs called the rebel Yukatekos *Wit'oo'*, synonymous with "bandits," and oral tradition tells of Itzaj participation in Guatemalan army action against the invaders (Hofling 1992; cf. Restall and Gabbert, this volume). The Yukateko presence was especially notable in San Andrés, which lies at the end of the *camino real* from Campeche, resulting in some sub-dialectal differences between San José and San Andrés (Schumann Gálvez 1971, 2000). The San Andrés dialect of Itzaj virtually disappeared in the 1960s. Perhaps several dozen older adults in San José and scattered about the region still speak Itzaj.

The ALMG has made considerable efforts to revitalize the language since the early 1990s, with mixed results. The effort has heightened San Joseños' self-awareness as descendents of the Itzajs (Hofling 1996). Itzajs recognize a connection to Yucatán and Campeche and trace their ancestry to the north. They call Yukatekos *Yuukajs*. They also recognize Mopans as Mayas (Schumann Gálvez 2000:16) but have little contact with them. Itzaj and Mopan are not fully mutually intelligible. The Itzajs also know of the Lakantuns, calling them *Caribes*, but they have not had significant contact with them in recent decades.

Mopan, which may have the etymology of *mo'* (macaw) and *pän* (toucan), was originally a toponym and is the name of a river in southern Petén. Prior to the conquest and congregaciones, Mopans were the southernmost Yukatekans and came into contact with Ch'olan groups—especially the Eastern Ch'olan groups, Ch'olti' and Ch'orti'—and with Q'eqchi's (Hofling 2007). Cano (1984) reports on a late-seventeenth-century journey from the Q'eqchi' Alta Verapaz through Cahabon across Manche Chol territory to Mopan territory and on to the Itzas. He notes that he encountered Mopans who were Chol-Mopan bilinguals (ibid.:9). After the conquest, the Spanish established a congregacion at San Luís, but apparently many Mopans fled into the forest. Peteneros in the Mopan region report periodic contact with Lakantuns up to modern times (Palka 2005:8).

According to the ALMG (2004), Mopan elders say their ancestors came from Tayasal, the Itza capital in Lake Petén–Itzá. A group emigrated south to the region of the Río Mopán because of disagreements among caciques and later migrated further south to San Luís. The people lived in a dispersed settlement pattern divided into the four quadrants of the cardinal directions. Gregorio Tzuncal, from the southern quadrant, encountered a group of animals scratching an incense tree on the top of a hill, which the elders considered a sign to found their town at that site, the modern San Luís (ibid.). Others say the founding lineages came from the Río Mopán region to the north and lived in four Naj Tuniches, "natural stone palaces," large caves at each of the cardinal directions—including the famous Naj Tunich to the east, near the Belizean border (Juan Idelfonso Coj Ical, personal communication, July 2008). Q'eqchi's came later from Cahabon, Alta Verapaz, the town Cano mentioned on his journey three centuries earlier.

The Q'eqchi's are now far more numerous in the area than Mopans. There has been extensive intermarriage, and Q'eqchi'-Mopan bilingualism is common. In recent decades Ladinos have dominated the region politically and economically. There is some tension between Mopans and Q'eqchi's, and they tend to live in separate districts. Mopans have also come into contact with K'ichee's and Kaqchikels through commerce. I now turn more directly to linguistic evidence relevant to understand this complex history of cultural contact and ethnogenesis.

LEXICON AND BORROWING

Mopans have been in intense contact with Q'eqchi' speakers since Colonial times and probably much longer. Many Mopans are also Q'eqchi' speakers. As a result of these contacts, Mopan has a number of Q'eqchi' loans not found in other Yukatekan languages shown in table 4.1 (Hofling 2007). Currently, some Mopan speakers are attempting to eliminate Q'eqchi' loan words from Mopan as part of the revitalization movement.[3] With the exception of g in table 4.1, Mopan is the only Yukatekan language to have these Q'eqchi' loan words, which include terms for social categories (table 4.1b, c, d).

In addition, Mopan has come into contact with Eastern Ch'olan (Ch'olti' and Ch'orti') more intensively than have other Yukatekan languages.[4] As a result, it has more lexical borrowings from Eastern Ch'olan (see table 4.2). It is also notable in table 4.2d that Mopan and Chorti' initial *k* corresponds to Itzaj and Yukateko *ch,* while in table 4.2e Mopan and Ch'orti' *t* corresponds to Itzaj and Yukateko *ch.* Similarly, in table 4.2g Mopan and Ch'orti' *r* corresponds to Itzaj and Yukateko *l* and in table 4.2h Mopan sibilants (*s* and *x*) correspond to Yukatekan nasals (*n* and *m*). Thus, phonological form also indicates Mopan contact with Eastern Ch'olan.

MOPAN LEXICON IN RELATION TO OTHER YUKATEKAN LANGUAGES

New evidence from Mopan (Hofling 2007, 2011a) shows that many terms for flora and fauna are reconstructable for Proto-Yukatekan (table 4.3). To reconstruct Proto-Yukatekan forms, they should be present in both Mopan and Yukateko, the most divergent varieties of Yukatekan. These data also indicate that the masculine noun classifier *aj-* and the feminine classifier *ix-* are more robust in Mopan and Itzaj than in other Yukatekan varieties. Some of the gaps in Lakantun may be the result of incomplete documentation. The large amount of vocabulary that can be reconstructed for Proto-Yukatekan confirms the general point that all Yukatekan

TABLE 4.1. Contact with Q'eqchi'

	Mopan	Q'eqchi'	Itzaj	Northern Lakantun	Southern Lakantun	Yukateko	Gloss
a.	chiw-chiw	ch'iwch'otk					'cheep cheep'
b.	ch'i'ip	ch'i'ip					'youngest child'
c.	ch'ajom	ch/ajom					'young man'
d.	tz'ub'	tz'ub'					'(grand)child'
e.	ch'ikwaan	ch'ikwan					'small bird'
f.	ixkuluk	kuluk					'caterpillar'
g.	poy-te'	poy-te'		poy'te'	poy-te'	poy-te (cy)	'raft'
h.	samaat	samat					'parsley'
i.	ajjonoon	jolo'on					'wasp'

TABLE 4.2. Contact with Eastern Ch'olan

	Mopan	Ch'orti'	Itzaj	Yukateko	Gloss
a.	näk'-chan	näk'-chan	näk'-chan		'roof beam'
b.	ajb'ub'	b'ub'		b'ub' (cy)	'tadpole'
c.	aj'usij	usij	aj'usil		'buzzard'
d.	ixkames	kamis	ixchemes	chemes	'centipede'
e.	pätaj	*pätah (pch')	pichi'	pichi'	'guava'
f.	t'ot'	*t'ot' (pch')	t'ot'		'snail'
g.	ajt'urich ~ajt'u'ul	t'ur	ajt'u'ul	t'u'ul	'rabbit'
h.	meles	merex	melen	meelem	'useless'

languages are closely related. As table 4.3c and table 4.3j indicate, Southern Lakantun has a tonal system on long vowels (with high tone in these examples), which is like Yukateko but contrasts with other Yukatekan languages, suggesting that their ancestors came from northern Yucatán.

There is also a substantial set of terms for flora and fauna that indicates areal contact (table 4.4), with a close relationship between Mopan and Itzaj and significant ties with Northern and Southern Lakantun, suggesting that some of the ancestors of modern Lakantuns included Mopans and Itzajs. Thus, there are areal features that distinguish southern Yukatekan varieties from northern Yukateko. In this list, items are shared among the southern varieties, in contrast to northern Yukateko. Northern and Southern Lakantun also appear in closer contact to

TABLE 4.3. Reconstructable for Proto-Yukatekan

	Mopan	Itzaj	Northern Lakantun	Southern Lakantun	Yukateko	Gloss
a.	ajch'umak	ajch'umak	äjch'ämäk		ch'omak	'gray fox'
b.	ajchupaat	ixchupaat	äjchup		chapáat	'milliped'
c.	chuluul	chuluul	chulul	churúur	chulúul	'heart of tree'
d.	ajch'anaan	ixchänay	äjch'anex		ixch'anan (cy)	'small cricket'
e.	ixch'ayuk	ixch'a'yuk		ch'a'uuk		'nightshade'
f.	ch'o'oj	ajch'o'	ch'o'	ch'o'	ch'o'	'rat'
g.	ajk'ok'o'-ta'	ixk'ok'	k'ok'-ta'		xk'ook'	'robin'
h.	ixpu'u'uk	ixpu'			xpu'	'chicken type'
i.	ixta'-maay	ta'-ma'ay			ta'a-maay	'tree species'
j.	ajtolok	ajtolok	äjtolok	tóorok	tóolok	'lizard type'
k.	pän		pän	pän	pan	'toucan'

TABLE 4.4. Southern versus Northern Yuketaken (areal)

	Mopan	Itzaj	Northern Lakantun	Southern Lakantun	Yukateko	Gloss
a.	ajtoy	ajtoy	äjtoy	tooy	am	'spider'
b.	ajxut'	ajxut'	xut'	xuut'		'frog species'
c.	chimun	chimun	äjchimon	chimoon		'wild fig'
d.	ixchuj-kib'	ajchukub'		chuukib'ir		'dove species'
e.	ixkookom			koomkom		'vine species'
f.	jach		jachil näl	jáach		'ear of corn'
g.	luwin	luwin	äjluwin			'tree species'
h.	tutu'	ajtutu'	t'unu'	t'unu'		'jute snail'
i.	tz'iy-a'		tzula-il ja	suura'		'otter'
j.	way			waay		'sopote seed'
k.	wät'äj		wäch'	wäch'		'wild tamarind'

one another than to Itzaj and Mopan, as indicated by items table 4.4c "wild fig," which contrasts Itzaj and Mopan *chimun* with Northern and Southern Lakantun *chimo(o)n*; table 4.4h "jute snail," which contrasts Mopan and Itzaj *tutu'* with Northern and Southern Lakantun *t'ut'u'*; and table 4.4k "wild tamarind," which contrasts Mopan *wät'äj* with Northern and Southern Lakantun *wäch'*.

TABLE 4.5. Lexicon Only in Mopan and Itzaj

	Mopan	Itzaj	Gloss
a.	ajkuri'	ajkuri'	'mole'
b.	ixteren-saak'	ixten-saak'	'itchy vine'
c.	ajtuwis	ajtuwi'is	'jumping bird'
d.	chikilab'	chikila'	'plantanillo palm'
e.	ixch'uw-ek'	ixch'uj	'bromeliad'
f.	ixkolool	ixmän-kolool	'tinamou'
g.	ajkele'-tux	ajk'ele'-tux	'tapir rib tree'
h.	ajnab'a'-ku'uk	ajnab'a'-ku'uk	'allspice seed'
i.	ixpuruwook	ixpuruwok	'ruddy ground dove'
j.	ixtukib'	tuki'	'sincuya tree'

A considerable number of terms for flora and fauna is unique to Mopan and Itzaj, indicating a long period of close contact (table 4.5). They retain the system of noun classification with the feminine prefix *ix-* and the masculine prefix *aj-*, and they are largely in agreement regarding noun class.

A considerable number of terms for flora and fauna are unique to Mopan (table 4.6) (of Yukatekan varieties). These, along with Mopan's shared vocabulary with Q'eqchi' and Ch'olan groups, are an indication both of Mopan's genetic linguistic distance from other Yukatekan varieties and its unique historical interactions with non-Yukatekan groups. A variety of other Mopan linguistic innovations point to the same conclusion (Hofling 2004, 2006a, 2006b, 2007, 2011b).

PATRONYMS

Grant Jones (1998:24–27) presents extensive evidence on Itza and Mopan patronyms recorded shortly after the conquest in 1697. Most patronyms are different in Mopan and Itza communities. Of the more than ninety patronyms listed, only nine, or about 10 percent (*Chan, K'in, Muwan, Ob'on, Pana, Tesukun, Tzak, Tzuntekun,* and *Tz'ib'*), were found in both Itza and Mopan communities. Most Kowoj patronyms were different from Itzaj patronyms. Of the five Kowoj patronyms, only one (*Kowoj*) was also found in Itza communities, and none were found in Mopan. Kejach patronyms were shared with Itza but not Mopan. I recently checked this list with modern Itzaj and Mopan speakers and discovered some interesting changes. Of the twenty-two Mopan patrynms listed, by Jones, twelve are no longer known in San Luís. However, eleven Itzaj patronyms not listed as Mopan patronyms are

TABLE 4.6 Lexicon Unique to Mopan

	Mopan	Gloss
a.	ajk'ijom	'small bird'
b.	ajk'iyon	'sentzontle'
c.	ajsul	'moth'
d.	ajt'el-us	'tortugilla bug'
e.	ajwen	'frog'
f.	ajxip'i'	'pig flea'
g.	ajxiyoj	'tree of San Juan'
h.	ixmorot'	'dwarf banana'
i.	ixkalalu'	'amaranth'
j.	t'ulij	'small bird'
k.	pumpu'	'bot fly'

now known in San Luís, including *Kante, Kowoj, May, Mo', Tun*, and *Tzin*. San José Itzaj has shown similar changes. Itzaj has lost about twenty-five patronyms listed by Jones but gained thirteen, including Tipuj patronyms (*Chi, Mas, K'u, Muk'ul, Pix*), Kowoj patronyms (*Kamal, Kawich, Ketzal*), and Mopan patronyms (*Ch'em, Jola, Kixchan, K'unil, Tzawi*). Certain patronyms are strongly associated with San José but not San Andrés (*B'atab', Chan, Kante, Kawich*), while others are associated with San Andrés but not San José (*Chab'in, Chata, Chi, Kinyokte, Kixchan, Po'ot, Tzin*). In addition, I discovered about twenty additional patronyms shared by modern Mopan and Itzajs, as well as fifteen new Mopan patronyms and a half dozen new Itzaj patronyms. These changes suggest a radical disjunction after the conquest, with congregaciones, flight and population loss, and movements back and forth among Yukatekan groups. Mopan oral histories confirm that many of the families in San Luís came from elsewhere and that the Kowojs in particular came from the north.

CONCLUSION

The linguistic data of Yukatekan languages are messy and reflect a complex history. An early split is indicated between Mopan and the rest of the Yukatekan varieties. I believe that Mopans are largely descendents of ancient Yukatekan populations living in the Petén in the Postclassic and possibly earlier. The toponym *Mopan* occurs in the area in the Classic period but is not necessarily a Yukatekan term. It could be that like Lakantun, it first referred to a Ch'olan group and was later transferred to

Yukatekan populations. It is clear that in the early Colonial period, Mopans were distinguished from, and enemies of, Itzas and Ch'ols. They have had unique contacts with Ch'olans and Q'eqchi's, which is reflected in their language. Their language was known as *Maayaj* and is now also known as *Mopan* or *Maayaj*.

The Itzajs are an ancient ethnic group and were dominant in the Petén until the conquest in 1697. Following congregaciones and the forced settlement of diverse ethnic groups, often enemies, Itzá became the name of surviving indigenous groups living around Lake Peten–Itzá, which appears to have included Kowojs, Kejaches, and Mopans. They also spoke Maayaj. It is not certain if they also called their language Itzaj, but modern Itzaj do recognize it as a language name as well. The presence of the term *Maayaj* in Mopan and Itzaj, while not definitive, suggests that its use as a language name can be reconstructed for Proto-Yukatekan.

While linguistic distances among Yukatekan groups in Petén were small, it is clear that differences in identity were significant. Just as the Books of Chilam Balam chronicle opposing Itza and Xiu factions with different histories, territories, and identities in northern Yucatán, named groups in Petén also had different histories, territories, and identities. Just as archaeological markers of identity can be subtle, linguistic differences need not be great for differences in identity to be substantial.

NOTES

1. Research on Itzaj and Mopan from 2005–7 has been supported by the National Science Foundation, grant number NSF-BCS-0445231. I am grateful to Norman Schwartz and the editors of this book for helpful comments on an earlier draft of this chapter. I use the term *Itzaj* to refer to the modern language and culture and Itzajs to refer to the Itzaj people. The ALMG adopted the term *Itza*,' but *Itzaj* is more accurate linguistically. Itza and Itzas refer to Colonial and precontact culture and people, respectively.

2. A k'atun is a period of twenty tuns (360 days), roughly twenty years. Thirteen k'atuns formed a 260-tun cycle called the *may*, roughly 256 years, and k'atun ending dates such as 8 Ajaw recurred ever 260 tuns (Rice 2004).

3. Mopan data for all tables were taken from Proyecto Lingüístico Francisco Marroquín (1971), Ulrich and de Ulrich (1976), Schumann Gálvez (1997), Academia de Lenguas Mayas de Guatemala (2003), Oxlajuuj Keej Maya' Ajtz'iib' (2003), and were elicited in the field (Hofling 2011a). Q'eqchi' data are from Proyecto Lingüístico Francisco Marroquín (2003). Data sources for Itzaj are Hofling and Tesucún (2000) and fieldwork since 2000. Northern Lakantun data come from a database I created based on Bruce (1968, 1974, 1975, 1976), Davis (1978), Borremanse (1998), and Cook and Carlson (2004). Southern Lakantun data are from Çanger (1995) and Hofling (2014). Information on modern Yukateko comes from Durbin (1999), Bricker, Po'ot Yah, and Dzul de Po'ot (1998), and Academia de

la Lengua Maya de Yucatán (2002). Barrera Vasquez and colleagues (1980) is the source of information on Colonial Yukateko.

    4. Data for Eastern Ch'olan and Proto-Ch'olan are from Kaufman and Norman, (1984), Kaufman 2003, and PLFM (1996).

REFERENCES CITED

Academia de la Lengua Maya de Yucatán (ALMY), AC. 2002. *Diccionario Maya Popular*. Merida, Yucatán: ALMY.

Academia de Lenguas Mayas de Guatemala (ALMG), Comunidad Lingüística Mopan. 2003. *Much't'an Mopan: Vocabulario Mopan*. Guatemala: ALMG.

Academia de Lenguas Mayas de Guatemala (ALMG), Comunidad Lingüística Mopan. 2004. Historia. http://www.almg.org.gt/Comunidades/mopan/mopan%202.htm.

Barrera Vásquez, Alfredo, Juan Ramon Bastarrachea Manzano, William Brito Sansores, Refugio Vermont Salas, David Dzul Gongora, and Dominzo Dzul Poot. 1980. *Diccionario Cordemex: Maya-Español, Español-Maya*. Merida, Yucatán: Ediciones Cordemex.

Blaha Pfeiler, Barbara, and Charles Andrew Hofling. 2006. "Apuntes Sobre la Variación Dialectal en el Maya Yucateco." *Peninsula* 1 (1): 27–43.

Boot, Erik. 2005. *Continuity and Change in Text and Image at Chichén Itzá, Yucatán, Mexico*. Leiden: CNWS Publications.

Borremanse, Didier. 1998. *Hach Winik: The Lacandon Maya of Chiapas, Southern Mexico*. Institute for Mesoamerican Studies, Monograph 11. Albany: State University of New York.

Bricker, Victoria R., Eleuterio Po'ot Yah, and Ofelia Dzul de Po'ot. 1998. *Dictionary of the Maya Language as Spoken in Hocabá, Yucatán*. Salt Lake City: University of Utah Press.

Bruce, Roberto D. 1968. *Gramática del Lakantun*. Mexico City: Instituto Nacional de Antropología e Historia.

Bruce, Roberto D. 1974. *El Libro de Chan K'in*. Mexico City: Instituto Nacional de Antropología e Historia Colección Científica Lingüística.

Bruce, Roberto D. 1975. *Lacandon Dream Symbolism*. Mexico City: Ediciones Euroamericanas Klaus Thiele.

Bruce, Roberto D. 1976. *Textos y dibujos Lacandones de Najá* (trilingual edition: Lacandón-Spanish-English). Departamento de Lingüística 45. Mexico City: Colección Científica Lingüística.

Çanger, Una. 1995. "Vocabulary of San Quintín." Unpublished manuscript, originally collected in 1969–70.

Cano, Agustín. 1984. *Manche and Peten: The Hazards of Itza Deceit and Barbarity*. Trans. Frank E. Comparato, Charles P. Bowditch, and Guillermo Rivera. Culver City, CA: Labyrinthos.

Cook, Suzanne, and Barry Carlson. 2004. "Ethnobiological Inventories: Birds, Fish, Mammals, Reptiles, Insects, Plants." http://web.uvic.ca/lacandon/language.htm. Accessed June 5, 2008.

Davis, Virginia Dale. 1978. "Ritual of the Northern Lacandon Maya." PhD dissertation, Department of Anthropology, Tulane University, New Orleans.

Durbin, Marshall E. 1999. "Yucatec Maya Dictionary." Unpublished manuscript, copy in author's possession.

Edmonson, Munro. 1986. *Heaven Born Merida and Its Destiny: The Book of Chilam Balam of Chumayel*. Austin: University of Texas Press.

Fischer, Edward F. 2001. *Cultural Logics and Global Economies*. Austin: University of Texas Press.

Hill, Jonathan D. 1996. "Ethnogenesis in the Northwestern Amazon: An Emerging Regional Picture." In *History, Power, and Identity: Ethnogenesis in the Americas, 1492–1992*, ed. Jonathan D. Hill, 142–60. Iowa City: University of Iowa Press.

Hofling, Charles Andrew. 1992. "Ukweentojil ajWit'oo': The Story of the Bandits." Told by Félix Fernando Tesucún. Unpublished manuscript, copy in author's possession.

Hofling, Charles Andrew. 1996. "Indigenous Linguistic Revitalization and Outsider Interaction: The Itzaj Maya Case." *Human Organization* 55 (1): 108–16. http://dx.doi .org/10.17730/humo.55.1.613j5q6p01836225.

Hofling, Charles Andrew. 2004. "Language and Cultural Contacts among Yukatekan Mayans." *Collegium Antropologicum* 28 (suppl. 1): 241–48.

Hofling, Charles Andrew. 2006a. "La historia lingüística y cultural del maya yucateco durante el último milenio." In *Los Mayas de Ayer y Hoy: Memorias del Primer Congreso Internacional de la Cultura Maya*, vol. 2, ed. Alfredo Barrera Rubio and Ruth Gubler, 1196–1216. Mexico City: Solar, Servicios Editoriales, S.A. de C.V.

Hofling, Charles Andrew. 2006b. "A Sketch of the History of the Verbal Complex in Yukatekan Mayan Languages." *International Journal of American Linguistics* 72 (3): 367–96. http://dx.doi.org/10.1086/509490.

Hofling, Charles Andrew. 2007. "Notes on Mopan Lexicon and Lexical Morphology." In *Proceedings of the Congreso de Idiomas Indígenas de Latinoamérica III*, ed. Nora C. England, Austin, TX. http://www.ailla.utexas.org/site/cilla3_toc.html. Accessed June 7, 2014.

Hofling, Charles Andrew. 2009. "The Linguistic Context of the Kowoj." In *The Kowoj of Central Peten*, ed. Prudence M. Rice and Don Rice, 70–79. Boulder: University Press of Colorado.

Hofling, Charles Andrew. 2011a. *Mopan Maya-Spanish-English Dictionary*. Salt Lake City: University of Utah Press.

Hofling, Charles Andrew. 2011b. "Voice and Auxiliaries in Mopan Maya." In *New Perspectives in Mayan Linguistics*, ed. Heriberto Avelino, 144–59. Newcastle upon Tyne: Cambridge Scholars Publishing.

Hofling, Charles Andrew. 2013. *El Maya Lacandón en el Siglo XXI*. Paper presented at the 9th Congreso Internacional de Mayistas, Campeche, Mexico, June 23–29.

Hofling, Charles Andrew. 2014. *Lacandon Maya-Spanish-English Dictionary*. Salt Lake City: University of Utah Press.

Hofling, Charles Andrew, and Félix Fernando Tesucún. 2000. *Tojt'an Maya' Itzaj: Diccionario Maya Itza'—Castellano*. Guatemala City: Cholsamaj.

Jones, Grant D. 1998. *The Conquest of the Last Maya Kingdom*. Stanford, CA: Stanford University Press.

Jones, Grant D. 2009. "The Kowoj in Ethnohistorical Perspective." In *The Kowoj of Central Peten*, ed. Prudence M. Rice and Don Rice, 55–69. Boulder: University Press of Colorado.

Kaufman, Terrence. 1976. "Archaeological and Linguistic Correlations in Mayaland and Associated Areas of Meso-America." *World Archaeology* 8 (1): 101–18. http://dx.doi.org /10.1080/00438243.1976.9979655.

Kaufman, Terrence. 2003. "A Preliminary Mayan Etymological Dictionary." http://www .famsi.org/reports/01051/pmed.pdf. Accessed June 7, 2014.

Kaufman, Terrence, and William M. Norman. 1984. "An Outline of Proto-Cholan Phonology, Morphology, and Vocabulary." In *Phoneticism in Mayan Hieroglyphic Writing*, ed. John S. Justeson and Lyle Campbell, 77–166. Institute for Mesoamerican Studies 9. Albany: State University of New York.

Litzinger, William J., and Robert D. Bruce. 1998. *Maya t'an, Spoken Maya*. Mexico City: Ediciones Euro-Americanos.

Oxlajuuj Keej Maya' Ajtz'iib'. 2003. *Vocabulario Comparativo*. Guatemala City: Cholsamaj.

Palka, Joel. 2005. *Unconquered Lacandon Maya*. Gainesville: University Press of Florida.

Proyecto Lingüístico Francisco Marroquín (PLFM). 1971. *Cuestionario lingüístico para la investigación de las variacoines de las lenguage de Guatemala (de Mopán)*. Antigua, Guatemala: PLFM.

Proyecto Lingüístico Francisco Marroquín (PLFM). 1996. *Diccionario Ch'orti', Jocotan, Chiquimula: Ch'orti'-Español*. Antigua, Guatemala: PLFM.

Proyecto Lingüístico Francisco Marroquín (PLFM). 2003. *Diccionario Q'eqchi*. Iximilew, Guatemala: PLFM.

Pugh, Timothy. 2001. "Architecture, Ritual, and Social Identity at Late Postclassic Zacpetén, Petén, Guatemala: Identification of the Kowoj." PhD dissertation, Department of Anthropology, Southern Illinois University at Carbondale.

Reed, Nelson. 1964. *The Caste War of Yucatan*. Stanford, CA: Stanford University Press.

Restall, Matthew. 2004. "Maya Ethnogenesis." *Journal of Latin American Anthropology* 9 (1): 64–89. http://dx.doi.org/10.1525/jlca.2004.9.1.64.

Rice, Prudence M. 2004. *Maya Political Science: Time, Astronomy, and the Cosmos*. Austin: University of Texas Press.

Rice, Prudence M., and Don Rice. 2009. "Introduction to the Kowoj and Their Petén Neighbors." In *The Kowoj*, ed. Prudence M. Rice and Don Rice, 3–15. Boulder: University Press of Colorado.

Schumann Gálvez, Otto. 1971. *Descripción estructural del maya itzá del Petén, Guatemala C.A.* Cuaderno 6, Centro de Estudios Mayas. Mexico City: Universidad Nacional Autónoma de Mexico.

Schumann Gálvez, Otto. 1997. *Introducción al Maya Mopan*. Mexico City: Universidad Nacional Autónoma de Mexico.

Schumann Gálvez, Otto. 2000. *Introducción al Maya Itzá*. Mexico City: Universidad Nacional Autónonma de Mexico.

Schwartz, Norman. 1990. *Forest Society: A Social History of Petén, Guatemala*. Philadelphia: University of Pennsylvania Press.

Tozzer, Alfred M. 1907. *A Comparative Study of the Mayas and Lacandones: Report of the Fellow in American Archaeology 1902–1905*. New York: Archaeological Institute of America.

Ulrich, Mateo, and Rosemary de Ulrich. 1976. *Diccionario Bilingüe Maya Mopán y Español, Español y Maya Mopan*. Guatemala: Impreso de los talleres del Instituto Lingüístico de Verano en Guatemala.

Voss N., Alexander W. 2002. "¿Qué significa maya?—Analysis etimológico de una palabra." *Investigaciones de la Cultura Maya* 10 (2): 380–98.

5

Maya Ethnogenesis and Group Identity in Yucatán, 1500–1900

MATTHEW RESTALL AND WOLFGANG GABBERT

INVENTING MAYAS

The Maya of Mexico's Yucatán Peninsula are considered heirs to one of the most famous ancient civilizations in the Americas by most outside observers—both scholars and the wider public.[1] The Yucatec Mayan–speaking population of the past and the present is seen as an ethnic community with deep historical roots. The term *Maya* does, in fact, appear in several Colonial documents as a designation of human beings. But this does not necessarily imply that it had the same meaning it has today, that of referring to all Yucatec Mayan speakers, or that Maya was the name of an ethnic community (i.e., a group united by a belief in a common heritage and destiny).[2]

We argue in this chapter that the Mayas of the Yucatán did not exist until the twentieth century, terminologically speaking. In terms of both the identities they claimed and those assigned to them, the Mayas were not Mayas.[3] Colonial period evidence shows that the native inhabitants of the peninsula, whom modern scholars identify as "Maya," did not consistently call themselves that or any other name that indicated they saw themselves as members of a common ethnic group.[4] This appears to have been true of the decades immediately before the Spanish invasion, as it was of the Colonial period and the early republican and Caste War period.[5]

We argue that the modern-day issues surrounding "Maya" as a "contested term" (Castañeda 1996:13) are relevant to the Colonial period, and vice versa. Our purpose is to approach this debate from the Colonial and Caste War periods, showing

DOI: 10.5876/9781607325673.c005

how evidence from the era disproves the commonly made assumption that for centuries Mayan speakers shared a sense of common ethnic identity—even saw themselves as "Mayas." Ernest Gellner (1964:168, original emphasis) has argued that "nationalism is not the awakening of nations to self-consciousness: it *invents* nations where they do not exist"; our position is that modern Maya ethnogenesis had to invent Maya ethnic identity because there was no Maya ethnic self-consciousness in former times to which Mayas could awake.

Because of its modern ubiquity, we begin with the term *Maya*, examining its meaning to the indigenous inhabitants of Yucatán in the Conquest and Colonial periods in Yucatán, using Yucatec Mayan–language sources to categorize its usage. We then briefly further explore the nature of Maya identity during these centuries, likewise using archival evidence primarily in Yucatec Maya, to search for possible alternative terms or bases of ethnic identification. We suggest that migration and demographic developments from the late sixteenth to late nineteenth centuries altered whatever cultural homogeneity Maya communities may have had before the Spanish invasions. Finally, we look very briefly at two circumstances that impacted "Maya ethnogenesis"—Colonial Spanish ethnoracial concepts and the Caste War—emphasizing the muted, gradual, or indirect nature of their impact.

"MAYA" IN THE COLONIAL PERIOD

If the image of a timeless Maya ethnic community is an illusion, what of the Colonial period use of the term *Maya*? Spanish Colonial sources frequently apply the term to the indigenous language spoken in Yucatán, occasionally to a region, but rarely to the inhabitants of a particular area (see, for example, Ponce [1897 (1588):447]). In general, Spaniards preferred the generic *indio* to refer to the natives of Yucatán. "Maya" does appear in Maya-language sources, but with little consistency or frequency. Table 5.1 gives examples of this usage, with types of usage categorized and listed according to frequency of attestation.

The primary category in table 5.1 is labeled "cultural," containing references to the Yucatec language, as the term was mostly used as an adjective to describe it (*maya-than*, "Mayan speech or language"); Landa's only reference to the term's etymology is to "the language of the land being known as Maya" (*la lengua de la tierra llaman maya*; Landa 1959 [1566]:13; Restall et al. n.d.). The persistence of this connotation as primary to the term among the Maya themselves is illustrated succinctly in the dictionary of present-day Yucatec by Victoria Bricker and her native collaborators (1998:181); the sole entry under "Maya" refers to the language.

The context of Landa's comment is the second category of usage, labeled "toponym" in table 5.1; the Franciscan asserts that the place name "Mayapan" was derived

TABLE 5.1. Uses of the term *Maya* in Colonial Mayan–language sources

Phrase	Reference Type	Date	Source: Genre, Town (Region) (Incidence)
mayathan	cultural: "the Maya language"	Colonial	quasi-notarial and notarial sources (numerous)*
maya cuzamil	toponym (Cozumel)	Colonial	Book of Chilam Balam, Chumayel (Xiu) (thrice)
mayapan	toponym (Mayapan)	Colonial	quasi-notarial and notarial sources (numerous)
uchben maya xoc	cultural/material: "the ancient Maya count"	Colonial	Book of Chilam Balam, Tizimin (east) (once)
maya pom	cultural/material: "Maya copal incense"	1669	*cabildo* petition, Calkiní (Calkiní) (once)
maya ciie	cultural/material: "Maya wine"	Colonial	Book of Chilam Balam, Chumayel (Xiu) (once)
maya zuhuye	cultural/material: "Maya virgin"	Colonial	Book of Chilam Balam, Chumayel (Xiu) (once)
maya ah ytzae	to others: "those Itzá Mayas"	Colonial	Book of Chilam Balam, Chumayel (Xiu) (once)
maya ah kinob	to others: "Maya priests"	Colonial	Book of Chilam Balam, Chumayel (Xiu) (once)
maya uinicob(i)	to others: "(the) Maya men/people"	Colonial	Book of Chilam Balam, Chumayel (Xiu) (eight times); Titles of the Pech, Chicxulub and Yaxkukul (Pech) (twice)
maya uinicob	to others: to commoners by nobles	Colonial (1769)	Titles of the Pech, Chicxulub and Yaxkukul (Pech) (once)
maya uinicob	to others: of another Yucatec region	Colonial (1769)	Titles of the Pech, Chicxulub and Yaxkukul (Pech) (once)
maya uinicob	to others: to Yucatec Mayas by Chontal Mayas	1567/1612	Title of Acalan-Tixchel (Chontal region) (once)
coon maya uinice	self-reference: "we Maya men/people"	1662	individual petition, Yaxakumche (Xiu) (once)

continued on next page

from the term *Maya*. However, no other toponym in Yucatán contains the element "Maya"; when in a single quasi-notarial source the term is attached to the name for Cozumel Island, the context is a sacred association to Mayapan (Edmonson 1986:47, 58–59). Indeed, we suspect that the reverse of Landa's suggestion is true, that "Maya" derived from "Mayapan." This hypothesis is consistent with six pieces

TABLE 5.1.—*continued*

Phrase	Reference Type	Date	Source: Genre, Town (Region) (Incidence)
coon maya uinice	self-references	1669	*cabildo* pedition, Baca (Pech) (once)[†]
con maya uinice	self-reference	Colonial	Book of Chilam Balam, Chumayel (Xiu) (once)
coon ah maya uinice	self-reference (as nobles of the Canul *chibal*)	Colonial (1595/1821)	Title of Calkiní (Calkiní) (once)

Sources: Edmonson (1982:169); AGI (*Escribanía* 317b, 9:folio 9); Roys (1933:28); TLH (*The Title of Calkiní*:folio 36); Roys (1933:57); Roys (1933:47, 58–59); Roys (1933:61); Roys (1933:58); Roys (1933:53, 55–56, 31, 27, 24, 56); TLH and TULAL (*Title of Chicxulub*:folios 6, 8, 15) and (*Title of Yaxkukul*:folios 3v, 4r, 8v); AGI (*México* 138, *Title of Acalan-Tixchel*:folio 76r); TLH (*Xiu Chronicle*:#35); AGI (*Escribanía* 317a, 2:folio 147); Roys (1933:20). For many of these examples, also see Restall (1997a:13–15; 1998a:35, 44, 74, 101, 116, 121, 124, 127, 134, 177, 233).

* A notarial example is in AGN (*Bienes Nacionales* 5, 35:folio 5); a quasi-notarial one is in Roys (1933:40).
† This is an example; the phrase appears several other times in nearly identical petitions from other northwest *cahob* in 1668–69 (AGI, *Escribanía* 317a, 2:various folios).

of evidence: (1) the term's association with, and primary usage in, the northwest, where Mayapan is located;[6] (2) the entry in the sixteenth-century dictionary from Motul, also in the northwest, that glosses *maya* as "nombre propio desta tierra" (see figure 5.1; Ciudad Real n.d., 1:folio 287v; Arzápalo Marín 1995, 1:489); and (3) the fact that several contemporary Spanish authors considered Maya a political entity.

Thus, Ponce (1872 [1588]:470), for example, speaks of the province of Maya (*provincia de Maya*) as the influence zone of the city of Mayapán. López de Cogolludo (writing in the 1650s) stated that at the time of the Spanish invasion, Yucatán "had no common name under which the area and its limits were known" but that it had earlier been "called *Mayapan* after the name of its capital where the king had his court" (López de Cogolludo 1957 [1654], book 2, chapter 1; see also book 4, chapter 3).

Our hypothesis is also consistent with (4) the term's vague link to the Itzás, who, like the site of Mayapan, were seen as part of the peninsula's semi-sacred, semi-mythic historical past; and (5) the following passage from the Chilam Balam of Chumayel (translation Restall's, but see Roys 1933:50, 140; Edmonson 1986:59; figure 5.2):

oxlahun ahau u katunil u	13 *Ahau* was the *katun* when they
he > cob cah mayapan: maya	founded the *cah* of Mayapan; they

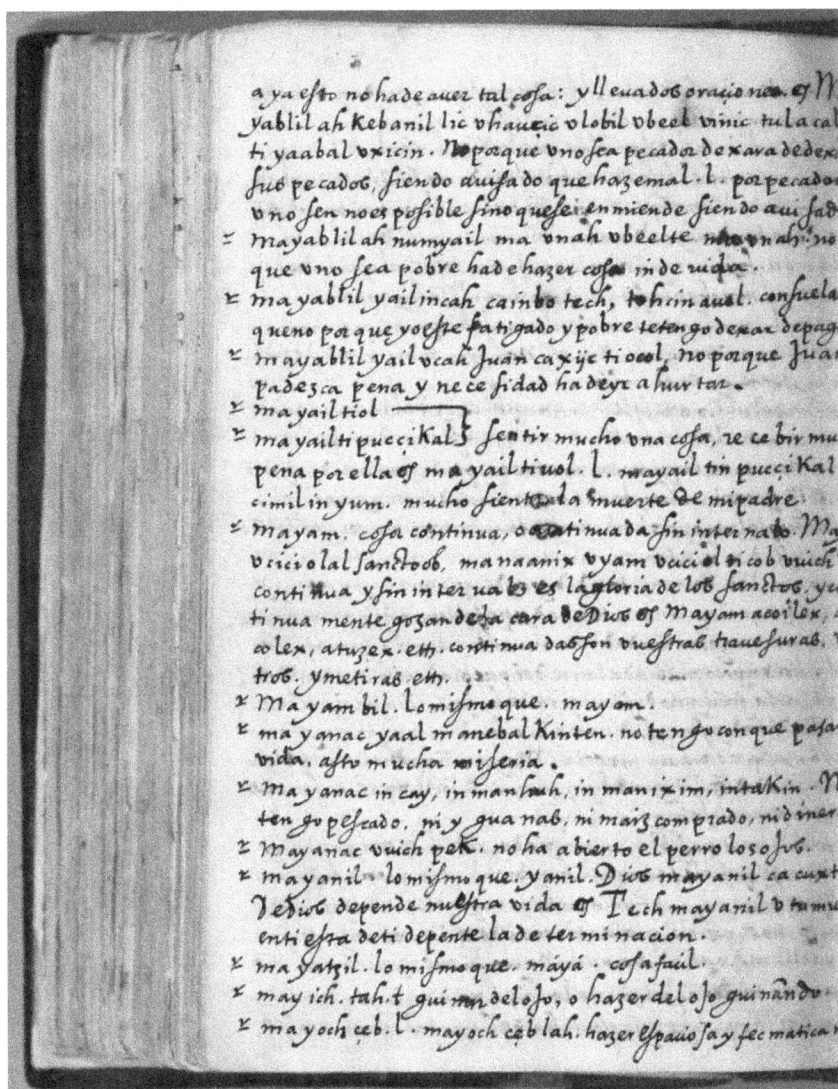

FIGURE 5.1. Motul Dictionary

uinic u kabaob: uaxac ahau
paxci u cabobi: ca uecchahi
ti peten tulacal: uac katuni
paxciob ca haui u maya

were [thus] called Maya men. In 8
Ahau their lands were destroyed
and they were scattered through
out the peninsula. Six *katun* after

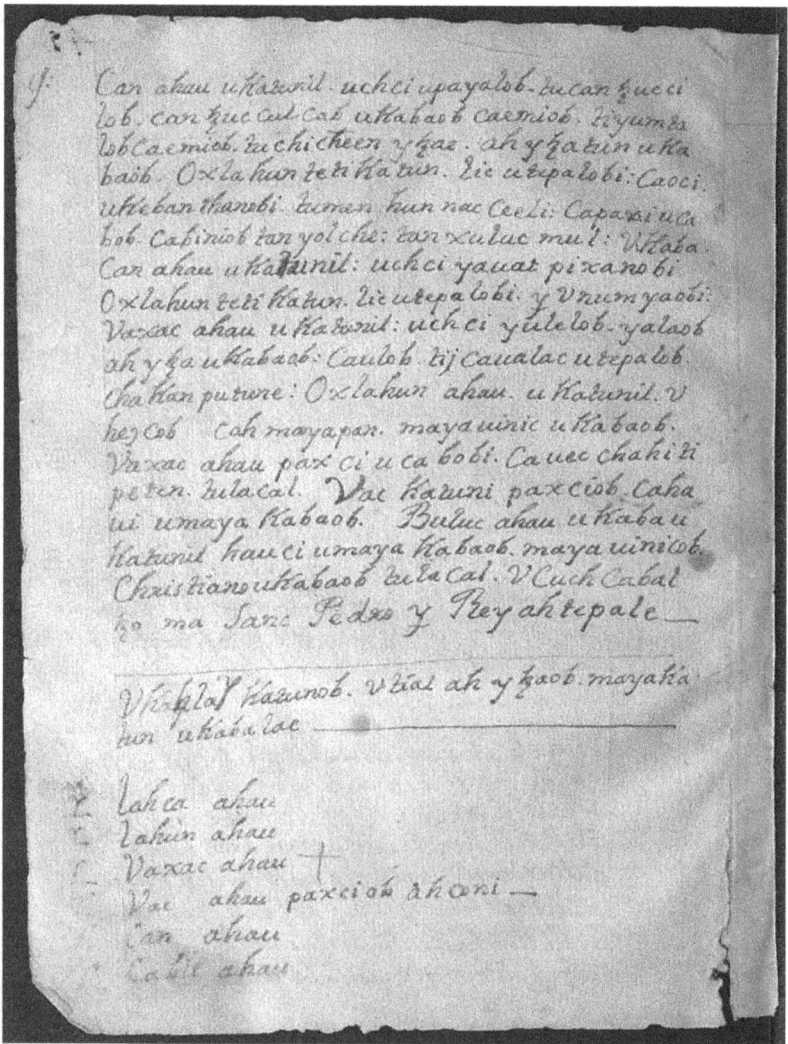

FIGURE 5.2. Chilam Balam of Chumayel

kabaob: bulub ahau u kaba
u katunil hauci u maya
kabaob maya uinicob:
christiano u kabaob

they were destroyed[;] they ceased
to be called Maya; 11 *Ahau* was
the name of the *katun* when the
Maya men ceased to be called Maya
[and] were called Christians.

These annual entries offer both an explanation of the diffusion of the term *Maya*—a product of the diaspora created by the fall and abandonment of Mayapan—and a clear association of the term with the pre-Conquest pagan past. This hypothesis on the origins of the term was also circulating in sixteenth-century Yucatán; a dozen years after Landa claimed the derivation was vice versa, an old conquistador of the province, the *encomendero* for the *cah* (Maya community) of Dzan, wrote in the *Relaciones Geográficas* that "this province speaks but one language, called Maya, its name derived from Mayapan" (RHGY 1983 1:156).[7] Our final piece of supportive evidence is (6) the kind of language used in the Maya sources. Groups of people are not categorized according to cultural (linguistic) criteria but by applying political or kinship affiliations, that is, the community of origin (cah)[8] and the relationship to a certain ruling lineage (as a member or vassal)[9] or polity (province).[10]

Of course, accepting that "Maya" comes from "Mayapan" begs the question as to the toponym's etymology. If "Mayapan" did indeed precede "Maya," then Landa's explanation of the toponym (*el pendón de la Maya*, "the banner of the Maya") would only have meaning after the site became a major city (Landa 1959 [1566]:13; Restall et al. n.d.). However, there are many possible alternative roots. May and Pan are both Maya patronyms, for example; *pan* also means "dig, sink [a well], plant [a tree]" and *ah pan* thus "he who digs," with *May Ah Pan*, "[the land of] May, the well digger." As *yapan* means "broken up," the origin could be a reference to the stony ground, with *ma yapan*, "not broken up, unbroken [terrain]."

The tertiary category of usages of "Maya," labeled "cultural/material" in table 5.1, consists of references to material objects native to the peninsula (such as *maya pom*, "Maya copal incense") or to local cultural practices (such as *uchben maya xoc*, "the ancient Maya count"). The significance of these types of references is that not only are they rare, but they all have sacred connotations and are consistent with the toponymic use of the term as rooted in semi-sacred myth and history. Although the Motul Dictionary lists a material item that seems to lack such associations—"*maya ulum* . . . gallina . . . de yucatan" and "gallina de la tierra: *ulum: mayaulum*"—in the references Mayas make to turkeys and chickens in their testaments, Restall and Christensen have never once seen *lum* qualified by *maya*; on the contrary, Mayas tend to qualify the imported fowl, the chicken, as *caxtillan u lum*, "Castilian turkey," abbreviated to *cax* by the seventeenth century.[11] The purpose of a dictionary like the Motul was for Franciscans to make themselves comprehensible to Mayas, and Mayas would certainly have understood *maya u lum*. But Mayas themselves would have used *lum* for "turkey" and the qualified or invented term for "chicken"; this would have been more logical from their perspective and consistent with the more esoteric associations of *maya*.

Equally rare, and comprising the fourth category in table 5.1, are instances where "Maya" refers to people. As references are so few, patterns can only be tentatively identified. But the examples suggest that the term was mostly applied by Mayas to Maya "others" or outsiders, specifically Yucatec natives of another region or class. One usage in this context was by nobles in reference to commoners, with the term seemingly somewhat derogatory. Thus, when applied to Mayan speakers of another region, the term sometimes implied that such people were of lesser status, although at other times the reference seems neutral. Native perspectives on the Spanish Conquest are the context for one such set of derogatory references, with "Maya" designating the natives of communities who were slower to accommodate the invaders.

The Pech nobles, for example, authors of one Conquest account, assert that they and their Spanish allies suffered much "because of the Maya people [*maya uinicob*] who were not willing to deliver themselves to God [*Dios*]" (i.e., surrender themselves to the new Colonial regime); these maya uinicob are ambiguously either local commoners or natives to the east of the Pech region or perhaps both (*Title of Chicxulub*, folio 15, from the translation in Restall 1998a:124). A similar perspective is found in the *Relaciones Geográficas* from Valladolid, a Spanish account based partly on oral native sources, which claims that the natives of Chikinchel (in the peninsula's northeast) called the Cupul and Cochuah (of the east and southeast, respectively) "*Ah Mayas*, insulting them as crude and base people of vile understanding and inclination [*soez y baja, de viles entendimientos e inclinaciones*]" (RHGY 1983 2:37).

This pattern incorporates the use of the term as a self-reference (the fifth and final category in table 5.1), in that the context in some of those cases is that of petitions, whose language was by tradition self-deprecating.[12] This tradition was Mesoamerican in scope, most clearly visible in petitions in Nahuatl and Yucatec Mayan. One of its central tropes was the presentation by nobles of themselves as children and commoners. In some Yucatec examples, this self-depiction is paralleled by a description of themselves as maya uinicob (Maya people or men). One group of such attestations is found in a series of petitions authored by *cahob* (plural of *cah*) across the entire colony in 1668–69, in response to *residencia* activities by Spanish officials—an investigation, in other words, into a governor's term of office. In this case, the administration under review was that of don Rodrigo Flores de Aldana, whose use of forced purchase operations had made him especially unpopular among Mayas and some colonist groups.

To view these attestations as simple indicators of ethnic self-identity, however, would be to remove them misleadingly from their context. That context was, first, the self-deprecating component of Maya petitionary discourse and, second, the similarity of these petitions across the series, suggesting the use of a template that may have been partly Spanish-authored (with maya uinicob thus a translation of a phrase such as indios) but was certainly aimed at a Spanish audience. Thus, by calling themselves "Mayas," the petitioners were ritually humiliating themselves within two parallel social structures—one a wholly native one in which "Maya" had negative class and region connotations, the other a Colonial ethnoracial one in which "Maya" was understood to have meaning *to Spaniards* as a marker of ethnic subordination.[13]

The region-class-"Maya" nexus has an additional dimension, one that further undermines the term as a monolithic ethnic designator. This dimension is the mythical tradition of foreign origin maintained by a number of Maya noble families—all families in the group of prominent ruling *chibalob* that Restall (2001) has elsewhere dubbed the "dynastic dozen" (the Caamal, Canul, Canche, Chan, Che, Chel, Cochuah, Cocom, Cupul, Iuit, Pech, and Xiu). Scholars have tended to take this tradition at face value, as simple historical evidence of the non-Yucatec (usually central Mexican) origins of the peninsula's native elite. However, there is no clear evidence beyond the tradition itself of any such invasion or migration. Furthermore, the metahistorical construction of the tradition by Maya dynasties conforms to the patterns of traditions of mythical elite foreign origins elsewhere in the world, what Sahlins has called "the ideology of external domination" (Sahlins 1985:77–78; see also Helms 1993, 1994, 1998; Henige 1982:90–96). We have argued, therefore, that this tradition was probably not rooted in a historic migration of ruling families into Yucatán but rather in pre-Conquest efforts to bolster legitimacy of status and rule through sacred, mythic associations with often-fictional distant places of origin (for the full development of this argument, see Restall 2001; Gabbert 2001a:28, 2004a:34–35).

These efforts were given renewed necessity and vitality by the Spanish Conquest, resulting in the frequent references to such mythic origins in sixteenth-century sources (e.g., in the *Title of Acalan-Tixchel*, folio 69v, *The Title of Calkiní*, 36, the *Book of Chilam Balam of Maní*, 134, and RHGY 1983 1:319; see Restall 1998a:58, 101, 140, 149). The fact that indigenous nobles referred to themselves as "conquerors" and tried to distance themselves from the local indigenous population can be better understood if considered from a perspective other than that of the modern nation-state ideology that asserts the cultural and biological sameness of rulers and the ruled. A comparison with the estate societies of Europe before the French Revolution, as well as with other continents, is more illuminating. In contrast to present-day concepts, these societies were based on the idea of a fundamental difference between rulers and the ruled, from the point of view of culture and descent.[14] This model of society was also common in Mesoamerica. By claiming to be both native and foreign, Yucatán's indigenous dynasties effectively problematized and undermined any incipient sense of Maya ethnic identity that may have otherwise developed in late Postclassic and Colonial times. In permitting and often fostering the survival of a Maya elite, Spaniards thereby colluded in the perpetuation of an identity differentiation that ran against their impulse to see natives as an undifferentiated mass—and softened the impact of that impulse on Maya ethnogenesis.

All the attested self-references of Mayas as "Maya" come from the regions of the west, seemingly confirming Munro Edmonson's suggestion (based on his reading of the Chilam Balam manuscript from Chumayel) that the Mayas were deemed to be the inhabitants of the peninsula's west and the Itzás those of the east.[15] However, the vast majority of extant Colonial Maya sources come from the peninsula's west, skewing the evidence. Furthermore, Edmonson's translation of *maya ah ytzae* as "O Maya / and Itza" is more likely "those Itzá Mayas" (or "Oh Maya Itza," as Ralph Roys has it). Elsewhere in the Chumayel manuscript the Yucatec language is called *u than maya ah ytzaob*, "the language of the Itzá Mayas," again suggesting that Maya and Itzá were not always mutually exclusive categories (Roys 1933:167, 40; Edmonson 1986:100, 222).

The regional association, therefore, of Mayas with the west and Itzás with the east is suggested but not well supported by this evidence. In some ways, the category of "Itzá" is comparable to that of "Maya"; both are ambiguous, used variously and usually to describe some other group of natives within the peninsula, with uncertain historical roots but a fairly clear connection to an important ancient city (Chichén Itzá and Mayapan, respectively). But there is also a crucial difference between the two terms: Itzá was, and still is, a Yucatec Maya patronym; "Maya" is not, and there is no sign that it ever was. Although this could be taken to suggest that "Itzá" connotes family and "Maya" ethnicity, in fact the difference between the two is more complex. Whereas "Maya" has various connotations, most of them not referring to people, "Itzá" is a category that primarily refers to people, both in the family sense (in the form of a patronym) and in an ethnic sense (in the form of the Itzá Mayas of the Petén region of northern Guatemala, whose name may have derived from the patronym of the kingdom's founders).[16]

Before we summarize the evidence offered by Mayan-language sources, it is worth turning briefly to the evidence of Colonial period dictionaries. This complex, bilingual, bicultural genre cannot be used as a simple window onto Colonial Yucatec; dictionaries merely suggest how Mayan was spoken in a particular time and region in the peninsula, as perceived and recorded by their Franciscan authors. Nevertheless, a search for *maya* entries in Colonial dictionaries is revealing, especially in the context of the evidence from Maya notarial sources discussed earlier (see Restall 2004:71–73 for a fuller discussion). Only in the Spanish-Maya sections of Colonial dictionaries does the term appear with any regularity, suggesting that while the term certainly existed in Colonial Maya, it was not commonly used by Mayan speakers. The types of applications of the term in Spanish-Maya vocabularies compare closely to the examples we grouped under "cultural" and "material" (as opposed to "human") in table 5.1, implying that to Spaniards the term was also an adjective conveying autochthony in a general sense rather than one specific to human beings. "Maya" remained uncommon as an ethnic designator through the end of the Colonial period (Ciudad Real n.d.; Arzápalo Marín 1995; Beltrán de Santa Rosa 1746; Pío Pérez 1898; Mengin 1972:folio 131v; Barrera Vásquez 1980:513).

We draw four conclusions from the evidence discussed so far and presented in table 5.1. First, *Maya* is not a common term in Colonial Maya sources. Second, it was used primarily to refer to the Yucatec language or to native material items, the latter mainly ones with sacred and historical associations. Third, when it was applied to people, it was never done in a way that explicitly indicated a peninsula-wide or macro-regional ethnic identity, suggesting instead smaller groups defined by region or class, with the term very possibly deriving from the toponym "Mayapan." Dictionary entries of the term as a macro-regional ethnic one are irregular, with no Colonial dictionary including it in both a Maya-Spanish and a Spanish-Maya vocabulary; its more common dictionary meanings are in reference to the Yucatec language and to local material items. Fourth, there are signs that the term has been viewed as derogatory by a section of Yucatán's speakers of Maya and by others as an archaic historical or literary term.

The apparent contradiction between uses of "Maya" with positive and negative connotations disappears if one realizes that the peninsula was subdivided politically—and to some degree also culturally—in pre-Conquest times. All positive references cited in table 5.1 for "Maya" that refer to rare or holy items come from regions once attached to Mayapan, while the negative uses are either from areas beyond Mayapan's influence or from a Colonial context in which native elites tried to distance themselves from the local commoners.

A MAYA BY ANY OTHER NAME?

If indigenous Yucatecans did not see themselves as "Mayas," what were the foundations of native self-identity? In addition to expected micro-identities, such as gender, age, class, and occupation, two fundamental units of social organization served as the basis of group and individual identity for Colonial Mayas—the municipal community (which Mayas called the cah) and the patronym-group (which they called the *chibal*). Mayas organized their lives and activities around these two units and consistently identified themselves and other Mayas according to cah and chibal affiliations.

The cah was a geographical entity, consisting of its residential core (what we would call a village or town) and its agricultural territory (the combination of the cultivated and forested lands held by cah members). But it was also a political and social entity, the focus of native political activity (regional politics was a Spanish monopoly during Colonial times) and the locus of social networks. At the primary level of the extended family, identity and social activity were generated at the meeting point of cah and chibal—built, in other words, around the members of a particular chibal in a particular cah. As chibalob were exogamous (in accordance with a deep-rooted native taboo broken only occasionally by dynastic-dozen couples), their members tended to form multi-chibal alliances that were inevitably class-based and related to political factionalism in the cah. As almost every aspect of an indigenous individual's life was determined by cah and chibal affiliations, it is not surprising that these units formed the native identity nexus and provided the references for identification; thus, someone might be *Ah Pech* or *Ah Pechob*, "of the Pech [chibal]," and Ah Motul, "of Motul [cah]" (Restall 1997a:15–50, 1998b) (see table 5.2).

One might argue that cah and chibal formed the basis of a kind of ethnic identity or a multiplicity of micro-ethnic identities, a notion reminiscent of an older historiographical tradition that saw the pre-Conquest Mayas as divided into various "tribes."[17] Furthermore, if all Mayas shared the same *type* of identity, as well as sharing the experience of Colonial subjection, then one could argue that they shared a kind of aggregate ethnic identity. This argument is not without merit, but it is hard to reconcile with the three fundamental aspects of Maya identities: (1) class differences persisted within each cah, as discussed above; (2) the cah was an open community, in that it was exogamous, it permitted settlers from other cahob, and it was part of the complex pattern of Maya mobility; as we shall see, it accepted other native Mesoamericans and people of African descent during the Colonial centuries; and (3) the chibal was diasporic in nature; its members were found in a variety of cahob, almost never in just one and often not even in a single region. Thus, to categorize cah and chibal as types of ethnic identity would seem to stretch the term too far.[18]

Another potential candidate for a term used by indigenous Yucatecans to imply ethnic identity is *macehual*, which in both Yucatec Mayan and Nahuatl meant "commoner." However, it would be a mistake to assume that macehual was effectively a Colonial cognate for "Maya" as used today (as Hervik [1999:39, 42] seems to suggest). By the mid-eighteenth century macehual appears in a Maya-Spanish dictionary glossed as indio, having been omitted entirely from earlier dictionaries (see Restall 2004:76 for a fuller discussion). A corresponding term, *dzul* (written >*ul* in Colonial orthography), meant "foreigner" and was often used to refer to Spaniards. Similarly, the Spanish word *vecino*, "resident," was mostly used by

TABLE 5.2. Maya terms of self-description containing possible ethnic implications

Term, with Variants	Meaning	Context of Usage
ah cahnal, cahnal, (ah) cahal / cahalnal, h cahala [late]	cah member, resident	all genres, non-rhetorical, often juxtaposed to vecino ("Spaniard")
ah otochnal	householder, native	same as ah cahnal
macehual, masehual	commoner	rhetorical usage implying "Maya"
mehen	(man's) children	same as macehual
almehen	noble	only to describe Maya nobility
uinic	man, person	sometimes means (Maya) person
kuluinic, u nucil uinic, noh uinic	a principal or elder	Maya person only
maya uinic	Maya man/person	rare; quasi-notarial sources only
mayathan	Yucatec Maya	the language
ah [cah name]	person of [cah]	Maya person only
ah [patronym]	person of [chibal]	Maya person only

Sources: Adapted from Restall (1997a:17), based on Colonial Mayan–language notarial and quasi-notarial sources.

Spaniards, and occasionally by Mayas too, to refer to non-natives (Restall 1997a:15–16, 1997b; Karttunen and Lockhart 1987; Lockhart 1992:86–89, 365–68; Gabbert 2004a:31–33).

This suggests that macehual and dzul did not become terms of ethnic identity comparable to the meaning we assign to "Maya" and "Spaniard." In table 5.2 we have denoted the "context of usage" of macehual in Mayan-language sources as a rhetorical one "implying 'Maya'" because native nobles typically styled themselves as commoners in petitions to Spaniards, as a political ploy and in accordance with Mesoamerican techniques of deferential discourse, in a way that was similar to their usage of "Maya" as an identity marker. Spaniards read such terms as ethnoracial because they defined the Colonial social structure ethnoracially (see also below). After the Conquest, Spanish colonialism established a social order in Latin America that can be characterized as an estate system. This means that fundamental social categories—Spaniards, Indians, and *castas* (people of presumed mixed ancestry, such as mestizos and mulattoes)—were legally defined and held specific rights and duties (e.g., Gabbert 2004a:19–20). Indigenous elites continued to see macehual as a class term because the social structure from their perspective was primarily a local one of native nobles and commoners and only secondarily a Colonial one featuring non-natives too.[19] The fact that Spanish officials read maya and macehual as indio was probably not lost on the native elite; indeed, this contributed to the efficacy of their rhetoric and its adaptation to the Colonial setting. But that does not mean that native elites thereby adopted Spanish perspectives and internalized the Spanish perception of them as Indians.

Nevertheless, the appearance of macehual in Colonial sources cannot simply be dismissed, any more than maya can. Indigenous Yucatecans did not see themselves as "Maya" or any other term or label that contained all natives in the peninsula, but the evidence presented so far suggests that during Colonial times they did develop an awareness of difference that more or less corresponded to Spanish ethnoracial distinctions. More specifically, this awareness can be better understood if we draw a distinction between two forms of ethnic awareness: *implied* ethnicity, whereby terms of self-identification imply membership in a loosely defined ethnic category within the context of broader social and ethnoracial structures, and *overt* ethnicity, characterized by the existence of social relations, solidarity, and cohesion among members. A community in this sense only exists if members orientate their actions to one another, based on their sense of a common fate.[20] Colonial evidence indicates that the Colonial experience gave rise to and fostered a sense of *implied* ethnicity among the natives who lived within the Spanish province but that *overt* ethnic awareness did not exist among them in either the Late Postclassic or Colonial periods and thus presumably not earlier either.

One dimension of this terminological bifurcation is the role played by ethnic boundaries: Maya terms of implied ethnicity are mostly inward-looking and concerned with social life in the cah, excluding Spaniards; overt ethnic markers tend to be outward-looking and reflect a keen awareness of ethnic borders. Jon Schackt (2001:4) proposes that "ethnogenesis should mean the drawing of new boundaries or, perhaps, some notable redrawing of old ones." The boundaries that defined community and identity among indigenous Yucatecans were not notably redrawn during the Colonial period, nor were new boundaries created; such boundaries continued to demarcate one cah, or group of cahob, from another without expanding outward to include the natives of all cahob.

By adding to the above analysis of Maya-language sources a reading of Spanish-language notarial sources from the Colonial archives (in Mérida, Mexico City, and Seville), it is possible to be more specific still in locating the Colonial conditions under which implied, but not overt, ethnic awareness developed. A survey of such sources reveals three pertinent types of condition. The first was the Colonial legal system itself. Its often-skillful manipulation by cah leaders suggests that one important reason for this bifurcated development was the natives' realization that Colonial identities and their various facets could be used as weapons in law courts or as tools to work away at the structures of Colonial administration. Under these circumstances, ethnic identity remained implied most of the time.

The second Colonial condition was the growing difference between urban and rural Maya communities. In rural cahob, identity remained rooted in community and family affiliations, as discussed. Colonialism reinforced this localization of identity through its suppression of regional native politics. But in the city of Mérida and the Colonial towns—the villas of Bacalar, Campeche, and Valladolid and the pueblos that became semi-urbanized toward the end of the Colonial period, such as Izamal—native identity developed urban variations on the implied/overt model. The multiracial setting and the concomitant process of miscegenation made indigenous ethnic identity increasingly overt in the late eighteenth and nineteenth centuries, even if that identity was increasingly labeled *mestizo* (e.g., Gabbert 2004a:74–75, 114–20).

Urban developments, therefore, incorporate the third condition under which implied ethnic awareness rather than overt ethnic self-identity developed. This was, simply put, time. Our hypothesis regarding the chronological development of the use of the term *Maya* and its implications for Maya ethnogenesis is the following.

In the Late Postclassic period, the term applied to all or some of the inhabitants of Mayapan or the region dominated by Mayapan; after that city's collapse in the 1440s, the term applied to the diaspora of families who migrated to various locations in the peninsula, but its application seems to have been vague and probably increasingly obscure, as such families did not maintain identities that were clearly distinct from other Maya families. At the time of the Spanish invasion, its primary use was probably in reference to the Yucatec language, in the form *mayathan*. By the late sixteenth century the term was applied both to the Yucatec language and to local material items but not to people, and even then it seems to have been more commonly used by Spaniards than Mayas. At the same time, there remained no other term in Yucatec Maya equivalent to our understanding of "Maya" as an ethnic designator; Maya identity remained more localized than that, lacking a clear ethnic component (see also ibid.:31).

As the Colonial period wore on, a sense of implied ethnic identity evolved in response to Colonial conditions and the influence of Spanish efforts to build a Colonial society based on ethnoracial principles. In the late seventeenth century the written record reveals evidence of "Maya" used in reference to people, but attestations are rare and dictionary entries are only in the Spanish-Maya listings. More common in the Late Colonial period is the term *macehual*, but its transition from a class term to an ethnoracial one was gradual and not complete by the end of Colonial rule (see also ibid.:31–32). By the early nineteenth century, there is little sign of this implied ethnic identity having become overt.

GENESIS OF MESO-MAYAS AND AFRO-MAYAS

We have argued thus far that the natives of Yucatán were not Mayas in name and can barely be said to have shared a common identity by another name (such as macehual). Our position on the putative central Mexican origins of elite dynasties in Yucatán is highly skeptical; we argue that the claim by such nobles was strategic rather than a literal one based on actual migration. In other words, we have *not* suggested that ethnic diversity in the peninsula undermined Maya ethnogenesis; on the contrary, unlike regions such as Oaxaca, with a marked degree of linguistic and cultural variation before and after the Spanish Conquest (Terraciano 2001; Yannakakis 2008), the Yucatán Peninsula was culturally and linguistically quite homogeneous. Even adjacent languages to the south, such as Chontal and Itzá, were arguably dialects of Yucatec spoken by descendents of migrants from the peninsula.

However, the sixteenth century brought rapid and complex ethnic diversity to the Yucatán. The arrival of Spaniards and the growth of a Spanish-native mestizo sector of the population is the most obvious dimension to that change, as mentioned. But two others have received little attention from historians: the arrival of other Mesoamericans in the 1540s and the arrival of Africans from the 1540s to the 1810s.

It has long been known that the three Franciscos de Montejo and their fellow Spaniards established a colony in Yucatán in the 1540s by bringing Nahua allies from central Mexico and recruiting Mayan speakers to fight each other. But the conventional view has long been that the Spaniards succeeded in colonizing the area largely by wearing down local resistance over three invasions and two decades (1527–46). More recently, the central role and multiple perspectives of Mayan speakers—including the claim of local nobles to the Spanish term *conquistador*—have been given more attention (Restall 1998a, 2003:44–51). And more recently still, the extent, diversity, and crucial roles played by Mesoamerican warriors and porters have been studied (Chuchiak 2007).

These allies were not Tlaxacalans, as previously claimed, but Nahuas from Azcapotzalco and Xochimilco (two towns held briefly as part of the Montejo *encomiendas*), with other central Mexican communities also represented. The Montejos also brought warriors, slaves, and porters from the regions where they had fought and attempted to establish colonies—primarily Honduras, Chiapas, and Tabasco. As table 5.3 shows, Spaniards brought 10,000 Nahuas with them, as well as another 3,000 or more warriors and porters from seventeen different Mesoamerican linguistic groups.

What was the fate of these thousands of indigenous newcomers? Evidence suggests that few, if any, returned to their native lands. Most probably died in the wars of the 1540s and from the disease epidemics that likewise hit Mayas during the period. The rest stayed in Yucatán, primarily in the Mérida-Tihó neighborhoods (or *cah-barrios*, as Restall has dubbed them; 1997a:31–37) of San Cristóbal and Santiago.

TABLE 5.3. Ethnic diversity of Mesoamericans brought into Yucatán in the 1540s

Ethnicity	Region of Origin	Number of Warriors	Number of Slaves and Porters	Totals
Nahuas	Central Mexico	2,500–3,000	5,000–7,000	up to 10,000
Zapotecs, Mixtecs, Mixes	Oaxaca	?	345	at least 345
Chontals, Popoluca, Zoque	Tabasco	200–300	800–1,000	up to 1,300
Tzeltal, Tzotzil, Chiapaneca	Chiapas	?	200–400	at least 300
Chorti, Xinka, Pilil	Guatemala and El Salvador	?	150	at least 150
Kaqchikel, K'iche'	Guatemala	100–200	?	at least 200
Lenca, Jicaque	Honduras	100	300	at least 400

Source: Chuchiak (2007), who draws on sixteenth-century sources in AGI.

In 1579 a group of fifty-six surviving veterans of the war, all residents of these two cah-barrios, put their names to a petition asking that their privileges as conquerors (primarily exemption from tribute payment) be restored.[21] The petitioners, all with Spanish or non-Maya Mesoamerican surnames, were born in central Mexico, Tabasco, Guatemala, and Honduras. The 1579 petition reflects the facts that (1) veterans had stayed, established communities in the Colonial capital, and were cohesive enough that some could still collaborate in legal action long after their initial arrival, despite (2) their ongoing ethnic diversity (in the sense of their intermixing with Mayas); but (3) their declining numbers suggested they had begun to be gradually absorbed into the larger indigenous population around them. Indeed, later evidence confirms this; San Cristóbal and Santiago appear in the archival record in the seventeenth and eighteenth centuries as Maya cah-barrios, not as separate ethnic, linguistic, or political entities. The Mesoamerican veterans lost their privileges and eventually their separate identity.

At the same time Spaniards were bringing thousands of Mesoamericans into Yucatán, they also started introducing Africans into the peninsula. There were only a few dozen brought in the early 1540s, greatly outnumbered by Nahuas and others; but whereas the influx of Mesoamericans soon stopped (or became negligible), the importation of Africans became a slow, steady trickle for centuries. The first century of the Yucatecan Colonial period (1540s–1640s) was also a period of intense slave importation into Mexico (when the Portuguese controlled the Atlantic slave trade and for most of that century the Portuguese and Spanish empires were united under the Spanish crown); even Yucatán, a relatively poor province of New Spain, witnessed a regular influx of black slaves, one that kept the black population at roughly the same level as the Spanish one. As Spaniards in Yucatán grew in number, partially by absorbing some "Spaniards" who had mixed ancestry, the Afro-Yucatecan population kept pace through parallel processes of immigration (in the African case, forced), reproduction, and racial mixing.

Thus, indigenous Mayan speakers remained the majority. But through the eighteenth century, Afro-Yucatecans (i.e., all those of African descent, from African-born slaves to Yucatán-born free coloreds) appeared in official colony-wide censuses as 12 percent to 15 percent of the total population. In 1779, Afro-Yucatecans were 11 percent of the population in and around Mérida and 27 percent in and around Campeche; in the rural districts that comprised the rest of the province, Afro-Yucatecans averaged 7 percent of the population. In the 1804 census, that number was 6 percent (Restall 2009:chapter 1). However, these numbers cannot be taken literally; all Spanish Colonial censuses must be subject to careful interpretation, and the official numbers from Yucatán need to be placed in the context of three further well-evidenced points.

First, Afro-Yucatecans were everywhere, even in the smallest villages. It is true that African slaves in the colony were auxiliary slaves attached personally to their owners (as opposed to plantation slaves), and both black slavery and the development of Afro-Yucatecan communities was more an urban than a rural phenomenon.[22] But even in the official church censuses of 1797–1813, there are people of African descent in 96 percent of the province's parishes; the actual figure was likely higher.

Second, the official numbers of Afro-Yucatecans undoubtedly *understate* their true numbers because the socio-racial ranking culture in the colonies (sometimes called "the casta system" by historians, a term not used in Colonial times) was race-conscious but fluid. It encouraged and permitted category "passing," which simultaneously reinforced ranking culture (the notion it was better to be a Spaniard than mulatto, better to be mulatto than black, and so forth) while also rendering its categories increasingly vague, broad, and unreliable (see also Gabbert 2004a:18–22). In Late Colonial Yucatán, Afro-Yucatecan categories such as *negro* and *moreno* (both "black" but with subtle distinctions) and *mulato* and *pardo* (both "mulatto") faded from usage as their real numbers continued to grow. Afro-Yucatecans themselves did not disappear; they became Spaniards, mestizos, and natives.

This brings us to the third point, one especially relevant to the question of Maya identity: Afro-Yucatecan men married Yucatecan Maya women throughout the Colonial period. The archival record contains evidence of specific examples (such as the African-born Manuel Bolio, who married Josepha Chan, a Maya resident of Mérida, in 1757; see Restall 2006 and 2009:chapter 5 for the full story). It also allows us to draw up statistical data; for example, over 2,000 marriages of Afro-Yucatecan in Colonial Mérida (1567–1797) show that 51 percent of black husbands chose Maya or mestiza wives, and 45 percent of colored husbands (pardo or mulato) did the same. Similar statistics out in the countryside show lower levels, as there were fewer Afro-Yucatecan men in Maya villages. But it took place everywhere; Afro-Maya marriage was a phenomenon that affected the entire province over centuries.[23] By 1800, in a manner of speaking, one can argue that Yucatán's Mayas had become Afro-Mayas (Restall 2009:chapter 7).

How, then, do the parallel stories of Mesoamerican and African arrivals in Colonial Yucatán impact questions of Maya identity? First, they strongly suggest that a process began in the 1540s whereby Yucatán's natives gradually became Meso-Mayas and Afro-Mayas—at least in terms of their ethnic or racial ancestry. This process of biological diversification was most intense in Mérida-Tihó and Campeche, but it had spread throughout the colony by 1800. But second, the numbers of, and diversity within, these two immigrants groups (Mesoamericans and black Africans) were such that separate, closed communities did not develop. Indigenous communities accepted and absorbed other indigenous and colored outsiders into their chibalob and cahob. In doing so, the cah and the chibal displayed strength through openness and flexibility, while a "Maya" identity continued to fail to develop.

ETHNIC CATEGORIES IN THE COLONY, 1542–1821

If the Colonial Maya evidence supports the notion of a lack of a broader ethnic consciousness among indigenous Yucatecans by the early nineteenth century, why have they been assigned such an identity with such regularity over the past five centuries? One of the most important factors is Colonial Spanish influence.

Spanish influence is rooted in the mid-sixteenth century, when repeated invasions finally resulted in the permanent establishment of a small colony in the peninsula. Directed by a presumptuous geography and a cavalier ethnocentrism, Spaniards imposed upon hundreds of native groups in the New World a blanket racial identity, that of indio, which indigenous people neither shared nor ever came to embrace. At the same time, Spaniards imagined that the "Indians" of particular regions, such as Yucatán, had a regional sense of identity that gave them particular characteristics in common.

Such characteristics were based less on systematic observation—investigations such as Diego de Landa's into native culture were the exception rather than the rule—and more on explaining phenomena related to the Spanish experience. For example, the protracted nature of the conquest—twenty years to establish a permanent hold on a mere corner of the peninsula (Clendinnen 1987; Restall 1998a)—was put down to

Maya bellicosity and duplicity, a paradigm that remained an undercurrent to Spanish discourse on Mayas throughout Colonial rule and one that would resurface with vehemence during the Caste War, when the Spanish Yucatecan Justo Sierra O'Reilly denounced the Mayas as "brutal, scheming, warlike savages, whose goal is nothing less than the destruction of civilization" (quoted in Chuchiak 1997:25).

Spaniards thus assigned the Yucatec Mayas what was in effect an ethnic identity, bounded by regionalism—in this case a Colonial province that more or less comprised the peninsula of Yucatán—or language and by perceived characteristics such as those cited above or those recorded by Landa.[24] Within the larger schema of the Colonial Spanish *sistema de castas*, or ethnoracial "caste" system, constructed ethnic units such as the Yucatec Mayas comprised the racial category "Indians." The importance of the latter—with "Indian" characteristics more significant than regional ones—was reflected in Spanish terms of reference; native groups were usually "the Indians of this province" or "the Indians of that land," with more specific references geographical (Landa sometimes refers to *los yucatanenses*; Landa 1959 [1566]:47, for example) or externally determined (there are so-called Chontal groups around the margins of the regions that were Nahuatl-speaking in the sixteenth century because *chontalli* is a Nahuatl term for "foreigner").

"Indians," as a subordinated but semi-civilized source of labor, were slotted into the ranking of the ethnoracial system between Spaniards, who as "people of reason" were destined to rule, and black Africans, whose inherent inferiority suited them to slavery. Because these "natural laws" were part of an evolving European ideology of Colonial justification, they had to be realized through a complex mixture of force, coercion, and co-optation. Furthermore, for the same reason, the system was never fully realized, leaving scholars of Colonial Spanish America to struggle with the complex contradictions between Colonial Spanish assertions and historical evidence on the nature of societies in these colonies. Some historians have argued that the Spanish-"Indian"-African ranking based on phenotype was, when it came to the functioning of social organizations, a Spanish-African-"Indian" system (Lockhart and Schwartz 1983:130). Others have argued that the growth in the mixed-race population, the people to whom the term *castas* properly refers, created a social structure in which class played a more significant role than race.[25] The point to be emphasized here is that there was, from the start and increasingly so, a disjuncture between social and cultural realities on the one hand and Colonial Spanish constructions and perceptions of ethnoracial identities on the other. One part of this phenomenon was the invention of an ethnic group of Yucatec "Indians," later Yucatec "Mayas," within the larger race of New World "Indians." The next few pages outline what happened to this complex situation after Yucatán had gained its independence from Spain in 1821.

ETHNIC CATEGORIES IN THE POST-COLONY, 1821–1900

Even after Mexico gained political independence, the population of Yucatán remained legally divided. The *repúblicas de indios*, established during Colonial times as special administrative units for the indigenous, tribute-paying population, survived. The Colonial tripartition—Spaniards, castas, and indios—was reduced to a system of administration that differentiated between people with total civil rights, the so-called vecinos, and natives (indios or indígenas) (Cline 1950 2:64). The repúblicas remained in the state of Yucatán until 1868, whereas in Campeche, which had separated from Yucatán in 1858, they were abolished around 1869.[26]

Nevertheless, the term *indígena* continued to be used in official documents and censuses (e.g., Padrón . . . Panaba, February 27, 1885, AGEY, PE, P, CP, RC). Everyday speech, in general, reflected the administrative dichotomy between "Indian" and "vecino." Frequently, however, the Spanish-speaking elite considered it not merely a legal but an ethnic or "racial" differentiation. Thus, Ancona writes that in Yucatán anyone who did not belong to the "pure Indian race" was called vecino (Ancona 1978 4:37n6). The terms *yucateco* and *blanco* (white) were also used to mean the opposite of indio or Maya: "In Yucatán whites are generally not only those in whose veins pure European blood runs but even those who mixed it with a quantity of Indian blood. Thus . . . our population is divided into two broad sections: the Indians and the whites. The first are the descendants of the Mayas who did not mix their blood with any other, and the second are the individuals of all other races" (ibid.:13n3; see also Stephens 1963 1:154–55).[27]

Another set of categories contrasted those dressed in European fashion (suits, dresses, shoes), the so-called *gente de vestido*, with people who wore folk costume, which had evolved from the garments worn by natives and mestizos during the Colonial period.[28] Social categories were also dichotomously structured in the Maya language. Members of the in-group were generally referred to as macehual or *otsil* (poor), those from the out-group were called dzul (see documents in Chi Poot 1982:237, 239, 278, 284–85, 287–88, 301–2; Tozzer 1982 [1907]:19; Cline 1950 5:149; Gabbert 2004a:62–64, 78–79, 111–15).[29]

Thus, the social categories employed in nineteenth-century Yucatán constitute a complex system composed of a number of sets, each referring to one or more dimensions of difference, including legal status, "race" (phenotype and descent), and clothing. A particular set was selected according to the context (census, everyday communication), the topic in question, and the language used (Spanish or Mayan). The analysis of this system is complicated by the fact that the social boundaries marked by the different traits did not coincide.[30] Data presented by Don Dumond (1997:41–43) for the first decades of the nineteenth century show that only the surname had a close relationship with legal status and administrative classification.

This apparently remained constant in the ensuing decades.[31] There was therefore a strong tendency to categorize anyone bearing a Maya patronymic as "Indian" or Maya. Phenotype was a completely different matter. After more than three centuries of miscegenation, any attempt to separate different population groups according to physical traits was a hopeless endeavor. These physical features, however, were by no means unimportant, since statistically there was indeed a relationship between, for example, wealth and skin color. But physical traits were not important for the categorization of individuals as such; only in combination with other features, including wealth, dress, occupation, and surname.

In post-Conquest Yucatán, Spanish was considered the language of civilization by the urban elite, which regarded Maya as the idiom of ignorance. Only a small part of the population in the few urban settlements and provincial towns understood and spoke Spanish. It was only in the southwest (western Campeche, Carmen, and Champoton) that Spanish was already dominant in the nineteenth century and where, in contrast to the situation in Mérida, some of the peasantry and farm laborers seem to have spoken it and domestic servants were forced to learn it (Aznar Barbachano and Carbó 1994:15; Cline 1950 5:307–8). Outside these areas, however, Mayan was universal (e.g., Norman 1843:68, 154; Tozzer 1977 [1921]:14–15, 1982 [1907]:54). It remained the sole or preferred language of people considered "Indian" and was also the mother tongue of many vecinos, particularly in the rural areas. Thus, the German linguist Carl Hermann Berendt, who visited Yucatán several times, noted in the 1870s: "[Mayan] is used not only by the Indians, but also by the greater part of the white and *mestizo* population; in the interior of Yucatán I have met with white families who do not understand one word of Spanish" (Tozzer 1977 [1921]:5n5; see also LNE, November 1, 1878:3–4; Stephens 1963 1:231; Aznar Barbachano and Carbó 1994:15; Anonymous 1997 [1866]:15).

Contemporary descriptions show that dress was an important status symbol in nineteenth-century Yucatán. Observers noted a division of society into two classes, those who wore pantaloons and those who went around in cotton breeches or drawers. The pantaloon was "the uniform of civilization," as US traveler B. M. Norman (1843:139) put it (see also Stephens 1963 2:71; Cline 1950 5:143–44). However, wearing European clothes was more widespread in large settlements, especially Mérida and Campeche, than in smaller towns and villages where, at best, a rich handful owned European-style garments (Stephens 1963 2:71; Norman 1843:3, 22). Moreover, in many cases they were only worn on holidays. Thus, the gente de vestido comprised only a small portion of the population. Even the majority of the vecinos dressed, like the indios, in folk costume (e.g., Anonymous 1997:15). Thus, the culture and living conditions of poorer indios and vecinos in the villages, ranches, and haciendas of Yucatán were in general similar (as contemporaries observed; see Aznar Barbachano and Carbó 1994:14–15; Anonymous 1997:14–15).

Dumond (1997:40–43) has shown that many indios and vecinos were not only culturally alike but also related by marriage or descent. In his sample of four communities in northern Yucatán between 1803 and 1840, more than 30 percent of the male vecinos were married to indigenous women, while 22 percent of women with Spanish names were married to men with Mayan names. This meant, as Dumond puts it, that "a significant number of rural Yucatecan vecinos must have had a preponderance of Indian relatives and must have been Indian in outlook" (ibid.:43). However, it would be premature to assume a *general* insignificance of status categories in the nineteenth century. Gabbert's analysis of entries in the registry office at Hopelchén, a town in the southern borderlands, confirms Dumond's conclusion in general, but beyond that it suggests that choice of spouse varied with class. In actual fact, status categories seem to have been of little importance in determining the behavior of poorer people (like farm laborers). No fewer than 37 (29.13%) of the 127 marriages registered in Hopelchén in selected years between 1875 and 1910 were exogamous, that is, marriages between spouses of different patronymics (Spanish or Maya). All the people involved in these marriages belonged to the lower class.[32] In contrast to the marriage pattern found among the lower class, the Spanish-speaking elite in Hopelchén was strictly endogamous. Of the 35 elite marriages registered, none of the spouses bore a Maya patronymic.

The data on choice of spouse demonstrate that the social distance between lower class indios and vecinos had already become minimal before the repúblicas de indígenas were completely abolished in the late 1860s. With the removal of the legal differentiation between both status categories, a relatively homogeneous Mayan-speaking lower class began to develop.[33] The elite, on the contrary, remained an almost completely closed social group.

As has been shown, the social categories used in nineteenth-century Yucatán were dichotomously structured. However, there were several categories denoting overlapping aggregates of people. There was no such thing, therefore, as bounded, separate ethnic communities. The category indio (indígena) was, for example, part of more than one set. It could refer to people of a certain legal status, to individuals of a certain descent/phenotype, or to individuals wearing a particular dress. Apart from surnames, legal or administrative distinctions (indio/vecino) did not coincide with either cultural differences or endogamous units. Maya, for example, was not only the language of legal "Indians" but was the mother tongue of the vast majority of the population. The most important cleavage separated the mainly urban Spanish-speaking elite from the Mayan-speaking lower class who dressed in folk costume. The elite considered the vast majority of peasants, farm laborers, and their

FIGURE 5.3. Caste War defense work in Iturbide. Photo by Ute Schüren

families to be indios, whereas vecinos in the interior, who frequently spoke nothing but Mayan, referred to people legally so defined (or people easily identifiable by a Maya patronymic) as indios when trying to claim a higher social status.[34] The subjectivity of this ascription helps us understand why a community consciousness encompassing everyone categorized as "Indian" or macehual did not develop. Yet there was another major factor that shaped the development of ethnic identification in Yucatán: the so-called Caste War.

THE CASTE WAR OF YUCATÁN AND ITS CONSEQUENCES

This conflict began in Yucatán in the 1840s as a civil war and during the course of 1847 was re-categorized and labeled a "caste" or race war by the peninsula's Hispanic leaders (see figures 5.3–5.5). In a long historical and historiographical tradition, running from Justo Sierra O'Reilly (see his 1848 quote above) to Lzaro Cárdenas (1972) to Nelson Reed (1964) and Victoria Bricker (1981), the war actually became a race war or war of ethnic liberation, with vengeful Maya rebels, later known as *cruzob*, almost regaining the lands taken from them by invading Spaniards and their descendents.[35] The counterview, articulated most notably by Terry Rugeley, is that divisions of region and class played a more important role than ethnic or racial antagonisms (Rugeley 1996; Cline 1950; Patch 1991).

FIGURE 5.4. Caste War fortifications in Bacalar. Photo by Ute Schüren

Questions of Maya ethnic identity are obviously at the heart of this debate, in the light of which our argument above on Colonial Maya identity has two possible applications.

One is that the Colonial period development of multiple ethnic categories laid a foundation for a Maya ethnogenesis during the Caste War. The other is that the bifurcation of implied and overt ethnic awareness persisted through the mid-nineteenth century, with the war failing to foster the emergence of an ethnic community consciousness that encompassed all Mayan speakers in Yucatán. As we have argued in other places (see Gabbert 2004a:46–59, 2004b; Restall 2004) and briefly outline below, we go even further than this, suggesting two major propositions: first, the fact that many Mayan speakers fought against the rebels or became victims of their attacks questions the characterization of the Caste War as a "race war" or the ethnic struggle of "the Maya." Many rebel leaders as well as rank-and-file soldiers were not considered "Indians" by their contemporaries. Rebels frequently attacked entirely indigenous hamlets and villages, killing people with Mayan surnames including men, women, and children. The units that fought the rebels frequently encompassed many people with Mayan surnames. While the majority of counterinsurgents were drafted, many were volunteers.[36]

Second, we suggest that the Caste War was of fundamental importance for the development of ethnic relations on the Yucatán Peninsula, but instead of promoting native unity, it caused a deep rift between Mayan speakers. This fostered, on one hand, the emergence of ethnic consciousness among the rebels and, on the other hand, the development of a socially and culturally homogeneous Mayan-speaking lower class to the north and west of Yucatán, which retained a localized sense of loyalty. Thus, the war hindered any tendencies toward the development of a broader Maya ethnic community encompassing all speakers of the language who lived in the peninsula.

In addition to the heterogeneous composition of the conflicting bands and the many natives who fell victim to rebel raids, the rebels' written expressions are similar evidence against the racial war thesis. In the surviving correspondence written in Maya, rebel leaders frequently employed the ethnically neutral term *enemies* (*enemigoob*) to designate their adversaries. Even the occasional use of *dzulob* does not necessarily support an ethnic interpretation (see the documents in Chi Poot 1982:230, 240, 243; Quintal Martín 1992:59; Florentino Chan, July 19, 1850, CAIHDY, Manuscritos, XLII, 011). This term had a multitude of meanings and cannot simply be translated as "white" or "Spanish," as is frequently the case in the relevant literature (e.g., Bricker 1981:187–218). It alludes to differences in lifestyle and status and particularly expresses the social distance from the speaker. In most cases the rebels called themselves *cristianoob* (Christians), *otsilob* (poor), or *masewalob* (see, e.g., the documents in ibid.:188–207; Chi Poot 1982:277–94). *Cruzob* (crosses), in comparison, which hints at the Cult of the Speaking Cross, appears rarely (ibid.:285; Dumond 1997:359). These terms referred to religious ties or a certain social position; *masewal* (or *macehual*) was a designation for the common people and, at least for the time being, not an ethnic category (ibid.:123–24; Gabbert 2004a:36, 54).

In the "Proclamation of Juan de la Cruz" of 1850, for example, the cruzob author refers to his followers either in paternal terms, as "my children" (*in sihsahbilob*, literally "my progeny," and *in sihsah uincilob*, "my engendered people") or in the same terms of the implied—not overt—ethnic awareness of the Colonial period (*Cristiano Cahex*, "you Christian cah members," and macehual, "commoner," or *in sihsah macehualilob*, "my commoner progeny"). Social and racial divisions are strongly implied—at one point Cruz lists four social categories, those of dzul, "foreigner, or rich," *box*, "black," macehual, "commoner," and *mulato*, "mulatto"—but the terms *indio*, *indígena*, and *Maya* never appear; and the bifurcated sociopolitical world of the letter seems to be between Cruz's community "children" and their "enemies" (enemigoob) (letter in Bricker 1981:187–207; glosses ours). The same language was used in Cruz's 1851 letter to Governor Barbachano (ibid.:208–18) and other documents (e.g., José María Barrera et al. to José Canuto Vela, Haas, April 7, 1850, in Chi Poot 1982:237; Cecilio Chi to Don Il. Ma. Díaz, Expec, November 11, 1847, and Eulogio Rosado to Secretario de Guerra y Marina, December 13, 1847, both in AGEY, PE, G, box 66, file Programa de indios sublevados).

As we have seen, ethnic identity did not create the two sides in the war because ethnic divisions did not characterize the makeup of its combatants or victims. The intense period of war (from 1847 to about 1853) was followed by a half century

FIGURE 5.5. Talking Cross in Felipe Carrillo Puerto. Photo by Wolfgang Gabbert

in which the Mayan-speaking population of Yucatec was as divided as it had ever been, with numerous native groups (cruzob, different *pacifico* groups, and so on) existing at various points along a spectrum between full incorporation into the Mexican state of Yucatán and complete autonomy. The so-called *bravos* or cruzob rebels proclaimed themselves masewalob in distinction to the "pacified" Mayas (Hervik 1999:42–46; Dumond 1997; Castro 2001; Gabbert 2004a:57–64). This political situation was partly a result of the state's inability to establish direct rule over the entire peninsula. But it also represented continuity in terms of the localized nature of Yucatán's indigenous identities. At the same time, it reflected the fact that the rebels' discourse was not built upon the kind of ethnopolitical ideas that have underpinned the late-twentieth-century ethnogenesis in Guatemala—such as the notion that promoting a pan-Maya identity is important, even essential, to the defense of individual Maya communities.

CONCLUSION

In the decades that followed independence, a Mayan surname remained the only reliable indicator of membership in the legal and administrative category of indio. In everyday interaction, other features such as phenotype, dress, language, and the occupation as a farmhand were frequently sufficient evidence to be considered and treated as "Indian" by elite Spaniards and, later, urban blancos. However, more nuanced social categories were employed among indios and people of mixed heritage. Thus, it was not possible to determine unequivocally the group of people regarded as indio, since ethnicity was subjective—it depended on the eye of the beholder. The Spanish-speaking urban elite considered the vast majority of peasants, farmhands, and their families to be indios.

On the other hand, the vecinos in the interior, who often spoke nothing but Mayan, regarded as "Indian" only those legally defined as such or those with a Maya patronym. This subjectivity of ascription helps explain why no indigenous community consciousness could develop. The same applies to the term *macehual* or *masewal*. It did not denote a strictly confined circle of individuals but was interpreted differently according to the speaker's social position and interest, as well as to the interactional context. The term *macehual* was generally related to a legally defined status category in the Colonial period. The primary social identification of the *macehualob* (or *masewalob)* was the community (cah) and the patronym group (chibal). In the west and northwest of the peninsula during the nineteenth century, macehual also referred to a status category and not to an ethnic community. Primary loyalty remained bound to the village or the hacienda.[37] It was only among the rebels in what is today Quintana Roo that an ethnic consciousness developed, which, however, excluded Mayan speakers from the rest of the peninsula. It was impossible for the majority of this population to identify with the rebels during the Caste War, since they constantly fought against them or were affected by their assaults on settlements in the territory controlled by the government. Thus, an identity and community consciousness of all native Yucatec Mayan speakers did not develop. Maya remained a category employed by others— the Spanish-speaking elite and, later, foreign linguists and anthropologists—but generally denied by Mayan speakers themselves. This has only begun to change, slowly and partially, in recent decades. Such a change is the result, among other things, of the adoption of ethnic rhetoric by the government, international organizations, and social movements.

Spanish ethnoracial concepts that developed in the sixteenth century, and the rhetoric of race and polarizing violence of the Caste War, reified Maya ethnic identity among non-Mayas and provided a false appearance of being an independent factor in the ordering of the Yucatec social world. While non-Mayas consistently saw "Indians" and "Mayas," the peninsula's natives themselves held to their own less monolithic identities. For centuries, indigenous Yucatecans have refused to accept categories of identity assigned to them. In a sense, then, the Maya struggled for centuries in the face of steady opposition *against* their own ethnogenesis.

What are our arguments' implications for diachronic research on indigenous (or other) populations? First, we are skeptical regarding the ubiquity of ethnicity (as defined above) in history. It is probably a form of political organization and legitimization of rule that emerged in tandem with the nation-state model of politics. While national as well as ethnic models of state society stress that rulers and ruled should be united by common descent and culture, elites in state societies before the late eighteenth century stressed their cultural and genealogical difference from the lower classes in their polities (Gabbert 2004a:34–35, 2006:91–93).

Further, elites in such societies should not be considered ethnic groups unto themselves. As Benedict Anderson (1991:6–7) has argued brilliantly for the European nobility prior to the French Revolution, they did not constitute a group that stressed cultural sameness but were divided into numerous genealogical branches of varying social status. Such a pattern is likely to have existed in many other societies as well.

The character of the commoners in such polities is exemplified by our discussion of Maya commoners. They identified themselves with their local community and their descent group and—in both the Colonial and pre-Conquest periods—as vassals of specific rulers. But they did not develop an overarching consciousness of belonging to an ethnic community. Such a consciousness only developed among the cruzob because of their traumatic experiences in the Caste War, resulting in a marked separation from both Spanish speakers and speakers of Yucatec alike. In addition, the religious "Cult of the Speaking Cross" provided an organizational form that tied the local cruzob communities into one body of believers and separated them from all others (Gabbert 2004a:57–59).

Researchers therefore face three challenges. First, we must abstain from reproducing the erroneous assumption by many nineteenth-century linguists and anthropologists that linguistic similarities or shared material culture constituted ethnic identity. Second, not each and every form of social categorization or identification (e.g., by locality, kinship, or polity) should be placed under the "ethnic" umbrella. Third, for various reasons, ethnicity can be detected in the empirical record only with major difficulties. It results from a complex interplay of self-identification and categorization by others. Ethnic categorization is context-dependent and *not directly* linked to overt markers, such as language, dress, or other items of material culture.[38] Since not all cultural traits are significant as symbols of difference, as Barth (1969) points out, and the meaning attributed to these symbols may vary among regions or situations, it seems highly problematic to infer ethnicity merely on the basis of material remains. Consequently, especially in cases where no written texts are available to complement archaeological findings, we will frequently be unable to reveal patterns of ethnic or other group identification.

NOTES

1. Earlier versions of some of the material presented here were published in Restall (2001, 2004) and Gabbert (2001a, 2001b, 2004a, 2004b).

2. As there is no agreement on the usage of the term *ethnicity*, a definition is necessary. It is understood here as referring to a phenomenon of social differentiation in which actors use cultural or phenotypical markers or symbols to distinguish themselves from others. It is a method of classifying people into categories that include individuals of both sexes and all age groups using (socially constructed) origin as its primary reference. These boundary processes can result in the development of a system of ethnic categories (i.e., classificatory units) or of ethnic communities (i.e., units of action). It is therefore of the utmost importance that *social categories* present in a specific society the *groups* or organizations based on such categories and the *individuals* using these categories in daily interaction be kept analytically separate. (See Gabbert 2004a:xii–xvii and 2006 for fuller discussions of the concept.)

3. In the following, the term *Maya* refers only to the speakers of Yucatec Maya unless otherwise indicated.

4. This is especially relevant since Barth (1969) rightly stressed that the specificity of ethnicity lies in the fact that *actors themselves* feel they belong to a common category.

5. The period of the Spanish invasions of the peninsula was 1527–46, the Colonial period lasted to 1821, and the Caste War era was 1847–1901; thus, we have given our chapter an approximate 1500–1900 time span.

6. Apparently, mayathan referred primarily to the language spoken in the north of Yucatán, since different terms were used in the surroundings of Campeche (*kampech than*),

in the extreme southwest (*putun than*), and in the southeast (*lengua de uaymil*). Maya than and kampech than did not differ a great deal, so mutual understanding was possible. The language of Uaymil resembled kampech than. The differences with putun than (Chontal), however, were much greater, making the language unintelligible to speakers of mayathan. See Landa (1959 [1566], chapters 3, 5); Ponce (1872 [1588]:393, 451–52, 468); Tozzer (1941:20n123).

7. A similar statement is made in the *relación* of "Quinacama" (RHGY 1983 1:254). See Gabbert (2001a, 2004a:28–31) for additional evidence. Munro Edmonson (1982:10) remarks that "the modern name of the Maya may be derived from Mayapan," but he cites Alfred Tozzer (1941:7, 9), who merely states that the peninsula was called "Maia" without speculating as to the term's etymology; later, Edmonson (1986:5, 9) suggested that the name was derived from the *may* cycle of 13 katuns.

8. Barrera Vásquez (1957:28–31, 72–73, 76–77, 80–81, 88–89); Roys (1939:356); Edmonson (1982:16, 37–38); Restall (1997a:15–17).

9. For example, ah Itzaob, Itza winikob, ah Canulob.

10. For example, ah Maniob, ah Ecabob, ah Chikinchelob. See, e.g., the Titles of Chicxulub and Yaxkukul (Restall 1998a); Roys (1933:53); Edmonson (1982:6–7, 10, 24, 33–34, 39, 54, 78–79, 82, 88, 94–95, 97–100, 143, 158, 174, 194); Roys (1939:78, 86). The name of a locality with the prefix *ah* (and the plural marker –ob) designates the inhabitants of a city or province. A patronym with the same affix refers to members of a lineage or patronym group (ch'ibal). The pre-Conquest provinces remained important for some time after the conquest (see also Gabbert 2004a:173n24). The inhabitants of the region around Valladolid and Chichén Itzá, for example, were called, at least until the seventeenth century, "people of ah Cupul" (*ah Cupul winikob*) after the ruling lineage of the same name (Roys 1939:78–79; Ponce 1872 [1588]:397).

11. In 2008 Restall and Mark Christensen re-read all extant Colonial Maya testaments surveyed earlier by Restall to double-check the assertions made here regarding terminological usage. The earliest attestation of cax that we saw is mid-seventeenth century; by Beltrán's time, it had become a dictionary term—"Gallo de Castilla *Ahcax*" and "Gallina de Castilla *Yxcax*" (Beltrán de Santa Rosa 1746). One could argue that turkeys did have sacred associations, as they were traditionally used in sacrificial rituals; but that does not mean turkeys were always imbued with sacred significance. Such an argument is stronger with respect to the *maya bat* entry in the seventeenth-century San Francisco dictionary, as *maya* is clearly used here to describe something historically distant and possibly with vague sacred associations—an ancient "Maya ax," as opposed to the metal axes Mayas had been using for a century by the time this dictionary was compiled (see mention of this entry, the dictionary's dating, and citations below) (Ciudad Real n.d. 1:folio 287v, 2:folio 119v; Arzápalo Marín 1995 1:489; Restall 1997a:125–26, 181, 365, 370).

12. However, as Gabbert has suggested, "maya uinicob" may also have been used by elites in some regions to claim descent from the ancient rulers of Mayapan, which was still held

as prestigious in most of northern Yucatán at least in the sixteenth century (see Gabbert 2004a:30–31, cf. also Landa 1959 [1566]:chapter 24; Barrera Vásquez 1957:28–31, 104–7).

13. On petitionary discourse among Mayas and Nahuas, see Restall (1997a:251–66, 1997b:255–59) and Karttunen and Lockhart (1987). The 1668–69 petitions are in the AGI (*Escribanía* 317a, 2, various folios). For a discussion of possible Spanish and Maya roles in the formulation of a series of petitions in Maya from a century earlier, see Restall (1998a:151–68).

14. See, for example, Rothschild (1981:11–14); Gellner (1983:1, 10–12). For Polynesia, see Sahlins (1985:73–103). For pre-Conquest Yucatán, see also Lincoln (1990:45–49).

15. Thus, the Chumayel phrases *ch'ibal c on maya uinic e* (which Edmonson glosses as "the ancestry of us Maya") and *u ch'ibal maya uinicob* ("the lineages of the Maya people") are a reference to the people of the peninsula's west (Edmonson 1986:109, 178).

16. On the Itzás of the Petén and their Yucatec origins, see Jones (1998:xix, 3–107). This would not be the only instance of a Maya people adopting as a group or ethnic label the name of a founding ruler or dynasty; the Quichés did it too (see Hill and Monaghan 1987:32–33).

17. Robert Chamberlain and Ralph Roys used the term *tribe* (see especially Roys 1943).

18. As Gabbert has argued elsewhere, it is necessary to differentiate between kinship and ethnicity. Both terms are related to (real or supposed) common descent. However, only those social categories that are related to ideas of common descent and integrate several families and kin groups should be referred to as "ethnic." Many scholars see ethnic collectivities as intermediate groups, larger than local communities but smaller than a nation (e.g., Tambiah 1989:337). Although there is no need to confine the meaning of the term *ethnic collectivities* to subnational groupings, it should be restricted to communities of a certain scale, to account for the different bases of cohesion. Only groups above the level of the local community should be referred to as "ethnic" because they have to integrate individuals who cannot be united directly through social, economic, or kin relationships (Gabbert 2006:88).

19. See Gabbert (2004a:16–25) for a discussion of the Colonial social structure and the role of the native nobility.

20. See Gabbert (2001b:463–64, 479–83, 2006:90–91) for a discussion of the differences between ethnic categories and ethnic communities.

21. AGI, *México* 100 (Restall thanks Robert Schwaller for transcribing and sharing this petition; also see Chuchiak 2007:175–78). This tale of betrayal and disappointment was repeated throughout Mesoamerica, as Spanish officials reneged on Conquest period promises and native veterans and their descendents fought in the law courts to regain some semblance of status (see Matthew 2004; Matthew and Oudijk 2007; Restall and Asselbergs 2007; Yannakakis 2008).

22. Restall defines and discusses these distinctions in general terms in Restall and Lane (2011:chapter 10) and Restall (2009:chapter 3).

23. In general, intermarriage was most common among the so-called castas, or mixed groups. However, status endogamy seems to have remained high among the Indian

population. A high rate of endogamous marriages is to be expected among Indians, since they made up the bulk of the population (cf. Gabbert 2004a:23).

24. Landa wrote a vast study of Yucatec Maya history and culture, called, according to its genre, his *Recopilación*; the work appears to have been lost in the late seventeenth century, with the only surviving traces the compilation of excerpts—some of which may not have been written by Landa himself—cited above as his *Relación* (see Restall and Chuchiak 2002). "Indios mayas" is used, for example, in a report from 1588 by the Spanish cleric Fray Alonso Ponce de León as a designation of all speakers of mayathan, excluding the Chontal and the inhabitants of several towns around Campeche and Bacalar (Ponce 1872 [1588]:407, 410, 413, 417–18, 420–22, 439, 441, 445, 447, 451, 462–64, 472, 474–75).

25. Most notably Cope (1994), but also see Boyer (1995) and Stern (1996), as well as additional citations on the race-class debate in Kellogg (2000).

26. The liberal constitution of 1841 formally abolished the repúblicas de indios, but in actual fact they continued to operate. In 1847 they were reestablished. For a discussion of the repúblicas de indios after independence, see Rugeley (1996) and Gabbert (2004a:60–62).

27. For the term *yucateco*, see Hernández 1846:291; Cline 1950 5:146–47.

28. This consisted, in the case of women, of a long skirt (*fustan* or *pik*) worn with a long, wide blouse with embroidery (*ipil*) on the square neckline and the hem below the waist. Men dressed in cotton shirts, trousers or drawers, and frequently sandals. The folk costume was also known as *traje de mestizo/a* (mestizo costume). This has confused many authors who suggested that the people known as "mestizos" in nineteenth-century Yucatán were a different social group than the Indians and whites (e.g., Cline 1950 5:145–46). This was, however, not the case. The traje de mestizo was *not* a garment specific to a social group but merely a term employed for the more elaborate variants of the folk costume. Differences in the quality of cloth and ornamentation reflected the economic situation of the wearer or were a result of the contrast between clothes worn on ordinary days and those worn on holidays (Gabbert 2004a:76–77). People wearing the folk costume were *not always* called "mestizos," as Redfield (1938:521) and Hansen (1980:123) suggest, but were frequently referred to as Indians (e.g., Norman 1843:145; Castillo 1845:295). While mestizo in other parts of Mexico and Latin America generally refers to the offspring of unions between Spaniards or whites and Indians or designates the culturally hispanicized section of the population in contrast to the Indian one, in Yucatán mestizo is used to refer to wearers of the folk costume and has become a symbol of Maya Indian identity.

29. Indio and Maya were not used as self-identifications (Tozzer 1982 [1907]:19). The use of dzul today is still variable and highly dependent on context. It is also used to refer to wealthy people irrespective of language spoken and style of dress (see Gabbert 2004a:114, 197n29.

30. Gabbert made this point for the first time in a paper presented at a meeting of the Deutsche Gesellschaft für Völkerkunde in 1995 (Gabbert 1995; see also 1997). Don

Dumond (1997:38–40) came to the same conclusion independently in his opus magnum on the Caste War.

31. On a taxpayer list from the Santiago quarter in Mérida in 1851, for example, only 13 (2.01%) of 630 indios bore a Spanish patronymic, and only 9 (2.35%) of 383 vecinos had a Maya surname (Dumond and Dumond 1982:155–56). All Indians listed in the Hunucmá birth register in 1873 had Maya surnames (AGEY, PE, P, CP, RC, box 185).

32. The entries analyzed are from RCHO 1875 (the beginnings of registration), 1880, 1885, 1890, 1895, 1900, 1905, and 1910. A relatively high proportion of exogamous marriages would not be sufficient to suggest the minor importance of the status categories indio and vecino for social interaction within the lower class. It could be explained by hypergamy (women of a subordinated social category marrying men from a higher category), which has been ascertained for the Colonial period. The exogamous marriages in Hopelchén, however, do not show a significant gender-specific variation. Spouses with Spanish patronymics were male in twenty cases and female in seventeen cases. For a detailed discussion of the data presented here, see Gabbert (2004a:72–73).

33. Similar tendencies toward the development of a common lower-class culture among people of different legal status have been reported, for example, for Colonial Mexico City (Cope 1994) and eighteenth-century Potosí, Bolivia (Abercrombie 1996).

34. This can be inferred from material presented by Redfield (1941:66–73, 375–77) and data collected during fieldwork by Gabbert (e.g., field notes, Hopelchén, January 11, 1995).

35. On Cárdenas's interpretation of the righteous role the "Maya race" played in the war, see Fallaw (1997:560–65).

36. See the full argument, data, and references in Gabbert (2004a:53–57, 2004b:97–104).

37. This is indicated, among other things, by the frequent conflicts between communities. See, e.g., Rugeley (1996:34, 161).

38. In addition to Gabbert (2006:90), see Michael Moerman's (1965) seminal article.

REFERENCES CITED

AGI	Archivo General de Indias, Seville, Spain
AGEY	Archivo General del Estado de Yucatán, Mérida, Yucatán
AGN	Archivo General de la Nación, Mexico City
CAIHDY	Centro de Apoyo a la Investigación Histórica de Yucatán, Mérida, Yucatán
CP	Censos y Padrones
G	Gobernación
JCBL	John Carter Brown Library, Brown University, Providence, RI
LNE	*La Nueva Era*, Campeche (newspaper)
P	Población
PE	Poder Ejecutivo

RC   Registro Civil
RCHO   Registro Civil de Hopelchén, Hopelchén
RHGY   *Relaciones Histórico-Geográficas de la Gobernación de Yucatán* (see below)
TLH   Tozzer Library, Harvard University, Cambridge, MA
TULAL   Latin American Library, Tulane University, New Orleans, LA

Abercrombie, Thomas A. 1996. "Q'aqchas and *la plebe* in 'Rebellion': Carnival vs. Lent in 18th Century Potosí." *Journal of Latin American Anthropology* 2 (1): 62–111. http://dx .doi.org/10.1525/jlca.1996.2.1.62.

Ancona, Eligio. 1978 [1879–80]. *Historia de Yucatán desde la época más remota hasta nuestros días*, vol. 4. Mérida: Universidad de Yucatán.

Anderson, Benedict. 1991. *Imagined Communities: Reflections on the Origin and Spread of Nationalism*. London: Verso.

Anonymous. 1997 [1866]. *Guerra de castas en Yucatán: Su orígen, sus consecuencias y su estado actual*. Ed. Melchor Campos García. Mérida: Universidad Autónoma de Yucatán.

Arzápalo Marín, Ramón. 1995. *Calepino de Motul: Diccionario Maya-Español*, 3 vols. Mexico City: Universidad Nacional Autónoma de México.

Aznar Barbachano, Tomás, and Juan Carbó. 1994 [1861]. *Memoria sobre la conveniencia, utilidad y necesidad de erigir constitucionalmente en estado de la confederación méxicana el antiguo distrito de Campeche*. Campeche: Ediciones de la LIV Legislatura.

Barrera Vásquez, Alfredo. 1957. *Códice de Calkiní*. Campeche: Gobierno del Estado.

Barrera Vásquez, Alfredo. 1980. *Diccionario Maya Cordemex*. Mérida, Yucatán: Ediciones Cordemex.

Barth, Fredrik, ed. 1969. *Ethnic Groups and Boundaries: The Social Organization of Cultural Difference*. London: Allen and Unwin.

Beltrán de Santa Rosa, Fray Pedro. 1746. *Arte de el Idioma Maya Reducido a Succintas Reglas, y Semilexicon Yucateco*. Mexico City: no pub.. John Carter Brown Library, Providence, RI, rare book B746/B453a.

Boyer, Richard. 1995. *Lives of the Bigamists: Marriage, Family, and Community in Colonial Mexico*. Albuquerque: University of New Mexico Press.

Bricker, Victoria Reifler. 1981. *The Indian Christ, the Indian King: The Historical Substrate of Maya Myth and Ritual*. Austin: University of Texas Press.

Bricker, Victoria Reifler, Eleuterio Po'ot Yah, and Ofelia Dzul de Po'ot. 1998. *A Dictionary of the Maya Language as Spoken in Hocabá, Yucatán*. Salt Lake City: University of Utah Press.

Cárdenas, Lázaro. 1972. *Ideario Político*. Mexico City: Era.

Castañeda, Quetzil. 1996. *In the Museum of Maya Culture: Touring Chichén Itzá.* Minneapolis: University of Minnesota Press.

Castillo, Gerónimo. 1845. "El indio yucateco: Carácter, costumbres y condición de los indios, en el departamento de Yucatan." *Registro Yucateco* 1: 291–97.

Castro, Inés de. 2001. "Die Geschichte der sogenannten Pacificos del Sur während des Kastenkrieges von Yucatan: 1851–1895: Eine ethnohistorische Untersuchung." PhD dissertation, Philosophische Fakultät, Friedrich-Wilhelms-Universität Bonn, Germany.

Chi Poot, María Bonifacia. 1982. *Medio siglo de resistencia armada maya: Fuentes documentales.* Etnolinguistica 27. Mexico City: SEP/INI.

Chuchiak, John F., IV. 1997. "Los intellectuales, los indios y la prensa: El periodismo polémico de Justo Sierra O'Reilly." *Saastun: Revista de Cultura Maya* (September): 3–41.

Chuchiak, John F., IV. 2007. "Forgotten Allies: The Origins and Roles of Native Mesoamericn Auxiliaries and Indios Conquistadores in the Conquest of Yucatan, 1526–1550." In *Indian Conquistadors: Indigenous Allies in the Conquest of Mesoamerica*, ed. Laura E. Matthew and Michael R. Oudijk, 175–225. Norman: University of Oklahoma Press.

Ciudad Real, Fray Antonio de. n.d. *Maya Motul Dictionary* [original manuscript untitled], 2 vols. Codex-Ind 8. Providence, RI: John Carter Brown Library.

Clendinnen, Inga. 1987. *Ambivalent Conquests: Maya and Spaniard in Yucatan, 1517–1570.* Cambridge: Cambridge University Press.

Cline, Howard F. 1950. *Related Studies in Early Nineteenth Century Yucatecan Social History,* Part 2: *The War of the Castes and Its Consequences,* and Part 5: *Regionalism and Society in Yucatan, 1825–1847.* Microfilm Collection of Manuscripts on Middle American Cultural Anthropology 32. Chicago: University of Chicago Library.

Cope, R. Douglas. 1994. *The Limits of Racial Domination: Plebeian Society in Colonial Mexico City, 1660–1720.* Madison: University of Wisconsin Press.

Dumond, Carol Streichen, and Don E. Dumond, eds. 1982. *Demography and Parish Affairs in Yucatan, 1797–1897: Documents from the Archivo de la Mitra Emeritense Selected by Joaquín de Arrigunaga Peón.* Anthropological Papers 27. Eugene: University of Oregon Press.

Dumond, Don E. 1997. *The Machete and the Cross: Campesino Rebellion in Yucatan.* Lincoln: University of Nebraska Press.

Edmonson, Munro S. 1982. *The Ancient Future of the Itza: The Book of Chilam Balam of Tizimin.* Austin: University of Texas Press.

Edmonson, Munro S. 1986. *Heaven Born Merida and Its Destiny: The Book of Chilam Balam of Chumayel.* Austin: University of Texas Press.

Fallaw, Ben. 1997. "Cárdenas and the Caste War That Wasn't: State Power and Indigenismo in Post-Revolutionary Yucatán." *Americas* 53 (4): 551–77. http://dx.doi.org/10.2307/1008148.

Gabbert, Wolfgang. 1995. "Die Entwicklung ethnischer Kategorien in Yukatán." Paper presented at the Gemeinsame Tagung der Deutschen Gesellschaft für Völkerkunde, der Österreichischen Ethnologischen Gesellschaft und der Anthropologischen Gesellschaft, Vienna, September 25–29.

Gabbert, Wolfgang. 1997. "El desarrollo de las categorias sociales y el problema de la etnicidad en Yucatán." *Revista de la Universidad Autónoma de Yucatán* 12 (202): 91–101.

Gabbert, Wolfgang. 2001a. "On the Term 'Maya.'" In *Maya Survivalism*, ed. Ueli Hostettler and Matthew Restall, 25–34. Markt Schwaben, Germany: Verlag Anton Saurwein.

Gabbert, Wolfgang. 2001b. "Social Categories, Ethnicity, and the State in Yucatán, México." *Journal of Latin American Studies* 33 (3): 459–84. http://dx.doi.org/10.1017/S0022216 X01005983.

Gabbert, Wolfgang. 2004a. *Becoming Maya: Ethnicity and Social Inequality in Yucatán since 1500*. Tucson: University of Arizona Press.

Gabbert, Wolfgang. 2004b. "Of Friends and Foes—the Caste War and Ethnicity in Yucatán." *Journal of Latin American Anthropology* 9 (1): 90–118. http://dx.doi.org/10 .1525/jlca.2004.9.1.90.

Gabbert, Wolfgang. 2006. "Concepts of Ethnicity." *Latin American and Caribbean Ethnic Studies* 1 (1): 85–103. http://dx.doi.org/10.1080/17486830500510034.

Gellner, Ernest. 1964. *Thought and Change*. London: Weidenfeld and Nicholson.

Gellner, Ernest. 1983. *Nations and Nationalism*. Oxford: Basil Blackwell.

Hansen, Asael T. 1980. "Change in the Class System of Merida, Yucatan, 1875–1935." In *Yucatán: A World Apart*, ed. Edward H. Moseley and Edward D. Terry, 122–41. Tuscaloosa: University of Alabama Press.

Helms, Mary. 1993. *Craft and the Kingly Ideal: Art, Trade, and Power*. Austin: University of Texas Press.

Helms, Mary. 1994. "Essays on Objects: Interpretations of Distance Made Tangible." In *Implicit Understandings*, ed. Stuart B. Schwartz, 355–77. Cambridge: Cambridge University Press.

Helms, Mary. 1998. *Access to Origins: Affines, Ancestors, and Aristocrats*. Austin: University of Texas Press.

Henige, David. 1982. *Oral Historiography*. London: Longman.

Hernández, Juan José. 1846. "Costumbres de las indias de Yucatan." *Registro Yucateco* 3: 290–98.

Hervik, Peter. 1999. *Mayan People within and beyond Boundaries: Social Categories and Lived Identity in Yucatán*. Amsterdam: Harwood.

Hill, Robert M., II, and John Monaghan. 1987. *Continuities in Highland Maya Social Organization: Ethnohistory in Sacapulas, Guatemala*. Philadelphia: University of Pennsylvania Press.

Jones, Grant D. 1998. *The Conquest of the Last Maya Kingdom*. Stanford, CA: Stanford University Press.

Karttunen, Frances, and James Lockhart. 1987. *The Art of Nahuatl Speech: The Bancroft Dialogues*. Los Angeles: Latin American Center, University of California.

Kellogg, Susan. 2000. "Depicting *Mestizaje*: Gendered Images of Ethnorace in Colonial Mexican Texts." *Journal of Women's History* 12 (3): 69–92. http://dx.doi.org/10.1353/jo wh.2000.0057.

Landa, fray Diego de. 1959 [1566]. *Relación de las cosas de Yucatán*. Mexico City: Editorial Porrúa.

Lincoln, Charles E. 1990. "Ethnicity and Social Organization at Chichen Itzá, Yucatán, Mexico." PhD dissertation, Department of Anthropology, Harvard University, Cambridge, MA.

Lockhart, James. 1992. *The Nahuas after the Conquest*. Stanford, CA: Stanford University Press.

Lockhart, James, and Stuart B. Schwartz. 1983. *Early Latin America: A History of Colonial Spanish America and Brazil*. Cambridge: Cambridge University Press.

López de Cogolludo, fray Diego. 1957 [1654]. *Historia de Yucatán*. Mexico City: Editorial Academia Literaria.

Matthew, Laura E. 2004. "Neither and Both: The Mexican Indian Conquistadors of Colonial Guatemala." PhD dissertation, Department of History, University of Pennsylvania, Philadelphia.

Matthew, Laura E., and Michael R. Oudijk, eds. 2007. *Indian Conquistadors: Indigenous Allies in the Conquest of Mesoamerica*. Norman: University of Oklahoma Press.

Mengin, Ernst, ed. 1972. *Bocabulario de Mayathan: Das Wörterbuch der Yukatekischen Mayasprache*. Graz, Austria: Akademische Druck- und Verlagsanstalt.

Moerman, Michael. 1965. "Ethnic Identification in a Complex Civilization: Who Are the Lue?" *American Anthropologist* 67 (5): 1215–30. http://dx.doi.org/10.1525/aa.1965.67 .5.02a00070.

Norman, B. M. 1843. *Rambles in Yucatan Including a Visit to the Remarkable Ruins of Chi-Chen, Kabah, Zayi, Uxmal &c*. New York: J. and H. G. Langley.

Patch, Robert W. 1991. "Decolonization, the Agrarian Problem, and the Origins of the Caste War, 1812–1847." In *Land, Labor, and Capital in Modern Yucatán: Essays in Regional History and Political Economy*, ed. Jeffrey Brannon and Gilbert Joseph, 51–81. Tuscaloosa: University of Alabama Press.

Pío Pérez, Juan. 1898. *Coordinación Alfabetica de las voces de la idioma maya que se hallan en el arte y obras del padre Fr. Pedro Beltrán de Santa Rosa*. Mérida, Yucatán: Imprenta de la Ermita.

Ponce, Alonso. 1872 [1588]. "Relación de las cosas que sucedieron al padre Fray Alonso Ponce en las provincias de la nueva España." In *Colección de documentos inéditos para la historia de España*, vol. 58, ed. Miguel Salva and the Marques de la Fuensanta del Valle. Madrid: Imprenta de la Viuda de Calero.

Quintal Martín, Fidelio. 1992. *Correspondencia de la Guerra de Castas*. Mérida: Universidad Autónoma de Yucatán.

Redfield, Robert. 1938. "Race and Class in Yucatan: Cooperation in Research." Pamphlet published by the Carnegie Institution of Washington, DC. *Publication* 501: 511–32.

Redfield, Robert. 1941. *The Folk Culture of Yucatán*. Chicago: University of Chicago Press.

Reed, Nelson. 1964. *The Caste War of Yucatan*. Stanford, CA: Stanford University Press.

Relaciones Histórico-Geográficas de la Gobernación de Yucatán. 1983 [1579–81]. 2 vols. Mexico City: Universidad Nacional Autónoma de México.

Restall, Matthew. 1997a. *The Maya World: Yucatec Culture and Society, 1550–1850*. Stanford, CA: Stanford University Press.

Restall, Matthew. 1997b. "Heirs to the Hieroglyphs: Indigenous Writing in Colonial Mesoamerica." *Americas* 54 (2): 239–67. http://dx.doi.org/10.2307/1007743.

Restall, Matthew. 1998a. *Maya Conquistador*. Boston: Beacon.

Restall, Matthew. 1998b. "The Ties That Bind: Social Cohesion and the Yucatec Maya Family." *Journal of Family History* 23 (4): 355–81. http://dx.doi.org/10.1177/0363199 09802300402.

Restall, Matthew. 2001. "The People of the Patio: Ethnohistorical Evidence of Yucatec Maya Royal Courts." In *Royal Courts of the Ancient Maya*, ed. Takeshi Inomata and Stephen Houston, 355–90. Boulder: Westview.

Restall, Matthew. 2003. *Seven Myths of the Spanish Conquest*. New York: Oxford University Press.

Restall, Matthew. 2004. "Maya Ethnogenesis." *Journal of Latin American Anthropology* 9 (1): 64–89. http://dx.doi.org/10.1525/jlca.2004.9.1.64.

Restall, Matthew. 2006. "Manuel's Worlds: Black Yucatan and the Colonial Caribbean." In *Slaves, Subjects, and Subversives: Blacks in Colonial Latin America*, ed. Jane G. Landers and Barry M. Robinson, 147–74. Albuquerque: University of New Mexico Press.

Restall, Matthew. 2009. *The Black Middle: Africans, Mayas, and Spaniards in Colonial Yucatan*. Stanford, CA: Stanford University Press.

Restall, Matthew, and Florine Asselbergs. 2007. *Invading Guatemala: Spanish, Nahua, and Maya Accounts of the Conquest Wars*. University Park: Pennsylvania State University Press.

Restall, Matthew, and John F. Chuchiak. 2002. "A Reevaluation of the Authenticity of Fray Diego de Landa's *Relación de las cosas de Yucatán*." *Ethnohistory* 49 (3): 651–69. http://dx.doi.org/10.1215/00141801-49-3-651.

Restall, Matthew, Amara Solari, John F. Chuchiak, and Traci Ardren n.d. *The Friar and the Maya: Fray Diego de Landa's Account of the Things of Yucatan*. Boulder: University Press of Colorado. Forthcoming.

Restall, Matthew, and Kris Lane. 2011. *Latin America in Colonial Times*. Cambridge: Cambridge University Press.

Rothschild, Joseph. 1981. *Ethnopolitics: A Conceptual Framework*. New York: Columbia University Press.

Roys, Ralph L. 1933. *The Book of Chilam Balam of Chumayel*. Washington, DC: Carnegie Institution of Washington.

Roys, Ralph L. 1939. *The Titles of Ebtun*. Washington, DC: Carnegie Institution of Washington.

Roys, Ralph L. 1943. *The Indian Background of Colonial Yucatan*. Washington, DC: Carnegie Institution of Washington.

Rugeley, Terry. 1996. *Yucatán's Maya Peasantry and the Origins of the Caste War*. Austin: University of Texas Press.

Sahlins, Marshall. 1985. *Islands of History*. Chicago: University of Chicago Press.

Schackt, Jon. 2001. "The Emerging Maya: A Case of Ethnogenesis." In *Maya Survivalism*, ed. Ueli Hostettler and Matthew Restall, 3–14. Markt Schwaben, Germany: Verlag Anton Saurwein.

Stephens, John L. 1963 [1843]. *Incidents of Travel in Yucatan*, vol. 1. New York: Dover.

Stern, Steve J. 1996. *The Secret History of Gender: Women, Men, and Power in Late Colonial Mexico*. Chapel Hill: University of North Carolina Press.

Tambiah, Stanley. 1989. "Ethnic Conflict in the World Today." *American Ethnologist* 16 (2): 335–49. http://dx.doi.org/10.1525/ae.1989.16.2.02a00090.

Terraciano, Kevin. 2001. *The Mixtecs of Colonial Oaxaca: Ñudhahui History, Sixteenth through Eighteenth Centuries*. Stanford, CA: Stanford University Press.

Tozzer, Alfred M. 1941. *Landa's Relación de las Cosas de Yucatán*. Papers 18. Cambridge: Peabody Museum.

Tozzer, Alfred M. 1977 [1921]. *A Maya Grammar*. New York: Dover.

Tozzer, Alfred M. 1982 [1907]. *Mayas y lacandones: Un estudio comparativo*. Mexico City: INI.

Yannakakis, Yanna. 2008. *The Art of Being In-between: Native Intermediaries, Indian Identity, and Local Rule in Colonial Oaxaca*. Durham, NC: Duke University Press. http://dx.doi.org/10.1215/9780822388982.

6

Differentiation among Mayan Speakers

Evidence from Comparative Linguistics and Hieroglyphic Texts

Martha J. Macri

Leonard Bloomfield (1933:318) cautioned that the comparative method of linguistic reconstruction can never claim to accurately describe the historical process. Winifred Lehmann (1962:84) likewise noted that it can never yield anything other than a dialect-free corpus. Fortunately, Mayan languages are recorded in a phonetic script from at least as early as 250 CE, so for some Mayan languages, hypothetical reconstructions can be checked against written records (e.g., Lacadena 2011). A careful comparison of hieroglyphic texts reveals the presence of differentiated speech communities at several periods for which linguistic reconstruction would predict only a small number of protolanguages. The data examined here demonstrate how languages found in written records can supersede hypothetical reconstructions of historical/comparative linguistics and provide insight into various forms of social organization.

Self-identification, of both individuals and society, is an ongoing and multilayered process. Ethnogenesis examines the beginnings of this process. Keeping in mind that language variation always reflects processes of social interaction, this chapter highlights linguistic variations reflected in the Maya texts of the Classic period—points at which certain portions of the lowland Maya community seem to have differentiated themselves from other communities. Evidence of these processes can be gleaned from a chronological and geographic comparison of Classic period hieroglyphic texts.

Earlier forms of languages can be discovered by comparing known related languages and hypothesizing features that were present in their common ancestor

DOI: 10.5876/9781607325673.c006

and by subgrouping language varieties according to shared phonological, morphological, syntactic, and lexical characteristics. In linguistics, cladistic classification expresses hypothesized evolutionary relationships based on the number of shared changes. Most readers are familiar with tree diagrams of the proposed development of Mayan languages from a hypothesized proto-Mayan, through various intermediary steps, to the thirty or so Mayan languages known today. Representing language change by a tree diagram, however, introduces a distortion of historical realities, since cladistic classifications based on the comparative method fail to detect variations that once existed but were lost. Two distinguished linguists have offered caution in this regard:

> The comparative method, then . . . would work accurately for absolutely uniform speech-communities and sudden, sharp cleavages. Since these presuppositions are never fully realized, the comparative method cannot claim to picture the historical process. (Bloomfield 1933:318)

> We lose information also in the complexity of the language we reconstruct. In normal use of the comparative method, we proceed backward by triangulation and eventually posit for each subgroup a dialect-free corpus . . . the method itself is not designed to yield anything other than a dialect-free corpus. (Lehmann 1962:84)

Figure 6.1 shows the hypothesized relationships between the language subgroups most relevant to this discussion of the Maya hieroglyphic script. Scholars agree that the majority of the Classic texts record a Ch'olan language (see discussion in Law 2014:16–18), though there remains a question of what role Yukatekan speakers may have played, not only in the early development of the script but continuing throughout its history. Certainly, when the Spanish arrived, the script was used in northern Yucatán by Yukatekan speakers.

This chapter offers evidence from several linguistic features for developments of regionally distinct social (ethnic) groups within Classic Maya civilization. The first relies on a comparison of person markers in contemporary and Colonial Mayan languages to suggest at least two distinct phases of contact between Ch'olan and Yukatekan speakers. Another has to do with phonological contrasts between Ch'olan and Yukatekan as evidenced in Classic hieroglyphic texts. A third describes the temporal and geographic distribution of two political titles. A comparison of prepositions used in hieroglyphic texts suggests a minor dialect variation both among and within Classic Maya sites. Finally, a possible spelling of *nun* 'foreign-speaking person' as part of epithets and personal names suggests that prestige was associated with certain non-local speech patterns.

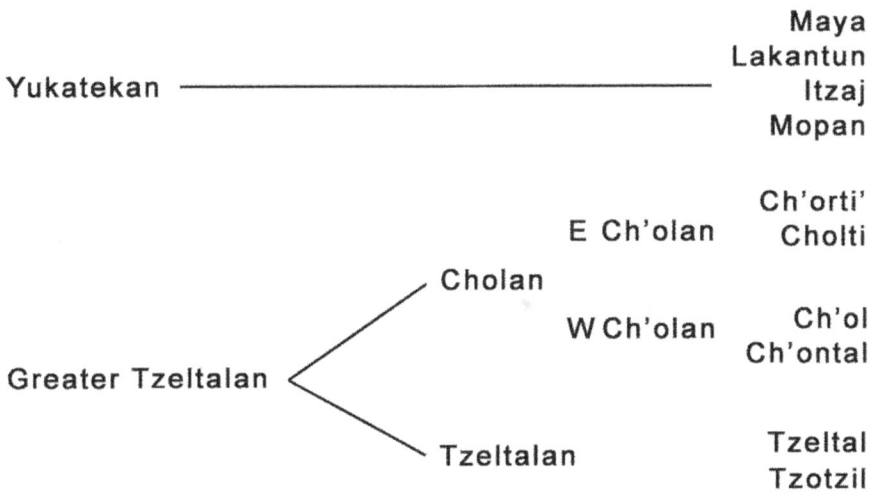

FIGURE 6.1. Mayan languages of the Yukatekan and Greater Tzeltalan subfamilies

PERSON MARKERS

Mayan languages differ among themselves most obviously in patterned sound change. They also differ in some cases in having completely different lexical items, that is, non-related words used to name the same item. The most complex features of comparison, however, are those related to morphology and syntax, that is, variation in word and sentence formation. A significant subset of grammatical morphemes in Mayan languages is the person markers. Generally, Mayan languages do not have obligatory freestanding pronouns occurring with verbs, as English does. Instead, they have two sets of person markers that are prefixed or suffixed to verb stems to indicate the subject of a verb. One set of person markers is used with ergative constructions (usually verbal constructions with both a subject and a direct object), and another set of person markers is used with absolutive constructions (usually verbal constructions with only a subject). For the person markers that occur as prefixes, there are forms that precede verbs beginning with a consonant—*preconsonantal forms*—and other forms (usually very similar) that modify verbs beginning with a vowel: *prevocalic forms*.

Table 6.1 shows all the person markers for the Greater Tzeltalan (also called Greater Ch'olan) and Yukatekan subgroups. They are arranged more or less geographically, beginning with Tzotzil and Tzeltal of the Chiapas highlands, followed by Ch'ol, Chontal, Acalan Chontal, Ch'orti', Ch'olti', then Mopan, Itzaj, Lakantun, and Yukatek (Maya). The premise of this arrangement is that the Tzeltalan and

TABLE 6.1. Person markers of Greater Tzeltalan and Yukatekan languages (does not include Set C person markers in Ch'orti')

	Tzotzil	Tzeltal	Ch'ol	Chontal	Acalan	Ch'orti'	Ch'olti'	Mopan	Itzaj	Lakantun	Yukatek
ERGATIVE (PRECONSONANTAL)											
1stSG	j-	j-	k-	kä-	ka-	in-	in-	in-	in-	in-	in-
2ndSG	a-	a-	a-	a-	a-	a-	a-	a-	a-	a-	a-
3rdS	s-	s-	i-	u-	u-	u-	u-	u-	u-	u-	u-
1stPLin	j..tik	j..tik	la(k)-	kä..la		ka-	ka-	ti..éex	ki..éex	k..éex	k-
1stPLex	j..(ti)kotik	j..kotik	k..lojon	kä..'okob'		—	—	ti-	ki-	k-	—
2ndPL	a..ik	a..ik	la'-	a..la	la-	i-	i-	a..éex	a..éex	a..eex	a..éex
3rdPL	s..ik	s..ik	i..ob'	u..ob'	u..ob'	u..ob'	u-	u..oo'	u..oo'	u..o'	u..óob'
ERGATIVE (PREVOCALIC)											
1stSG	k-	k-	k-	k-	k-	inw-	inw-	inw-	inw-	inw-	inw-
2ndSG	av-	aw-	aw-	aw-	-aw	aw-	aw-	aw-	aw-	aw-	aw-
3rdSG	y-	y-	i-	y-(j-)	y-	uy-	uy-	uy-	uy-	uy-	uy-
1stPLin	k..tik	k..tik	la(k)	k-	k-	kaw-	kaw-	tiw..éex	kiw..éex	k..eex	k-
1stPLex	k..(ti)kotik	k..kotik	k..lojon	k-	—	—	—	tiw-	kiw-	(dual k-)	—
2ndPL	aw..ik	aw..ik	la'w	aw..la	la-	iw-	iw-	aw..éex	aw..éex	aw..eex	aw..éex
3rdPL	y..ik	y..ik	y..ob'	y..ob'	y..ob'	uy..ob'	uy-	uy..oo'	uy..oo'	y..o'	uy..óob'
ABSOLUTIVE											
1stSG	-on (-i-)	-on	-on	-on	-on	-é'n	-in	-(e)en	-(e)en	-en	-en
2ndSG	-ot (-a)	-at	-et	-et	-et	-é't	-et	-(e)ech	-(e)ech	-ech	-ech

continued on next page

TABLE 6.1.—continued

	Tzotzil	Tzeltal	Ch'ol	Chontal	Acalan	Ch'orti'	Ch'olti'	Mopan	Itzaj	Lakantun	Yukatek
ABSOLUTIVE—continued											
3rdSG	Ø	Ø	Ø	-Ø,-i	Ø	Ø	Ø	(-ij),Ø	(-ij),Ø	(-i'),Ø	Ø
1stPLin	-otik	-otik	-onla	-la	—	-o'n	-on	-o'on..e'ex	-o'on-e'ex	-oonex	ó'on
1stPLex	-otikotik	-otikotik	-on lojon	-t'okob'	—	—	—	-o'on	-o'on	-eno' (dual -oon)	
2ndPL	-oxuk	-ex	etla	-la	—	-o'x	-ox	-e'ex	-e'ex	-eex	-é'ex
3rdPL	-ik	-ik/lah-	-ob'	-(j)ob'	Ø	-ob'	Ø	-oo'	-oo'	-iho',Ø	-ó'ob'

Abbreviations: 1st = first person (I, we); 2nd = second person (you); 3rd = third person (he/she/it/they); A = absolutive (subject of intransitive verb); C = preconsonantal (before a consonant); E = ergative (subject of transitive verb); ex = exclusive (we, excluding you); in = inclusive (we, including you); PL = plural; SG = singular; V = prevocalic (before a vowel).

Sources: Tzotzil (Aissen 1987:49); Tzeltal (Kaufman 1971:103); Ch'ol (Aulie and Aulie 1998:234–36); Chontal (Knowles 1984:77); Chontal (Keller and Plácido 1997:444); Acalan Chontal (Smailus 1975:188); Ch'orti' (Fought 1984:47; K'ulb'il Yol Twitz Paxil 2004:61); Mopan (Hofling 2011:10); Itzaj (Hofling and Tesucún 1997:9); Lakantun (Bruce 1968:48); Yukatek (Bricker et al. 1998:329).

Yukatekan languages represent two historically distinct groups and that the Ch'olan languages represent language varieties of Tzeltalan that were formed as a result of contact between a group of Tzeltalan and Yukatekan speakers. In addition to the person markers, this relationship is confirmed by other morpho-syntactic features, such as split ergative systems of subject marking, and in a significant subset of vocabulary shared between the Ch'olan and Yukatekan groups (e.g., Justeson et al. 1985:7–28).

With a simple exercise in visual inspection, it is possible to observe in the person markers several stages of language change in the development of Ch'olan languages. First, boxes are drawn around identical or nearly similar forms. Then, those person markers that have similar patterns (e.g., those that have all Ch'olan forms agreeing with Yukatekan) are grouped together. These two steps in the comparison are not illustrated here. The result of this exercise is shown in table 6.2, in which all of the person markers with shared patterns, presumably representing several proposed stages of contact, have been grouped together.

In the first group, the second-person ergative singular preconsonantal, *a-*, and prevocalic, *aw-*, and the third-person absolutive, Ø, are the same across all of the languages. These forms are very close to what has been reconstructed for proto-Mayan, the language of origin common to all Mayan languages: *aa- *aaw- *Ø, respectively (Kaufman and Norman 1984:91). Because these forms are identical (or nearly so), they do not provide any information about language prehistory other than that all of these languages share a common origin in the distant past.

In the second group, all of the Ch'olan forms agree with Yukatekan. Only the Tzelatalan forms are distinctive. Five forms—the ergative third-person preconsonantal and the ergative third-person plural preconsonantal and prevocalic, the absolutive third-person plural and the absolutive first-person inclusive—pattern in exactly the same way. A question arises as to whether the *s-* prefix is the original one for proto–Greater Tzeltalan and was subsequently changed in Ch'olan as a result of Yukatekan influence or whether the *s-* was introduced only into Tzeltal and Tzotzil (and Tojolab'al, Chuh, and Popti') after Ch'olan languages had separated. One argument in favor of *s-* as the original form is that two absolutive person markers also follow the same pattern, that is, for the third-person absolutive plural and the first-person absolutive inclusive, all Ch'olan forms follow Yukatekan, not Tzeltalan. Because the first group of changes happened in all Ch'olan languages, these changes appear to date from the earliest period of contact between Greater Tzeltalan and Yukatekan, well before the Ch'olan languages had begun to differentiate.

Group 3 shows those forms in which only the Eastern Ch'olan languages follow Yukatekan. The changes that happened at this stage reflect additional Yukatekan influence only on Eastern Ch'olan languages. These changes must have occurred subsequent to the separation of Eastern and Western Ch'olan.

TABLE 6.2. Person markers grouped according to possible source patterns

	Tzotzil	Tzeltal	Ch'ol	Chontal	Acalan	Ch'orti'	Ch'olti'	Mopan	Itzaj	Lakantun	Yukatek
GROUP 1. ALL FORMS ARE THE SAME.											
EC2ndSG	a-	a-	a-	a-	a-	a-	a-	a-	a-	a-	a-
EV2ndSG	av-	aw-	aw-	aw-	aw-	aw-	aw-	aw-	aw-	aw-	aw-
A3rdSG	Ø	Ø	Ø	-Ø,-i	Ø	Ø	Ø	(-ij), Ø	(-ij), Ø	(-i'), Ø	Ø
GROUP 2. ALL CH'OLAN FORMS FOLLOW YUKATEKAN.											
EC3rdS	s-	s-	i-	u-	u-	u-	u-	u-	u-	u-	u-
EC3rdPL	s.ik	s.ik	i.ob'	u.ob'	u.ob'	u-	u-	u.oo'	u.oo'	u.o'	u.óob'
EV3rdPL	y.ik	y.ik	y.ob'	y.ob'	y.ob'	uy.ob'	uy-	uy.oo'	uy.oo'	y.o'	uy.óob'
A3rdPL	-ik	-ik/lah-	-ob'	-(j)ob'	Ø	-ob'	Ø	-oo'	-oo'	-ihó, Ø	-óob'
A1stPLin	-otik	-otik	-onla	-la	-	-o'n	-on	-óon.é'ex	-óon-é'ex	-oonex	óon
GROUP 3. EASTERN CH'OLAN FORMS FOLLOW YUKATEKAN.											
EV1stSG	k-	k-	k-	k-	k-	inw-	inw-	inw-	inw-	inw-	inw-
EC1stSG	j-	j-	k-	kä-	ka-	in-	in-	in-	in-	in-	in-
EV3rdSG	y-	y-	i-	y- (j-)	y-	uy-	uy-	uy-	uy-	uy-	uy-
A1stSG	-on (-i-)	-on	-on	-on	-on	-é'n	-in	-een	-(e)en	-en	-en
GROUP 4. CH'OLAN FORMS ARE UNIQUE.											
EC2ndPL	a.ik	a.ik	la-	a.la	la-	i-	i-	a.é'ex	a.é'ex	a.cex	a.é'ex
EV2ndPL	aw.ik	aw.ik	la'w	aw.la	la-	iw-	iw-	aw.é'ex	aw.é'ex	aw.cex	aw.é'ex
EC1stPLin	j.tik	j.tik	la(k)-	kä.la	ka-	ka-	ka-	ti.é'ex	ki.é'ex	k.cex	k-

continued on next page

TABLE 6.2.—*continued*

	Tzotzil	Tzeltal	Chʼol	Chontal	Acalan	Chʼortiʼ	Chʼoltiʼ	Mopan	Itzaj	Lakantun	Yukatek
GROUP 4. CHʼOLAN FORMS ARE UNIQUE.—*continued*											
EV1stPLin	k..tik	k..tik	la(k)	k-	—	kaw-	kaw-	tiw..eʼex	kiw..eʼex	k..eex	k-
EC1stPLex	j..(ti)kotik	j..kotik	k..lojon	kä..tʼokobʼ	—	—	—	—	ki-	k-	—
EV1stPLex	k..(ti)kotik	k..kotik	k..lojon	k-	—	—	—	—	kiw-	(dual k-)	—
A1stPLex	-otikotik	-otikotik	-on lojon	-tʼokobʼ	—	—	—	-ʼon	-ʼon	-enoʼ (dual -oon)	—
A2ndSG	-ot (-a)	-at	-et	-et	-et	-eʼt	-et	-eech	-(e)ech	-ech	-ech
A2ndPL	-oxuk	-ex	-etla	-la	—	-oʼx	-ox	-ʼex	-ʼeʼex	-eex	-ʼeʼex

In Group 4 the patterning is much less regular, with the Ch'olan forms reflecting independent developments within Ch'olan languages. These changes do not appear to have occurred directly as a result of Yukatekan contact; since the patterns differ for each of the languages, they must have occurred after Eastern and Western Ch'olan groups had differentiated into the subsequent language varieties we are familiar with today.

Several conclusions can be drawn from these data. First, they support the idea of Tzeltalan and Yukatekan as two distinct groups, with Ch'olan as a Greater Tzeltalan language heavily influenced by Yukatekan. Second, these data suggest two distinct periods of influence: an initial phase of influence prior to the separation of Eastern and Western Ch'olan and a later phase of influence only on Eastern Ch'olan languages. The final grouping illustrates changes that took place during a time of no or minimal influence from Yukatekan languages. It does not appear that the person markers in Yukatekan languages, or in Tzeltal and Tzotzil, were changed as a result of contact. Ch'olan languages, in contrast, underwent at least two major periods of contact with Yukatekan that resulted in significant changes to their system of person markers.

Mayan linguists and epigraphers differ in assigning dates to the formation of proto-Ch'olan and the differentiation of Ch'olan into eastern and western forms. An early estimate would place proto-Ch'olan in the Late Preclassic period, perhaps as early as 150 BCE, and the differentiation of Ch'olan languages in the Early Classic period, perhaps around 300 CE. Some estimates place these changes several hundred years later. This discussion of language change illustrates that Ch'olan communities underwent repeated phases of language contact and differentiation. The example of the variation in person markers reflects changes in self-identification for major populations. This is not, however, a deliberate behavior in the same way the use of "Maya" suggests an emerging identity (Restall and Gabbert, this volume). These unconscious variations reflect the existence of distinct speech communities that have resulted from changes in social interaction between large segments of the lowland populations. Most of the following examples reflect comparatively minor changes that affected much smaller groups.

YUKATEKAN AND CH'OLAN SPELLINGS

Maya epigraphers agree that at least the bulk, if not all, of the Classic texts represent Ch'olan languages. Since the Maya script is a mixture of both logographic (word) signs and syllabic signs, it is sometimes possible to find phonological evidence for a Ch'olan form of a particular word that contrasts with the Yukatekan form of that word. For example, the word for 'house' in Yukatekan is *yotoch*, but in Ch'olan languages it is *yotot*. In Classic texts the word is most often represented by a

yo otoch   yo otoch ti   yo to ti   ta yo to ti
yotot?   *yotot*   *yotot*   *ta yotot*

a

k'a/k'ahk   k'ahk   ti k'a k'a
k'ahk   *k'ahk*   *ti k'ak'*

b

FIGURE 6.2. a. Four spellings of yotoch 'house'; b. glyphs for 'fire'

combination of syllabic and logographic signs (the graphemes are identified below by the three-digit codes developed for the Maya Hieroglyphic Database and published as the *New Catalog of Maya Hieroglyphs* [Macri and Looper 2003a; Macri and Vail 2009]): the first sign is usually syllabic *yo* (1SA or MZC) followed by a logograph of a house (ZY5), frequently followed by the syllabic sign for *ti* (3M2) (figure 6.2a). Since the Yukatekan word ends in *–ch*, clearly the Ch'olan pronunciation is intended. In nineteen examples, most often at Chichén Itzá, the word is spelled completely with syllabic signs *yo-to-ti* (MZC 33A 2M1). This spelling confirms a Ch'olan pronunciation for the word for house. Evidence from the Maya codices is less decisive. Although the codices contain evidence of both Yukatekan and Ch'olan forms, the sign for *ti* never follows the house glyph.

One example of a variant spelling that occurs at Chichén Itzá is the word for 'fire', *k'áak'* in Yukatekan but *k'ahk* in Ch'olan languages. That is, in all Ch'olan languages except Chontal, the final *k* has lost glottalization. In nearly all of the Classic texts the word for fire is represented by some variant of the logograph for fire *k'ahk* (2S6) with no doubling of the fire sign (figure 6.2b). However, at the site of Chichén

ka-yo-ma   a-k'a-ba   chak ch'o-ki k'uhul

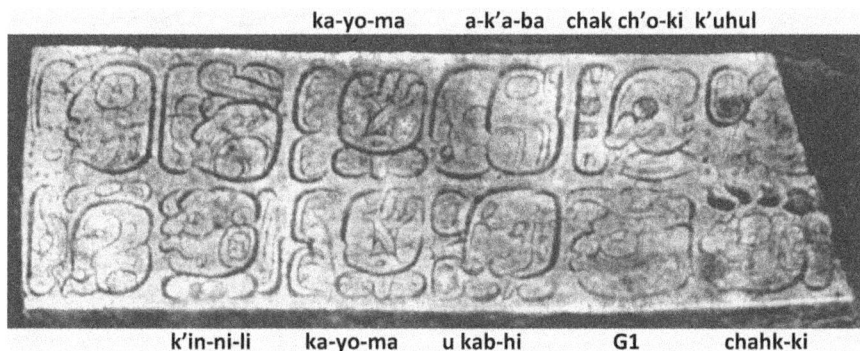

k'in-ni-li   ka-yo-ma   u kab-hi   G1   chahk-ki

FIGURE 6.3. Creation Tablet from Palenque. Merle Greene Robertson; used with permission.

Itzá, the word for 'fire' is spelled with repeated syllabic signs, *k'a-k'a* (MZ3 MZ3). Whether this spelling represents a Yukatekan pronunciation *k'áak'* or simply a Chontal or other dialectal variant is not clear, but it does contrast with the representation of 'fire' in other Classic texts where the grapheme is never duplicated.

Another seemingly incongruent example is the word *ka-yo-ma kayom* 'fisherman' (AA1 MZC 32A) (figure 6.3). It occurs twice on the Creation Tablet from the site of Palenque in a context relating to the Maya day and night paddler deities, in which it is clear that the word 'fisherman' is intended. It comes from the word *kay* 'fish' and a suffix *–oma*, which means to do something regularly or customarily (see Kaufman 1971:58 for a discussion of a related suffix in Tzeltal). What is unexpected is that the word for 'fish' in Ch'olan languages in *chay*; *kay* is the Yukatekan pronunciation. The presence of this Yukatekan pronunciation in an otherwise Ch'olan text remains unexplained, though there are other anomalous spellings at Palenque (see the discussion of Kan B'ahlum below).

Additional evidence for Ch'olan pronunciations of words can be seen in substitution patterns. One such substitution occurs among graphemes representing 'sky', 'snake', and the number 'four'. As can be seen from the data set below, the Ch'olan words are nearly homophonous, while each of the Yukatekan forms is distinctive in vowel quality, and the forms would thus be less likely to substitute one for another.

ká'an	*chan*	'sky; high; tall'
kàan	*chan*	'snake'
kan	*chan ~chän*	'four'

Ch'olan speakers were in close contact with Yukatekan speakers, with numerous examples of borrowing between the two groups. The Classic period Ch'olan scribes

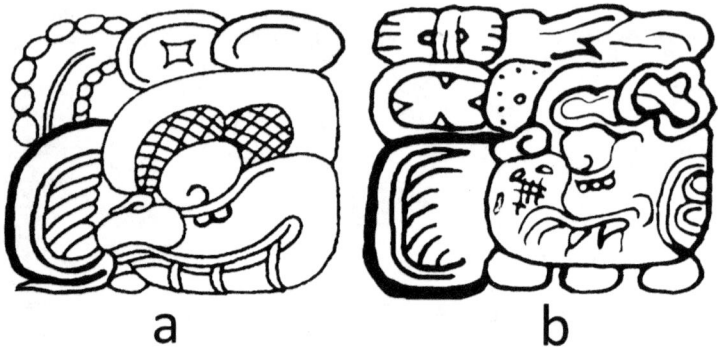

FIGURE 6.4. a. Glyphs for Calakmul with AA1 ka; b. Kan B'ahlam's name with AA1 ka

indicated a "foreign" pronunciation of 'snake' as *kàan* rather than the expected *chan* by prefixing the comb-like *ka* sign to the head of a snake in the site name for Calakmul (figure 6.4a) and in several personal names, including that of Kan B'ahlam at Palenque (figure 6.4b).

The contrasts noted here reflect simple sound correspondences between two subgroups of Mayan languages. Syllabic spellings and substitution patterns show that the Classic Maya texts of the southern lowlands, with rare exceptions, were written and read by a population that understood itself to be distinct from speakers of Yukatekan languages. The evidence for this level of identification spans a rather large area and reflects an identity that probably grew over several centuries. Comparative linguistic data suggest this phenomenon was caused by the intrusion of a Tzeltalan-speaking population into the greater Petén region. The resulting mixed population, although very much hybridized, subsequently began to identify itself as distinct from non-hybridized Yukatekan speakers.

LIMITED DISTRIBUTIONS OF LEXICAL ITEMS

Yet another sort of differentiation can be seen in the distribution of specific lexical items, not necessarily pointing to different languages but minimally to different traditions of language use. One example is the title *b'akab'*. It is spelled with syllabic signs *b'a-ka-b'a*; it follows personal names and other titles, nearly always the final sign in a statement—in a few examples it follows the emblem glyph (figure 6.5a). The translation is uncertain, but only one *b'akab'* is named at a site at any given time. In several cases the title is preceded by the profile of a woman, indication a female *b'akab'*. Of

FIGURE 6.5. a. Glyphs ba'-ka-b'a spelling the title b'akab'; b. glyphs te-ku-yu spelling the title tekuy(u)

180 examples coded in the Maya Hieroglyphic Database (Macri, Looper, and Vail 2001–12), none occur before 640 CE, and most are from the Usumacinta and Pasión regions. Few occur at Palenque, few if any occur at the site of Calakmul (data for that site are incomplete), and none are known from any monuments at Tikal.

What conclusions can be drawn from the uneven distribution of the title? The full significance is not known, but its presence/absence would seem to be deliberate. One possibility is that by 640 CE the title *b'akab'* became important to record as part of a ruler's name phrase. It may be that the title did not exist before that time or that it was not previously considered important enough to record. The title first appears in western and southern sites in the Usumacinta River drainage; it then spreads throughout the Maya region. Its absence (or near absence) from Tikal and Calakmul inscriptions may provide evidence of a significant political difference between rulers at those sites and rulers elsewhere by 640 CE. It may be one of the few explicit confirmations from hieroglyphic texts that by the mid-seventh century, rulers from Tikal and Calakmul constituted a distinct superior category.

Another example of a limited title also originates in the Usumacinta area. Examples of the title *te-ku-yu* (2G1/XGC ZC1 32D) currently total twelve (figure 6.5b). The earliest example is dated to 9.15.5 (736 CE) in the Maya long count at Yaxchilan on the hieroglyphic stairway of Structure 44. The latest example is from 9.17.10 (780 CE) at the site of Naranjo. Nine of the occurrences are a part of expanded name phrases for the same person, the Yaxchilan ruler Yaxun B'ahlam.

Since the date of the event for the earliest example is a century before the others, it is not part of Yaxun B'ahlam's name but is better defined as a title. The latest known occurrence is at Naranjo within a parentage statement that could conceivably refer to a descendant of Yaxun B'ahlam, though that is not certain. Two additional possible examples occur much earlier, 9.0.0.0.0 about 445 CE, on Stela 31 at Tikal.

There is no Mayan word *tekuy(u)*, but a nearly identical word does exist in Nahuatl, *-te:kuiyo:* 'lordship'. It is the possessed form of the word *te:uk-tli* 'lord, member of the high nobility' (Karttunen 1983:218, 237). It appears in an early vocabulary as part of two greetings (Arenas 1611:1):

> *Dios sea en esta casa—Ma to Tecuiyo Dios nican amochantzinco moyetztic*
> [May Our Lord God be in this house.]

> *Dios sea con todos—Ma to Tecuiyo Dios amotlan myoetztic*
> [May Our Lord God be with everyone.]

The appearance of this title in the early eighth century is consistent with the seventh- and eighth-century dates for several other Nahua words spelled syllabically in Maya texts (Macri and Looper 2003b). These words suggest that certain Maya regions experienced possibly several episodes of influence from Nahua speakers. *Tekuy(u)* provides yet another example of how differences in the histories of individual Maya regions or communities are reflected in differences in the written texts.

"TI" AND "TA" AS EVIDENCE FOR DIALECT VARIATION

In a logosyllabic script, phonetic contrasts can be difficult to detect. Nevertheless, slight syntactic differences can provide important clues to language variation. Differences in the use of signs for *ti* or signs for *ta* as prepositions and complementizers (introducers of dependent clauses) provide one example of such variation. A preliminary discussion of *ti* and *ta* appeared in Macri (1991). The subsequent development of the Maya Hieroglyphic Database (Macri, Looper, and Vail 2001–12) has provided many additional examples along with their associated dates and locations. This compilation has allowed a much more complete picture to emerge than was available at that time. Figure 6.6 shows the most common graphemes in the substitution sets that represent *ti* and *ta*. Whatever may have accounted for the origin of the graphemes 3M2 and BV3 (most likely originally *ta* or *ta'* from *täh* 'torch; pine' and *ta'* 'excrement', respectively [Kaufman and Norman 1984:131]), by the height of the Classic period they occur in spellings with the syllabic value *ti*, suggesting that by that time, at most sites, the locative preposition was, as it is in Yukatekan and some Ch'olan languages today, *ti*. However, in texts from at least three sites, we find

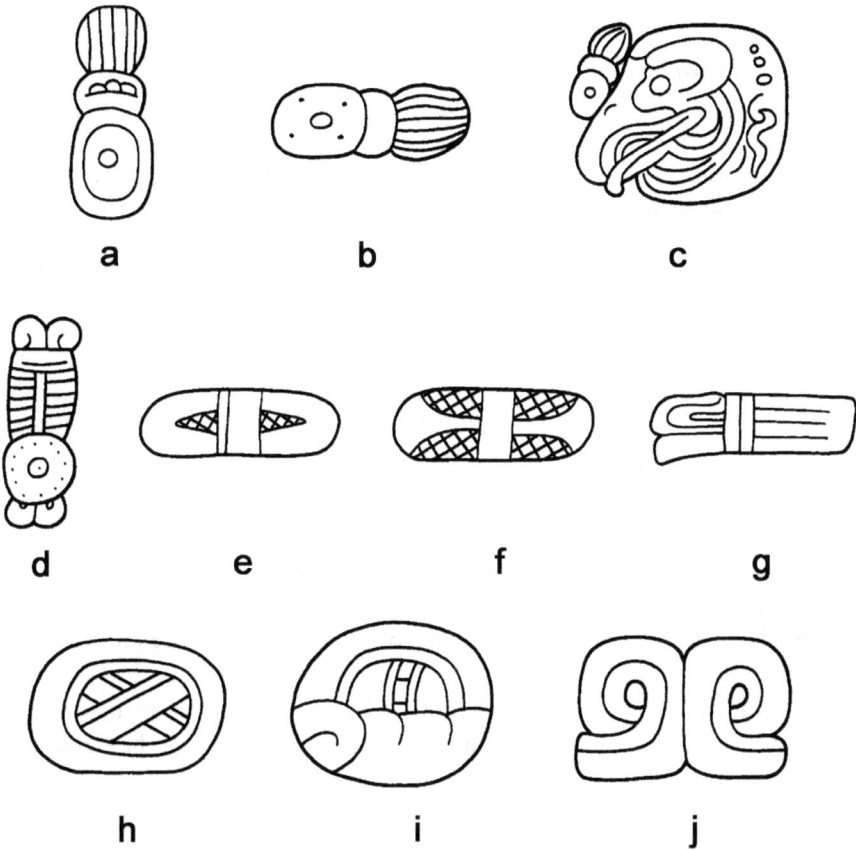

FIGURE 6.6. a–c. Graphemes for ti: 3M2.1, 3M2.2, BV3; d–j. graphemes for ta: 3M3, 1B1.2, 1B1.1, 1B1.3, XQB, YM2, ZS1. Drawings by Matthew G. Looper (Macri and Looper 2003a)

clear evidence of a contrast between *ti* and *ta*. In inscriptions at those sites, variations of the syllabic sign *ta* occur in both prepositional contexts and syllabic spellings, while *ti* occurs only in syllabic spellings or as an introduction to a subordinate clause but not as a locative preposition.

At the site of Palenque, variants of *ta* occur in the following phrases:

ta ajaw-le	*ta ajawlel*	'as ajaw (in ajawship)'
u-na-ta-la	*unatal*	'the first time'

The only times *ti* occurs, it appears to function to spell out words with *t* but never as a preposition. The most frequent example is:

u-ti	*uht*	'it happened'

But a variety of other words spelled syllabically include *ti*:

3-lu-ti-ch'uh	*oxlut? ch'ul*	'divine triad'?
mu-ti	*mut*	'bird'
ti-sa-ku	*tisak*	'Tisak' (personal name)
u-pa-ti	*upätil*	'his work'?
u-chi-li-ti-ni	*uchitinil*	'their sweatbath'

The clearest examples of the contrast between functions of *ti* and *ta* at Palenque and Chichén Itzá occur in the phrase 'in his house,' which begins with the preposition *ta* and ends with the syllabic sign for the spelling of *yotot* (see figure 6.2a for an illustration of the example from Chichén Itzá).

ta yo-otot-ti	*ta yotot*	'in his house'

Phrases that include *tu* are ambiguous in two respects. First, *tu* represents a contraction of either *ti* or *ta* with the third-person marker *u*. Second, by far the most frequent example is **tu-b'a(-hi)** *tub'äh*, the exact translation of which is somewhat uncertain. It may be a benefactive reflexive 'for himself' or an instrumental reflexive 'by himself'.

A similar contrast between the functions of *ti* and *ta* occurs at the site of Naranjo. Here, graphemes for *ta* occur as the preposition up to the Maya date 9.13.10.0.0 (702 CE), at which time the texts change to reflect the more common usage of *ti* for the preposition. Examples of the contrast between *ta* and *ti* from the earlier texts include:

HS1 Step 6	**ta 3-te-tun-ni**	*ta oxte tun*	'at the 3 stone place'
Altar 1 B11	**ta 13 Ix**	*ta oxlajun ix*	'on 13 Ix'
Altar 1 D7	**u-ti**	*uti*	'it happened'
Stele 24 A2	**1 Sotz' ta k'in-ni**	*jun sotz' ta k'in*	'on the day 1 Sotz'

From 593 to 702 CE, the only exception to *ta* used as a locative/temporal preposition is that *ti* precedes the half-period sign on Stelae 22 and 24 for the date 9.13.10 (702 CE). On Stela 24, however, *ti* occurs as a complementizer, that is, it introduces a dependent clause:

ti xa-k'uh	*ti xak'*	'by standing over'

(see Martínez Hernández 1929:915 454r)

By 702 CE, only *ti* occurs as a preposition:

ti pet	*ti pet*	'on the island'?
ti ajaw-le	*ti ajawlel*	'as ajaw (in ajawship)'

ti yotot	*ti yotot*	'in his house'
ti 5 Ak'b'al	*ti ho Ak'b'al*	'on 5 Ak'b'al'

and *ta* only occurs in syllabic spellings:

yi-ta-hi	*yitah*	'his companion'
ya-ta-na	*yatan*	'his wife'

The differing use of *ti* and *ta* is not diagnostic of either the Ch'olan or Yukatekan language family, but it does reflect a difference among varieties of Ch'olan dialects. The substitution of the set of *ti* graphemes for the *ta* set would not have seriously impaired one's ability to read the text, but it does reflect the usage of the author of a text. Literate people would have no difficulty reading texts written in a variety of dialects. In the case of Palenque, the use of *ta* as a preposition seems to suggest the presence of speakers of a dialect somewhat different from that of other Classic Maya sites. The change from the preposition *ta* to *ti* at the site of Naranjo might reflect language change within a constant population or the influx of a new population (or a new scribal tradition) whose dialect is in agreement with the majority of Maya sites. Again, from our vantage point we recognize the distinctions but are not certain of their causes or their social significance. Did the people at Palenque speak in a way that sounded odd to their neighbors along the Usumacinta River and the central Petén? Did the people of Naranjo speak (or write) significantly differently after 702 CE, and was this in some way tied to the presence or the demise of Lady Six Sky? What we can infer from the differences in the representation of prepositions at Palenque, Naranjo, and Chichén Itzá is that distinctive speech communities did exist among the lowland Maya during the Classic period.

GEOGRAPHIC AND LINGUISTIC IDENTIFICATION
OF LADY SIX SKY AT NARANJO

The hieroglyphic text on Stela 24 from the site of Naranjo provides a glimpse into the life of Lady Six Sky up to the ritual celebration of the period ending 9.13.10.0.0 (702 CE), at which time her son was about nine years old (figure 6.7). The text on the sides of the monument begins with her arrival at Naranjo, then continues with the birth of her son and the celebration of the period ending on 9.13.10, and ends with a parentage statement that gives the names of her mother and her father, the ruler of the site of Dos Pilas.

In a phrase modifying her name in the parentage expression, there is the phrase **u-b'a-hi-li aj-nu-na-ja ta-li-chan** *ub'ahil ah nun (n)ah tali chan* (figure 6.8). The first root *b'ah* or *b'äh* is part of the general phrase translated variously as 'her image', 'she does it', 'herself', and the like.

FIGURE 6.7. Drawing of Naranjo, Stele 24, front, by Ian Graham © President and Fellows of Harvard College, Peabody Museum of Archaeology and Ethnology number 2004.15.6.2.45 (digital file #99100038)

The second part of the phrase is unique to this text. It begins with the agentive *aj* 'he/she who (is) . . .' followed by *nu-na* or *nunah*. Published attestation of the root *nun* itself is limited to Yukatek, that is, I have not found it in dictionaries for other Mayan languages. On the contrary, Kaufman (2002:727) reconstructs **meem* 'mudo [dumb]' for Central (Eastern + Western) Mayan languages. The Motul Dictionary provides several relevant entries:

> *nun, ah nun* boçal, que no sabe la lengua de la tierra o que es balbuciente o tar-tamudo; y el rudo que no aprovecha enseñarle [someone who does not know the language of the land or speaks poorly; a coarse person who doesn't learn]. (Martínez Hernández 1929:695, 337r)

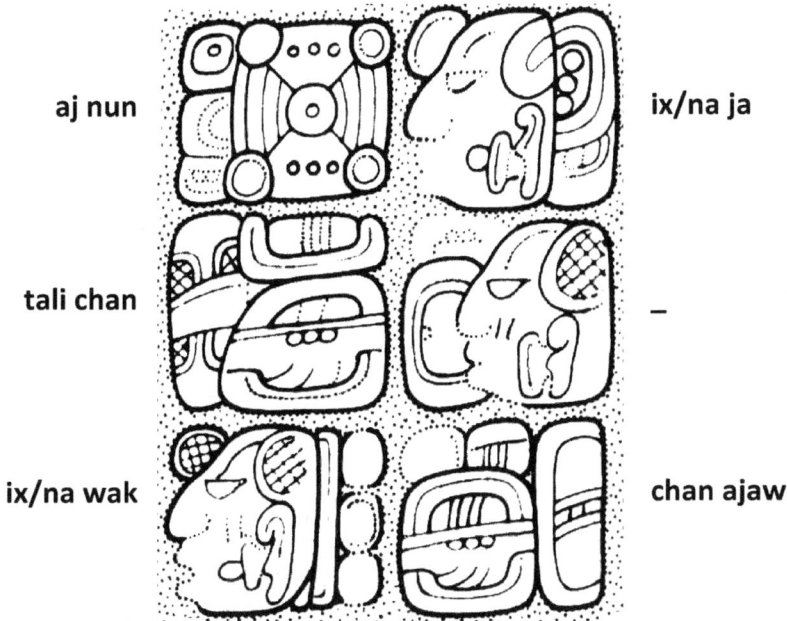

FIGURE 6.8. Drawing of Naranjo, Stela 24, right side, D4–D7, by Ian Graham © President and Fellows of Harvard College, Peabody Museum of Archaeology and Ethnology, PM# 2004.15.6.2.47 (digital file # 99320005)

nunum vagabundo y perdido que no quiere asenta casa [a vagabond; an incorrigible person who won't settle down]. (ibid.)

The Cordemex offers additional examples including 'mudo [mute]' from a number of sources (Barrera Vasquez et al. 1980:588). At least one contemporary Maya dialect has the word *nùum* 'ignorant, stupid, lazy, retarded' (Bricker, Po'ot Yah, and Dzul de Po'ot 1998:202)—for a discussion of final *n* > *m* variation in Yukatek, see Blaha Pfeiler (1992).

These words appear to be related to the Nahuatl word *no:n-tli* 'someone mute' (Karttunen 1983:174), which may, in fact, be the source. Molina (1944:73v) lists *nontli* 'mudo [mute]' and several related forms such as *nonti* 'hazerse mudo [to become mute]' and *nontilia* 'hazer mudo a otro [to act mute to another]'.

In other words, Lady Six Sky is described by a phrase suggesting she speaks the language of Naranjo poorly, as if she were a foreigner. At one time this suggested to me that there was a language or dialect difference between Naranjo and Dos Pilas. Possibly, Naranjo spoke a Ch'olan dialect closer to Yukatek and Dos Pilas a dialect with fewer similarities to Yukatek.

However, the following phrase may illuminate this epithet: *ta-li-chan*. This phrase begins with the locative *ta* instead of the more common *ti*, a sure sign of a dialect distinction (this also occurs on the front of Stela 24 in the phrase *ta k'in*). The word *chan*, in addition to meaning 'sky', can also mean 'tall' or 'high'. It sometimes occurs with the meaning 'highland'. The phrase occurs in Yukatek as *tali ka'analil* 'from the highlands [para arriba]' and *tali ka'anal k'uchuk ti kab'* 'from high to low [de alto abajo]' (Martínez Hernández 1929:832, 409v). Although Dos Pilas is indeed south of Naranjo toward the Guatemalan highlands, it is only slightly higher in elevation than the central Petén, and the environment is not appreciably distinct, so the phrase remained puzzling.

Recent archaeological evidence suggests that some Pasión region rulers appear to have taken elite highland women as wives. So rather than the *tali chan* referring to Dos Pilas as a highland location, it may refer to the fact that Lady Six Sky's mother originated from an Eastern Mayan– (K'ichean or Mamean) speaking community in the mountains of Guatemala. If this reading of Lady Six Sky as a "person who speaks poorly, "as a "foreign-speaking woman," is correct, it would be yet another feature from the hieroglyphic texts that shows a self-awareness of the Classic Maya of Naranjo as an identifiable group separate from other Mayan-speaking peoples. Even more important, since this phrase occurs on a stela celebrating Lady Six Sky, the designation as *ah nun* 'foreign speaker' would have had to have been a mark of status. Whether her "accent" in Naranjo derives from her association with a different lowland dialect spoken by elite families at Dos Pilas or even ultimately from Tikal or whether it is a result of her mother having been a native speaker of a highland language, *ah nun* is a quality that contributes to her importance—it carried prestige.

The Naranjo text is not the only one on which the word *nun* is spelled with syllabic signs. It also occurs at Chichén Itzá on Lintel 2 of the Las Monjas structure. After the name of *K'ak'upakal K'awil* is the phrase **u-nu-na-li ??-la b'a-te ajaw-wa-li** *ununal ?? b'ate ajwal* 'foreign-speaking ?? ballplayer/warrior ajaw' (figure 6.9). In this case the context offers nothing to support a reading of 'foreign', but it does occur in association with a name, thus it is a phrase referring to a person.

A discussion of *nun* as represented by the logograph 3M9 and associated with several early rulers, most famously Yax Nun Ayin of Tikal, the son of Sihyaj K'ahk', a military captain associated with Teotihuacan (Houston and Inomata 2009:10; Stuart 2000), is beyond the scope of this chapter, but it does invite some intriguing speculation about his non-local origins and about the effect a foreign intrusion would have had on the political and social boundaries of the Classic Maya. The word *nun* "someone who does not know the language of the land or speaks poorly" appears later in name phrases and titles from several other sites (including Chichén Itzá, Copán, Dos Pilas, Pusilha, and Yaxchilan). The reappearance of *nun* in later texts may have been the result of move-ment among populations or of elite persons speaking different Maya language varieties (languages or dialect), and it may also have resulted from repeated intrusions of Mexican groups into various parts of the Classic Maya region known from the Early Classic, the seventh century, and the Postclassic period.

Nun in the name of the early Tikal ruler represents an unusually early date for a possible loan from a Nahua language into the vocabulary of the Classic Maya, adding to a growing body of data that suggests an early form of Nahua was present in central Mexico and the Gulf region from as early as the Late Preclassic and was at least one of the languages used at Teotihuacan (Dakin and Wichmann 2000; Macri and Looper 2003b; Macri 2005). Perhaps more important for a

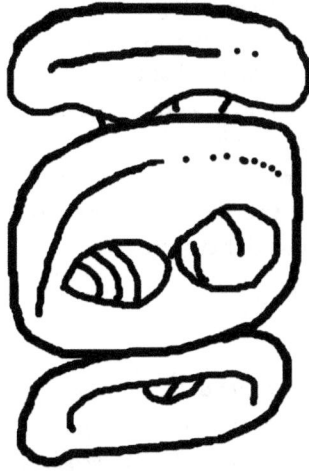

FIGURE 6.9. Chichén Itzá, Las Monjas, Lintel 2aA C1. Drawing by Ian Graham (Bolles 1977:269)

discussion of ethnogenesis, the use of the term *nun* "someone who does not know the language of the land" in names of prominent individuals suggests an acknowledgment of the presence of those who speak differently from the local population and the prestige associated with those persons.

CONCLUSION

In summary, rigorous examination of both comparative linguistics and the written hieroglyphic record provides insight into multiple levels of social, political, and intellectual differentiation of the Classic Maya. Some of these traits are broad, such as changes in the system of person markers; others are quite limited, either spatially or temporally, such as the titles *b'akab'* and *tekuy(u)*. Identifying clusters of such traits or matching them with parallel developments or changes in ceramics, architecture, burial customs, or population density can provide useful information about how various groups of Maya people understood themselves in relation to those around them and what sorts of interactions may have transpired both among Maya groups and between Maya groups and speakers of languages from other language families.

We can no longer labor under the illusion that the Classic Maya were a monolithic or homogeneous group or even that their texts represent a single "prestige" language variety (Houston, Robertson, and Stuart 2000). Social variation, as evidenced by language change and written texts, offers evidence that the Classic Maya under-stood themselves through multiple layers of identification. From the written record, it is evident that these multiple layers were not static but changed gradually—even in some cases dramatically—over time. There is a tendency to under-differentiate the people and events of the past, to try to understand them more simply than they were. The more fine-grained our data about the past become and the more layers of their various identifications we see, the more closely we approach an accurate view of who they were.

<h2 style="text-align:center">REFERENCES CITED</h2>

Aissen, Judith L. 1987. *Tzotzil Clause Structure*. Dordrecht, Germany: D. Reidel. http://dx .doi.org/10.1007/978-94-009-3741-3.

Arenas, Pedro de. 1611. *Vocabulario Manual de Las Lenguas Castellana y Mexicana*. Mexico: Enrico Martinez.

Aulie, H. Wilbur, and Evelyn W. de Aulie. 1998. *Diccionario Ch'ol de Tumbalá, Chiapas, con variaciones dialectales de Tila y Sabanilla*, ed. Emily Scharfe de Stairs. Serie de vocabu-larios y diccionarios indígenas, Mariano Silva y Aceves 121. Mexico City: Instituto Lingüístico de Verano.

Barrera Vasquez, Alfredo, Juan Ramón Bastarrachea Manzano, William Brito Sansores, Refugio Vermont Salas, David Dzul Góngora, and Domingo Dzul Poot. 1980. *Diccionario Maya Cordemex: Maya-Español, Español-Maya*. Mérida, Mexico: Ediciones Cordemex.

Blaha Pfeiler, Barbara. 1992. "Así som, los de Yucatam: El proceso fonológico Vn—> m/__ (#,C) en dos lenguas en contacto." In *Memorias del Primer Congreso Internacional de Mayistas*, ed. Barbara Blaha Pfeiler, 110–22. Mexico City: UNAM.

Bloomfield, Leonard. 1933. *Language*. New York: Henry Holt.

Bolles, John S. 1977. *Las Monjas: A Major Pre-Mexican Architectural Complex at Chichén Itzá*. Norman: University of Oklahoma Press.

Bricker, Victoria R., Eleuterio Po'ot Yah, and Ofelia Dzul de Po'ot. 1998. *A Dictionary of the Maya Language as Spoken in Hocabá, Yucatán*. Salt Lake City: University of Utah Press.

Bruce, Robert D. 1968. *Gramática del Lacandón*. Mexico City: Instituto Nacional de Antropología e Historia.

Dakin, Karen, and Søren Wichmann. 2000. "Cacao and Chocolate: A Uto-Aztecan Perspective." *Ancient Mesoamerica* 11 (1): 55–75. http://dx.doi.org/10.1017/S0956536 100111058.

Fought, John. 1984. "Cholti Maya: A Sketch." In *Handbook of Middle American Indians: Linguistics, Supplement 2*, ed. Victoria Reifler-Bricker and Munro S. Edmonson, 43–55. Austin: University of Texas Press.

Graham, Ian, and Eric von Euw. 1975. *Corpus of Maya Hieroglyphic Inscriptions:* Vol. 2, Part 1: *Naranjo*. Peabody Museum of Archaeology and Ethnology. Cambridge, MA: Harvard University.

Hofling, Charles Andrew. 2011. *Mopan Maya–Spanish-English Dictionary*. Salt Lake City: University of Utah Press.

Hofling, Charles Andrew, with Félix Fernando Tesucún. 1997. *Itzaj Maya–Spanish-English Dictionary*. Salt Lake City: University of Utah Press.

Houston, Stephen D., and Takeshi Inomata. 2009. *The Classic Maya*. Cambridge: Cambridge University Press.

Houston, Stephen D., John Robertson, and David Stuart. 2000. "The Language of Classic Maya Inscriptions." *Current Anthropology* 41 (3): 321–56. http://dx.doi.org/10.1086 /300142.

Justeson, John S., William M. Norman, Lyle Campbell, and Terrence Kaufman. 1985. *The Foreign Impact on Lowland Mayan Language and Script*. Middle American Research Institute 53. New Orleans: Tulane University Press.

Karttunen, Frances. 1983. *An Analytical Dictionary of Nahuatl*. Norman: University of Oklahoma Press.

Kaufman, Terrence S. 1971. *Tzeltal Phonology and Morphology*. Publications in Linguistics, vol. 61. Berkeley: University of California Press.

Kaufman, Terrence S. 2002. *A Preliminary Mayan Etymological Dictionary*. With the assistance of John Justeson. Accessed April 27, 2009. http://www.famsi.org/reports/01051 /index.html.

Kaufman, Terrence S., and William M. Norman. 1984. "An Outline of Proto-Cholan Phonology, Morphology, and Vocabulary." In *Phoneticism in Mayan Hieroglyphic Writing*, ed. John S. Justeson, 77–166. Institute for Mesoamerican Studies, State University of New York Publication 9. Albany: State University of New York.

Keller, Kathryn C., and Luciano G. Plácido. 1997. *Diccionario Chontal de Tabasco*. Serie de vocabularios y diccionarios indígenas, Mariano Silva y Aceves, no. 36. Tucson, AZ: Summer Institute of Linguistics.

Knowles, Susan. 1984. "A Descriptive Grammar of Chontal Maya (San Carlos Dialect)." PhD dissertation, Department of Anthropology, Tulane University, New Orleans, LA.

K'ulb'il Yol Twitz Paxil. 2004. *U'tirache Ojroner Maya Ch'orti': Gramática Descriptiva Ch'orti*. Guatemala City: Academia de las Lenguas Mayas de Guatemala.

Lacadena, Alfonso. 2011. "Maya Hieroglyphic Texts as Linguistic Sources." In *New Perspectives in Mayan Linguistics*, ed. Heriberto Avelino, 343–73. Newcastle upon Tyne: Cambridge Scholars Publishing.

Law, Danny. 2014. *Language Contact, Inherited Similarity, and Social Difference: The Story of Linguistic Interaction in the Maya Lowlands*. Amsterdam: John Benjamins.

Lehmann, Winifred P. 1962. *Historical Linguistics: An Introduction*. New York: Holt, Rinehart, and Winston.

Macri, Martha J. 1991. "Prepositions and Complementizers in the Classic Period Inscriptions." In *Sixth Palenque Round Table, 1986*, ed. Virginia M. Fields, 266–72. Palenque Round Table Series, vol. 8, Merle Greene Robertson, gen. ed. San Francisco: Pre-Columbian Art Research Institute.

Macri, Martha J. 2005. "Nahua Loanwords from the Early Classic: Words for Cacao Preparation on a Río Azul Ceramic Vessel." *Ancient Mesoamerica* 16: 321–26.

Macri, Martha J., and Matthew G. Looper. 2003a. *The New Catalog of Maya Hieroglyphs*, vol. 1: *The Classic Period Inscriptions*. Norman: University of Oklahoma Press.

Macri, Martha J., and Matthew G. Looper. 2003b. "Nahua in Ancient Mesoamerica: Evidence from Maya Inscriptions." *Ancient Mesoamerica* 14 (2): 285–97. http://dx.doi .org/10.1017/S0956536103142046.

Macri, Martha J., Matthew G. Looper, and Gabrielle Vail. 2001–2012. *The Maya Hieroglyphic Database*. Current beta-version available at the Native American Language Center. Davis: University of California.

Macri, Martha J., and Gabrielle Vail. 2009. *The New Catalog of Maya Hieroglyphs*, vol. 2: *The Codical Texts*. Norman: University of Oklahoma Press.

Martínez Hernández, Juan. 1929. *Diccionario de Motul, Maya-Español Atribuido a Fray Antonio de Ciudad Real*. Mérida, Mexico: Compañía Tipográfica Yucateca.

Molina, Fray Alonso de. 1944. *Vocabulario en lengua mexicana y castellana*. Facsimile of 1571 edition. Colección de Incunables Americanos, vol. 4. Madrid: Ediciones Cultura Hispanica.

Smailus, Ortwin. 1975. *El Maya-Chontal de Acalan: analisis lingüístico de un documento de los años 1610–1612*. Centro de Estudios Mayas, Cuaderno 9. Mexico City: UNAM.

Stuart, David. 2000. "'The Arrival of Strangers': Teotihuacan and Tollan in Classic Maya History." In *Mesoamerica's Classic Heritage: From Teotihuacan to the Aztecs*, ed. David Carrasco, Lindsay Jones, and Scott Sessions, 465–513. Boulder: University Press of Colorado.

PART II

Archaeological Explorations of Identity Construction

7

Establishing the Preconditions for Ethnogenesis among the Classic Maya of the Upper Belize River Valley

LISA J. LECOUNT

Ethnicity is an uncomfortable topic for many Maya archaeologists, particularly those who work with groups pre-dating the Late Postclassic Kowoj or Itza. The subjective nature of ethnicity does not easily lend itself to the study of ancient groups understood only through patterning in material cultural and practices. For cultural anthropologists, ethnicity is "the most general identity determined by origin and background" (Barth 1969:13) that can be narrowed or broadened to fit the specific needs of a social group as it mobilizes to negotiate social relations and access to resources (Cohen 1978:391). Identities, therefore, are situational depending on the context and scale of interaction and who is doing the categorizing. If ethnic group membership is fluid, then it seems that archaeologists are ill-equipped to examine it. However, I argue that this is not the case because the processes that give rise to ethnic groups, as well as the shared practices of cultural differentiation and common descent that maintain boundaries and structure social interactions, can be recognized by archaeologists through careful analysis of archaeological patterning (Jones 1997). Although cultural anthropologists are correct in pointing out the problematic nature of ethnicity, ethnicity is "not random within particular sociohistorical contexts" (ibid.:125). The study of ancient Maya ethnicity, therefore, can contribute specific case examples surrounding the development and maintenance of identities, as exemplified in the chapters that follow in this volume.

Some researchers may deny the existence of ancient Maya ethnic groups, but it seems to me simplistic to suggest that Classic period peoples who occupied the vast

DOI: 10.5876/9781607325673.c007

terrain of southern Mesoamerica somehow lacked it. To do so assumes an undifferentiated cultural group without regard for social differences based on languages, histories, geopolitics, and adaptations to diverse highland-lowland environments. Given that boundary maintenance and political opposition trigger ethnogenesis, it is plausible to postulate that the roots of ethnicity were established in the Classic period when states attempted to consolidate control over people and tribute. Maya archaeologists, therefore, are in a good position to document the preconditions under which identity groups arose, the range of identities they achieved, and the processes of assimilation, hybridity, and creolization that blur identities and ethnicity in the archaeological record.

Others may reject the presence of Classic Maya ethnicities because epigraphers have yet to recognize named ethnic groups. When the Classic Maya identified themselves in hieroglyphics, it was in terms of places, ruling dynasties, specific royal individuals, and deities linked to local landscapes (Tokovinine 2013:98). Emblem glyphs, titles, and names speak more about places and individuals than peoples; however, the Mayan term *tzuk* is considered the best candidate for indexing membership in larger groups. Following Dmitri Beliaev (2000), Alexander Tokovinine (2013) suggests that *tzuk* meant a person from a "part" or "division" of a specific geographical area that was evoked only when one's political status was subverted. In other words, it was an explicit reference to "the other" as opposed to the implicit reference to the in-group. In this regard, the term's use is similar to the way historical Native Americans recognized differences between themselves and others. In-group members were called by the linguistic term for "people," but "the other" was a named entity, such as the title Anasazi, which means "ancient enemies," "enemy ancestors," or simply "ancient non-Navajos" to Navajos. Given that there were no explicitly named Classic Maya groups, it might be prudent to avoid the term *ethnic group* altogether. However, I continue to use it because in this chapter I attempt to demonstrate that the processes that gave rise to ethnogenesis are evident in the Classic period.

From an archaeological perspective, an argument for ethnicity must be built up from a number of intersecting lines of evidence documenting differences in cultural practices, boundary maintenance, and conflicting interests. Gone are the days when archaeologists could simply assume that ancient ethnic groups constituted a homogeneous society of bounded and discreet practices and material cultures on either side of a geographical boundary (Jones 1997). While some ethnographic studies document strong material culture patterning at ethnic boundaries, the expression of ethnic differences more often involves a limited range of marked styles or practices (Hodder 1985). Although some actively communicate difference (Wobst 1977), others are recognizable only to those people who have intimate knowledge of them (Wiessner 1983, 1985). Differences in ethnic practices and symbols may also be so completely habituated, subconscious, or hidden that analyses of production techniques are required to discover them (Gosselain 2000; Stark 1998). Little wonder that attempts to map the distribution of styles and practices across cultural landscapes result in blurred boundaries (Jones 1997:124; Lightfoot and Martinez 1995:487). Rather than bemoan our ambiguous data, archaeologists should embrace these patterns as reflecting multiple and overlapping interactions between groups at the nexus of social boundaries.

Today, social boundaries are conceptualized as zones of cross-cutting networks where interactions between and within groups result in cultural dynamism. The dynamic character of boundaries is one reason many ethnoarchaeological studies have demonstrated no necessary correlation between diacritics (marked material culture or community practices) and identities (Dietler and Herbich 1998; Gosselain 2000; Hodder 1979). In fact, social boundaries may actually display *greater* diversity in these items and practices than those found in cultural heartlands. Frontier communities can contain diacritics that reify those in homelands, as well as display entirely new or hybrid styles and practices that reflect novel involvements experienced in these locations (Jones 1997; Schortman and Nakamura 1991). Given this dynamism, it may be more productive to first establish the saliency of long-term traditions within specific domains, such as house layouts, pottery styles, and burial practices within a particular region, before charting how the processes of ethnogenesis lead to material cultural change, similar to the way Richard Reycraft (2005) identified ethnogenesis among the Chiribaya of Far South Coastal Peru.

More straightforward is the task of documenting the hegemonic processes of conflict and oppression that give rise to ethnic affiliation and attribution. Oppression—whether by empire, state, or other foreign agents—sets in motion strategies to resist subordination that is foundational to the construction of identity. But given that conflict and oppression do not necessarily result in ethnogenesis, the question remains: what actions or series of actions trigger strong emotional attachments to homeland, people, and symbols that underlie collective identity and promote the mobilization of resources in support of it (Cohen 1978:396)? Although archaeologists may never know these details, they can document the degree to which the hegemonic process materializes differences between, as well as groupness among, peoples. To that end, in the next sections I discuss the ways social boundary maintenance, communities of practices, and conflict have been shown to lead to ethnogenesis in the anthropological literature and then apply these insights to archaeological data from the upper Belize River valley to argue for the creation of a social boundary along the eastern periphery of Petén in the Classic period.

SOCIAL BOUNDARIES

Fredrik Barth's (1969) seminal work on boundaries is a logical starting point because he was more interested in exploring boundaries as expressions of cultural differences than in defining ethnic units and content (Hegmon 1998:271). Barth identified three important factors— sustained interaction, complementarity, and interdependence—that lead to the creation of social categories and how this process results in boundary maintenance.

For Barth (1969:10; also Naroll et al. 1964), ethnic categories originate not from conjecture but from a clear understanding of social differences. These differences arise from sustained interaction, since without it there can be no basis for dichotomous classification of groups into exclusive categories. Although Barth does not fully explain why differences emerge from sustained interactions, once they do, members of exclusive categories express a separate range of "value standards" or "orientations." Members canonize roles because they are reluctant to act outside them for "fear that such behavior might be inappropriate for a person of their identity" (Barth 1969:18). In this way, categories naturalize differences and take on the "appearance of being an autonomous factor in the ordering of the social world" (Comaroff 1987:313).

Ethnogenesis involves complementarity and interdependence, since without them there is either "no interaction or interaction without reference to ethnic identity" (Barth 1969:18). Barth dichotomized the social roles of males versus females, and John Comaroff discussed how elite and common classes underpin many societies. At the polity level, Barth (ibid.:19–21) approached these processes from ecological and demographic perspectives. For him, ecological interdependence may have several forms. Emerging ethnic groups may occupy distinct environmental zones, in which case they are in minimal competition for resources and interdependence is sustained through trade goods. Or they may occupy separate territories in the same environmental zone, in which case they are in direct competition for resources, especially along their borders. In this case, each group may produce and trade important goods and services in a classic symbiotic relationship in which it monopolizes a particular economic resource. These forms of ecological interdependence refer to stable landscapes, where persistent and sustained interaction leads to close contact between groups and boundary maintenance. Although social differences can be attributed to ecological adaptations, rarely are they the source of cultural boundaries. Even in situations where boundaries may be rigidly maintained, people continually flow across them as competition for resources or labor stimulates migrations. The recruitment and assimilation of individuals often hinge on incentives for changing identity, including access to economic resources, and the presence of mechanisms that ease incorporation, such as shared religion and kin relations (ibid.:22–24).

Ancient Maya groups illustrate Barth's mechanisms associated with social categorization and boundary maintenance. Rosemary Joyce (2000, 2001) suggests that social categories—particularly gender, age, and status—are evident in monumental images and small-scale human figurines that illustrate people and activities. As early as the Early Preclassic period, costume ornaments cast in pottery, stone, and shell were particularly salient mediums for the creation of social identities. In terms of differences between social classes, Mayanists fiercely debate the nature of social stratification but not the existence of endogamous royal, noble, and commoner groups (Sharer 1993:93). Asserted status was displayed through the differential distribution of prestige goods, a pattern that has its beginnings in the Preclassic villages (Clark and Hansen 2001; Demarest 2003; Garber et al. 2004; Hammond 1991; Healey 1990).

Interdependence with outside groups is also well documented for the Maya. Sustained interactions with other Mesoamerican groups were foundational to ideas about the nature of the universe and society, which were expressed, modified, and contested through material styles and practices. Olmec-style pottery and figurines, as well as standardized site plans and civic monument styles, were widespread from the highlands to the lowlands during the Early to Middle Preclassic period (Flannery and Marcus 2000), and Maya populations actively engaged in their creation and manipulation by 1000 BC (Inomata et al. 2013). Highland-lowland interactions were also pronounced in the Early Classic period when Teotihuacanos and/or Teotihuacan-inspired groups influenced politics, architecture, and art at major Maya capitals including Kaminaljuyu, Tikal, and Copán (Braswell 2003). Similarly, interaction between Maya and Mexican groups also occurred in the Postclassic period. According to William Ringle and colleagues (1998), the much debated Toltec-Maya connection is best understood as the expansion of a world religion focused on the feathered serpent deity called Kukulcan by the Maya and Quetzalcoatl by Nahuatl speakers. The international character of the religion, the influx of elite pilgrims who belonged to distinct ethnic groups, and the increase in trade relations resulted in similar architecture and art styles at Chichén Itzá and Tula. Long-distance trade and international relationships continued in the Late Postclassic when Mayapan maintained or renewed economic ties with central Mexico (Masson and Peraza Lope 2010). On the Southeast Periphery of the Maya lowlands, Copán may have always been a frontier center where lowland Maya interacted with non-Maya peoples living in the area (Fash 2004; Schortman and Nakamura 1991).

Most Classic period political boundaries were not new frontiers between settled and unsettled lands but rather zones through which people and goods moved. Recent strontium isotope research provides detailed examples of elite leaders and brides who traveled long distances from homelands to their final resting point (Buikstra 1997; Wright 2004; Wright and White 1996). Most of this research focuses on individuals within royal tombs in a few large sites, specifically Tikal, Kaminalujuyu, Copán, and Teotihuacan; but Lori Wright's work at Tikal also demonstrates the presence of several non-local skeletons in non-elite domestic contexts. She contends that "the multiethnic nature of ancient Mesoamerican states is becoming increasingly apparent, as are the extent and intensity of interactions between distant cities" (Wright 2004:207).

Cross-cutting social networks are most easily seen at the nexus of environmental zones where trade goods were bulked and shipped. Highland obsidian and jade, coastal salt, shell, fish, and lowland high-status goods such as cotton and cacao established interdependence between regional groups through trade relations. Arthur Demarest (2013) illustrates how Cancuen nobles regulated the supply of highland Guatemalan obsidian and jade into the lowlands from their port at the head of navigation on the Pasión River. Distinct artifact distributions within the site are associated with city sectors and architectural features, including a highland-style ballcourt, that suggest multiethnic populations. Hybrid styles indicative of frontier dynamism are also found at nearby sites that exhibit synchronized religious architecture, such as the "lowlandized" mountain shrine at Raxruja Viejo.

When populations reached their apogee in the Classic period, groups occupying the same environmental zones were in direct competition for good farmland, fresh water, and labor. Some populations colonized remote regions, such as southern Belize, to gain access to land (Braswell 2007), but those in Petén were largely circumscribed on all sides by existing groups. Conflicts between Tikal and Calakmul and their allies for control of people and tribute are recorded in Late and Terminal Classic hieroglyphs (Martin and Grube 2008). However, peripheral centers they subjugated often did not figure prominently in Petén hieroglyphic texts, presumably because they were unfamiliar or alien people.

Based on this brief summary of Maya social categories and boundaries, it is apparent that Barth's prerequisites for ethnogenesis among the Maya were in place by the Classic period. But from a practice perspective, ethnogenesis also involves the construction of groupness not addressed by an adaptationalist model. More recent anthropological models focus on the ways conventional ways of understanding and acting in the world give rise to collective sentiments and actions within ethnic groups.

COMMUNITIES OF PRACTICE

Ethnicity is the mechanism by which groups use "culture to symbolize their within-group organization in opposition to and in competition with other interest groups"

(Hodder 1979:452). Similarly, G. Carter Bentley (1987:26) suggests that ethnicity involves recognition of likeness and differences that derive from *habitus*, the lifestyle, values, and dispositions of particular social groups internalized early in life and reified through life experiences. Habitus, as defined by Pierre Bourdieu (1990), provides cognitive distinctions of difference because the emotional responses to unfamiliar situations or people are not voluntary but come from internalized expectations. Development of schemas of perception, thought, and action constitutes the "microprocesses by which collectivities of interest and sentiment come into existence that dispose people to act, think and feel in different ways" (Bentley 1987:26). These schemas constrain how people respond to phenomena and supply the sentiments and symbols by which shared identities are recognized.

Working from this perspective, Siân Jones (1997:13) suggests that ethnicity is based on shifting categorizations of self and others, "which are rooted in ongoing daily practice and historical experience of community members." The term *community* in this context is not a small village or town but a social field, a network of likeminded people such as a class, religion, region, and other associations (Roseberry 1996). Given its unbounded nature, a community can be imagined (Anderson 1991:15), but William Roseberry (1996:83) concedes that social fields within "primordial villages of face-to-face contact" are not. They exist in Bourdieu's (1977:80) "commonsense world" and as such are grounded in the social nature of learning in groups. By participating, people negotiate identities and cultural meaning and produce material culture that reflects shared experience in communities of practice (Lave 1988; Wenger 1998).

Ethnic symbols and practices, as well as those that embody other identities, commonly derive from widely available practices or objects. For Roseberry (1996:82), they are the "words, images, symbols, forms, organization, institutions, and movements used by subordinate populations to talk about, understand, confront, accommodate themselves to, or resist their domination." They draw upon primordial associations that illicit an emotional response and convey ideological frameworks understood by all members of a community. Language, food, clothing styles, burial practices, and other dimensions of common ancestry and cultural tradition provide these internal sources of identification as well as differentiation.

Symbols and practices that convey explicit references about groups of people have been called emblemic (Wiessner 1983). Portable or personal items are effective for signifying identity, since members may encounter affiliates in widely dispersed locations (Schortman, Urban, and Ausec 2001:314). The same can be said of practices, such as speech patterns and bodily gestures. However, emblemic symbols and practices need not derive from local contexts or common items; nor do they need to be portable or obvious to all. Elites may select foreign symbols and goods to symbolize relations to distant supernatural or unknown powers (Helms 1993). These may be large, immovable objects requiring high labor costs or esoteric knowledge to impede emulation by non-members (Schortman, Urban, and Ausec 2001:314). More problematic is the fact that very few symbols and practices communicate explicit meanings. Most don't "mean" something; rather, they "evoke" emotion and intellectual responses (Dietler and Herbich 1998:244). Recent ethnoarchaeological studies demonstrate how basic level features of material culture, such as the color of pottery framing lines (Bowser 2000) or design symmetry (Washburn 1989), signify social and political boundaries. However, while designs can provide group members with clues as to the makers of these items, outsiders may only recognize their foreignness (Bowser 2000:237; Wiessner 1983:269). Further, some community practices or symbols are not at all obvious to outsiders, such as burial practices or house-building techniques that are hidden from view most of the time (Reycraft 2005). They are learned through relationships with family, kin, and community members and prescribed by ritual. They endure because they are rooted in habitus, unlike emblemic or assertative styles and practices that are situational and fluid, rapidly changing depending on the circumstances of time and place.

Community styles and practices can materialize social boundaries, but often they do so through the expression of dialectical opposition *within* ethnic groups. Genders, age cohorts, kin groups, and polities can be marked by symbols, and trade relations may distribute them widely beyond group boundaries. Boundaries become marked not because they are emblematic of political or ethnic differences but because these items are less popular outside the group. For instance, Polly Wiessner (1983) illustrates how a shared projectile point style among the San of South Africa helped to resolve rival claims to animal kills between hunting partners and to distribute meat widely within the group rather than establish hunting territories between themselves and outsiders. Similarly, Ian Hodder's (1985) research on Kenyan calabash designs found that styles had more to do with tensions between men and women over children and economic activities than with ethnic tensions. In both cases, "emblemic" attributes were those that played the most salient role in negotiating social relations inside, rather than outside, the group.

Among the Classic Maya, community symbols and practices reflect the nested and overlapping nature of social relations expected for highly sophisticated, state-level societies. Membership in international circles was expressed through the display and exchange of elite symbols (Schortman, Urban, and Ausec 2001). A prime example is illustrated by the elaborately painted and inscribed Classic period vases, which are easily tracked across political boundaries based on their distinctive iconography and paste composition (Reents-Budet 1994:153–57). The most widely recognized political symbols are emblem glyphs, which describe kings as divine lords of a particular kingdom, found inscribed on monuments (Martin and Grube 2008) and possibly abstract motifs painted on pottery vessels (Ball and Taschek 2004; Schortman, Urban, and Ausec 2001:321).

A community identity, one based in the commonsense world of practice, has also been identified through patterned aspects of ancient Maya settlement organization, house orientation, and access to water and other resources. Jason Yaeger (2000) illustrates multiple lines of evidence for community identity at the rural settlement of San Lorenzo near the provincial capital of Xunantunich in Belize. There, houses cluster together along the alluvial terraces of the Mopan River, and their orientation is statistically different that those in nearby settlement clusters in a way that suggests they were laid out using a reference point such as a celestial body or prominent landmark. Further, all members used a local chert quarry to make their stone tools, which were distinct from those manufactured at other sources nearby. Within the Copán Valley, communities were defined by waterholes, which based on Maya hieroglyphs are referred to by place names (Fash and Davis-Salazar 2006). Copán residential clusters shared waterholes in ways similar to the modern Maya at Zinacantán, Chiapas, where kin-based residential units formed social groups (Vogt 1969). These groups maintained the waterhole and performed offerings to ancestors and water deities who resided there (ibid.:387). At Chan Nòohol, located in the greater Xunantunich hinterlands, houses were also situated adjacent to a waterhole and formed waterhole groups (Robin 1999). These studies suggest that ancient Maya community symbols and practices occurred at multiple societal scales and among many social categories.

THE HEGEMONIC PROCESS

If micro-processes shape the practices and symbols of communities, past and present, macro-processes of domination and subordination trigger ethnogenesis. Subordinate populations are subject to forms of prejudice, discrimination, segregation, and persecution at the hands of the dominant group that triggers the psychological dichotomization of "us" versus "them" (Vincent 1974). To counter these forces, they mobilize common symbols, cosmological frameworks, and everyday practices that allow them to confront or accommodate domination (Roseberry 1996:80). William Roseberry and Jay O'Brien call the strategies and outcomes of competition and conflict with outside groups, as well as internal conflict and contention within a community, the hegemonic process (Roseberry and O'Brien 1991). It is a dual process involving the internal dynamics of affiliation, in which individuals self-identify as members of an ethnic group, and external processes of attribution, in which individuals are placed in social categories by outsiders.

State leaders and bureaucracies are important agents in the hegemonic process because they have the power "to name, to identify, to categorize, to state what is what and who is who" (Brubaker and Cooper 2000:15). Leaders may instigate aggression or defend against it by allocating public goods and other resources, and they have the authority to declare the official stance in relations with outsiders (Barth 1994:19). They may allocate or deny valued resources to particular factions, fomenting self-awareness of subaltern groups and their formal legal status. In this process, some practices and symbols must be masked and others must be discovered to create dichotomous groups. It is erroneous to suggest that social cohesion, solidarity, and group consciousness are automatic within groups (Gabbert 2004:xii); rather, they must be forged through collective social action and practice. Strategies may also be implemented to foment ethnic attribution and discrimination against outsiders. For instance, the Inka and Aztec states attempted to naturalize differences between themselves and subordinate populations as a means of social and ideological control (Brumfiel 1994; Patterson 1991; Rodman and Fernandez Lopez 2005). Indeed, some of the best-recognized archaeological examples of ethnogenesis are found on the margins of expanding states (see Emberling 1997:308).

Most archaeologists agree that salient identities are forged in the face of unresolved contests and stress associated with group competition (DeBoer 1990; Hodder 1979; Jones 1997; Longacre 1991; Shennan 1989; Wiessner 1983; Wobst 1977). Among the Classic Maya, conflicts between polities are well documented in hieroglyphic texts and the building of defensive earthworks (Webster 1993). At contact, warfare was "carried out for land, slaves, control of trade routes, and for elite prestige, revenge, intrapolity political advantage, and tribute" (Webster 1999:349). With help from their allies, the Late Classic centers of Tikal and Calakmul engaged in conflicts for similar reasons. Political aggression created powerful "overkings" who brought subordinates under their control (Martin and Grube 2008). Subordinate and dominant relations were cemented through marriage and military threat. By the Terminal Classic period, warfare and raiding were endemic in many parts of the central lowlands, creating an ever-shifting landscape of political power.

Political titles and possessive prefixes that denote vassalage of one ruler to another also illustrate subordinate-dominant relations (ibid.:19). Paramount rulers held the title *k'uhul ajaw* (divine lord) or *kaloomte'* (no translation available), establishing themselves at the top of the political hierarchy that included *ajawtaak* (lords), *sajalob'* (loosely translated as regional governors, war captain, or feared one), and possibly *aj-k'uhuun* (often referred to as the "God C" title) (Houston and Inomata 2009; Jackson 2013). Possessive prefixes on titles, as illustrated by the verb clause *u-kab'jiiy* or "it was done by him," were used to refer to actions and relations between paramount and subordinate kings (Martin and Grube 2008:19).

In contrast to practices surrounding domination and subordination, resistance to oppression is not well understood for the Classic Maya. After centers were defeated in war, they often experienced architectural hiatuses, suggesting that labor and authority were siphoned off by the victors; but others, particularly those involved in status rivalries between kings, sustained only low-level effects (Webster 1993:428). Less frequently, centers were completely abandoned (Inomata 2006). Therefore, resistance may be best understood by the *consistency* of local practices through time within polities most heavily involved in conflicts. Along the peripheries of powerful regional states, kings of smaller polities were only loosely bound into multi-polity networks or eschewed interactions with paramount capitals altogether (Braswell 2007; LeCount and Yaeger 2010).

For these reasons, ethnogenesis may have occurred first in geographical regions at the boundaries of core polities in Petén. In peripheral areas, members may have maintained numerous interconnected affiliations across social networks, marked by the proliferation of community practices and symbols and the creation of new or hybrid forms. In the next section I demonstrate these ideas using data from sites in the upper Belize River valley.

CASE STUDY: SOCIAL BOUNDARIES IN THE UPPER BELIZE RIVER VALLEY

The upper Belize River valley sits at the nexus of ecological and political boundaries along the eastern periphery of the Maya lowlands (map 7.1). Comprising the area bounded by the Mopan and Macal tributaries of the Belize River, it is positioned between the hilly karst plateau of Petén and the coastal plain. Although freshwater is more abundant in Belize than it is in Petén, both have well-drained uplands and rich Mollisol soils capable of providing high returns in crop yields. As a consequence, settlement densities in the well-drained uplands of the upper Belize River valley are nearly as high as those in Petén (Ford and Fedick 1992:39). However, Petén was the home of the largest Maya cities, which far exceeded the size and population densities of centers in the eastern periphery. Nonetheless, upper Belize River valley sites, particularly Actuncan, Xunantunich, and Buenavista del Cayo overlooking the Mopan River, were strategically located and long-lived.

In the Late and Terminal Classic periods (AD 600–1000), people in this area were referred to as members of a distinct geopolitical group called the *Huk Tzuk*, or "Seven Divisions," in hieroglyphic inscriptions (Tokovinine 2013:98). Huk Tzuk people resided in Holmul, Yaxha, Naranjo, and Buenavista but were also differenti-ated into western and eastern groups. By the sixteenth and seventeenth centuries this region was part of a native province called Tz'ul Winikob, occupied by Mopan Mayan–speaking peoples (Jones 1998:3–5). It stretched from the New River in the

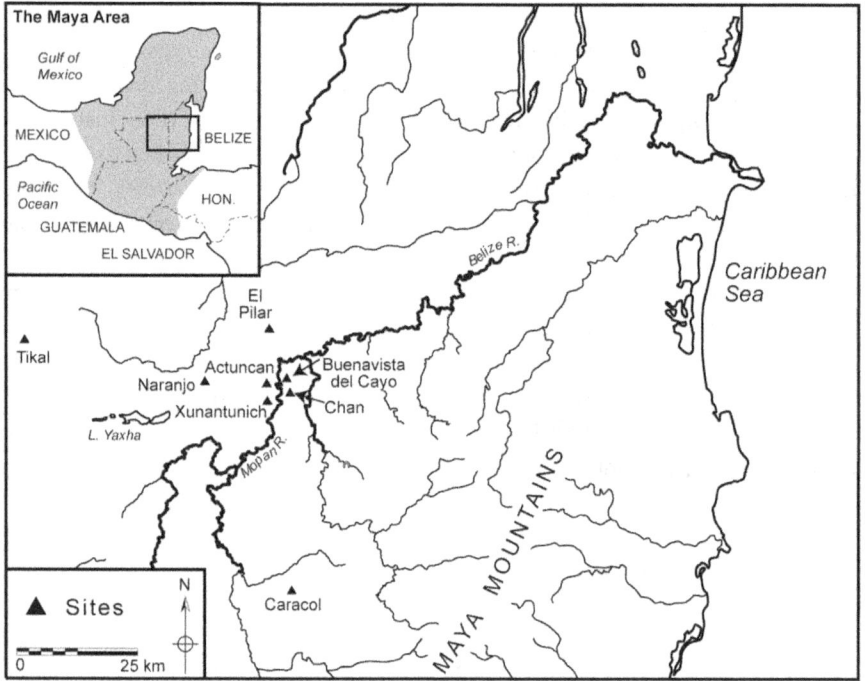

MAP 7.1. Upper Belize River valley and sites mentioned in the text

north to the Sittee River in the south and from the present-day Guatemalan border in the west to the sea. Tipuj, the political center, was located east of modern Benque Viejo del Carmen in the upper Belize River valley. It is interesting that the modern-day border between Belize and Guatemala lies very close to an ancient boundary established as early as the Classic period by the eastern Huk Tzuk people and reified by Mopan Mayan speakers of Tz'ul Winikob.

Languages spoken in the eastern periphery changed through time. Based on phonetic differences identified in hieroglyphic texts, Søren Wichmann (2006:283) suggests that Classic Ch'olan had split into eastern and western languages by AD 600. Petén texts, as well as Caracol's, contain features of both, while those within the upper Belize river valley do not demonstrate strong eastern or western features (ibid.). Apparently, Belizean texts remained linguistically neutral or followed the lingua franca of the dominant state discourse. These patterns suggest that Mayan speakers in Petén may have spoken multiple languages, but it is difficult to determine what language was spoken in the eastern periphery. The residents may have been Mopan Mayan speakers. But regardless of what language they spoke, the dynamic nature of Petén texts is in stark contrast to the texts of the upper Belize River valley and other Belizean sites.

The boundary between the upper Belize River valley and Petén regions can be explored through the three factors discussed above for ethnogenesis: sustained interaction, communities of practice, and the hegemonic process.

SUSTAINED INTERACTION

Actuncan, Xunantunich, and Buenavista del Cayo are located on hilltops above the fall line of the Mopan River and thus oversaw the flow of people and goods, as well as participated in ideas, moving along the major transportation route from the Caribbean Sea to Petén. The distribution of obsidian, perhaps more than any other trade item, illustrates sustained interaction between upper Belize Valley and Petén sites. Imported from highland Guatemala, Honduras, and Mexico, it was used by lowland populations for making fine cutting tools, projectile points, and esoteric cache objects. Availability of particular obsidian sources to centers depended on trade relations, politics, and exchange modes that shifted over time (Hammond 1972; McKillop 2004). The two most common sources—El Chayal and Ixtepeque— were traded through competing routes in the Classic period. El Chayal obsidian was transported overland from the Guatemalan highlands to the lowlands, while Ixtepeque obsidian traveled inland from the Yucatán coast after it was transported down from the highlands via the Motagua River. According to Geoffrey Braswell (2010:135), Tikal controlled interregional trade in the central lowlands.

At Actuncan and Xunantunich, populations had adequate amounts of obsidian required for daily activities and rituals, but access was more limited in scope than that reported for Petén sites (Keller 2006:474; Shults 2012). El Chayal obsidian dominates Actuncan's household assemblages, making up 77 percent of all sources, while Ixtepeque (20 percent) and other sources make up the rest. These data are consistent with those from other eastern periphery sites (Bill and Braswell 2005:311), lending evidence to suggest that much of the obsidian arrived from inland routes controlled by Tikal. In exchange, eastern periphery sites may have traded cacao and staple crops grown in the rich alluvial river valleys (Ashmore 2010:61; also McAnany et al. 2002) or served as middlemen for marine items such as shell, dried fish, and salt. Upper Belize River valley sites, therefore, may have been in direct competition with Petén polities for control over coastal resources moving along the river, or they may have established interdependent relationships with them through trade.

People, however, moved more freely across the eastern periphery boundary. What is perhaps most telling about upper Belize River valley settlements is the abundance of small house sites. Roughly 61 percent of all settlement is made up of one- or two-mound house sites (Robin, Yaeger, and Ashmore 2010). Although some of this growth was a result of household developmental cycles, it is possible that new sites in the hilly uplands east of Xunantunich housed recent immigrants (LeCount and Yaeger 2010). Here, evidence points to homogeneous settlements composed of self-sufficient, single-family households, a pattern suggestive of recently founded communities (VandenBosch, LeCount, and Yaeger 2010). Although homogeneous settlements are not definitive evidence of migrant status, they are unusual in a mature landscape as historically deep and densely populated as the upper Belize River valley.

Carolyn Freiwald's (2011) strontium isotope studies also provide evidence for the movement of peoples in this area during the Late and Terminal Classic periods. She found that 24 percent of individuals in her upper Belize River valley samples were not born near the site in which they were buried, and more than 40 percent of the Xunantunich burial population had non-local origins, the highest non-local population in her sample. Non-local individuals at Xunantunich have strontium values similar to the central Petén region, and these people were buried in non-standard body positions and orientations for the upper Belize River valley (ibid.:94). These data indicate that valley sites experienced high rates of in-migration from Petén.

Architectural styles indicate that interaction between the upper Belize River valley and Petén had a long history beginning in the Late Preclassic period around 400 BC. At Actuncan (map 7.2), the presence of Petén-style monuments attests to the site's close affiliation with other centers to the west (Mixter, Jamison, and LeCount 2013). The E-group is comparable to that found at the site of Cenote near Lake Petén Itzá (Chase and Chase 1995:93), and the "Capitoline" Triadic Group is diagnostic of Triadic Groups elsewhere in the central lowlands (von Faulkenhausen 1985:120), as is Stela 1, which depicts a dancing individual rendered in a style similar to murals at San Bartolo (Fahsen and Grube 2005). At Xunantunich, the construction of a Petén-style royal compound indicates that Xunantunich's Late Classic ruler participated in the same sociopolitical kingship system as that found in larger lowland sites (Yaeger 2010).

Pottery assemblages at Actuncan and Xunantunich contain both Petén and local Belize Valley types (Gifford 1976; LeCount 1996). Starting as early as 1000 BC, these sites shared types and styles linked to central lowland ceramic spheres, a pattern interpreted by archaeologists as indicative of widespread interaction (McAnany 2001). Types did not diverge significantly until the Classic period, when many ceramic complexes in the eastern periphery developed local style zones (Gifford 1976; LeCount 1996). Marilyn Masson (2001) also documents shrinking Classic period interaction spheres across the central lowlands in her study of common slipped wares. Royalty and nobles, nonetheless, continued to exchange pottery and ideas about what luxury pottery should look like.

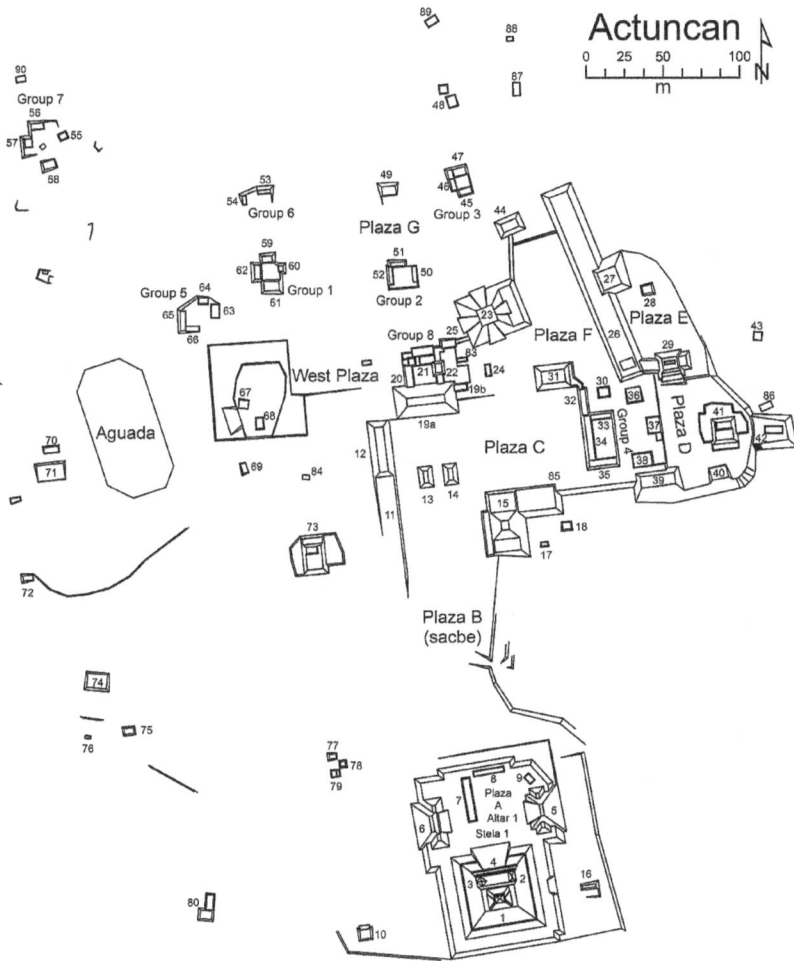

MAP 7.2. Site of Actuncan. Note the styles of the Triadic Group of Plaza A and the Cenote-style E-Group of Plaza F

One of the best examples of international-style pottery in the upper Belize River valley is the Juancy vase, which displays a Holmul dancer and a primary standard (hieroglyphic) sequence along the rim. Based on the translation of the text, it was a gift from a Naranjo k'uhul ajaw to a subordinate king who lived at Buenavista del Cayo (Houston, Stuart, and Taube 1992; Reents-Budet 1994; Taschek and Ball 1992). Sites in the region also share a black-on-cream fine-line painting style, possibly associated with members of the Naranjo ruling lineage (Reents-Budet 1994:156).

These vessels indicate that elites interacted through exchanged gifts across polity boundaries in the eastern periphery of the Maya lowlands.

ANCIENT MAYA COMMUNITIES OF PRACTICE

Although Petén influence was widespread in the eastern periphery, material culture in the area is best understood as an amalgamation of local- and Petén-style cannons. Acropolises, such as those found at Xunantunich, Caracol, and Altun Ha, were constructed in a particular eastern style, with broad and terraced platforms supporting range structures on medial terraces and multiple-story buildings on summits. In Petén, in contrast, acropolises were built on relatively low platforms and funerary structures were freestanding, such as Tikal's Temple 1 and Temple 2, which are taller and narrower than eastern pyramids. Indeed, city architecture is easily identified based on its distinctive monumental styles (Miller 1999). Monumental art programs also played an important role in creating visually distinctive regional styles. Virginia Fields (2004) suggests that a localized tradition of modeled stucco architectural sculpture occurred at Xunantunich in the Late Classic period. It combines the large facade masks reminiscent of the Late Preclassic period with the narrative style of Late Classic architectural relief sculpture.

Community identities rooted in concepts of home, village, and place on the landscape are also evident by the Late Classic period. In previous publications, I have focused on how common pottery used to cook and serve food figured prominently in the formation of a social identity (LeCount 2010a, 2010b). Common pottery displayed identity through the use of bold, simple colors, similar to the way modern Maya today express community identity on common pottery and dress (Reina and Hill 1978). Bold colors and shapes create a lasting impression of group prosperity and unity in contested environments (DeBoer 1990; Hodder 1979; Longacre 1991; Sackett 1985, 1990; Wiessner 1983). In the upper Belize River valley, two common pottery groups—Garbutt Creek and Mount Maloney—display either red- or black-slipped surfaces on similar sturdy vessel forms. These dichotomously colored pottery groups segregate into distinct style zones in the valley. The black-slipped Mount Maloney is prevalent around Xunantunich (figure 7.1), and the red-slipped Garbutt Creek is prevalent downstream (Connell 2010). Masson (2001) also documents shrinking Classic period interaction spheres across the central lowlands in her study of common slipped wares.

Other pottery styles have been postulated to signal local political affiliations. According to Joseph Ball and Jennifer Taschek (2004), Buenavista del Cayo in the upper Belize River valley expressed its political identity through the display of an emblematic device painted on fine-ware pottery. Classic period pottery motifs

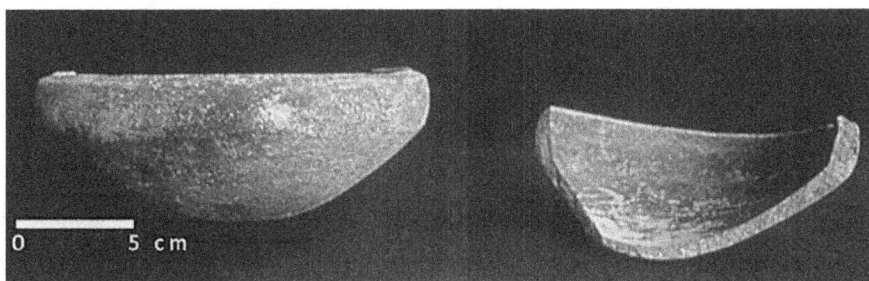

FIGURE 7.1. Mount Maloney Type bowl from Actuncan

may have acted as emblematic devices because they are based on the same kind of explicit symbolism seen in Postclassic Aztec town glyphs, Classic Mayan emblem glyphs, and modern Maya *huipil* elements. If these motifs were toponyms, they were fundamental to the way ancient people expressed place and territory (Marcus 1992:153). It is also possible that they may represent totems, a practice identified through the animal surnames of K'iche' houses (Braswell 2008) and Lacandon patrilineages (Soustelle 1935).

More hidden community practices, including burial patterns, reflect local identities. In the Belize Valley, individuals were consistently buried in an extended position with the head to the south (Awe and Helmke 2005). At Actuncan, this burial practice was maintained for more than 1,000 years, from the Terminal Preclassic through the Terminal Classic periods (figure 7.2). In Petén, Late Classic internments were more often buried oriented in the opposite direction (north), albeit there is greater variation in burial practices across Petén than in other parts of the lowlands—possibly because of greater differences in class, gender, or ethnicity in this area (Welsh 1988:221; figure 7.1).

Classic Maya Hegemonic Process

The large centers of Naranjo and Caracol are located within a day's walk of sites in the upper Belize River valley, a distance that placed Xunantunich, Actuncan, Buenavista del Cayo, and other sites easily within their sphere of influence (Schele and Mathews 1991). Naranjo's incursions into the eastern periphery are well-documented through hieroglyphic texts that describe this region as part of Naranjo's hegemony (Audet and Awe 2005:362; Houston, Stuart, and Taube 1992; Reents-Budet et al. 2005). Naranjo's rival in the area was Caracol, whose leaders also attempted to claim portions of western Belize (Iannone 2005). Caracol's efforts were aimed particularly at Cahal Pech, Baking Pot, and Pacbitun. Accounts

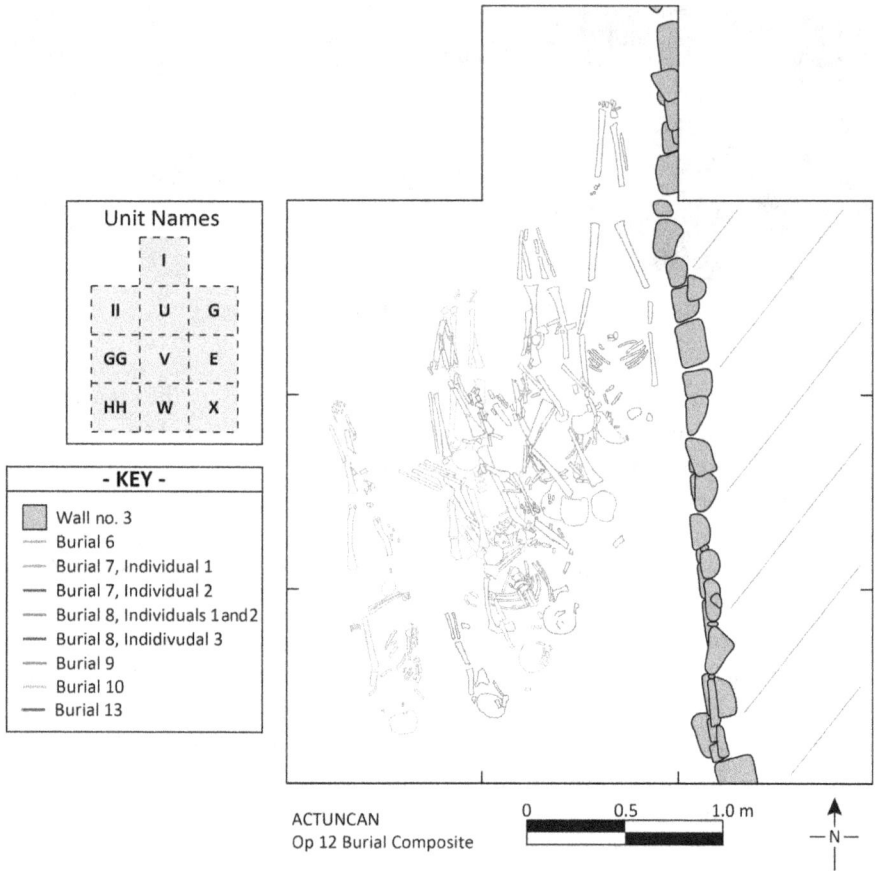

Unit Names

	I	
II	U	G
GG	V	E
HH	W	X

- KEY -

▢ Wall no. 3
Burial 6
Burial 7, Individual 1
Burial 7, Individual 2
Burial 8, Individuals 1 and 2
Burial 8, Indidivudal 3
Burial 9
Burial 10
Burial 13

ACTUNCAN
Op 12 Burial Composite

0   0.5   1.0 m

— N —

FIGURE 7.2. Upper Belize River valley burial practices at Actuncan Group 1. Courtesy, Kara Fulton, Carolyn Freiwald, and Destiny Micklin

of warfare between sites within the upper Belize River valley centers and adjacent regions indicate that competing polities struggled to maintain autonomy from the advances of both local and foreign kings (Helmke and Awe 2008).

During the Terminal Classic period, the political landscape balkanized as the hegemonies maintained by the most powerful states collapsed, and smaller polities claimed regional authority. At Xunantunich, leaders displayed their own local emblem glyph starting sometime after AD 800 and began erecting stelae not long thereafter (Helmke, Awe, and Grube 2010). At Xunantunich, Panel 2 contains a full emblem glyph, including phonetic complements and a main sign toponym translated as "divine mountainous place lord" (ibid.:106). Panel 2 also mentions a place called

Monpan, which may reference the river or possibly a region where Mopan Mayan was spoken. The final statement on the panel tells of a triple alliance of lords involved in a martial conflict, possibly a raid within the greater Naranjo area (ibid.:107). This statement appears to have been a harbinger of things to come or a commentary on continuing disputes. During the final years of the Late Classic period, Structure A-11, the ruler's residence, was marked by a desecratory termination of the kind that signaled a site's conquest (Yaeger 2010:156). Palace rooms were dismantled, vessels were smashed on the floors, and an adult male was sacrificed and left on the floor to be buried when the building was entirely filled with marl. A non-local red-slipped bowl, probably Garbutt Creek Red type, was placed on top of the marl fill. This desecratory termination, along with its symbolically charged diacritic, may have been one of many emotional actions that sparked identity politics in the region.

CONCLUSION

In sum, I make a case for Classic Maya ethnogenesis based on three cultural processes: sustained interaction, practices of identity, and the hegemonic process. Evidence for sustained interaction across lowland populations can be seen in shared material culture, religious ideology, and concepts of kingship developed by the Preclassic period. Though time, polythetic identities developed, as evidenced by the emergence of nested and overlapping symbols of international, political, and class statuses and community practices by the Late Classic period. Hegemonic processes associated with expansionistic states may have been the trigger that resulted in more explicitly differentiated cultural groups. Although elites may have continued to share cultural and political ways of understanding and acting in the world, they prompted ethnogenesis within regional populations through political aggression and subordination. Powerful polities such as Tikal and Calakmul may have facilitated the creation of basic identity groups as they subsumed allies and enemies into their hegemonic sphere of influence.

In the upper Belize River valley, the coalescence of a social boundary by the Late Classic period is marked by (1) the proliferation of symbols linked to complex networks including kin, class, and political identities, (2) stylistic diversity representing social dynamism along a zone of interaction, (3) substantial population movements, and (4) internal differentiation in the form of political groups. In the Late and Terminal Classic periods, upper Belize River valley sites were dynamic places displaying amalgamated architecture, sculpture, and pottery styles that reflected their border zone status.

Does this mean that ethnic groups can be identified in the upper Belize River valley? Part of the reason this is such a difficult question to answer is that ethnic groups in the past may have been fundamentally different from modern ethnic groups that inform our models and definitions. Modern ethnic groups arose from interactions with Colonial powers and are embedded in capitalistic social, political, and economic structures. This situation makes extrapolating our definitions of ethnicity, ethnic identity, and ethnic groups into the past problematic. Another problem is our lack of understanding of the relationships between leaders and followers, which are not recorded in Maya hieroglyphic texts and not easily elucidated from the archaeological record. Leadership is a critical component of ethnogenesis because the creation of group identity requires the mobilization of images, symbols, and actions to resist assimilation by dominant forces. Although recognizing a common enemy or foreign people is a relatively straightforward process, creating ethnic unity is not. It requires charismatic leadership and coordination. Among the historic Yucatán "Maya," kinship and town interests superseded ethnic concerns even in the face of hundreds of years of Colonial oppression (Restall 2004). Therefore, for the Classic Maya of the eastern periphery, ethnicity may have been more implicit than explicit (ibid.:75), not developing fully until the Postclassic period when groups like the Itza arose.

ACKNOWLEDGMENTS

The ideas presented here were refined after conversations with graduate students Ted Nelson, Jessica Kowalski, Emma Koenig, and Luke Donohue in a seminar on ethnicity at the University of Alabama. I also appreciate the comments of two anonymous reviewers. Bernadette Cap, David Mixter, and Kara Fulton were instrumental in producing the illustrations. Data from the Actuncan Archaeological Project were gathered with support from a National Science Foundation grant (BSC-0923747), as well as National Geographic Society Committee for Research and Exploration (9279-13) and University of Alabama College of Arts and Sciences grants.

REFERENCES CITED

Anderson, Benedict. 1991. *Imagined Communities: Reflections on the Origins and Spread of Nationalism*, 2nd ed. London: Verso.

Ashmore, Wendy. 2010. "Antecedents, Allies, Antagonists: Xunantunich and Its Neighbors." In *Classic Maya Provincial Politics: Xunantunich and Its Hinterlands*, ed. Lisa J. LeCount and Jason Yaeger, 46–66. Tucson: University of Arizona Press.

Audet, Carolyn, and Jaime Awe. 2005. "The Political Organization of the Belize Valley: Evidence from Baking Pot, Belize." *Research Reports in Belizean Archaeology* 2: 357–64.

Awe, Jaime J., and Christophe G.B. Helmke. 2005. "Alive and Kicking in the 3rd to 6th Centuries AD: Defining the Early Classic in the Belize River Valley." *Research Reports in Belizean Archaeology* 2: 39–52.

Ball, Joseph W., and Jennifer T. Taschek. 2004. "Buenavista del Cayo: A Short Outline of Occupational and Cultural History at an Upper Belize Valley Regal-Ritual Center." In *The Ancient Maya of the Belize Valley: Half a Century of Archaeological Research*, ed. James F. Garber, 149–67. Gainesville: University Press of Florida.

Barth, Fredrik. 1969. "Introduction." In *Ethnic Groups and Boundaries*, ed. Fredrik Barth, 9–38. Oslo, Norway: Johansen and Nielsen Boktrykkeri.

Barth, Fredrik. 1994. "Enduring and Emerging Issues in the Analysis of Ethnicity." In *The Anthropology of Ethnicity: Beyond "Ethnic Groups and Boundaries,"* ed. Hans Vermeulen and Cora Govers, 11–32. Long Grove, IL: Waveland.

Beliaev, Dmitri D. 2000. "Wuk Tsuk and Oklahun Tsuk: Naranjo and Tikal in the Late Classic." In *The Sacred and the Profane: Architecture and Identity in the Maya Lowlands*, ed. Pierre Robert Colas, 63–81. Markt Schwaben, Germany: A Saurwein.

Bentley, G. Carter. 1987. "Ethnicity and Practice." *Comparative Studies in Society and History* 29 (1): 24–55. http://dx.doi.org/10.1017/S001041750001433X.

Bill, Cassandra R., and Geoffrey E. Braswell. 2005. "Life at the Crossroads: New Data from Pusilha, Belize." *Research Reports in Belizean Archaeology* 2: 301–12.

Bourdieu, Pierre. 1977. *Outline of a Theory of Practice*. Cambridge: Cambridge University Press. http://dx.doi.org/10.1017/CBO9780511812507.

Bourdieu, Pierre. 1990. *The Logic of Practice*. Cambridge: Polity.

Bowser, Brenda. 2000. "From Pottery to Politics: An Ethnoarchaeological Study of Political Factionalism, Ethnicity, and Domestic Pottery Style in the Ecuadorian Amazon." *Journal of Archaeological Method and Theory* 7 (3): 219–48. http://dx.doi.org/10.1023/A:1026510620824.

Braswell, Geoffrey. 2003. "Understanding Early Classic Interaction between Kaminaljuyu and Central Mexico." In *The Maya and Teotihuacan: Reinterpreting Early Classic Interaction*, ed. Geoffrey Braswell, 105–42. Austin: University of Texas Press.

Braswell, Geoffrey. 2007. "Late and Terminal Classic Occupation of Pusilha, Toledo District, Belize: Site Planning, Burial Patterns, and Cosmology." *Research Reports in Belizean Archaeology* 4: 67–77.

Braswell, Geoffrey. 2008. "The Construction of K'iche'an Identity and the Problem of Ethnicity." Paper presented at the symposium (Re)constructing Identity; the Archaeology of the Pacific Coast and Highlands of Chiapas and Guatemala, organized by Claudia Garcia-Des Lauriers and Michael Love, Vancouver, BC, March 26–30.

Braswell, Geoffrey. 2010. "The Rise and Fall of Market Exchange: A Dynamic Approach to Ancient Maya Economy." In *Archaeological Approaches to Market Exchange in Ancient*

Societies, ed. Christopher P. Garraty and Barbara L. Stark, 127–40. Boulder: University Press of Colorado.

Brubaker, Rogers, and Fredrick Cooper. 2000. "Beyond Identity." *Theory and Society* 29 (1): 1–47. http://dx.doi.org/10.1023/A:1007068714468.

Brumfiel, Elizabeth M. 1994. "Ethnic Groups and Political Development in Ancient Mexico." In *Factional Competition and Political Development in the New World*, ed. Elizabeth M. Brumfiel and John W. Fox, 89–102. Cambridge: Cambridge University Press. http://dx.doi.org/10.1017/CBO9780511598401.009.

Buikstra, Jane E. 1997. "Studying Maya Bioarchaeology." In *Bones of the Maya: Studies of Ancient Skeletons*, ed. Stephen Whittington and David Reed, 221–28. Washington, DC: Smithsonian Institution Press.

Chase, Arlen F., and Diane Z. Chase. 1995. "External Impetus, Internal Synthesis, and Standardization: E Group Assemblages and the Crystalization of Classic Maya Society in the Southern Lowlands." *Acta Mesoamericana* 8: 87–101.

Clark, John E., and Richard D. Hansen. 2001. "The Architecture of Early Kingship and the Origins of the Mesoamerican Royal Court." In *The Royal Courts of the Ancient Maya*, vol 2: *Data and Case Studies*, ed. Takeshi Inomata and Stephen D. Houston, 1–45. Boulder: Westview.

Cohen, Ronald. 1978. "Ethnicity: Problem of Focus in Anthropology." *Annual Review of Anthropology* 7 (1): 379–403. http://dx.doi.org/10.1146/annurev.an.07.100178.002115.

Comaroff, John L. 1987. "Of Totemism and Ethnicity: Consciousness, Practice and the Signs of Inequality." *Ethnos* 3–4: 310–23.

Connell, Samuel. 2010. "A Community to Be Counted: Negotiating the Place of Chaa Creek in the Emerging Xunantunich Polity." In *Provincial Politics: The Classic Maya Center of Xunantunich and Its Hinterlands*, ed. Lisa J. LeCount and Jason Yaeger, 295–314. Tucson: University of Arizona Press.

DeBoer, Warren. 1990. "Interaction, Imitation, and Communication as Expressed in Style: The Ucayali Experience." In *Uses of Style in Archaeology*, ed. Margaret W. Conkey and Christine A. Hastorf, 82–104. Cambridge: Cambridge University Press.

Demarest, Arthur A. 2003. *Ancient Maya: The Rise and Fall of a Rainforest Civilization*. Cambridge: Cambridge University Press.

Demarest, Arthur A. 2013. "Ideological Pathways to Economic Exchange: Religion, Economy, and Legitimation at the Classic Maya Royal Capital of Cancuen." *Latin American Antiquity* 24 (4): 371–402. http://dx.doi.org/10.7183/1045-6635.24.4.371.

Dietler, Michael, and Ingrid Herbich. 1998. "Habitus, Techniques, Style: An Integrated Approach to the Social Understanding of Material Culture and Boundaries." In *The Archaeology of Social Boundaries*, ed. Miriam T. Stark, 232–63. Washington, DC: Smithsonian Institution Press.

Emberling, Geoff. 1997. "Ethnicity in Complex Societies: Archaeological Perspectives." *Journal of Archaeological Research* 5 (4): 295–344. http://dx.doi.org/10.1007/BF02229256.

Fahsen, Federico, and Nikolai Grube. 2005. "The Origins of Maya Writing." In *Lords of Creation: The Origins of Sacred Maya Kingship*, ed. Virginia Fields and Dorie Reents-Budet, 74–79. Los Angeles: Los Angeles County Museum of Art and Scala Publishers.

Fash, Barbara W., and Karla L. Davis-Salazar. 2006. "Copán Water Ritual and Management: Imagery and Sacred Place." In *Precolumbian Water Management: Ideology, Ritual, and Power*, ed. Lucy J. Lucero and Barbara W. Fash, 126–43. Tucson: University of Arizona Press.

Fash, William L. 2004. "Toward a Social History of the Copán Valley." In *Copán: The History of an Ancient Maya Kingdom*, ed. E. Wyllys Andrews and William L. Fash, 73–102. Santa Fe: School of American Research Press.

Fields, Virginia. 2004. "The Royal Charter at Xunantunich." In *The Ancient Maya of the Belize Valley: Half a Century of Archaeological Research*, ed. James F. Garber, 180–90. Gainesville: University Press of Florida.

Flannery, Kent V., and Joyce Marcus. 2000. "Formative Mexican Chiefdoms and the Myth of the 'Mother Culture.'" *Journal of Anthropological Archaeology* 19 (1): 1–37. http://dx.doi.org/10.1006/jaar.1999.0359.

Ford, Anabel, and Scott L. Fedick. 1992. "Prehistoric Maya Settlement Patterns in the Upper Belize River Area: Initial Results of the Belize River Archaeological Settlement Survey." *Journal of Field Archaeology* 19 (1): 35–49. http://dx.doi.org/10.1179/009346992791549012.

Freiwald, Carolyn. 2011. "Patterns of Population Movement at Xunantunich, Cahal Pech, and Baking Pot during the Late and Terminal Classic (AD 600–900)." *Research Reports in Belizean Archaeology* 8: 89–100.

Gabbert, Wolfgang. 2004. *Becoming Maya: Ethnicity and Social Inequality in Yucatan since 1500*. Tucson: University of Arizona Press.

Garber, James F., M. Kathryn Brown, W. David Driver, David M. Glassman, Christopher J. Hartman, F. Kent Reilly III, and Lauren A. Sullivan. 2004. "Archaeological Investigations at Blackman Eddy." In *The Ancient Maya of the Belize Valley: Half a Century of Archaeological Research*, ed. James F. Garber, 48–69. Gainesville: University of Florida Press.

Gifford, James C. 1976. *Prehistoric Pottery Analysis and the Ceramics of Barton Ramie in the Belize Valley*. Memoirs of the Peabody Museum of Archaeology and Ethnology, vol. 18. Cambridge, MA: Harvard University.

Gosselain, Olivier P. 2000. "Materializing Identities: An African Perspective." *Journal of Archaeological Method and Theory* 7 (3): 187–217. http://dx.doi.org/10.1023/A:1026558503986.

Hammond, Norman. 1972. "Obsidian Trade Routes in the Mayan Area." *Science* 178 (4065): 1092–93. http://dx.doi.org/10.1126/science.178.4065.1092.

Hammond, Norman. 1991. "The Maya and Their Civilization." In *Cuello: An Early Maya Community in Belize*, ed. Norman Hammond, 1–7. Cambridge: Cambridge University Press.

Healey, Paul. 1990. "Excavations at Pacbitun, Belize: Preliminary Report on the 1986 and 1987 Investigations." *Journal of Field Archaeology* 17: 247–62.

Hegmon, Michelle. 1998. "Technology, Style, and Social Practices: Archaeological Approaches." In *The Archaeology of Social Boundaries*, ed. Miriam T. Stark, 264–80. Washington, DC: Smithsonian Institution Press.

Helmke, Christophe, and Jaime Awe. 2008. "Organizacion Territorial de los Antiguos Maya de Belice Central: Confluencia de Datos Argueologicos y Epigraficos." *Mayab* 20: 65–91.

Helmke, Christophe, Jaime Awe, and Nikolai Grube. 2010. "The Monuments and Inscriptions of Xunantunich: Implications for Terminal Classic Socio-Political Relationships in the Belize Valley." In *Provincial Politics: The Late and Terminal Classic Maya Site of Xunantunich and Its Hinterlands*, ed. Lisa J. LeCount and Jason Yaeger, 97–121. Tucson: University of Arizona Press.

Helms, Mary W. 1993. *Craft and the Kingly Ideal: Art, Trade, and Power*. Austin: University of Texas Press.

Hodder, Ian. 1979. "Economic and Social Stress and Material Culture Patterning." *American Antiquity* 44 (3): 446–54. http://dx.doi.org/10.2307/279544.

Hodder, Ian. 1985. "Boundaries as Strategies: An Ethnoarchaeological Study." In *The Archaeology of Frontiers and Boundaries*, ed. S. W. Green and S. M. Perlman, 141–59. New York: Academic. http://dx.doi.org/10.1016/B978-0-12-298780-9.50013-8.

Houston, Stephen D., and Takeshi Inomata. 2009. *The Classic Maya*. New York: Cambridge University Press.

Houston, Stephen D., David Stuart, and Karl Taube. 1992. "Image and Text on the 'Jauncy Vase.'" In *The Maya Vase Book: A Corpus of Rollout Photographs of Maya Vases*, vol. 3, ed. Justin Kerr, 498–513. New York: Kerr Associates.

Iannone, Gyles. 2005. "The Rise and Fall of an Ancient Maya Petty Royal Court." *Latin American Antiquity* 16 (1): 26–44. http://dx.doi.org/10.2307/30042485.

Inomata, Tasheki. 2006. *Warfare and the Fall of a Fortified Center: Archaeological Investigations at Aguateca*. Nashville, TN: Vanderbilt University Press.

Inomata, Takeshi, Daniela Triadan, Kazuo Aoyama, Victor Castillo, and Hitoshi Yonenobu. 2013. "Early Ceremonial Constructions at Ceibal, Guatemala, and the Origins of Lowland Maya Civilization." *Science* 340 (6131): 467–71. http://dx.doi.org /10.1126/science.1234493.

Jackson, Sarah E. 2013. *Politics of the Maya Court: Hierarchy and Change in the Late Classic Period*. Norman: University of Oklahoma Press.

Jones, Grant D. 1998. *The Conquest of the Last Maya Kingdom*. Stanford: Stanford University Press.

Jones, Siân. 1997. *The Archaeology of Ethnicity*. London: Routledge. http://dx.doi.org/10 .4324/9780203438732.

Joyce, Rosemary. 2000. *Gender and Power in Prehispanic Mesoamerica*. Austin: University of Texas Press.

Joyce, Rosemary. 2001. "Negotiating Sex and Gender in Classic Maya Society." In *Gender in Pre-Hispanic America*, ed. Cecelia F. Klien, 109–41. Washington, DC: Dumbarton Oaks.

Keller, Angela H. 2006. "Roads to the Center: The Design, Use, and Meaning of the Roads of Xunantunich, Belize." PhD dissertation, Department of Anthropology, University of Pennsylvania, Philadelphia.

Lave, Jean. 1988. *Cognition in Practice: Mind, Mathematics, and Culture in Everyday Life*. Cambridge: Cambridge University Press. http://dx.doi.org/10.1017/CBO9780511609268.

LeCount, Lisa J. 1996. "Pottery and Power: Feasting, Gifting, and Displaying Wealth among the Late and Terminal Classic Lowland Maya." PhD dissertation, Department of Anthropology, University of California, Los Angeles.

LeCount, Lisa J. 2010a. "Mount Maloney People? Domestic Pots, Everyday Practice, and the Social Formation of the Xunantunich Polity." In *Provincial Politics: The Classic Maya Center of Xunantunich and Its Hinterlands*, ed. Lisa J. LeCount and Jason Yaeger, 209–32. Tucson: University of Arizona Press.

LeCount, Lisa J. 2010b. "Ka'kaw Pots and Common Containers: Creating Histories and Collective Memories among the Classic Maya of Xunantunich, Belize." *Ancient Mesoamerica* 21 (2): 341–51. http://dx.doi.org/10.1017/S095653611000026X.

LeCount, Lisa J., and Jason Yaeger. 2010. "Conclusions: Placing Xunantunich and Its Hinterland Settlements in Perspective." In *Provincial Politics: The Classic Maya Center of Xunantunich and Its Hinterlands*, ed. Lisa J. LeCount and Jason Yaeger, 337–69. Tucson: University of Arizona Press.

Lightfoot, Kent, and Antoinette Martinez. 1995. "Frontiers and Boundaries in Archaeological Perspective." *Annual Review of Anthropology* 24 (1): 471–92. http://dx .doi.org/10.1146/annurev.an.24.100195.002351.

Longacre, William A. 1991. "Sources of Ceramic Variability among the Kalinga of Northern Luzon." In *Ceramic Ethnoarchaeology: An Introduction*, ed. William A. Longacre, 95–111. Tucson: University of Arizona Press.

Marcus, Joyce. 1992. *Mesoamerican Writing Systems*. Princeton, NJ: Princeton University Press.

Martin, Simon, and Nikolai Grube. 2008. *Chronicle of the Maya Kings and Queens: Deciphering the Dynasties of the Ancient Maya*, 2nd ed. New York: Thames and Hudson.

Masson, Marilyn A. 2001. "Changing Patterns of Ceramic Stylistic Diversity in the Pre-Hispanic Maya Lowlands." *Acta Archaeologica* 72 (2): 159–88. http://dx.doi.org/10.1034/j.1600-0390.2001.720207.x.

Masson, Marilyn A., and Carlos Peraza Lope. 2010. "Evidence for Maya-Mexican Interaction in the Archaeological Record of Mayapan." In *Astronomers, Scribes, and Priests: Intellectual Interchange between the Northern Maya Lowlands and Highland Mexico in the Late Postclassic Period*, ed. Gabrielle Vail and Christine Hernandez, 77–114. Washington, DC: Dumbarton Oaks.

McAnany, Patricia. 2001. "Cosmology and the Institutionalization of Hierarchy in the Maya Region." In *From Leaders to Rulers*, ed. Jonathan Haas, 125–48. New York: Kluwer Academic/Plenum. http://dx.doi.org/10.1007/978-1-4615-1297-4_7.

McAnany, Patricia, Polly Peterson, Ben Thomas, Steve Morandi, and Eleanor Harrison. 2002. "Praise the Ajaw and Pass the Kakaw: Xibun Maya and the Luxury Economy of Cacao." In *Ancient Maya Political Economies: Essays in Honor of William L. Rathje*, ed. Marilyn Masson and David Freidel, 123–39. Walnut Creek, CA: Altamira.

McKillop, Heather. 2004. "The Ancient Maya Trading Port on Moho Cay." In *The Ancient Maya of the Belize Valley: Half a Century of Archaeological Research*, ed. James F. Garber, 257–72. Gainesville: University Press of Florida.

Miller, Mary Ellen. 1999. *Maya Art and Architecture*. London: Thames and Hudson.

Mixter, David, Thomas Jamison, and Lisa J. LeCount. 2013. "Actuncan's Noble Court: New Insights into Political Strategies of an Enduring Center in the Upper Belize River Valley." *Research Reports in Belizean Archaeology* 10: 93–106.

Naroll, Raoul, Ronald M. Berndt, Frank D. Bessac, Eliot D. Chapple, Gertrude E. Dole, Harold E. Driver, Paul Ducey, Melvin Ember, Helmuth Fuchs, Hans Hoffmann et al. 1964. "On Ethnic Unit Classification." *Current Anthropology* 5 (4): 283–312. http://dx.doi.org/10.1086/200501.

Patterson, Thomas C. 1991. *The Inca Empire: The Formation and Disintegration of a Pre-Capitalist State*. Oxford: Berg.

Reents-Budet, Dorie. 1994. *Painting the Maya Universe: Royal Ceramics of the Classic Period*. Durham, NC: Duke University Press.

Reents-Budet, Dorie, Ronald L. Bishop, Carolyn Audet, Jaime Awe, and M. James Blackman. 2005. "Act Locally, Think Internationally: The Pottery of Baking Pot, Belize." *Research Reports in Belizean Archaeology* 2: 365–86.

Reina, Rueben E., and Robert M. Hill II. 1978. *The Traditional Pottery of Guatemala*. Austin: University of Texas Press.

Restall, Matthew. 2004. "Maya Ethnogenesis." *Journal of Latin American Anthropology* 9 (1): 64–89. http://dx.doi.org/10.1525/jlca.2004.9.1.64.

Reycraft, Richard M. 2005. "Style Change and Ethnogenesis among the Chiribaya of Far South Coastal Peru." In *Us and Them: Archaeology and Ethnicity in the Andes*, ed. Richard M. Reycraft, 54–77. Monograph 53. Los Angeles: Cotsen Institute of Archaeology, University of California.

Ringle, William M., Tomás Gallareta Negrón, and George J. Bey. 1998. "The Return of Quetzalcoatl." *Ancient Mesoamerica* 9 (2): 183–232. http://dx.doi.org/10.1017/S095 6536100001954.

Robin, Cynthia. 1999. "Towards an Archaeology of Everyday Life: Ancient Maya Farmers of Chan Nòohl and Dos Chombitos Cikín." PhD dissertation, Department of Anthropology, University of Pennsylvania, Philadelphia.

Robin, Cynthia, Jason Yaeger, and Wendy Ashmore. 2010. "Political Assertion, Settlement Expansion, and Everyday Life in the Xunantunich Hinterland." In *Provincial Politics: The Classic Maya Center of Xunantunich and Its Hinterlands*, ed. Lisa J. LeCount and Jason Yaeger, 315–36. Tucson: University of Arizona Press.

Rodman, Amy O., and Gioconda A. Fernandez Lopez. 2005. "North Coast Style after Moche: Clothing and Identity at El Brujo, Chicama Valley, Peru." In *Us and Them: Archaeology and Ethnicity in the Andes*, ed. Richard M. Reycraft, 115–33. Los Angeles: Cotsen Institute of Archaeology, University of California.

Roseberry, William. 1996. "Hegemony, Power, and Languages of Contention." In *The Politics of Difference*, ed. Edwin N. Wilmsen and Patrick McAllister, 71–85. Chicago: University of Chicago Press.

Roseberry, William, and Jay O'Brien. 1991. "Introduction." In *Golden Ages, Dark Ages: Imaging the Past in Anthropology and History*, ed. Jay O'Brien and William Roseberry, 1–8. Berkeley: University of California Press.

Sackett, James R. 1985. "Style and Ethnicity in the Kalahari: A Reply to Wiessner." *American Antiquity* 50 (1): 154–59. http://dx.doi.org/10.2307/280642.

Sackett, James R. 1990. "Style and Ethnicity in Archaeology: The Case for Isochrestism." In *Uses of Style in Archaeology*, ed. Margaret W. Conkey and Christine A. Hastorf, 32–43. Cambridge: Cambridge University Press.

Schele, Linda, and Peter Mathews. 1991. "Royal Visits and Other Intersite Relationships among the Classic Maya." In *Classic Maya Political History: Hieroglyphic and Archaeological Evidence*, ed. T. Patrick Culbert, 226–52. Cambridge: Cambridge University Press.

Schortman, Edward, and Seiichi Nakamura. 1991. "A Crisis of Identity: Late Classic Competition and Interaction on the Southeast Maya Periphery." *Latin American Antiquity* 2 (4): 311–36. http://dx.doi.org/10.2307/971781.

Schortman, Edward M., Patricia A. Urban, and Marne Ausec. 2001. "Politics with Style: Identity Formation in Prehispanic Southeastern Mesoamerica." *American Anthropologist* 103 (2): 312–30. http://dx.doi.org/10.1525/aa.2001.103.2.312.

Sharer, Robert. 1993. "The Social Organization of the Late Classic Maya: Problems of Definition and Approaches." In *Lowland Maya Civilization in the Eighth Century AD*, ed. Jeremy A. Sabloff and John S. Henderson, 91–110. Washington, DC: Dumbarton Oaks.

Shennan, Steven J. 1989. "Introduction." In *Archaeological Approaches to Cultural Identity*, ed. Steven J. Shennan, 1–32. London: Unwin and Hyman.

Shults, Sara C. 2012. "Uncovering Ancient Maya Exchange Networks: Using the Distributional Approach to Interpret Obsidian Exchange at Actuncan, Belize." Master's thesis, Department of Anthropology, University of Alabama, Tuscaloosa.

Soustelle, Jacques. 1935. "Le Totemisme des Lacandones." *Maya Research* 2: 325–44.

Stark, Mirian T., ed. 1998. *The Archaeology of Social Boundaries*. Washington, DC: Smithsonian Institution Press.

Taschek, Jennifer, and Joseph W. Ball. 1992. "Lord Smoke-Squirrel's Cacao Cup: The Archaeological Context and Socio-Historical Significance of the Buenavista 'Jauncy Vase.'" In *The Maya Vase Book*, vol. 3, ed. Justin Kerr, 490–98. New York: Kerr Associates.

Tokovinine, Alexandre. 2013. *Place and Identity in Classic Maya Narratives*. Studies in Pre-Columbian Art and Archaeology 37. Washington, DC: Dumbarton Oaks.

VandenBosch, Jon, Lisa LeCount, and Jason Yaeger. 2010. "Integration and Interdependence: The Domestic Economy of the Xunantunich Polity." In *Provincial Politics: The Classic Maya Center of Xunantunich and Its Hinterlands*, ed. Lisa J. LeCount and Jason Yaeger, 272–94. Tucson: University of Arizona Press.

Vincent, Joan. 1974. "The Structuring of Ethnicity." *Human Organization* 33 (4): 375–79. http://dx.doi.org/10.17730/humo.33.4.2k10l667117p4513.

Vogt, Evon Z. 1969. *Zinacantan: A Maya Community in the Highlands of Chiapas*. Cambridge, MA: Harvard University Press. http://dx.doi.org/10.4159/harvard.978 0674436886.

von Faulkenhausen, Lothar. 1985. "Architecture." In *A Consideration of the Early Classic Period in the Maya Lowlands*, ed. Gordon R. Willey and Peter Mathews, 111–34. Institute for Mesoamerican Studies, Publication 10. Albany: State University of New York Press.

Washburn, Dorothy. 1989. "The Property of Symmetry and the Concept of Ethnic Style." In *Archaeological Approaches to Cultural Identity*, ed. Stephen Shennan, 157–73. London: Allen and Unwin.

Webster, David. 1993. "The Study of Maya Warfare: What It Tells Us about the Maya and What It Tells Us about Maya Archaeology." In *Lowland Maya Civilization in the Eighth*

Century AD, ed. Jeremy A. Sabloff and John S. Henderson, 415–44. Washington, DC: Dumbarton Oaks.

Webster, David. 1999. "Ancient Maya Warfare." In *War and Society in the Ancient and Medieval Worlds*, ed. Kurt Raaflaub and Nathan Rosenstien, 333–60. Cambridge, MA: Harvard University Press.

Welsh, W. Bruce M. 1988. *An Analysis of Classic Lowland Maya Burials.* BAR International Series 409. Oxford: British Archaeological Reports.

Wenger, Etienne. 1998. *Communities of Practice: Learning, Meaning, and Identity.* Cambridge: Cambridge University Press. http://dx.doi.org/10.1017/CBO97 80511803932.

Wichmann, Søren. 2006. "Mayan Historical Linguistics and Epigraphy: A New Synthesis." *Annual Review of Anthropology* 35 (1): 279–94. http://dx.doi.org/10.1146/annurev.ant hro.35.081705.123257.

Wiessner, Polly. 1983. "Style and Social Information in Kalahari San Projectile Points." *American Antiquity* 48 (2): 253–76. http://dx.doi.org/10.2307/280450.

Wiessner, Polly. 1985. "Style or Isochretic Variation—a Reply to Sackett." *American Antiquity* 50: 160–66.

Wobst, H. Martin. 1977. "Stylistic Behavior and Information Exchange." In *For the Director: Research Essays in Honor of James B. Griffin*, ed. Charles E. Cleland, 317–42. Anthropological Papers, vol. 61. Ann Arbor: Michigan Museum of Anthropology.

Wright, Lori E. 2004. "Osteological Investigations of Ancient Maya Lives." In *Continuities and Changes in Maya Archaeology: Perspectives at the Millennium*, ed. Charles W. Golden and Greg Borgstede, 201–15. New York: Routledge.

Wright, Lori E., and Christine D. White. 1996. "Human Biology in the Classic Maya Collapse: Evidence from Paleopathology and Paleodiet." *Journal of World Prehistory* 10 (2): 147–98. http://dx.doi.org/10.1007/BF02221075.

Yaeger, Jason. 2000. "The Social Construction of Communities in the Classic Maya Countryside: Strategies of Affiliation in Western Belize." In *The Archaeology of Communities: A New World Perspective*, ed. Marcello A. Canuto and Jason Yaeger, 123–42. London: Routledge.

Yaeger, Jason. 2010. "Shifting Political Dynamics as Seen from the Xunantunich Palace." In *Classic Maya Provincial Politics: Xunantunich and Its Hinterlands*, ed. Lisa J. LeCount and Jason Yaeger, 145–60. Tucson: University of Arizona Press.

8

He's Maya, but He's Not My Brother

Exploring the Place of Ethnicity in Classic Maya Social Organization

DAMIEN B. MARKEN, STANLEY P. GUENTER, AND DAVID A. FREIDEL

> Ethnic distinctions do not depend on an absence of social interaction
> and acceptance, but are quite to the contrary often the very foundations
> on which embracing social systems are built. Interaction in such a social
> system does not lead to its liquidation through change and acculturation;
> cultural differences can persist despite inter-ethnic contact and interde-
> pendence. (Barth 1969:10)

Several years ago, while excavating a large temple at Palenque in Chiapas, Mexico, a
local workman asked one of the authors, "What happened to the Maya?" Slightly
confused, Marken asked what he meant. He said he was curious as to why the Maya
"disappeared." So Marken explained, in general terms, that while the large Classic
period centers such as Palenque and Tikal were largely abandoned, the Maya as a
people did not really go anywhere. In fact, Marken pointed out, the man himself
was Maya, as were most of the project's workmen. With an odd look, he responded
adamantly that no, he was not Maya, he was Tzeltal. So were the other workmen
from his *ejido*. A few workmen from another ejido were Chol. He did finally con-
cede that maybe the Lacandon selling wares at the site entrance were Maya, but he
certainly was not.

This conversation, experienced by many archaeologists working throughout the
Maya area, illustrates contemporary ethnic boundary maintenance in the Maya lowlands. But who or what does the term *Maya* describe? Although a seemingly simple

DOI: 10.5876/9781607325673.c008

question, it is anything but, and answers are greatly dependent upon one's own subjective perspective.[1] Despite the best efforts of the pan-Maya movement, numerous "Maya" groups still refuse to recognize a common ethnic ancestry (Samson, this volume). Linguistic and cultural differences continue to separate communities, even those located in spatial proximity.

With Fredrik Barth (1969:11) as a starting point, we define an ethnic group as a population that recognizes itself "as constituting a category distinguishable from other categories of the same order." As this implies and as the Maya case demonstrates, ethnic affiliation can also be ascribed to a group by others. The emic and etic identifying markers of difference may or may not diverge widely, which can carry strong implications for analysis (e.g., Eidheim 1969). Differentiating ethnic groups from other forms of social identity is the emic perception that members share a culturally constructed common ancestry that includes groups larger than family, lineage, or "house" (Emberling 1997:302–3).

To incorporate the greatest overlap and disjunction between potential emic and etic criteria, we envision "the Maya" as a macro-ethnic group composed of numerous smaller and localized ethnic groupings. As applied here, this "macro-ethnicity" is of necessity a simplified and academic etic designation based on a common linguistic family, rough geographic contiguity, and broadly shared similarities in subsistence techniques, including the centrality of maize to the diet. In contrast, the localized ethnic groups that jointly form Maya macro-ethnicity are defined emically and do not necessarily recognize a common ethnic affiliation with each other.[2] Often, a shared connection to a specific physical or mythic place and bonds created by speaking a specific Mayan language forms the basis of these localized identities (e.g., Siverts 1969; Vogt 1993). A critical aspect of localized Maya ethnicities is that they are defined not only by inclusion but also by those excluded from membership (see Barth 1969).

Considering Colonial, as well as post-Colonial, attempts to assimilate and integrate Maya groups as a whole into "modern" society, it seems unlikely that the existence of ethnic divisions between various Maya peoples is a recent phenomenon (Watanabe 2004:38). Assuming that Maya ethnic differentiation does have its roots in the deep past, the ancient social and political landscape would have been far more complex than currently conceived by most Mayanists. In this chapter we attempt to enhance current models of ancient Maya social organization by evaluating the potential input from perspectives of ethnic group formation and maintenance. The often-unexplored theoretical potential of ethnicity in archaeology can open new interpretive doors into the material interpretation of processes effecting intra-polity social bonds (influencing elite-elite, elite-commoner, and commoner-commoner relations). In this vein, our goals are twofold: (1) to demonstrate the interpretive benefits and pitfalls of incorporating conceptions of ethnic identity in modeling the social relations comprising Classic Maya polities, and (2) to begin inquiry into the interplay between ethnic and class identity at the Classic site of Palenque, Chiapas. These goals expand the theoretical territory for explaining the increasingly apparent regional variability across the Maya lowlands.

ETHNICITY IN THE MAYA LOWLANDS

Research on ethnicity in several world regions demonstrates the great difficulty in identifying ethnic groups archaeologically (e.g., Aldenderfer and Stanish 1993; Bernardini 2005; Emberling 1997; Emberling and Yoffee 1999; Hegmon 1998; Jones 1997; Stanish 1989). Ethnic identifications and boundaries can shift and change rapidly (though see Wilson [1993:122]). Furthermore, they can often be expressed in media that preserve poorly (e.g., Schortman 1989:56). Theoretically, the multi-focal and situational nature of ethnicity hampers the scope with which any single perspective can inform *all* aspects of ethnic identity. Primordialist, instrumentalist, subjectivist, and objectivist perspectives each focus on different relational dimensions of the form of social groupings cataloged under the rubric of ethnicity (Banks 1996; Barth 1994; Eriksen 1991; Jones 1997:13; Wade 1997; Wilson 1993).[3]

In attempting to circumvent these theoretical difficulties, several researchers advocate documenting changes and differences in *habitus* between and within archaeological spatial groups (Bourdieu 1977; see Aldenderfer and Stanish 1993; Janusek 2003; Jones 1997:88–96; Stanish 1989; Stark 2008). Jones (1997:13, 96) in particular emphasizes the importance of intersections between habitus and social context. While this chapter focuses largely on ways particular cultural symbols are manipulated to advance group-specific interests, their interpreted impact is nevertheless grounded in a *potentially* shared habitus between multiple, hierarchically organized local populations (ibid.:75; McAnany 1995). The difficulty in generalizing about polity-wide material processes generated by habitus in the tropical lowlands somewhat mitigates the applicability of giving primacy to practice theory in reconstructing ancient Maya ethnic categorizes. There have been relatively few systematic comparative studies of the social import of daily activities in constructing identities—as reconstructed from archaeological data—between multiple residential groups at a particular Maya site (e.g., Gerstle 1988; Hendon 1991; LeCount 2001; Piehl 2005; Sheets et al. 1990; see also Janusek 2003, 2008).

Moreover, the opening anecdote unfortunately typifies several potential limitations to simplistically distinguishing ethnic habitus materially, even among contemporary Maya groups. While Lacandon dress is visibly distinct, Tzeltals and Chol individuals dress similarly, perform the same jobs, and eat the same foods. Their houses are built of similar materials and contain many of the same general items. Instead, cultural elements such as language, place of residence, and a sense of common history define group identity.[4] Recent diachronic theoretical and empirical considerations of ethnic differentiation in Mesoamerica support the significance of "place" in defining prehispanic ethnic and political affiliations (e.g., Berdan 2008a; Stark and Chance 2008; see also Grosby 1995). Ethnohistoric and ethnographic data confirm the continuing weight specifically given to conceptions of common history and geographic origin in defining ethnic group membership (e.g., Berdan 2008b; Montejo 1999; Roosens 1994:85; Wade 1997:18; Watanabe and Fischer 2004:13). Extensive textual data from inscriptions indicate that Palenque's ruling family shared similar concerns in communicating its local roots and connections.

Previous research incorporating ethnicity theories in the Maya lowlands has concentrated on interactions between elite Maya and ethnically distinct foreign groups. Studies have been largely restricted to two analytical foci: (1) investigation of ethnic enclaves within sites and regions and (2) reconstructions of inter-societal interactions at the peripheries of the Maya lowlands. Possible ethnic enclaves and foreign intrusions into the lowlands have been the topic of recurring debate and will not be dealt with here (see Braswell 2003; Kidder, Jennings, and Shook 1946; Kowalski and Kristan-Graham 2007; Spence 1989, 1992, 1996; Stark 2008; Stark and Chance 2008:15–18; Stuart 2000; Wright 2005). Meanwhile, research on Maya and non-Maya interaction within a region has been almost exclusively restricted to the southeastern periphery of the Maya area (e.g., Canuto and Bell, this volume; Gerstle 1988; Schortman and Nakamura 1991; Schortman, Urban, and Ausec 2001). These studies however, have done little to confront the possibility of ethnic interaction *between* Classic Maya groups.

This is not to say that regional variability has gone unrecognized in the Maya lowlands. Maya scholars acknowledge the great diversity in local material culture from region to region. However, this diversity is often downplayed or attributed to political or ecological factors. Beyond the work of Schortman and his colleagues, little discussion has been devoted to the inherently conflicting balance of affiliations affected by the Classic elite to maintain their prominence both locally and among elites from other centers (figure 8.1; Sharer and Golden 2004:42). On the one hand, Maya elites needed to participate in the shared elite culture linking them into spatially expansive salient identity networks (see Blanton et al. 1996; Clark and Blake 1994; Schortman 1989:60). Manipulation and monopolization of this horizontal network were necessary for elites and rulers to differentiate themselves locally from non-elites and exclude them from positions of authority (ibid.). Conversely, Maya rulers and elites could not entirely distance themselves from their local supporting population in an agrarian-based economy.

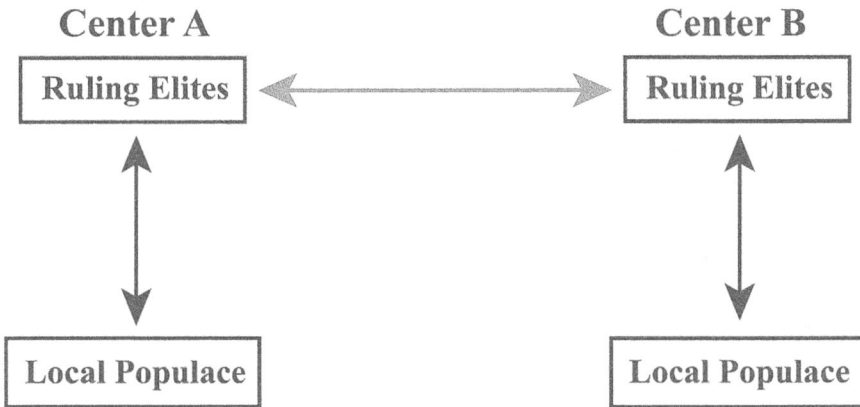

FIGURE 8.1. Schematic of vertical and horizontal interaction networks operating across the Maya region

MODELING THE ROLE OF ETHNIC IDENTITY IN CLASSIC POLITICAL AND SOCIAL ORGANIZATION

General descriptions of Classic Maya civilization highlight the shared aspects of elite high culture, what Schortman (ibid.:58) describes as a class-based salient identity (see also Baines and Yoffee 1998). Key characteristics marking this horizontal affiliation between elites are a common written language, similar art styles and architectural elements, and related political structures, including the *ajaw* concept (Andrews 1975; Freidel and Schele 1988; Freidel, Schele, and Parker 1993; Houston, Robertson, and Stuart 2000; Kubler 1975; Martin and Grube 2000; Roys 1934; Sharer 1993; Sharer and Golden 2004). A shared cosmology is often cited as another trait defining the Classic high culture, despite the fact that no unified cosmological tradition existed across the lowlands. Certain deities held a critical place in the ideologies of particular cities but were absent at other centers.

The fact that interaction between elites from different centers occurred within this shared framework in a sense diverts attention from investigation of horizontally distributed, *ethnic* divisions within the Maya lowlands through interaction, as advocated by Barth (1969). Furthermore, clear evidence for interaction between geographically separated non-elite groups—individuals excluded from elite class identities—is sparse across the Maya lowlands.[5]

In most interpretations of Classic Maya society, vertical integration is conceived as a system of basic community identities, sometimes contested, often generated through shared ritual spectacle. While a well-documented class-based elite shared culture existed, the regional variation in material culture across the lowlands likely also reflects the manifestation of distinct Maya ethnicities. But identifying group membership by specific, "intrinsic" criteria is both theoretically and analytically suspect (e.g., ibid.; Jones 1997). To circumvent the pitfalls of cultural trait lists, we concentrate on (largely elite) expressions of both class and ethnic practice and boundaries (Berdan 2008b:6; Stark and Chance 2008:27).

Class, Ethnicity, and Place

Although theoretical and analytical disagreements remain, well-established criteria define "social classes" in Mesoamerican scholarship (e.g., Berdan 2008b; Chase and Chase 1992; Clark 2000; Schortman and Urban 2003; Sharer 1993:95; Willey and Leventhal 1979). Prehispanic class differences are noted by material differentials in wealth and power structures (e.g., Rick 2005). Archaeologically, ancient Maya classes are most easily identified by the social context of, and quantitative differences in, access to labor, wealth, imports, and cultural capital[6] (e.g., Abrams 1989; Blanton et al. 1996; Chase 1992; DeMarrais, Castillo, and Earle 1996; Haviland and Moholy-Nagy 1992; Hendon 1991; Marcus 1993; Sanders 1992:280; Scarborough 2005; Sharer 1993:94; Willey et al. 1965; Willey and Leventhal 1979; also White [1999] for additional dietary evidence). These studies indicate that Classic Maya society was in general composed of at least two social classes: elites and commoners.[7]

Investigation of "class" in Maya archaeology has been especially profitable in interpreting vertical stratification at the local level and elite interactions at the polity level (cf. Sharer and Traxler 2006). While forming the initial basis to define ancient class divisions, quantitative measures of social status are more easily simplified analytically than are interpretations of differential access to cultural capital (table 8.1). However, distinctions based on raw quantitative data may lack marked divisions and represent merely the analytical beginning. Linking wealth-based variation in practice to materializations of power and authority (Anderson 1983; Bourdieu 1977; DeMarrais, Castillo, and Earle 1996; Stark and Chance 2008:7) elucidates cognitive aspects of class identity formation and maintenance (e.g., Houston et al. 2003; Yaeger 2000; Yaeger and Canuto 2000). Furthermore, tracking how elites and rulers manipulated aspects of cultural capital—ideology, history, and political authority—highlights its multidimensional potential. In particular, specific symbols and rituals can activate both class and ethnic group identities across multiple social contexts.

Recent discussions of ethnic identity in prehispanic Mesoamerica indicate the significance of "place" in defining group membership (e.g., Berdan 2008a; Brumfiel 1994; McAnany 1995; Stark and Chance 2008; see also Roosens 1994). It is the centrality of "place" in Maya ethnic identity formation that distinguishes ethnicity from class. Although incomplete and fragmentary, empirical evidence supports

TABLE 8.1. Common archaeological measures to distinguish class

Context	Archaeological Measure	Social Implication
Mortuary	Grave goods	Greater access to material wealth
	Health and nutrition	Greater access to subsistence resources
Architecture: domestic/ monumental	Building size	Greater ability to conscript labor
	Masonry quality	Greater access to specialized labor

envisioning numerous Maya ethnic groups organized across the lowlands during the Classic period. Moreover, the manifestation of ethnic identity significantly influenced local political structure, despite often being suppressed in inter-polity elite interactions.

By recognizing that social group markers are not arbitrary (Bentley 1987; Wilson 1993), it may be possible to distinguish the function(s) of particular symbol types. Primacy should not, however, be attributed to any particular potential practice or symbol.[8] The ways markers/symbols actively or passively fostered class and ethnic group membership should instead be examined to define their communicative import. Moreover, the historical and polity-specific significance of potential identity-confirming practices and symbols needs to be viewed as part of a process by which elites maintained bonds with, yet justified their domination over, local populations.

EXPRESSIONS OF IDENTITY: ETHNICITY VERSUS CLASS

Myriad strategies were available for ruling families to establish and maintain an ethnic affiliation with their local populations. The most effective manner likely involved creating shared notions of history, values, and place as materialized in habitus (e.g., Berdan 2008a; Jones 1997). However, as mentioned, reconstructing and comparing habitus across the entire Maya lowlands is well beyond the scope of this chapter. Instead, we evaluate how some symbols may have been employed by Palencano rulers to communicate affiliation and distinction with local groups (sometimes simultaneously). Assessing the potential of particular classes of archaeological data to mark group identity is a first step to better comprehend Palencano social organization. As will be seen, some commonly invoked material classes to distinguish between Maya groups fall short of the necessary criteria to identify ethnicity (Banks 1996; Barth 1969, 2000; Jones 1997). In particular, simple typologies of architecture style and *written* language are unfortunately inadequate archaeological indicators of ethnic group affiliation. The focus should instead be on how aspects of material culture were employed to communicate and affirm group identities (Aldenderfer and Stanish 1993; Jones 1997; Rapoport 1988).

Maya rulers went to great lengths to legitimize their power locally, continually reinforcing local roots and emphasizing the temporal depth of their dynasties. These practices served to create and maintain local identities affiliating rulers with their resident elite *and* non-elite populations. Recurrent themes connecting "place" with "people" associated with certain elite symbols strongly suggest their ethnic qualities. As noted, recognizing the multidimensionality of these symbols is critical. Ethnic and class markers can overlap, potentially communicating multiple or variable meanings to different individuals. This necessitates considering audience when interpreting the social import of practices and symbols. Archaeologically, audience can be inferred from the spatial context and distribution of social markers and inform the intertwined meanings communicated by specific markers (Inomata and Coben 2006; Moore 1996).

The extensive public and private declaration of the ties between rulers and local deities in ritual, sculpture, and writing indicates a dynastic preoccupation with demonstrating a long-standing connection to place and local history. In writing, often in restricted visual contexts, the Palencano sovereigns used emblem glyphs, toponyms, and relations to local deities to connect with local elites (e.g., Baudez 1989, 1996b; Stuart 2005). To demonstrate their ethnic affiliation to non-elites, rulers employed highly visible monumental sculpture and spectacle (e.g., Baudez 1989, 1996a; Greene Robertson 1983, 1985a, 1985b, 1991; Griffin 1978; Pollock 1965; A. Smith 2003). At the same time, by emphasizing the temporal depth of their local roots, these markers also differentiated the rulers from the ruled.

PALENQUE, CHIAPAS

Nestled in the foothills of the Sierra de Chiapas, the Classic period site of Palenque, Chiapas, Mexico, is most celebrated for its extensive hieroglyphic corpus, elegant stucco sculpture, delicate architecture, and the impressive tomb of its most renowned ruler, K'inich Janaab' Pakal I. As the largest center of the western periphery of the Maya lowlands, Palenque has been the focus of considerable archaeological investigation since the early 1900s (Mathews 2007:3–5). Over the years, several scholars have commented that Palenque's material culture is distinctive among Classic Maya sites. Beyond basic technological similarities, Palenque's architectural, sculptural, and ceramic traditions have little in common with contemporaneous traditions to the east. In this regard, the work of Robert Rands and his colleagues with Palenque ceramics has been the most systematic. Rands has convincingly demonstrated the region's ceramic isolation throughout much of the Classic period (e.g., Rands 1967, 2007; Rands and Bishop 1980). However, few scholars have viewed these data with the intention of identifying clues that suggest ethnic diversity across the Maya lowlands. We argue that elite expressions and, more important, use of cultural symbols indicate that Classic period Palencanos were ethnically distinct from other lowland Maya groups.

Although we choose not to discuss in detail Palenque's ceramic isolation (see Bishop 1975, 1994; Rands 1967, 1969, 1987; Rands and Bishop 1980), the apparent low importance of ceramic vessels as mortuary offerings at Palenque, especially polychromes, is suggestive. Royal Palencano tombs, lavishly decorated with art and jade, were ceramically impoverished compared with their Petén contemporaries. Pakal's tomb, for example, contained only five vessels, two with geometric polychrome designs. Non-royal burials throughout the site also contain few vessels (López Bravo 2003; Marken 2003; Rands and Rands 1961), indicating that, at least in death, the inhabitants of Palenque did not regard pottery as particularly valuable. This stark contrast with much of the rest of the Maya lowlands suggests that an alternate value system regarding pottery was at work in Classic Palenque. While difficult to reconstruct archaeologically, such systems—linked to reconstructions of habitus—may be productive indicators of ethnic affiliation.[9]

ARCHITECTURE

Since the reports of the earliest explorers, scholars have remarked at length on how Palenque's architectural and sculptural traditions differ from those at other Maya sites. Architecturally, the wide galleries and lattice-type roofcombs of Palenque are distinctive of what George Andrews (1995) has called the Northwestern Maya architectural tradition. Some of these architectural traits are also seen at several other centers of the western lowlands, including Tonina, Piedras Negras, and Yaxchilan (see Marken and Straight 2007:291–94). However, while the architectural styles of Tonina and the Usumacinta sites share elements with Palenque's tradition, their floor plans and vaulting have more in common with Petén architecture. To the west, much has been made of similarities to Palenque in the vault and roofing styles of Comacalco temples (Andrews 1975, 1989; Gallegos Gomora 1997). It would thus appear that a particular architectural tradition, or sets of traditions, characterizes the western Maya lowlands, with perhaps some blending of styles along the Usumacinta.

Though suggestive, monumental architecture is not as secure a line of evidence to identify ethnic diversity across the Maya lowlands as it may seem. By now we should be wary of simple stylistic comparisons to define particular Maya ethnic types. The nature of Maya constructions, not to mention the expense of large-scale excavation and restoration, often limits archaeologists' capability to fully investigate the development of a particular architectural style from beginning to end. This is the

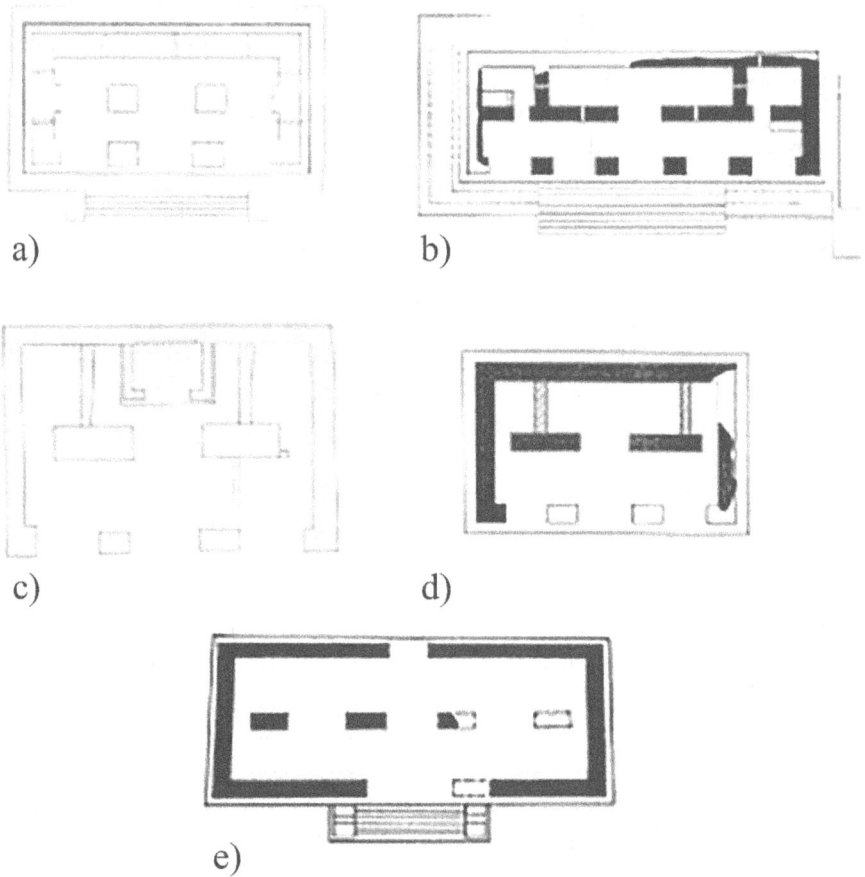

FIGURE 8.2. Temple plans at Palenque through time (after Marken 2007): (a) Temple Olvidado, (b) Temple V, (c) Temple XVII, (d) Temple XII, (e) Temple XXI

case at Palenque, where the known architectural sequence appears fully developed and spans a mere 150 years (Marken 2007). Moreover, the architectural traditions of individual sites, such as Palenque, are generally more diverse and varied than we often admit. Architectural forms rarely remain static through time (figure 8.2).

The regional distribution of particular building types may instead provide a more fruitful research avenue to examine Maya ethnic differences. Along these lines, Mark Child (2007) has suggested that a sweatbath cult operated in the western Maya lowlands during the Classic period. Although sweatbaths have been identified archaeologically throughout the Maya lowlands, the architectural form saw its

FIGURE 8.3. Perspective cross-section of Temple of the Sun, Palenque, showing interior symbolic sweatbath (after Holmes 1896)

greatest refinement in the west, namely at the sites of Palenque and Piedras Negras (Child 2006). Specifically at Palenque, architects constructed symbolic sweatbaths within the inner galleries of several temple structures. These are small, vaulted structures situated within the rear vaulted galleries of larger temple structures (figure 8.3). Associated inscriptions identify these structures, called sanctuaries by numerous scholars, as post-natal "sweatbaths" or "ovens" used to heat specific Palenque deities after their mythological births (Houston 1996). Symbolic and functional sweatbaths were also paired in two excavated elite residential compounds (Marken and González Cruz 2007). The distribution of these symbolic sweatbaths is limited to the western lowlands; other examples are known from Comalcalco, Xupa, and El Retiro, all within the Palenque realm (Andrews 1989; Liendo Stuardo 1999). While more abundant and diverse data sets would be necessary to connect this architectural form to ethnic practice (as opposed to class-based, elite practice), the confinement of this structure type to an isolated geographic zone does suggest some form of shared regional belief/ritual system.

HIEROGLYPHS AND LANGUAGE

While monumental architectural style may be a poor marker of Maya ethnic identity, a number of scholars have attempted to recover ethnic affiliation through linguistic analyses of the hieroglyphic texts carved in stone and recorded in stucco inscriptions. Although early epigraphers debated whether the hieroglyphic inscriptions recorded the broad language families of either Yukatek or Ch'olan (Schele 1982; Justeson and Campbell 1984), Houston and colleagues (2000) have presented evidence that almost all Maya texts are recorded in a single, particular prestige language whose most direct descendent is modern Ch'orti, which they term "Classic Ch'olti'an." This proposal has met with general acceptance in the epigraphic community (Wichmann 2004) but significantly complicates the use of inscriptions to determine ethnic identity. Just as medieval German, French, and English authors wrote in Latin, ancient Maya scribes apparently wrote in a class-confirming prestige language, despite whatever vernacular languages they may have spoken day to day in their home communities.

While Maya inscriptions as a whole appear to have been written in a prestige language, a number of epigraphers have noted that local variant spellings may provide clues as to the vernacular languages spoken at specific sites, a phenomenon known elsewhere in which aspects of the vernacular languages "percolate" into the prestige language of official texts (see Macri, this volume). Zachary Hruby and Mark Child (2004) examined the influence of one of these Classic period vernacular languages by focusing on grammatical peculiarities in texts, in particular the *-wa-ni* verbal suffix, an intransitive positional affix. Houston and colleagues (2000) noted that since this *-wan* suffix could not be reconstructed back to Common Mayan or Classic Ch'olti'an, it was most likely adopted from another language, which they propose was Chontal, where it is well attested from the early Colonial period. Hruby and Child tracked the adoption of this suffix across the southern Maya lowlands in the Late Classic period and detected a pattern where the earliest attestation of the *-wan* suffix is at the sites of Tortuguero and Palenque and sites in the Chontal region as discovered by the Spaniards in the sixteenth century (figure 8.4). According to Hruby and Child, the *-wan* suffix made its way up the Usumacinta River, progressively adopted at the sites of Yaxchilan and Cancuen in the middle and late eighth century, respectively, even appearing at distant Copán. Hruby and Child interpret this pattern as reflective of Palenque's social and political influence in the eighth century and, by extension, suggest that Palenque was a center of Chontal speakers.

There are a number of problems with this proposal. First, the data used by Hruby and Child are fragmentary, and their pattern of adoption of the –*wan* suffix ignores several examples that invalidate their claim of a progression from the Palenque region (figure 8.5). One of the earliest attestations outside of Palenque and Tortuguero is at Dos Pilas, in the Pasión region of southwest Petén, and dates to, or prior to, AD 727 (Stela 8). This example comes before the –*wan* suffix is attested at sites on the Usumacinta between Palenque and the Pasión region. Skepticism can also be raised regarding the emphasis on a late date provided for the first use of –*wan* at Cancuen. There are no early texts from Cancuen, the earliest

FIGURE 8.4. Early attestation of the –wan suffix from Palenque's Temple of the Inscriptions East Tablet, in a passage relating the accession of K'inich Janaab' Pakal I. The first glyph is the verb chum, "was seated," with the suffix waniiy spelled –wa-ni-ya. Drawing by Linda Schele

inscriptions not carved until after the mid-eighth century, and so data from this site will be of little use for the types of diachronic analyses attempted by Hruby and Child.

Even more problematic is the basic notion that the –*wan* suffix was a Chontal invention. Alfonso Lacadena Garcia-Gallo and Søren Wichmann (2002) have suggested that the –*wan* suffix is actually an invention of Classical Western Ch'olan and not specifically Chontal. To some this may appear little more than a matter of semantics, but it is actually a very important distinction, especially considering arguments that Palenque was a Chontal-speaking region. The modern Ch'olan languages Ch'orti', Ch'ol, and Chontal all derive from the same proto-Ch'olan language spoken about 2,000 years ago. When these languages diverged is uncertain, but in examining the percolation of vernacular languages into the hieroglyphic inscriptions that occurred during the Classic period, Lacadena Garcia-Gallo and Wichmann have identified clues that there was a dialectical difference between Eastern and Western Ch'olan. As both modern Ch'ol and Chontal descend from this Western Ch'olan of the Late Classic, it is not certain that the –*wan* suffix originated in and was adopted from the Palenque region. In fact, Lacadena Garcia-Gallo and Wichmann suggest that Calakmul may have been the center from which Western Ch'olan linguistic features such as the –*wan* suffix derived. Unfortunately, Calakmul's monuments are so badly eroded that this suggestion cannot as yet be

FIGURE 8.5. Early attestation of –wan suffix from Dos Pilas Stela 8. Drawing by Ian Graham

confirmed, but this proposal is more parsimonious than deriving this linguistic feature from the Palenque region, given its known political relationships during the Late Classic period (Marken and Straight 2007:296–304). There is little evidence for Palenque having had as wide an influence as would be suggested by the spread of the –*wan* suffix, while there is plenty of epigraphic information for Calakmul's broad political sway during the Late Classic period (Martin and Grube 2000). What this means is that, at least for the present, the best-known linguistic analysis of hieroglyphic texts at Palenque provides little concrete data for inquiry into ethnic identity (although see Macri, this volume, for future avenues of investigation). Instead, they confirmed both inter-elite class identity and elite-commoner distinctions.

Hieroglyphs and Place

There are other ways, however, in which the inscriptions may provide clues as to how elites evoked class and ethnic identities. One potential avenue, introduced here, is the active use of Emblem Glyphs by Maya rulers. At Palenque, rulers, like those of a number of ancient Maya states, carried two Emblem Glyphs (figure 8.6).

Emblem Glyphs are titles carried by rulers that identify them as lords of named polities (Berlin 1958). As Stuart and Houston (1994) have shown, many polity names derive from local toponyms. The more common of Palenque's two emblem glyphs is K'uhul Baakal Ajaw, or "Divine Bone (Kingdom) Lord," and it follows this pattern. While the local Palenque toponym was Lakam Ha' (meaning "Big Water"), a passage referring to the year AD 353 on Monument 6 from the nearby site of Tortuguero[10] records an event occurring at a specific location in Baak, demonstrating the toponymic nature of this Emblem Glyph.

The K'uhul Baakal Ajaw title was the most important title of the rulers of Palenque, and it is significant that this is a regional title based on an ancient toponym. This contrasts with the most important titles of the rulers of many other ancient states across the world. For example, Egyptian royal titles refer only obliquely to the two major divisions of the country, Upper and Lower Egypt, through reference to titulary deities of these regions, but there seems to have been little ethnic identity

FIGURE 8.6. Two Palenque Emblem Glyphs from the Palace Tablet. The first is K'uhul Matwiil Ajaw and the second is K'uhul Baakal Ajaw. Drawing by Linda Schele

associated with these broad subdivisions of the Egyptian nation (Gauthier 1907–17). In ancient Cambodia, rulers did take royal titles based on the names of the polities they ruled over, but these polity names were derived from the names of their capital cities, which in most cases seem to have simply been named after the kings who founded them or after Hindu deities (Briggs 1951:39–52; Vickery 1998:24–25). The K'uhul Baakal Ajaw title of Palenque, then, is likely a prominent title that references a connection to a specific place, one that does not simply identify rulers as the highest-ranking members of the upper class but that would also connect them to, while elevating them above, local populations.

Palenque's second emblem glyph is K'uhul Matwiil Ajaw, where Matwiil is a word that incorporates the name for cormorant, *mat*, and a suffix –*wil* of unknown function. While the translation of Matwiil is unclear, it is named as a supernatural location where the patron gods of Palenque touched down after their births in the mythological past. It is possible that the mountain behind the Temple of the Inscriptions was considered the earthly portal to this location (Freidel and MacLeod 2000; Freidel, Schele, and Parker 1993:283–84). The labeling of a conch shell from which the Maize God emerges as Matwiil on the Tablet of the Foliated Cross seems a particularly explicit reference to this supernatural location as a place of origin (Stuart 2005:169). The use of Matwiil as an Emblem Glyph indicates that Palenque's rulers considered this location a source of their identity.

Central Mexican parallels may provide insight as to how the Matwiil identity functioned at Palenque. The Mixtec lords of Oaxaca believed their ancestors emerged from sacred trees in particular valleys, especially Apoala (Jansen and Pérez Jiménez Gabina 2007:124). However, while the Mixtec lords claimed descent from these ancestral trees, the commoners, who spoke the same languages as their lords and by western terms would be considered part of the same ethnicity, were believed to have emerged from the earth itself and had a completely separate and autonomous origin from the elite (ibid.:135). In contrast, the various groups that formed the Aztecs of the Valley of Mexico claimed to have emerged as tribes from the seven caves of Chicomoztoc in Aztlan (M. Smith 2003:38–39). The Aztecs did not have a separate origin story for their elite, as did the Mixtec.

If we accept that the lords of Palenque identified themselves through an association with the Matwiil location, the question remains as to whether the commoners of Palenque shared in this identity, following the Aztec analogy, or whether they, like Mixtec commoners, were thought to have had a separate origin. Unfortunately, no firm evidence is presently known to determine which of these Mexican analogies, if either, is applicable to the Maya case.

GODS AND PLACE

Another manner in which the rulers of Palenque may have attempted to emphasize their inclusion in local ethnic identities is indicated through their manipulation and display of the patron gods of their city and polity. Heinrich Berlin (1963) was the first to identify the three principal gods of Palenque, whose main shrines were the three major temples of the Cross Group.[11] While early scholars were prone to view the "Palenque Triad" as a pan-Maya set of deities worshipped throughout the lowlands, it has since become evident that the Triad is a set of local deities (Stuart 2005, 2007). These gods, while manifestations of more universal deities, such as the gods of the sun, maize, and rain, were incarnated at Palenque in very local forms (ibid.). Investigations throughout the site of Palenque have uncovered evidence of the worship of these gods, indicating that these deities were worshipped not just by the site's ruling elite but by a large portion of the city's population (López Bravo 2000).[12] Moreover, the gods' prominently displayed association with rulers on highly visible temple facades and roofcombs suggests that elite identification with local deities served multiple purposes (e.g., Rapoport 1988).

Numerous studies have examined the ways Palencano rulers evoked their intimate association with the Triad Gods to assert their dominant political status, especially through highly visible monumental sculptural programs (e.g., Baudez 1996a; Schele and Miller 1986). Beyond the legitimization of authority, however, these monumental sculptures, as well as rituals as materialized by recovered *incensarios* (Cuevas García 2007), also likely communicated messages of common affiliation bonding rulers to the ruled. Palencano rulers used their access to and control of the city's patron gods to signal both their privileged and exclusionary position over the site and their common identity with the other residents. The rulers commemorated not just any gods but a set of deities specific to the site of Palenque (Stuart 2007). The restriction of certain gods to particular locales suggests their strong connections to place and thus, in a Mesoamerican context, to ethnicity as well.

The worship of specific deities has long been known as a manner in which groups of people formed a new ethnic identity. We suspect that the worship of the Palenque Triad Gods by a wide swathe of Palenque's population would have served to form a specifically "Palencano" ethnic identity that could span class divisions. Thus, while Palenque's ruling elite likely maintained class-based connections with contemporary rulers of other sites, even going so far as intermarrying with other royal families (Schele and Freidel 1990:320), concomitantly they would have continued to differentiate themselves from foreign elites by their devotion to a specific set of deities worshipped along with the other citizens of Palenque, regardless of social rank.

CONCLUSION

Studies of ethnicity and ethnic difference in several ancient complex societies have benefited tremendously from the analysis of written texts. In some areas, historic documentation is often the best or even the only indicator of ethnic divisions in the past (e.g., Emberling and Yoffee 1999). In the Maya lowlands, carved and painted hieroglyphic texts should ultimately serve as a vital data source to differentiate distinct Maya ethnic types. At present, subtle linguistic variations within Maya texts only seem to follow broad language divisions, as we have discussed. The inscriptions can, however, potentially identify other means by which ethnic affiliation is commonly established and maintained, in particular a common place of origin and ancestors. Unfortunately, unlike the case in some other areas of the world, Maya texts primarily deal with elites, precluding easy textual demonstration of vertical connections between elites and local populations in the inscriptions. If we are able to identify subtle ethnic divisions between various Maya elites, however, we can then begin to examine how elites were able to integrate local populations into cohesive social units in a broader perspective than political and economic control.

We have clarified some potential misconceptions regarding how the Palenque data may demonstrate a distinct ethnic affiliation and, at the same time, highlighted particular cultural phenomena we feel reflect potential ethnic diversity among the Classic Maya. It is becoming clear that traditional methods to identify disparate ethnic groups in the archaeological record of the Maya lowlands may be largely inadequate. Clear-cut ethnic markers are difficult to discern between Classic Maya sites, and simple comparisons of multiple types of material culture are unlikely to advance our understanding. It is not enough to note differences in architecture, pottery, verbal endings, or other cultural materials between sites. But by identifying differences in how these cultural items were used, we may gain some insight into Maya ethnic types. In this vein, we have mentioned how epigraphic, iconographic, and ritual "symbols" could have been used by elites to highlight both class and ethnic identities. The dual and perhaps competing elite maintenance of their local connection to place and their extra-polity relationships with other elite individuals suggest these conclusions:

1. Inter-polity elite relationships operated in a class-based network, fostered by shared access to wealth, political authority, ideology, and social status. Ethnic distinctions may or may not have been suppressed or overlooked in this arena, but considering the political, social, and economic broadness of inter-polity elite interactions, it appears that class-based requirements dominated inter-elite group membership.

2. Depending on context and audience, intra-polity elite relationships, to varying degrees, were likely structured by both ethnic and class identities. Internal elite competition and cooperation must have been negotiated within complicated networks of ethnic and class affiliations.

3. Without sufficient data to examine class-cutting connections as embodied by habitus, local elite-commoner relationships are more difficult to reconstruct. Class identities certainly framed a large portion of interactions, especially those in which hierarchical authority structures played a prominent role. Nevertheless, simple economic and ideological power relationships strike us as inadequate and overly one-sided explanations for the multigenerational sustainability of Maya polities. Numerous studies indicate that Maya rulers exerted limited influence over local subsistence, or utilitarian, economic systems (e.g., Bishop 1975; Clark 2003; Rands 1967; West 2002), while there is abundant evidence for their control of ideology. However, if couched within a shared ethnic framework, ideological and religious messages can create more concrete integrative bonds across class divisions.

It is acknowledged that much of this could indeed be deemed largely theoretical speculation from a pure scientific perspective. Yet despite decades of research and interpretation (much of which is also speculative), the internal organization of Classic Maya polities has eluded reconstruction (Marken and Fitzsimmons 2015). Our hope is that the present work will foster new interpretive frameworks that incorporate more nuanced theoretical approaches recognizing the inherent social dilemma(s) facing rulers and their subjects: how and why are class distinctions sustained while maintaining some semblance of integrated social unity? Internal ethnic affiliation, coupled with constructed perceptions of external ethnic difference, may provide Mayanists with one solution to this question. It is hoped that new research will attempt to empirically confirm or disprove its applicability to the Maya case.

NOTES

1. In contemporary discourse, the cultural designation "Maya" is generally used to describe the indigenous peoples (and their ancestors) of the Yucatán Peninsula, encompassing the modern nations of Guatemala and Belize; the states of Yucatán, Quintana Roo, Campeche, Chiapas, and Tabasco in Mexico; and the western portions of El Salvador and Honduras (e.g., Sharer and Traxler 2006). While many members of these groups may speak a Mayan language, this is not always a necessary prerequisite, especially when government or academic authorities are the designators. As this definition illustrates, there is often a strong underlying etic tone to the term *Maya* as an ethnic or cultural classification. Beginning with European contact, *Maya* has been a term employed for disparate groups within larger states who nevertheless often lacked an overarching group identity (see Emberling 1997:297–98, 304). Moreover, the degree to which Maya individuals and communities identify themselves as "Maya" and recognize a common ethnicity with other Maya varies widely between individuals and can be highly situational (Montejo 1999; see also Barth 1969).

2. The degree to which these localized identities are "nested" within a Maya macro-ethnic identity is subject to debate and should be evaluated case by case (e.g., Montejo 1999; see also Ferguson and Mansbach 1996).

3. Fortunately, primordialist/instrumentalist and subjectivist/objectivist approaches can be paired to create four distinct theoretical expectations. However, the applicability of each perspective to a particular archaeological case will vary and will always be somewhat dependent upon levels of preservation and the manner and societal contexts used to express specific identities.

4. These elements leave difficult-to-specify material residues with which to differentiate ethnic versus other local groups in the archaeological record (see also Bowser 2000). Most researchers thus argue that multiple lines of archaeological evidence must be brought to bear upon issues of ethnic interaction (e.g., Bernardini 2005; Hegmon 1998; Jones 1997; Stark and Chance 2008). Among the available forms of archaeological data, written records, settlement patterns, material and osteological data from burials, household organization, and ritual practices provide potential evidentiary classes with which to identify ethnic identities (Aldenderfer and Stanish 1993). In the Maya area, research has unfortunately tended to overly stress similarities in cultural traits across the lowlands. The application of the type-variety system to Maya ceramics is a complicated example of the inclination among Maya scholars to search for similarities and connections between sites as opposed to differences (e.g., Henderson and Agurcia 1987; Willey, Culbert, and Adams 1967).

5. Regional utilitarian ceramic distribution patterns suggest that highly localized economies existed across the southern lowlands (e.g., Bishop 1975, 1994; Drennan 1984; Fry 1969; McAnany 1989; Rands 1967, 1969, 1987). The strong support for economic explanations of *utilitarian* ceramic distribution largely precludes applying the same data to certain aspects of social identities, namely ethnicity. Nevertheless, compositional and stylistic sourcing of *prestige* vessels, likely distributed within a complex gifting system, demonstrates the political importance of class-confirming, elite inter-polity interactions (e.g., Reents-Budet 1994, 2001).

6. Cultural capital is principally defined by the ability to manipulate controllable cultural "assets" encompassing ideology, ritual, and history (writing, monumental architecture, ritual practice). Displays of quantitative differences in wealth (housing, diet, pottery—i.e., conspicuous consumption) also enhance cultural capital.

7. Debate continues as to the nature of Classic Maya stratification (see Chase and Chase 1992; Lohse and Valdez 2004). Despite the apparent disagreement, however, most researchers who advocate a two-class system (as opposed to a more complex system of three or more classes) accept that these classes can be further subdivided and were likely internally ranked or stratified (e.g., Hammond 1991:270; Jackson and Stuart 2001; Marcus 1993; Sharer 1993).

8. The term *symbol* is meant in its broadest definition. Culturally derived symbols include not only material objects but actions, including those associated with habitus and the memory of past rituals and historical events (e.g., Berdan 2008b; Jones 1997; Stanton and Magnoni 2008; Stark and Chance 2008; Wilson 1993).

9. Also beyond the scope of this chapter, comparison of dental mutilation and cranial deformation styles and rates across class lines could also prove fruitful in elucidating other sets of shared or dissimilar aspects of habitus between and within elite and commoner groups.

10. The lords of Tortuguero shared the use of the Baak Emblem Glyph with Palenque's rulers, indicating some sort of relationship between the two polities, although that relationship is not yet clear.

11. However, recent research has demonstrated that several monumental structures at Palenque, not only the Cross Group temples, were dedicated, or "belonged," to individual Triad Gods (Stuart 2005, 2007).

12. Incensarios depicting these deities have been discovered in similar elite and non-elite ritual contexts across the site (Cuevas García 2007), suggesting these objects signified some shared meaning(s) for elites and commoners.

REFERENCES CITED

Abrams, Elliot. 1989. "Architecture and Energy: An Evolutionary Approach." In *Archaeological Method and Theory*, vol. 1. ed. Michael Schiffer, 47–87. Tucson: University of Arizona Press.

Aldenderfer, Mark S., and Charles Stanish. 1993. "Domestic Architecture, Household Archaeology, and the Past in the South-Central Andes." In *Domestic Architecture, Ethnicity, and Complementarity in the South-Central Andes*, ed. Mark S. Aldenderfer, 1–12. Iowa City: University of Iowa Press.

Anderson, Benedict. 1983. *Imagined Communities*. London: Verso.

Andrews, George F. 1975. *Maya Cities: Placemaking and Urbanization*. Norman: University of Oklahoma Press.

Andrews, George F. 1989. *Comalaclco, Tabasco, Mexico: Maya Art and Architecture*, 2nd ed. Culver City, CA: Labyrinthos.

Andrews, George F. 1995. "Arquitectura maya." *Arqueología Mexicana* 2 (11): 4–12.

Baines, John, and Norman Yoffee. 1998. "Order, Legitimacy, and Wealth in Ancient Egypt and Mesopotamia." In *Archaic States*, ed. Gary M. Feinman and Joyce Marcus, 199–260. Santa Fe: School of American Research Press.

Banks, Marcus. 1996. *Ethnicity: Anthropological Constructions*. London: Routledge. http://dx.doi.org/10.4324/9780203417935.

Barth, Fredrik. 1969. "Introduction." In *Ethnic Groups and Boundaries*, ed. Fredrik Barth, 9–38. Long Grove, IL: Waveland.

Barth, Fredrik. 1994. "Enduring and Emerging Issues in the Analysis of Ethnicity." In *The Anthropology of Ethnicity*, ed. Hans Vermeulen and Cora Govers, 11–32. Amsterdam: Het Spinhuis.

Barth, Fredrik. 2000. "Boundaries and Connections." In *Signifying Identities*, ed. Anthony P. Cohen, 17–36. London: Routledge.

Baudez, Claude F. 1989. "House of the Bacabs: An Iconographic Analysis." In *House of the Bacabs: Copan, Honduras*, ed. David Webster, 73–81. Washington, DC: Dumbarton Oaks Research Library and Collection.

Baudez, Claude F. 1996a. "The Cross Group at Palenque." In *Eighth Palenque Round Table—1993*, vol. 10, ed. Merle Greene Robertson, Martin Macri, and Jan McHargue, 121–28. San Francisco: Pre-Columbian Art Research Institute.

Baudez, Claude F. 1996b. "Arquitectura y escenografía en Palenque: un ritual de entronización." *RES* 29-30: 172–79.

Bentley, G. Carter. 1987. "Ethnicity and Practice." *Comparative Studies in Society and History* 29 (1): 24–55. http://dx.doi.org/10.1017/S001041750001433X.

Berdan, Frances F. 2008a. "Concepts of Ethnicity and Class in Aztec-Period Mexico." In *Ethnic Identity in Nahua Mesoamerica*, ed. Frances F. Berdan, 105–32. Salt Lake City: University of Utah Press.

Berdan, Frances F., ed. 2008b. *Ethnic Identity in Nahua Mesoamerica*. Salt Lake City: University of Utah Press.

Berlin, Heinrich. 1958. "El glifo emblema en las inscripciones mayas." *Journal de la Société des Americanistes* 47 (1): 111–19. http://dx.doi.org/10.3406/jsa.1958.1153.

Berlin, Heinrich. 1963. "The Palenque Triad." *Journal de la Société des Americanistes* 52 (1): 91–99. http://dx.doi.org/10.3406/jsa.1963.1994.

Bernardini, Wesley. 2005. "Reconsidering Spatial and Temporal Aspects of Prehistoric Cultural Identity: A Case Study from the American Southwest." *American Antiquity* 70 (1): 31–54. http://dx.doi.org/10.2307/40035267.

Bishop, Ronald L. 1975. "Western Lowland Maya Ceramic Trade: An Archaeological Application of Nuclear Chemical Geological Data Analysis." PhD dissertation, Department of Anthropology, Southern Illinois University, Carbondale.

Bishop, Ronald L. 1994. "Pre-Columbian Pottery: Research in the Maya Region." In *Archaeometry of Pre- Columbian Sites*, ed. David A. Scott and Pieter Meyers, 15–66. Los Angeles: Getty Conservation Institute.

Blanton, Richard E., Gary M. Feinman, Stephen A. Kowalewski, and Peter N. Peregrine. 1996. "A Dual-Processual Theory for the Evolution of Mesoamerican Civilization." *Current Anthropology* 37 (1): 1–14. http://dx.doi.org/10.1086/204471.

Bourdieu, Pierre. 1977. *Outline of a Theory of Practice*. Cambridge: Cambridge University Press. http://dx.doi.org/10.1017/CBO9780511812507.

Bowser, Brenda J. 2000. "From Pottery to Politics: An Ethnological Study of Political Factionalism, Ethnicity, and Domestic Pottery Style in Ecuadorian Amazon." *Journal of Archaeological Method and Theory* 7 (3): 219–48. http://dx.doi.org/10.1023/A:10265 10620824.

Braswell, Geoffrey E., ed. 2003. *The Maya and Teotihuacan*. Austin: University of Texas Press.

Briggs, Lawrence Palmer. 1951. *The Ancient Khmer Empire*. Philadelphia: Transactions of the American Philosophical Society.

Brumfiel, Elizabeth M. 1994. "Factional Competition and Political Development in the New World: An Introduction." In *Factional Competition and Political Development in the New World*, ed. Elizabeth M. Brumfiel and John W. Fox, 3–14. Cambridge: Cambridge University Press. http://dx.doi.org/10.1017/CBO9780511598401.002.

Chase, Arlen F. 1992. "Elites and the Changing Organization of Classic Maya Society." In *Mesoamerican Elites*, ed. Diane Z. Chase and Arlen F. Chase, 30–49. Norman: University of Oklahoma Press.

Chase, Arlen F., and Diane Z. Chase. 1992. "Mesoamerican Elites: Assumptions, Definitions, and Models." In *Mesoamerican Elites*, ed. Diane Z. Chase and Arlen F. Chase, 3–17. Norman: University of Oklahoma Press.

Child, Mark. 2006. "The Symbolic Space of the Ancient Maya Sweatbath." In *Space and Spatial Analysis in Archaeology*, ed. Elizabeth C. Robertson, Jeffrey D. Seibert,

Deepika C. Fernandez, and Marc U. Zender, 157–67. Albuquerque: University of New Mexico Press.

Child, Mark. 2007. "Ritual Purification and the Ancient Maya Sweatbath at Palenque." In *Palenque: Recent Investigations at the Classic Maya Center*, ed. Damien B. Marken, 233–62. New York: Altamira.

Clark, John E. 2000. "Towards a Better Explanation of Hereditary Inequality: A Critical Assessment of Natural and Historic Human Agents." In *Agency in Archaeology*, ed. Marcia-Anne Dobres and John Robb, 92–112. London: Routledge.

Clark, John E. 2003. "A Review of Twentieth-Century Mesoamerican Obsidian Studies." In *Mesoamerican Lithic Technology*, ed. Kenneth G. Hirth, 15–54. Salt Lake City: University of Utah Press.

Clark, John E., and Michael Blake. 1994. "The Power of Prestige: Competitive Generosity and the Emergence of Rank Societies in Lowland Mesoamerica." In *Factional Competition and Political Development in the New World*, ed. Elizabeth M. Brumfiel and John W. Fox, 17–30. Cambridge: Cambridge University Press. http://dx.doi.org/10.1017/CBO9780511598401.003.

Cuevas García, Martha. 2007. *Los Incensarios Efigie de Palenque: Deidades y Rituales Mayas*. Mexico City: Universidad Nacional Autónoma de México.

DeMarrais, Elizabeth, Luis Jamie Castillo, and Timothy Earle. 1996. "Ideology, Materialization, and Power Strategies." *Current Anthropology* 37 (1): 15–31. http://dx.doi.org/10.1086/204472.

Drennan, Robert D. 1984. "Long-Distance Transport Costs in Pre-Hispanic Mesoamerica." *American Anthropologist* 86 (1): 105–12. http://dx.doi.org/10.1525/aa.1984.86.1.02a00100.

Eidheim, Harald. 1969. "When Ethnic Identity Is a Social Stigma." In *Ethnic Groups and Boundaries*, ed. Fredrik Barth, 39–57. Long Grove, IL: Waveland.

Emberling, Geoff. 1997. "Ethnicity in Complex Societies: Archaeological Perspectives." *Journal of Archaeological Research* 5 (4): 295–344. http://dx.doi.org/10.1007/BF02229256.

Emberling, Geoff, and Norman Yoffee. 1999. "Thinking about Ethnicity in Mesopotamian Archaeology and History." In *Fluchtpunkt Uruk: Archaologische Einheit aus methodischer Vielfalt: Schriften fur Hans Nissen*, ed. Hartmut Kuhne, Reinhard Bernbeck, and Karin Bartl, 272–81. Rahden, Germany: Marie Leidorf.

Eriksen, Thomas Hylland. 1991. "The Cultural Contexts of Ethnic Differences." *Man* 26 (1): 127–44. http://dx.doi.org/10.2307/2803478.

Ferguson, Yale H., and Richard W. Mansbach. 1996. *Polities: Authority, Identities, and Change*. Columbia: University of South Carolina Press.

Freidel, David A., and Barbara MacLeod. 2000. "Creation Redux: New Thoughts on Maya Cosmology from Epigraphy, Iconography, and Archaeology." *PARI Journal* 1 (2): 1–8.

Freidel, David A., and Linda Schele. 1988. "Kingship in the Late Preclassic Maya Lowlands: The Instruments and Places of Ritual Power." *American Anthropologist* 90 (3): 547–67. http://dx.doi.org/10.1525/aa.1988.90.3.02a00020.

Freidel, David A., Linda Schele, and Joy Parker. 1993. *Maya Cosmos*. New York: William Morrow.

Fry, Robert E. 1969. "Ceramics and Settlement in the Peripheries of Tikal, Guatemala." PhD dissertation, Department of Anthropology, University of Arizona, Tucson.

Gallegos Gomora, M. Judith. 1997. "Forma, Materiales y Decoracion: La Arquitectura de Comalcalco." *Los Investigadores de la Cultura Maya* 5 (1): 212–26.

Gauthier, Henri. 1907–17. *Le livre des rois d'Egypte: Recueil de tigres et protocoles royaux, noms propres de rois, reines, princes et princesses, noms de pirámides et de temples solaires, suivi d'un index alphabétique*. Cairo, Egypt: L'Institut Français d'Archéologie Orientale.

Gerstle, Andrea I. 1988. "Maya-Lenca Ethnic Relations in Late Classic Period Copan, Honduras." PhD dissertation, Department of Anthropology, University of California at Santa Barbara.

Griffin, Gillett G. 1978. "Cresterias of Palenque." In *Tercera Mesa Redonda de Palenque*, vol. 4, ed. Merle Greene Robertson and Donnan Call Jeffers, 139–46. San Francisco: Pre-Columbian Art Research Institute.

Grosby, Steven. 1995. "Territoriality: The Transcendental, Primordial Feature of Modern Societies." *Nations and Nationalism* 1 (2): 143–62. http://dx.doi.org/10.1111/j.1354-5078 .1995.00143.x.

Hammond, Norman. 1991. "Inside the Black Box: Defining Maya Polity." In *Classic Maya Political History: Hieroglyphic and Archaeological Evidence*, ed. T. Patrick Culbert, 253–84. Cambridge: Cambridge University Press.

Haviland, William A., and Hattula Moholy-Nagy. 1992. "Distinguishing the High and Mighty from Hoi Polloi at Tikal, Guatemala." In *Mesoamerican Elites*, ed. Diane Z. Chase and Arlen F. Chase, 50–60. Norman: University of Oklahoma Press.

Hegmon, Michelle. 1998. "Technology, Style, and Social Practices: Archaeological Approaches." In *The Archaeology of Social Boundaries*, ed. Miriam Stark, 264–79. Washington, DC: Smithsonian Institution Press.

Henderson, John S., and Richardo Agurcia. 1987. "Ceramic Systems: Facilitating Comparison in Type-Variety Analysis." In *Maya Ceramics*, ed. Prudence M. Rice and Robert J. Sharer, 431–38. BAR International Series 345. Oxford: British Archaeological Reports.

Hendon, Julia A. 1991. "Status and Power in Classic Maya Society: An Archaeological Study." *American Anthropologist* 93 (4): 894–918. http://dx.doi.org/10.1525/aa.1991.93.4 .02a00070.

Holmes, William H. 1896. *Archaeological Studies among the Ancient Cites of Mexcio*, Part 2: *Monuments of Chiapas, Oaxaca and the Valley of Mexico*, vol. 1, no. 2. Field Columbian Museum pub. 16. Chicago: Field Columbian Museum.

Houston, Stephen D. 1996. "Symbolic Sweatbaths of the Maya: Architectural Meaning in the Cross Group at Palenque, Mexico." *Latin American Antiquity* 7 (2): 132–51. http://dx.doi.org/10.2307/971614.

Houston, Stephen D., Héctor Escobedo, Mark Child, Charles W. Golden, and René Muñoz. 2003. "The Moral Community: Maya Settlement Transformation at Piedras Negras, Guatemala." In *The Social Construction of Ancient Cities*, ed. Monica L. Smith, 212–53. Washington, DC: Smithsonian Institution Press.

Houston, Stephen D., John Robertson, and David Stuart. 2000. "The Language of Classic Maya Inscriptions." *Current Anthropology* 41 (3): 321–56. http://dx.doi.org/10.1086/300142.

Hruby, Zachary, and Mark Child. 2004. "Chontal Linguistic Influence in Ancient Maya Writing: Intransitive Positional Verbal Affixation." In *The Linguistics of Maya Writing*, ed. Søren Wichmann, 13–26. Salt Lake City: University of Utah Press.

Inomata, Takeshi, and Lawrence S. Coben. 2006. "Overture: An Invitation to the Archaeological Theater." In *Archaeology of Performance*, ed. Takeshi Inomata and Lawrence S. Coben, 11–44. New York: Altamira.

Jackson, Sarah, and David Stuart. 2001. "The *Aj K'uhun* Title." *Ancient Mesoamerica* 12 (2): 217–28. http://dx.doi.org/10.1017/S0956536101122030.

Jansen, Maarten, and Aurora Pérez Jiménez Gabina. 2007. *Encounter with the Plumed Serpent: Drama and Power in the Heart of Mesoamerica*. Boulder: University Press of Colorado.

Janusek, John W. 2003. "The Changing Face of Tiwanaku Residential Life." In *Tiwanaku and Its Hinterland*, vol. 2, ed. Alan L. Kolata, 264–95. Washington, DC: Smithsonian Institution Press.

Janusek, John W. 2008. *Ancient Tiwanaku*. New York: Cambridge University Press.

Jones, Siân. 1997. *The Archaeology of Ethnicity*. London: Routledge. http://dx.doi.org/10.4324/9780203438732.

Justeson, John S., and Lyle Campbell, eds. 1984. *Phoneticism in Mayan Hieroglyphic Writing*. Institute for Mesoamerican Studies Publication 9. Albany: State University of New York.

Kidder, Alfred V., Jesse D. Jennings, and Edwin M. Shook. 1946. *Excavations at Kaminaljuyu, Guatemala*. Publication 561. Washington, DC: Carnegie Institution of Washington.

Kowalski, Jeff K., and Cynthia Kristan-Graham, eds. 2007. *Twin Tollans: Chichén Itzá, Tula, and the Epiclassic to Early Postclassic Mesoamerican World*. Washington, DC: Dumbarton Oaks Research Library and Collection.

Kubler, George. 1975. *The Art and Architecture of Ancient America*, 2nd ed. Baltimore: Penguin Books.

Lacadena Garcia-Gallo, Alfonso, and Søren Wichmann. 2002. "The Distribution of Lowland Maya Languages in the Classic Period." In *La Organización Social Entre los Mayas Prehispánicos, Colonials y Modernos*, ed. Vera Tiesler Blos, Rafael Cobos, and Merle Greene Robertson, 275–320. Mexico City: Instituo Nacional de Antropología e Historia.

LeCount, Lisa J. 2001. "Like Water for Chocolate: Feasting and Political Ritual among the Late Classic Maya of Xunantunich, Belize." *American Anthropologist* 103 (4): 935–53. http://dx.doi.org/10.1525/aa.2001.103.4.935.

Liendo Stuardo, Rodrigo. 1999. "The Organization of Agricultural Production at a Classic Maya Center: Settlement Patterns in the Palenque Region, Chiapas, Mexico." PhD dissertation, Department of Anthropology, University of Pittsburgh, Pittsburgh, PA.

Lohse, Jon C., and Fred Valdez Jr., eds. 2004. *Ancient Maya Commoners*. Austin: University of Texas Press.

López Bravo, Roberto. 2000. "La Vereración de los Ancestros en Palenque." *Arqueología Mexicana* 8 (45): 38–43.

López Bravo, Roberto. 2003. "Del Motiepa al Picota: La primera temporada del Crecimiento Urbano de la antigua ciudad de Palenque (PCU)." *Lakamha* 2 (9): 10–15.

Marcus, Joyce. 1993. "Ancient Maya Political Organization." In *Lowland Maya Civilization in the 8th Century AD*, ed. Jeremy A. Sabloff and John S. Henderson, 111–84. Washington, DC: Dumbarton Oaks Research Library and Collection.

Marken, Damien B. 2003. "Elite Political Structure at Late Classic Palenque, Chiapas, Mexico." Paper presented at the Fifth World Archaeology Congress, Washington, DC, June 23–26.

Marken, Damien B. 2007. "The Construction Chronology of Palenque: Seriation within an Architectural Form." In *Palenque: Recent Investigations at the Classic Maya Center*, ed. Damien B. Marken, 57–81. New York: Altamira.

Marken, Damien B., and James Fitzsimmons, eds. 2015. *Classic Maya Polities of the Southern Lowlands: Integration, Interaction, Dissolution*. Boulder: University Press of Colorado.

Marken, Damien B., and Arnoldo González Cruz. 2007. "Elite Residential Compounds at Late Classic Palenque." In *Palenque: Recent Investigations at the Classic Maya Center*, ed. Damien B. Marken, 135–60. New York: Altamira.

Marken, Damien B., and Kirk D. Straight. 2007. "Conclusion: Reconceptualizing the Palenque Polity." In *Palenque: Recent Investigations at the Classic Maya Center*, ed. Damien B. Marken, 279–324. New York: Altamira.

Martin, Simon, and Nikolai Grube. 2000. *Chronicles of the Maya Kings and Queens: Deciphering the Dynasties of the Ancient Maya*. London: Thames and Hudson.

Mathews, Peter. 2007. "Palenque Archaeology: An Introduction." In *Palenque: Recent Investigations at the Classic Maya Center*, ed. Damien B. Marken, 3–14. New York: Altamira.

McAnany, Patricia A. 1989. "Stone Tool Production and Exchange in the Eastern Maya Lowlands: The Consumer Perspective from Pulltrouser Swamp, Belize." *American Antiquity* 54 (2): 332–46. http://dx.doi.org/10.2307/281710.

McAnany, Patricia A. 1995. *Living with the Ancestors*. Austin: University of Texas Press.

Montejo, Victor. 1999. *Voices from Exile: Violence and Survival in Modern Maya History*. Norman: University of Oklahoma Press.

Moore, Jerry D. 1996. *Architecture and Power in the Ancient Andes: The Archaeology of Public Buildings*. Cambridge: Cambridge University Press. http://dx.doi.org/10.1017/CBO9780511521201.

Piehl, Jennifer C. 2005. "Performing Identity in an Ancient Maya City: The Archaeology of Houses, Health and Social Differentiation at the Site of Baking Pot, Belize." PhD dissertation, Department of Anthropology, Tulane University, New Orleans, LA.

Pollock, Harry E.D. 1965. "Architecture of the Maya Lowlands." In *Handbook of Middle American Indians*, vol. 2: *Archaeology of Southern Mesoamerica, Part 1*, ed. Robert Wauchope and Gordon R. Willey, 378–440. Austin: University of Texas Press.

Rands, Barbara C., and Robert L. Rands. 1961. "Excavations in a Cemetery at Palenque." *Estudios de Cultura Maya* 1: 87–106.

Rands, Robert L. 1967. "Ceramic Technology and Trade in the Palenque Region, Mexico." In *American Historical Anthropology: Essays in Honor of Leslie Spier*, ed. Carroll L. Riley and Walter W. Taylor, 137–51. Carbondale: University of Southern Illinois Press.

Rands, Robert L. 1969. *Maya Ecology and Trade: 1967–1968: A Progress Report of Work Carried Out under the Auspices of the National Science Foundation Grant of 1455X*. Carbondale: University Museum, Southern Illinois University.

Rands, Robert L. 1987. "Ceramic Patterns and Traditions in the Palenque Area." In *Maya Ceramics: Papers from the 1985 Maya Ceramic Conference*, ed. Prudence M. Rice and Robert J. Sharer, 203–38. BAR International Series 345(i). Oxford: Hadrian Books.

Rands, Robert L. 2007. "Chronological Chart and Overview of Ceramic Developments at Palenque." In *Palenque: Recent Investigations at the Classic Maya Center*, ed. Damien B. Marken, 17–23. New York: Altamira.

Rands, Robert L., and Ronald L. Bishop. 1980. "Resource Procurement Zones and Patterns of Ceramic Exchange in the Palenque Region, Mexico." In *Models and Methods in Regional Exchange*, ed. Robert E. Fry, 19–46. SAA Papers 1. Washington, DC: Society for American Archaeology.

Rapoport, Amos. 1988. "Levels of Meaning in the Built Environment." In *Cross-Cultural Perspectives in Non-Verbal Communication*, ed. Fernando Poyatos, 317–36. Toronto: C. J. Hogrefe.

Reents-Budet, Dorie. 1994. *Painting the Maya Universe: Royal Ceramics of the Classic Period*. Durham, NC: Duke University Press.

Reents-Budet, Dorie. 2001. "Classic Maya Concepts of the Royal Court: An Analysis of Renderings on Pictorial Ceramics." In *Royal Courts of the Ancient Maya*, vol. 1, ed. Takeshi Inomata and Stephen D. Houston, 195–233. Boulder: Westview.

Rick, John. 2005. "The Evolution of Authority and Power at Chavín de Huántar, Peru." In *Foundations of Power in the Prehispanic Andes*, ed. Kevin J. Vaughn, Dennis Ogburn, and Christina A. Conlee, 71–89. Archaeological Papers of the American Anthropological Association 14. Arlington, VA: American Anthropological Association. http://dx.doi .org/10.1525/ap3a.2005.14.071.

Robertson, Merle Greene. 1983. *The Sculpture of Palenque*, vol. 1: *The Temple of the Inscriptions*. Princeton, NJ: Princeton University Press.

Robertson, Merle Greene. 1985a. *The Sculpture of Palenque*, vol. 2: *The Early Buildings of the Palace and Wall Paintings*. Princeton, NJ: Princeton University Press.

Robertson, Merle Greene. 1985b. *The Sculpture of Palenque*, vol. 3: *The Late Buildings of the Palace*. Princeton, NJ: Princeton University Press.

Robertson, Merle Greene. 1991. *The Sculpture of Palenque*, vol. 4: *The Cross Group, the North Group, the Olvidado, and Other Pieces*. Princeton, NJ: Princeton University Press.

Roosens, Eugeen. 1994. "The Primordial Nature of Origins in Migrant Ethnicity." In *The Anthropology of Ethnicity*, ed. Hans Vermeulen and Cora Govers, 81–104. Amsterdam: Het Spinhuis.

Roys, Lawrence. 1934. "The Engineering Knowledge of the Maya." In *Contributions to American Archaeology*, vol. 2, no. 6, 27–105. Washington, DC: Carnegie Institution of Washington.

Sanders, William T. 1992. "Ranking and Stratification in Mesoamerica." In *Mesoamerican Elites*, ed. Diane Z. Chase and Arlen F. Chase, 278–91. Norman: University of Oklahoma Press.

Scarborough, Vernon L. 2005. "The Power of Landscapes." In *A Catalyst for Ideas: Anthropology, Archaeology, and the Legacy of Douglas W. Schwartz*, ed. Vernon L. Scarborough, 209–28. Santa Fe: School of American Research Press.

Schele, Linda. 1982. *Maya Glyphs: The Verbs*. Austin: University of Texas Press.

Schele, Linda, and David Freidel. 1990. *A Forest of Kings: The Untold Story of the Ancient Maya*. New York: William Morrow.

Schele, Linda, and Mary Miller. 1986. *The Blood of Kings*. New York: George Braziller.

Schortman, Edward M. 1989. "Interregional Interaction in Prehistory: The Need for a New Perspective." *American Antiquity* 54 (1): 52–65. http://dx.doi.org/10.2307/281331.

Schortman, Edward M., and Seiichi Nakamura. 1991. "A Crisis of Identity: Late Classic Competition and Interaction on the Southeast Maya Periphery." *Latin American Antiquity* 2 (4): 311–36. http://dx.doi.org/10.2307/971781.

Schortman, Edward M., and Patricia A. Urban. 2003. "Coping with Diversity." In *Perspectives on Ancient Maya Rural Complexity*, ed. Gyles Iannone and Samuel V. Connell, 131–37. Los Angeles: Cotsen Institute of Archaeology, University of California.

Schortman, Edward M., Patricia A. Urban, and Marne Ausec. 2001. "Politics with Style: Identity Formation in Prehispanic Southeastern Mesoamerica." *American Anthropologist* 103 (2): 312–30. http://dx.doi.org/10.1525/aa.2001.103.2.312.

Sharer, Robert J. 1993. "The Social Organization of the Late Classic Maya: Problems of Definition and Approaches." In *Lowland Maya Civilization in the 8th Century AD*, ed. Jeremy A. Sabloff and John S. Henderson, 91–109. Washington, DC: Dumbarton Oaks Research Library and Collection.

Sharer, Robert J., and Charles W. Golden. 2004. "Kingship and Polity: Conceptualizing the Maya Body Politic." In *Continuities and Changes in Maya Archaeology: Perspectives at the Millennium*, ed. Charles W. Golden and Greg Borgstede, 23–50. New York: Routledge.

Sharer, Robert J., with Loa Traxler. 2006. *The Ancient Maya*, 6th ed. Palo Alto, CA: Stanford University Press.

Sheets, Payson D., Harriet F. Beaubien, Marilyn Beaudry, Andrea Gerstle, Brian McKee, C. Dan Miller, Hartmut Spetzler, and David B. Tucker. 1990. "Household Archaeology at Ceren, El Salvador." *Ancient Mesoamerica* 1 (1): 81–90. http://dx.doi.org/10.1017/S0956536100000092.

Siverts, Henning. 1969. "Ethnic Stability and Boundary Dynamics in Southern Mexico." In *Ethnic Groups and Boundaries*, ed. Fredrik Barth, 101–16. Long Grove, IL: Waveland.

Smith, Adam T. 2003. *The Political Landscape: Constellations of Authority in Early Complex Society*. Berkeley: University of California Press.

Smith, Michael E. 2003. *The Aztecs*, 2nd ed. Oxford: Blackwell.

Spence, Michael E. 1989. "Excavaciones Recientes en Tlailotlaca, El Barrio Oaxaqueño de Teotihuacan." *Arqueología* 5: 81–104.

Spence, Michael E. 1992. "Tlailotlacan: A Zapotec Enclave in Teotihuacan." In *Art, Ideology, and the City of Teotihuacan*, ed. Janet C. Berlo, 59–88. Washington, DC: Dumbarton Oaks Research Library and Collection.

Spence, Michael E. 1996. "A Comparative Analysis of Ethnic Enclaves." In *Arqueología Mesoamericana: Homenaje a William T. Sanders*, vol. 1, ed. A. Guadalupe Mastache, Jeffrey R. Parsons, Robert S. Santley, and Mari Carmen Serra Peche, 333–53. Mexico City: Instituto Nacional de Antropología e Historia.

Stanish, Charles. 1989. "Household Archaeology: Testing Models of Zonal Complementarity in the South-Central Andes." *American Anthropologist* 91 (1): 7–24. http://dx.doi.org/10.1525/aa.1989.91.1.02a00010.

Stanton, Travis, and Aline Magnoni, eds. 2008. *Memories of the Past: The Use of Abandoned Structures by the Ancient Maya.* Boulder: University Press of Colorado.

Stark, Barbara L. 2008. "Archaeology and Ethnicity in Postclassic Mesoamerica." In *Ethnic Identity in Nahua Mesoamerica*, ed. Frances F. Berdan, 38–63. Salt Lake City: University of Utah Press.

Stark, Barbara L., and John K. Chance. 2008. "Diachronic and Multidisciplinary Perspectives on Mesoamerican Ethnicity." In *Ethnic Identity in Nahua Mesoamerica*, ed. Frances F. Berdan, 1–37. Salt Lake City: University of Utah Press.

Stuart, David. 2000. "The Arrival of Strangers." In *Mesoamerica's Classic Heritage: From Teotihuacan to the Aztecs*, ed. David Carrasco, Lindsay Jones, and Scott Sessions, 465–513. Boulder: University Press of Colorado.

Stuart, David. 2005. *The Hieroglyphic Inscriptions from Temple XIX at Palenque: A Commentary.* San Francisco: PreColumbian Art Research Institute.

Stuart, David. 2007. "Gods and Histories: Mythology and Dynastic Succession at Temples XIX and XXI at Palenque." In *Palenque: Recent Investigations at the Classic Maya Center*, ed. Damien B. Marken, 207–32. New York: Altamira.

Stuart, David, and Stephen D. Houston. 1994. *Classic Maya Place Names.* Washington, DC: Dumbarton Oaks Research Library and Collection.

Vickery, Michael. 1998. *Society, Economics, and Politics in Pre-Angkor Cambodia: The 7th–8th Centuries.* Tokyo: Centre for East Asian Cultural Studies for UNESCO.

Vogt, Evon Z. 1993. *Tortillas for the Gods: A Symbolic Analysis of Zinacanteco Rituals*, 2nd ed. Norman: University of Oklahoma Press.

Wade, Peter. 1997. *Race and Ethnicity in Latin America.* London: Pluto.

Watanabe, John M. 2004. "Culture History in National Contexts: Nineteenth-Century Maya under Mexican and Guatemalan Rule." In *Pluralizing Ethnography*, ed. John M. Watanabe and Edward F. Fischer, 35–65. Santa Fe: School of American Research Press.

Watanabe, John M., and Edward F. Fischer. 2004. "Introduction: Emergent Anthropologies and Pluricultural Ethnography in Two Postcolonial Nations." In *Pluralizing Ethnography*, ed. John M. Watanabe and Edward F. Fischer, 3–33. Santa Fe: School of American Research Press.

West, Georgia. 2002. "Ceramic Exchange in the Late Classic and Postclassic Maya Lowlands: A Diachronic Approach." In *Ancient Maya Political Economies*, ed. Marilyn A. Masson and David A. Freidel, 140–96. Walnut Creek, CA: Altamira.

White, Christine D., ed. 1999. *Reconstructing Maya Diets.* Salt Lake City: University of Utah Press.

Wichmann, Søren, ed. 2004. *The Linguistics of Maya Writing*. Salt Lake City: University of Utah Press.

Willey, Gordon R., William R. Bullard Jr., John B. Glass, and James C. Gifford. 1965. *Prehistoric Settlement in the Belize Valley*. Papers of the Peabody Museum of Archaeology and Ethnology, vol. 54. Cambridge, MA: Harvard University Press.

Willey, Gordon R., T. Patrick Culbert, and Richard E.W. Adams. 1967. "Maya Lowland Ceramics: A Report from the 1965 Guatemala City Conference." *American Antiquity* 32 (3): 289–315. http://dx.doi.org/10.2307/2694659.

Willey, Gordon R., and Richard M. Leventhal. 1979. "Prehistoric Settlement at Copán." In *Maya Archaeology and Ethnohistory*, ed. Norman Hammond and Gordon R. Willey, 75–102. Austin: University of Texas Press.

Wilson, Richard. 1993. "Anchored Communities: Identity and History of the Maya-Q'eqchi." *Man* 28 (1): 121–38. http://dx.doi.org/10.2307/2804439.

Wright, Lori E. 2005. "Identifying Immigrants to Tikal, Guatemala: Defining Local Variability in Strontium Isotope Ratios of Human Tooth Enamel." *Journal of Archaeological Science* 32 (4): 555–66. http://dx.doi.org/10.1016/j.jas.2004.11.011.

Yaeger, Jason. 2000. "The Social Construction of Communities in the Classic Maya Countryside: Strategies of Affiliation in Western Belize." In *The Archaeology of Communities: A New World Perspective*, ed. Marcello A. Canuto and Jason Yaeger, 123–42. London: Routledge.

Yaeger, Jason, and Marcello A. Canuto. 2000. "Introducing an Archaeology of Communities." In *The Archaeology of Communities: A New World Perspective*, ed. Marcello A. Canuto and Jason Yaeger, 1–15. London: Routledge.

9

Considering the Edge Effect

Ethnogenesis and Classic Period Society in the Southeastern Maya Area

MARCELLO A. CANUTO AND ELLEN E. BELL

THE EDGE EFFECT: DEFINING POPULATIONS PAST AND PRESENT

From the outset of archaeological investigations in western Honduras, researchers have grappled with questions about the relationship between the "ancient Maya" and the modern nation-state of Honduras. As early as 1834, explorer, political operative, and archaeologist Juan Galindo (1945:219) asserted that Copán represented an incursion by foreigners into Honduran territory: "Copán fué originario de una colonia tulteca; su rei dominó el país que se estiende al Oriente del de los mayas o Yucatán, alcanzando desde el golfo de Honduras hasta cerca del Oceano Pacífico."[1] The untrained but enthusiastic Apostolic Nuncio to Honduras, Federico Lunardi, devoted years of research to counteract these dominant views, claiming in his peculiar tome *Honduras Maya* that "hacía ocho años que sabía que Honduras era toda Maya y maestra del Mayab; pero, no solamente los extranjeros, que de ordinario ven las cosas superficialmente, sino los propios hijos de honduras, le negaban a su madre lo que hay más precioso, la maternidad, y una tan noble como la de los Mayas"[2] (Lunardi 1948:ii).

Despite Lunardi's protestations, the area that became known prosaically as "the southeast Maya periphery" came to be broadly understood as a borderland region where Maya groups based in the large centers of Copán and Quiriguá interacted with non-Maya populations to the east (Hay et al. 1940; Kirchoff 1943; Longyear 1947; Lothrop 1939). These non-Maya populations were assumed to have spoken different languages, produced and used stylistically different material culture, and

DOI: 10.5876/9781607325673.c009

engaged in traditions and practices distinct from those of their Maya neighbors. The boundaries between them were conceptualized (actively or passively) as impermeable, monolithic, and unchanging. Interactions were modeled as unidirectional and hierarchically defined, with the Maya "high culture" acting as a donor culture to the "low culture" non-Maya recipients of Maya-style pottery and other material goods as well as intangible concepts of political, economic, and social organization. In this approach, identity was viewed as *primordial*—a response to an innate human need for connection and belonging that was shaped by cultural norms.

Needless to say, subsequent research efforts have argued that this characterization is too simplistic and that it relied on the heavy-handed use of material culture trait lists typical of early culture history approaches to describe the interactions among the inhabitants of this area (Boone and Willey 1988; Robinson 1987; Schortman and Urban 1986:2). In time, processualist approaches reshaped these conceptualizations so the image of a monolithic border erratically shuffling back and forth was replaced by models that recognized interaction spheres. These spheres were defined by the common presence of certain pottery types throughout a delineable region (Andrews 1976:181; Demarest 1986:163; Demarest and Sharer 1986). Based on archaeologically recovered ceramic data, these interaction spheres were found to have extended back to the Preclassic period, where, for example, the Providencia/Miraflores and the Uapala ceramic spheres suggested the existence of separate but contemporaneous interaction zones in central highland Guatemala–western El Salvador and in central Honduras. It became clear that as early as the Late Preclassic, southeastern Maya elites were engaged in the construction of elaborate architecture, the erection of public sculptural monuments, and the exchange of prestige goods through long-distance trade routes (Dixon 1992; Sheets 1984:90–91; 2000:420). It was also clear that those interactions were more frequent within each sphere than between spheres, thus impacting group identities. While these ceramic spheres were vaguely associated with ethnic groups, they were conceived as the result of processes of socioeconomic interaction, elite prestation, and social competition or emulation, which helped explain the rise of sociopolitical complexity throughout the southeastern Maya area in the Late Preclassic period.

Beyond the Late Preclassic, research showed that interactions within and between ceramic spheres became even more complex, revealing a complicated network of interactions between different non-kin social groups. These interactions included cohabitation of ethnic groups in the same areas (Gerstle 1988), the local use and manipulation of interregional foreign objects and styles (Reents-Budet et al. 2004), the regional adoption of highly visible symbols of identity (Schortman 1989; Viel 1999), and, a tight cohesion, organization, and interaction among area elites (Ashmore 1984; Sharer 1978).

Although these processualist and transactionalist approaches, which modeled identity as *instrumental*—one of many tools deployed to achieve goals—opened many new avenues of investigation, several applications continued to emphasize elements (including, for example, monumental architecture, fine-ware pottery, sculpted monuments, inscribed texts) whose production is thought to have been under elite control. Characteristics like monumental art and ceramic style principally represent the activities, declared affinities, kinship, and public tastes of the powerful class. Furthermore, the active identities reflected in these attributes do not necessarily fully represent the complexity of this manipulation of styles, nor do they include all members of the group. Undoubtedly, commoners displayed their own identities and affiliations, and while these often intersected with those of the elites, they diverged in important ways. It is also likely that commoner identities were expressed in less ostentatious ways or by using perishable items such as clothing, which are less recognizable archaeologically. Nevertheless, these identities are part of the daily negotiations and interactions that occurred at all levels of the hierarchy in ancient centers. In other words, the new paradigms failed to assess the extent and diversity of salient social identities in the southeastern Maya area. They also failed to systematically explore the salience of different identities or changes in that salience through time (see Canuto 2002; Schortman 1989; Willey 1986).

ARCHAEOLOGY AND SOCIAL GROUPS

The archaeology of complex societies has had great success in recognizing and studying multiple forms of past societal organization, especially as it relates to class or status. These particular societal distinctions are often fixed within the material world to facilitate acceptance of a historical contingency as a natural fact. As a consequence, archaeology can recognize societal distinctions commonly expressed (and reinforced) by conscious manipulation of the material world. For instance, differences of *economic* class or *political* status were encoded in the built environment in an attempt to naturalize differences between groups—that is, to help "make inequality enchant" (Geertz 1980:123). In this way, the elements of material culture grouped within the old culture history "trait lists" can provide meaningful information about past identities. They serve as visible markers of choices made and actions undertaken in the past. For this reason, the study of a building's iconographic program can inform us about political changes within a polity, and an energetics analysis of a building's construction can help determine the extent of the residents' resource wealth.

NORMATIVE IDENTITY

Complex societies, however, consist of more than just status groups, economic classes, communities, and families. These societies are rife with large non-kin groups—such as *factions* or *ethnicities*—constituted of people who "think themselves into difference" (Cohen 1985:117). Such distinctions, also known as *salient social identities* (Schortman 1989; Schortman and Nakamura 1991), are collectives whose members often deploy a mutually recognized, exchanged, and manipulated subset of symbols to mark themselves.

While these symbols, also known as *diacritics* (Cohen 1978), might appear arbitrary from an etic perspective, the emic perception of them as representative of an imminent (almost normative) culture transforms them into effective and readily recognizable icons of identity. In fact, their normative quality often involves some form of materialization—such as architectural style, decoration, emblems, insignia, or even written language—that leaves an archaeological signature (in residential structures, building facades, prestation goods, or texts) of the group's self-proclamation.

TRANSACTIONALISM

It is also true that such social groups do not develop in a vacuum; they are situational, often defined in relation to others: *we are X because we are not Y* (Barth 1966; Bourdieu 1977; Shennan 1994). In fact, Dell Upton (1996:5, original emphasis) urges that archaeologists must not treat such diacritics "as something that can be held and nurtured, then photographed or excavated and identified, [but rather as processes] by which . . . groups form themselves by *choosing* to commodify their identities and to attach them to equally conscious chosen material signs."

Fredrik Barth (1969), in fact, noted that the specific "content" of any particular group is only a means to maintain boundaries of distinction. Interactions among individuals who share an affiliation erase subtle differences and reinforce similar dispositions based on a perception of shared material conditions of existence. Conversely, interactions between individuals who do not share such an affiliation reinforce their distinction, especially if those interactions are strictly limited and designed to highlight differences between them. In other words, Barth suggests that social groups are simply the consequence of interactions that form social groups, as in the case of *factionalization* or *ethnogenesis*.

This process is highlighted and even accelerated in situations of culture contact. Boundaries are formed through the negotiation of points of difference, and while ethnogenesis is often conceptualized as a slow, steady process, it can, in the proper circumstances, occur extremely quickly. Barbara Voss (2008), for example, traces the emergence within a single generation of a new "Californio" identity among the Mexican soldiers and their families sent by the Spanish Crown to fortify and guard the Presidio of San Francisco, California, in 1776. Full members of neither the Spanish political system they represented nor the indigenous Native North American populations they were charged with overseeing, the Mexican soldiers forged an independent identity that occupied the conceptual interstices of the multiethnic landscape in which they lived. The frontier zone along the southeast edge of the Maya area may have presented similarly intense and intrusive interrelations and likely resulted in swiftly forming, fluid social affiliations as individuals and groups sought to position themselves within the new sociopolitical milieu created by the expansion of Mayan-speaking groups into non-Maya territory in the Early Classic period.

SALIENCE AND AGENCY

In terms of archaeology, therefore, the dual strategy of identifying diacritics and evaluating the formation of boundaries provides some of the most useful and effective ways to consider the importance and impact of non-kin social groups in the past. It is not enough to identify which diacritics—such as architecture, decoration, emblems, or insignia—were used in a particular context. It is also important to assess how and for what reason these arbitrary symbols were deployed.

Nevertheless, the combination of normative and transactional approaches does not consider the fact that identity manipulation can often be the result of *individual* rather than *collective* strategies. It is important to acknowledge, therefore, the role of individuals in manipulating archaeologically visible diacritics rather than assuming that such assertions of normative identity characterize an entire population. The static, normative, monolithic identity asserted through the use of diacritics could be the result of a particular *negotiation of identity* despite a daily reality that reflects a more complicated and dynamic system of intercalated identities. To link normative and transactionalist definitions of identity with a practice-oriented approach, the manipulation of diacritics should be seen as a negotiation or declaration of a social identity rather than a result of the identity itself.

LATE CLASSIC IDENTITY: THE SOUTHEASTERN MAYA AREA

In Classic Maya society (AD 250–900), for example, groups such as lineages, political factions, or ethnicities reflect some of the potential salient identities used to integrate people into large, non-local, extra-kin groups. To investigate how identities were formed, tolerated, and maintained within the southeastern Maya area's

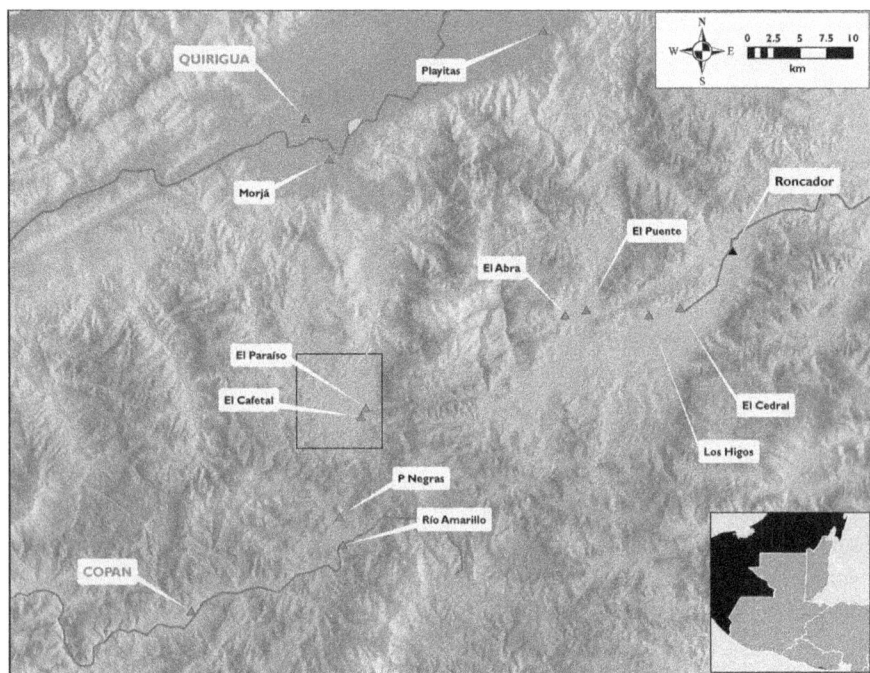

MAP 9.1. Southeast Maya area

multiethnic landscape, the Proyecto Arqueólogico Regional El Paraíso (PAREP; Bell, Canuto, and Ramos 2001; Canuto and Bell 2008, 2013; Canuto, Charton, and Bell 2010; von Schwerin 2010) conducted nine years of archaeological investigations at two Classic period sites in the El Paraíso Valley, western Honduras (map 9.1). This valley is located between Copán and Quiriguá along a trade route that also provided access to central Honduras. The well-watered, fertile, alluvial bottomlands are more extensive than those in the Copán Valley (Fash 1983), suggesting that the present high agricultural productivity likely extended into the past.

When archaeological research first began at Copán, only the site of El Paraíso was known in the valley (Lothrop 1926; Morley 1917, 1920; Sapper 1898; Yde 1936, 1938). Early reports noted that this site was an important regional center located between Copán and Quiriguá and that this importance was underscored by the presence of standing architecture and plentiful evidence of architectural sculpture. Given the rarity of both attributes throughout the Copán hinterlands, it became apparent that the El Paraíso elites were important members of regional Classic Maya society. These early reports supported the impression that Copán influence (and the Maya ethnicity associated with it) extended homogeneously throughout the region.

In the 1980s, however, a far more complex picture of regional identity began to emerge when David Vlcek and William Fash (1986) reported a second large site in the valley that differed in significant ways from El Paraíso. The second site, known as El Cafetal, is located a scant 1.5 km southwest of El Paraíso; while the two sites are largely coeval, they differ from one another in significant and pervasive ways. As both sites appear to have been the settings for the same range of residential and administrative activities, their dissimilarity cannot be ascribed to differences in function or status alone. Instead, we suggest that these centers reflect the presence of two distinct social groups living side by side in the valley during the Late Classic period. To explore this possibility, we discuss several of the more archaeologically visible ways affiliation and identity can be expressed, including site plan, construction techniques, architectural embellishment, the use of open space, and portable material culture. We conclude with a discussion of the implications of this pattern for our understanding of ethnogenesis and interaction in the region and beyond.

EL PARAÍSO AND EL CAFETAL: A STUDY IN CONTRASTS

The El Paraíso Valley contains two linked but culturally distinct contemporaneous Late Classic centers, El Cafetal and El Paraíso (map 9.2). Differences in settlement patterns, site plans, architectural design, construction techniques, sculpture, and portable material culture indicate that El Cafetal was a long-lived, autochthonous center, while El Paraíso was established by Copán elites (or at least under their auspices) in the mid-seventh century A D and likely served as an administrative outpost. Available data suggest that this administrative strategy, which highlighted cultural distinctions, is unique among Maya polities and appears to have been limited to southeast Mesoamerica, where it may have been replicated by the centers of El Puente and El Abra in the La Venta Valley, 29 km southeast of the El Paraíso Valley (Nakamura, Aoyama, and Uratsuji 1991), and possibly by the centers of Morja and Quiriguá in the Motagua Valley, 30 km to the north (Ashmore 2007). These patterns suggest that PAREP has documented an administrative strategy particular to Copán rulers. Such findings support, complement, and expand research in other Maya kingdoms, including Yaxchilan and Piedras Negras (Golden et al. 2008, 2012), in which distinct local administrative strategies have been documented. We suggest that this strategy was tailored to and necessitated by the presence of multiple salient social identities in the region and that, in essence, it was specifically designed to meet the unique challenges present in a multiethnic frontier zone.

Extensive excavations in the valley have shown the sites to be markedly different in nearly every respect investigated. By the mid-seventh century A D, stark

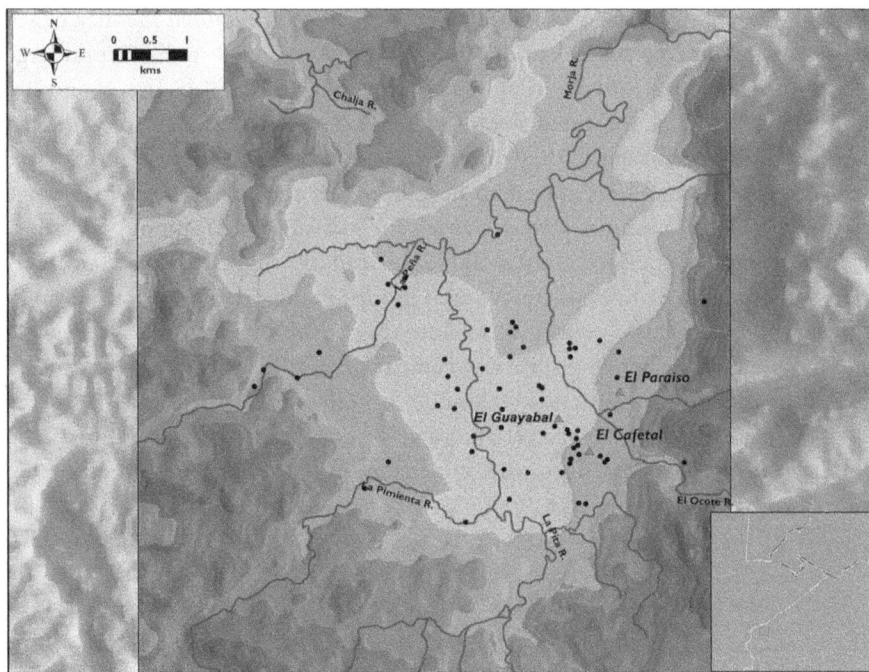

MAP 9.2. Settlement in the El Paraíso Valley, western Honduras

differences between the two major Late Classic settlements were very apparent and would have shaped the lives of residents at each center.

EL PARAÍSO: A COPÁN ENCLAVE IN THE EL PARAÍSO VALLEY

The site of El Paraíso (map 9.3), which we believe was established as an enclave by or in association with the Copán elite, is a quadrangular center situated in the foothills along the southeastern edge of the valley. Its site plan is characterized by enclosed, sunken patios surrounded by monumental architecture and elite residences. The buildings are composed of stone-faced substructure platforms topped by stone structures, many of which include dressed volcanic tuff (*toba*) masonry and Copán-style mosaic sculpture. Elite residences contain built-in architectural features commonly found in elite Maya residences, including benches, "curtain holders," and niches. Many of the buildings retain traces of the stucco (in at least one instance red-painted) that covered superstructure walls, floors, and benches. Water flow out of (and possibly into) the stucco-surfaced main plaza was facilitated

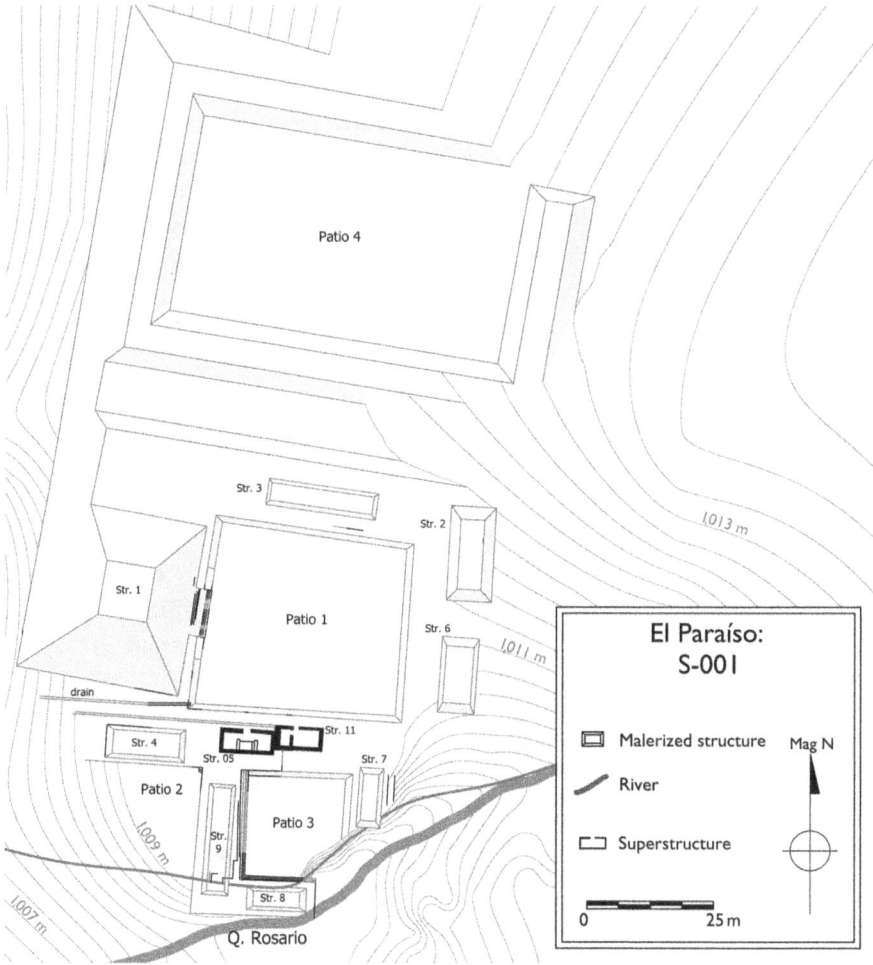

MAP 9.3. El Paraíso site map

by an elaborate drainage system integrally constructed with the southwest corner of the sunken court.

At El Paraíso, open spaces appear to have been swept clean, and phosphate analysis within the sunken courts suggests that they may not have been used for phosphate-rich activities such as food preparation, consumption, or disposal (Canuto, Charton, and Bell 2010). El Paraíso residents did, however, cache objects, including large ceramic jars, beneath the surface of these open spaces. Like the architecture, portable material culture at El Paraíso suggests that the residents were closely tied to the Copán ceramic economy, with Copán pottery types comprising as much as 95 percent of the fine wares, 80 percent of the censers, and even a striking 70 percent of the utilitarian wares found at the site analyzed to date. These types include Copador polychromes, black-brown Surlo carved wares, and Copán jars (Bill et al. 2006; Bill, Levan, and McFarlane 2007). Settlement at El Paraíso also appears to have been limited to the Classic period, with no evidence of occupation before that time and very ephemeral traces of any activity in the Postclassic period. In sum, El Paraíso exhibits all the hallmarks of a Copán-style center that may have served as an outpost for further Copán administrative strategies in the region.

El Cafetal: A Long-Lived Local Center

The nearby center of El Cafetal (map 9.4), located a mere 1.5 km to the south and west of El Paraíso, provides stark contrasts with its neighbor. At El Cafetal, the site plan may best be characterized as an open plaza plan: no known corners are closed, there are ample points of access into and out of the site core, and the northern portion of the site appears to have included a formalized entrance that opens to the northwest, onto the bottomlands that comprise the vast majority of the valley. This entrance is defined by a cobble-paved plaza bordered by two low structures (Structures 12 and 13) and bounded to the south by a low platform (Structure 9) and steps that lead into the Main Plaza. Phosphate analysis combines with spatial patterning to suggest that space within the site was organized in loosely defined areas that served as the settings for a variety of open-air activities (Canuto, Charton, and Bell 2010). At El Cafetal, buildings are composed of cobble-faced substructure platforms with earth and cobble fill. Low cobble-faced steps or terraces provide access to the summits, while side and rear walls are steep and narrow. These substructures are topped by perishable buildings seated on cobble foundations, and most include large, open interior rooms.

In contrast to the portable material culture at El Paraíso, pottery at El Cafetal boasts a large percentage of locally made ceramic vessels, including both fine and utilitarian wares. There is also, however, a significant amount of pottery, especially fine wares, imported from Copán. Local wares include jars, modeled and scored censers, and small orange-slipped bowls. When seen side by side, the ceramic frequencies at El Paraíso and El Cafetal present a stark contrast, highlighting the strong connections with the Copán ceramic economy enjoyed by El Paraíso residents and the vibrant local ceramic economy in which those who lived at El Cafetal participated (Bill et al. 2006; Bill, Levan, and McFarlane 2007). El Cafetal also appears to have had a much longer occupation history than El Paraíso, with extensive deposits of Preclassic pottery found below the Late Classic plaza floors. In sum, El Cafetal

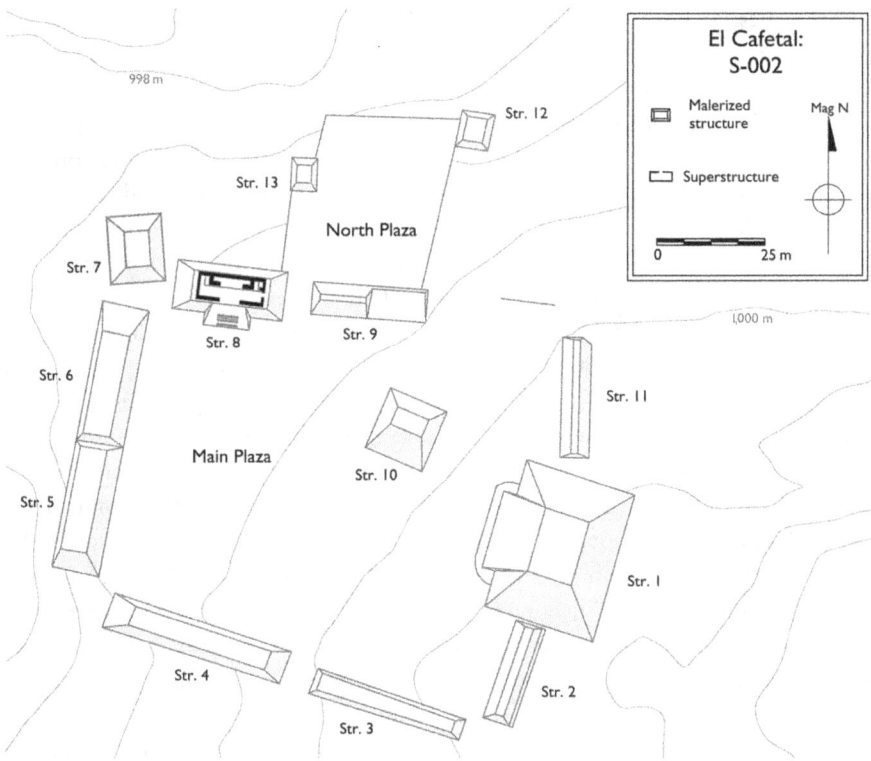

MAP 9.4. El Cafetal site map

appears to have been a long-lived local center whose residents marshaled their own strategies vis-à-vis Copán elites—both in the valley and beyond.

ETHNOGENESIS ON THE EDGE OF THE COPÁN KINGDOM

Much of the PAREP research in the El Paraíso Valley has developed from a transactionalist paradigm. When we started in 2001, we focused on the strategic location of the El Paraíso Valley along routes connecting Copán, Quiriguá, and settlements in central Honduras and the dynamic frontier zone interactions this location likely fostered. By intensively investigating the region, we recovered not only evidence for the deployment of salient social identities in interactionalist strategies to secure privileges and resources but also evidence of the salience of social identity altogether. In other words, although we have attempted to identify the processes that led to the use and deployment of critical group-marking diacritics, we also noted a pervasiveness of difference that extended beyond the predicted scope of a "strategic" (or transactionalist) deployment of such diacritics. How, then, might this unexpected emphasis on difference be explained? Rather than attribute it to an irreducible primordial normative distinction between two groups that could not help but be encoded in the archaeological record, we turned to broader and more complex models of the role of ethnicity and ethnogenesis in the negotiation of difference.

The forging of ethnicity and the shared identities it can create is a complex, dynamic, and multidirectional process and must be understood as such. As Wolfgang Gabbert (2004:xii) notes, ethnic identity does not automatically result in group integration, solidarity, or shared awareness of a unifying identity; and Barbara Voss (2008) has demonstrated that ethnogenesis can be employed both as a means of resistance and in the assertion of dominance. As a supra-ordinate identity, Lisa LeCount (this volume) suggests that ethnicity subsumes many facets of selfhood whose members are unevenly connected through nested and overlapping affiliation; that is, "given that members of any ethnic group share some identities with oppositional groups, nested and overlapping affiliations contribute to the often amorphous and unbounded character of ethnicity." As such, ethnic groups are better understood as "imagined communities" that provide few opportunities for group-wide face-to-face interaction. Furthermore, in complex societies, where people of different ethnic backgrounds come into daily contact, individuals are prompted to develop and express multiple affiliations—such as social status, craft specializations, or gender—that cross-cut or even undermine ethnic boundaries. As a consequence, ethnic affiliation is not necessarily encouraged; in some cases, it might not be salient at all.

What might therefore impel the construction or discovery of similarities among people who otherwise perform conflicting identities and whose differences are not necessarily resolved by ethnic affiliation? In essence, what are the conditions for *ethnogenesis*? Fredrik Barth (1969:18) has suggested that ethnic distinction becomes relevant in conditions where a large number of social roles and values are canalized and standardized. These conditions simultaneously foment *communitas* among those who would otherwise express obvious differences and impel the exclusion of those who do not share the most salient social values.

We contend that in the Classic period, the El Paraíso Valley—and much of the Copán region more broadly—demonstrates many of the conditions under which ethnic identity would have been rendered broadly meaningful, despite (or, perhaps more appropriately, as a response to) intense intra-regional interaction. In other words, ethnic attribution would have been part of the public discourse, perhaps pervasively and prevailingly so. As such, we have suggested (Bell, Canuto, and Ramos 2001; Canuto and Bell 2008, 2013; Canuto, Bell, and Bill 2007; Canuto,

Charton, and Bell 2010) that *identity politics* played a key role in the development and management of Copán's Classic period polity.

ETHNOGENESIS AT EL PARAÍSO

How and why do we interpret the archaeological record in this fashion? We use Barth (1969) as a guide to determine if the conditions for *ethnogenesis*—the rendering salient of distinct ethnic identities—were present in the southeastern Maya area during the Classic period. Barth (ibid.) claimed that conditions needed for ethnogenesis between groups include structural complementarity, interdependence of resource management, and mutual and sustained interaction. We have found patterns that suggest these processes were present in the El Paraíso Valley and consider each of them below. Data from a wider region, including the centers of Copán, Quiriguá, Los Higos, El Puente, and Río Amarillo, also suggest that such conditions were present in much of the area Copán dynasts controlled during the Classic period, providing venues for further investigation of these processes.

COMPLEMENTARITY

Groups living side by side in the El Paraíso Valley were indeed structurally complementary. All data suggest that the residents of both El Paraíso and El Cafetal were organized hierarchically by status and wealth. Despite the different ways they were manifested, residents of both centers shared concepts of private versus public space, elite versus commoner identities, sacred versus profane places, and fine versus utilitarian goods. In the case of El Paraíso and El Cafetal, the differences between these two groups were "stable, so that the complementary differences on which the systems rest can persist in the face of close inter-ethnic contact" (ibid.:19).

INTERDEPENDENCE

For the further canalization in intergroup interaction to occur, some co-dependence must develop between groups as they vie for access to limited resources. In the case of the El Paraíso Valley and broadly throughout the southeastern Maya area, residents of El Paraíso and El Cafetal occupied the same environmental zone, likely leading to competition for similar resources that fomented border formation and border politics. The location of El Cafetal along an important communication route likely led to the establishment of El Paraíso in the same region, sharing the economic and strategic value of the valley. This paring was repeated at other important transportation chokepoints in the Copán region, such as in the Río Amarillo,

La Florida, and La Venta Valleys. The intermixing of these groups led to the development of several flashpoints where "border politics" was paramount.

MUTUAL SUSTAINED INTERACTION

A final requisite for the encouragement of ethnic identity formation would appear counterintuitive—continued intense interaction. That is, for Barth, the practice that enjoins identity formation is knowledge and acknowledgment of the "Other." Interaction across boundaries, whether physical, social, political, or economic, provides opportunity for both, allowing for the recognition and refinement of differences. This is especially true if those interactions are limited despite being frequent. Moreover, this interaction also provides the opportunity for code switching, assimilation, and incorporation—all forms of interaction that lead to the explicit, assertive, and active use of difference markers. For the El Paraíso Valley and, indeed, the larger Copán region, there is little evidence that population movement was restricted or hindered. Considering the intermixing of utilitarian vessels and lithic tool styles found in the household middens of both sites in the El Paraíso Valley, it is clear that the exchange of everyday goods—and the interactions that accompanied it—was commonplace.

PERFORMING AND MAINTAINING ETHNICITIES: CREATING AND CROSSING ETHNIC BOUNDARIES

Considering that the Classic period El Paraíso Valley presented the proper conditions for ethnogenesis, we now turn to the evidence that supports the notion that the predominant public discourse in the Classic period Copán polity involved the development, maintenance, and allusion to ethnic identity. Like LeCount (this volume), we suggest that ethnogenesis would result in a marked rise in the deployment of materialized and standardized symbols of affiliation. Since there is no fundamental set of symbols that inherently represent social difference (Emberling 1997), any argument that depends on the use of such symbols—diacritics—must ensure that they were indeed meaningful.

We have discussed in detail (Bell, Canuto, and Ramos 2001; Canuto and Bell 2008, 2013; Canuto, Bell, and Bill 2007; Canuto, Charton, and Bell 2010) the large-scale differences between the two major Classic period sites in the El Paraíso Valley. We have noted major differences regarding access, site plan, architectural style, spatial organization, decorative motifs, use of open spaces, elite ceramics, and other portable material culture. Along all these distinct lines of evidence, we note that the site of El Paraíso consistently reproduced "Copán-style" attributes, such as red-painted plastered buildings, enclosed patios, mosaic sculpture decoration, and Surlo ceramics. In almost symmetrical contradistinction, the site of El Cafetal reflected attributes more commonly associated with Honduran sites located along the Chamelecon, Sula, and Cacaulapa drainages, including un-stuccoed buildings made of perishable materials or lightly shaped stone, open plazas, no mosaic sculpture of any kind, and a preponderance of locally produced utilitarian and fine-ware ceramics.

The differences exhibited by these two coeval and neighboring centers reflect both isochrestic (unconscious) variation (Sackett 1990) and distinct assertive styles (Wiessner 1990). Certain attributes, such as Copán-style architectural sculpture, represent an assertion by leading El Paraíso families of participation and membership in a Copán-centered elite group. These decorative features likely could be and were bestowed on rulers, families, or groups that adopted a certain factional allegiance to Copán. In other words, the leading residents of El Paraíso were affiliated with the Late Classic ruling elite of Copán. They may even have been members of a noble house from Copán sent to the El Paraíso Valley to guard the socioeconomic interests of the Copán dynasty. The El Cafetal paramounts, conversely, likely shared no such affiliation with Copán elite.

These active (or assertive) stylistic differences are also accompanied by several examples of isochrestic (or unconscious) variation, including building techniques, spatial plans, and the use of open space. These latter distinctions support the proposition that differences between the inhabitants of these two sites reflect aesthetic and cultural distinctions among their respective inhabitants. In other words, these material differences between the centers are typical of groups that define themselves according to ethnic differences. These findings might be interpreted as suggesting that the residents of El Cafetal and its surrounding settlements did not see themselves as Maya (or, more specifically, as part of the social and ethnic group headed by Copán elites).

The combination of passive and active stylistic differences between these two centers speaks to differences of primordial as well as instrumental identity between their occupants. Not only did shared identities foster a sense of connection and belonging tied to shared traditions and experiences, but they could also be deployed strategically to achieve specific goals. The differences between these two groups asserted across the material and behavioral categories discussed above suggest the mutual participation of valley residents in boundary maintenance. This boundary did not separate two territories; rather, it was the consequence of local ethnogenesis that highlighted a local version of a Lowland Maya elite identity and a local version of a non-Maya identity.

In our model, ethnogenesis is an unintended consequence of the political expansion of the Copán polity. As Geoff Emberling (1997:308) claims: "A new ethnic identity often develops when a state conquers or otherwise encompasses previously independent groups . . . The newly formed ethnic groups in these situations thus arise on the margins of expanding states. States very often attempt to dramatically increase the rigidity of cultural differences between these groups, as a strategy of control."

In the complex, multicultural milieu of the Classic period, Copán dynasts forged an administrative strategy that exacerbated rather than diminished difference. El Paraíso, the outpost center Copán elites built on the southeastern edge of the valley, was designed to contrast with local patterns at El Cafetal in nearly every way possible, standing out in stark relief against them. The research discussed above has suggested that these patterns extend beyond the two large centers to characterize at least some of the settlements that surrounded each. Copán elites drove wedges across cultural boundaries to gain access to trade routes, agricultural surpluses, and raw materials rather than seeking to fully assimilate regional populations and mask ethnopolitical differences.

DYNAMICS OF IDENTITY POLITICS

Although intergroup interaction, interdependence, and competition may fuel the *creation* of diacritics, their deployment is a fluid and recursive process prone to modification. In mature sociopolitical landscapes, some diacritics are discarded while others creep semantic value into other symbolic fields through forms of identity politics similar to those described above for ethnogenesis. The malleability of diacritics can be seen in the way ethnopolitical distinctions between Maya and non-Maya peoples eroded rapidly in the second half of the eighth century AD and old symbols of ethnicity were repurposed for new political ends. Stark differences between the two groups were carefully crafted and maintained from AD 600 to 750. However, in the middle of the eighth century AD, the multiethnic landscape of the Copán kingdom was plunged into political conflict. Given the El Paraíso Valley's location and cultural configuration, its residents would have had to have confronted the host of cultural, political, and economic upheavals that transformed the southeastern Maya area during the ninth century AD.

At the height of the Classic period, Copán's thirteenth ruler, Waxaklajuun Ubaah K'awiil, met his untimely end. In AD 738 he warred unsuccessfully against his longtime ally K'ahk' Tiliw Chan Yopaat (AD 724–85), the ruler of Quiriguá. As a result of this military misadventure, he was beheaded, leaving the erstwhile subordinate lord of Quiriguá in control of the entire region. Furthermore, the Quiriguá ruler not only claimed to have destroyed his rival's gods but also subsequently adopted Copán's royal titles, claiming himself as the rightful successor to Copán's dynasty (Martin and Grube 2008). He also claimed control over paramounts of several nearby centers to bolster his assertion of regional supremacy. References to these centers (including one nicknamed "Xkuy" mentioned in texts found at both Copán and Quiriguá) have yet to be linked to archaeologically known sites, but centers in the El Paraíso Valley and the larger region are possible candidates.

During this period of political turmoil, the distinctions between El Cafetal and El Paraíso faded somewhat. Several new residential, ceremonial, and administrative buildings—Structures 6, 7, and 8—that have no stylistic precedent were constructed at El Cafetal. Their platforms and superstructures are made of cut stone. Their facades and floors were coated with stucco. The buildings were not, however, embellished with any mosaic sculpture.

The unusual floor plan of the Structure 8 superstructure warrants additional attention. Its interior consists of a single transverse room that gives access to three much smaller rooms or niches whose floors are raised above that of the transverse room, all of which have plaster floors and stuccoed walls. Although smaller in size, this building is reminiscent of Structure 10L-22 at Copán and Structure 1B-5 at Quiriguá—both considered throne rooms for their rulers, Waxaklajun Ubaah K'awil (Ruler 13 of Copán) and K'ahk' Tiliw Chan Yopaat (ruler of Quiriguá), respectively. Moreover, both buildings date to the same time period in which El Cafetal Structure 8 was constructed.

While the specific affiliation of El Cafetal paramounts with Copán or Quiriguá kings requires further investigation, it is clear that at some time during the eighth century AD a building that fits perfectly within the Late Classic Maya elite aesthetic of the southeast Maya area was constructed at El Cafetal, perhaps as a reward for the paramounts' support. It resembles the architecture found at El Paraíso; and its construction techniques, architectural embellishment, and spatial organization contrast strongly with almost all other buildings at El Cafetal. Along with the contemporaneous Structures 6 and 7, which exhibit similar construction styles and embellishment, Structure 8 anchors a new elite ward within the center, possibly reflecting new opportunities and affiliations marshaled by El Cafetal paramounts even as direct Copán influence in the region faltered.

The Copán-Quiriguá conflict likely cleaved the region into at least two political factions (elite groups) with mutually exclusive and competing interests, both of which used the same diacritics to signal membership. The political conflict in the region gave El Cafetal paramounts access to resources, technology, and labor that in the Copán hinterlands had been limited previously to specific centers, such as El Paraíso. Consequently, the Late Classic Mayanization of the Copán region might be related more to the political fission between Copán and Quiriguá in AD 738 than to the (inexorable) enculturation of non-Maya peoples.

CONCLUSION

Questions about the salience of ethnic identity are broadly applicable throughout the Copán polity rather than just within the El Paraíso Valley. Identity was not so localized as to be limited to small geographic entities such as individual river valleys. Rather, the El Paraíso Valley is a space in which ongoing processes of ethnogenisis were foregrounded and intensified as Copán diacritics were marshaled for use in interactions outside the Copán Valley. The deployment of Copanec affiliation and identity in the El Paraíso Valley was a reflection of the assertiveness with which inhabitants of the region found it necessary to stake their claim. Heightened, perhaps even literally loud, proclamations of their identity throughout the region would have resulted in the marked differences between the sites that we have documented not only in the El Paraíso Valley but potentially throughout the Copán region.

With the conflict between Copán and Quiriguá in the mid-eighth century AD, the salience of these distinctions drained away as new and perhaps more chaotic and contingent networks of political alliance were developed. What likely had been predictable, canalized, and standardized interactions throughout the Classic period "might have become impossible with so many people linked in ever more complicated configurations" (Schortman and Ashmore 2007:23). The situation could only have been exacerbated by the seeming instability of the resulting networks, given that each included subgroups in active or potential competition with one another (ibid.).

The Copán-Quiriguá conflict undermined the canalized and restricted forms of interaction between the two groups in such a way that diacritics came under the aegis of political alliance rather than ethnic affiliation. Furthermore, group solidarity within these volatile networks would have been more difficult to maintain because there would have been much less impetus to establish cooperative, complementary, interdependent, and sustained forms of interaction. In the finale decades of the Classic period, the area would have been awash with now ambiguous symbols of affiliation that likely accelerated the collapse of the regional political system, the increase in self-sustaining communities, the reduction of interregional interaction, and a fading of the salience of ethnic identity.

In this way, research in the El Paraíso Valley brings an additional dimension to discussions of the "Mayanization" of Honduras in the present day. By providing a model in which the salience of ethnic affiliation and identity must be demonstrated rather than assumed and by demonstrating that diacritics commonly interpreted as direct indicators of the performance of ethnicity may be marshaled across etically defined ethnic boundaries as events warrant, this research underscores the complexities of identity formation and expression. It provides a broader framework within which to explore the use of "Maya-style" images, iconography, architectural forms, and embellishments in modern practice in Honduras. Perhaps some modern ethnic identities prove to be the result of modern-day state-formation strategies.

However, it is also just as true that the incorporation (or co-option) of Copán-style architectural cannons by El Cafetal elites in the mid-eighth century AD may be understood not as the adoption of a new ethnic identity but rather as the marshaling of potent elite markers in a political milieu in which they become both accessible and salient. It follows, therefore, that the modern-day assertive use of "Maya-style" imagery in daily practice in Honduras could also be understood in the same light. In other words, the adoption of these symbols does not necessarily signal the erasure of difference and the (self-)denial of one's own identity. Rather, the symbols can be understood as modern examples of the long-enduring and effective strategy of pragmatic co-option of master narratives and symbols made available through the public sphere.

NOTES

1. "Copán was founded as a Toltec colony; its king dominated the country that extends to the east of the Maya of Yucatán, stretching from the Gulf of Honduras to near the Pacific Ocean" (translation by authors).

2. "For eight years I've known that Honduras was completely Maya and [the] teacher/master of Mayab; but not only foreigners, who usually see things superficially, but also Honduras's own sons deny their mother country that which is most precious, the maternal role, and one as noble as that of the Maya" (translation by authors).

REFERENCES CITED

Andrews, E. W., V. 1976. *The Archaeology of Quelepa, El Salvador*. New Orleans: Middle American Research Institute.

Ashmore, W. A. 1984. "Quirigua Archaeology and History Revisited." *Journal of Field Archaeology* 11: 365–86.

Ashmore, W. A. 2007. *Settlement Archaeology at Quirgua, Guatemala*. Philadelphia: University of Pennsylvania Museum of Archaeology and Anthropology.

Barth, F. 1966. *Models of Social Organization*. London: Royal Anthropological Institute.

Barth, F. 1969. "Introduction." In *Ethnic Groups and Boundaries*, ed. F. Barth, 9–38. Boston: Little, Brown.

Bell, E. E., M. A. Canuto, and J. Ramos. 2001. "El Paraíso: Punto Embocadero de la Periferia Sudeste Maya." *Yaxkin* 19: 41–75.

Bill, C. R., E. E. Bell, M. A. Canuto, and P. L. Geller. 2006. "From the Edge of the Copan Kingdom: Recent Research in the El Paraíso Valley." Paper presented at the 71st Annual Meeting of the Society for American Archaeology, San Juan, Puerto Rico, April 26–30.

Bill, C. R., L. Levan, and W. J. McFarlane. 2007. "Local Traditions and Imported Ceramics in the El Paraíso Valley, Honduras, during the Classic Period." Paper presented at the 72nd Annual Meeting of the Society for American Archaeology, Austin, TX, April 25–29.

Boone, E. H., and G. R. Willey, eds. 1988. *The Southeast Classic Maya Zone*. Washington, DC: Dumbarton Oaks.

Bourdieu, P. 1977. *Outline of a Theory of Practice*. Trans. R. Nice. Cambridge: Cambridge University Press. http://dx.doi.org/10.1017/CBO9780511812507.

Canuto, M. A. 2002. "A Tale of Two Communities: Social and Political Transformation in the Hinterlands of the Maya Polity of Copan." PhD dissertation, Department of Anthropology, University of Pennsylvania, Philadelphia.

Canuto, M. A., and E. E. Bell. 2008. "Ties That Bind: Administrative Strategies in the El Paraiso Valley, Department of Copan, Honduras." *Mexicon* 30 (1): 10–20.

Canuto, M. A., and E. E. Bell. 2013. "Archaeological Investigations in the El Paraíso Valley: The Role of Secondary Centers in the Multiethnic Landscape of Classic Period Copan." *Ancient Mesoamerica* 24 (1): 1–24. http://dx.doi.org/10.1017/S0956536113000011.

Canuto, M. A., E. E. Bell, and C. R. Bill. 2007. "Desde el Limite del Reino de Copán: Modelando la integración socio-política de los Mayas del clásico." In *XX Simposio de Investigaciones Arqueológicas en Guatemala*, ed. J. P. Laporte, B. Arroyo, and H. Mejía, 737–52. Guatemala City: Ministerio de Cultura y Deportes, Instituto de Antropología e Historia, Asociación Tikal, Fundación Arqueológica del Nuevo Mundo.

Canuto, M. A., J. A. Charton, and E. E. Bell. 2010. "Let No Space Go to Waste: Comparing the Uses of Space between Two Late Classic Centers in the El Paraiso Valley, Copan, Honduras." *Journal of Archaeological Science* 37 (1): 30–41. http://dx.doi.org/10.1016/j.jas.2009.08.021.

Cohen, A. P. 1985. *The Symbolic Construction of Community*. London: Routledge. http://dx.doi.org/10.4324/9780203323373.

Cohen, R. 1978. "Ethnicity: The Problem and Focus in Anthropology." *Annual Review of Anthropology* 7 (1): 379–403. http://dx.doi.org/10.1146/annurev.an.07.100178.002115.

Demarest, A. A. 1986. *The Archaeology of Santa Leticia and the Rise of Maya Civilization*. Middle American Research Institute Monograph 52. New Orleans: Middle American Research Institute, Tulane University.

Demarest, A. A., and R. J. Sharer. 1986. "Late Preclassic Ceramic Spheres, Culture Areas, and Cultural Evolution in the Southeastern Highlands of Mesoamerica." In *The Southeast Maya Periphery*, ed. P. A. Urban and E. M. Schortman, 194–223. Austin: University of Texas Press.

Dixon, B. 1992. "Prehistoric Political Change on the Southeast Mesoamerican Periphery." *Ancient Mesoamerica* 3 (1): 11–25. http://dx.doi.org/10.1017/S0956536100002261.

Emberling, G. 1997. "Ethnicity in Complex Societies: Archaeological Perspectives." *Journal of Archaeological Research* 5 (4): 295–344. http://dx.doi.org/10.1007/BF 02229256.

Fash, W. L. 1983. "Maya State Formation: A Case Study and Its Implications." PhD dissertation, Department of Anthropology, Harvard University, Cambridge, MA.

Gabbert, W. 2004. *Becoming Maya: Ethnicity and Social Inequality in Yucatán since 1500.* Tucson: University of Arizona Press.

Galindo, J. 1945. "Informe de la comisión científica formada para el reconomcimiento de Copán, por Decreto de 15 de enero de 1934." *Anales de la Sociedad de Geografía e Historia* 20: 217–28.

Geertz, C. 1980. *Negara: The Theater State in Nineteenth Century Bali.* Princeton, NJ: Princeton University Press.

Gerstle, A. 1988. "Maya-Lenca Ethnic Relations in Late Classic Period Copan, Honduras." PhD dissertation, Department of Anthropology, The Pennsylvania State University, State College.

Golden, C. M., A. Scherer, A. R. Muñoz, and Z. Hruby. 2012. "Polities, Boundaries, and Trade in the Classic Period Usumacinta River Basin." *Mexicon* 34 (1): 11–19.

Golden, C. M., A. Scherer, A. R. Muñoz, and R. Vásquez. 2008. "Piedras Negras and Yaxchilan: Divergent Political Trajectories in Adjacent Maya Polities." *Latin American Antiquity* 13 (3): 249–74.

Hay, C. L., R. L. Linton, S. K. Lothrop, H. L. Shapiro, and G. C. Vaillant, eds. 1940. *The Maya and Their Neighbors: Essays on Middle American Anthropology and Archaeology.* New York: Dover.

Kirchoff, P. 1943. "Mesoamerica: Its Geographical Limits, Ethnic Composition, and Cultural Characteristics." *Acta Americana* 1 (1): 92–107.

Longyear, J. M. 1947. *Cultures and Peoples of the Southeastern Maya Frontier.* Cambridge, MA: Division of Historical Research, Theoretical Approaches to Problems, Carnegie Institution of Washington.

Lothrop, S. K. 1926. "Stone Sculptures from the Finca Arevalo, Guatemala." *Indian Notes* 3 (3): 147–71.

Lothrop, S. K. 1939. "The Southeastern Frontier of the Maya." *American Anthropologist* 41 (1): 42–54. http://dx.doi.org/10.1525/aa.1939.41.1.02a00040.

Lunardi, F. 1948. *Honduras Maya, Etnología de Honduras (Estudios Mayas-Orientaciones).* Tegucigalpa: Biblioteca de la Sociedad de Antropología y Arqueología de Honduras y del Centro de Estudios Mayas.

Martin, S., and N. Grube. 2008. *Chronicle of the Maya Kings and Queens*, 2nd ed. London: Thames and Hudson.

Morley, S. G. 1917. "Archaeology." *Year Book* 16: 285–89.

Morley, S. G. 1920. *The Inscriptions at Copan*. Publication 219. Washington, DC: Carnegie Institution of Washington.

Nakamura, S., K. Aoyama, and E. Uratsuji, eds. 1991. *Investigaciones Arqueológicas en la Región de La Entrada, Primera Fase*. San Pedro Sula, Honduras: Servicio de Voluntarios Japoneses para la Cooperación con el Extranjero and Instituto Hondureño de Antropología e Historia.

Reents-Budet, D., E. E. Bell, R. L. Bishop, and L. P. Traxler. 2004. "Early Classic Ceramic Offerings at Copan: A Comparison of the Hunal, Margarita, and Sub-Jaguar Tombs." In *Understanding Early Classic Copan*, ed. E. E. Bell, M. A. Canuto, and R. J. Sharer, 159–90. Philadelphia: University of Pennsylvania Museum.

Robinson, E. J., ed. 1987. *Interaction on the Southeast Mesoamerican Frontier*. 2 vols. Oxford: British Archaeological Reports.

Sackett, J. R. 1990. "Style and Ethnicity in Archaeology: The Case for Isochrestism." In *The Uses of Style in Archaeology*, ed. M. W. Conkey and C. A. Hastorf, 32–43. Cambridge: Cambridge University Press.

Sapper, Karl. 1898. "Die Ruinen von Mixco (Guatemala)." *Internationales Archiv für Ethnographie* 11: 1–6, pl. 2, 5 plans.

Schortman, E. M. 1989. "Interregional Interaction in Prehistory: The Need for a New Perspective." *American Antiquity* 54 (1): 52–65. http://dx.doi.org/10.2307/281331.

Schortman, E. M., and W. A. Ashmore. 2007. "Reaching beyond Boundaries: A Network Perspective on Political Competition in the Late and Terminal Classic Lower Motagua Valley, Guatemala." Paper presented at the 72nd Annual Meeting of the Society for American Archaeology, Austin, TX, April 25–29.

Schortman, E. M., and S. Nakamura. 1991. "A Crisis of Identity: Late Classic Competition and Interaction on the Southeast Maya Periphery." *Latin American Antiquity* 2 (4): 311–36. http://dx.doi.org/10.2307/971781.

Schortman, E. M., and P. A. Urban. 1986. "Introduction." In *The Southeast Maya Periphery*, ed. P. A. Urban and E. M. Schortman, 1–14. Austin: University of Texas Press.

Sharer, R. J. 1978. "Archaeology and History at Quirigua, Guatemala." *Journal of Field Archaeology* 5: 51–70.

Sheets, P. D. 1984. "The Prehistory of El Salvador: An Interpretive Summary." In *The Archaeology of Lower Central America*, ed. F. Lange and D. Stone, 85–112. Albuquerque: University of New Mexico Press.

Sheets, P. D. 2000. "The Southeast Frontiers of Mesoamerica." In *The Cambridge History of the Native Peoples of the Americas*, vol. 2: *Mesoamerica, Part 1*, ed. R. E. W. Adams and M. J. Macleod, 407–48. Cambridge: Cambridge University Press.

Shennan, S. J. 1994. *Archaeological Approaches to Cultural Identity: One World Archaeology*. London: Routledge.

Upton, D. 1996. "Ethnicity, Authenticity, and Invented Traditions." *Historical Archaeology* 30 (2): 1–7.

Viel, R. H. 1999. "The Pectorals of Altar Q and Structure 11: An Interpretation of the Political Organization at Copán, Honduras." *Latin American Antiquity* 10 (4): 377–99. http://dx.doi.org/10.2307/971963.

Vlcek, D. T., and W. L. Fash. 1986. "Survey in the Outlying Areas of the Copan Region, and the Copan-Quirigua 'Connection.'" In *The Southeast Maya Periphery*, ed. P. A. Urban and E. M. Schortman, 102–13. Austin: University of Texas Press.

von Schwerin, J. 2010. "The Problem of the 'Copan Style' and Political Identity: The Architectural Sculpture of El Paraiso, Honduras, in a Regional Context." *Mexicon* 32 (3): 56–66.

Voss, B. L. 2008. *The Archaeology of Ethnogenesis: Race and Sexuality in Colonial San Francisco*. Berkeley: University of California Press.

Wiessner, P. 1990. "Is There Unity in Style?" In *Uses of Style in Archaeology*, ed. M. W. Conkey and C. A. Hastorf, 105–12. Cambridge: Cambridge University Press.

Willey, G. R. 1986. "Copán, Quiriguá, and the Southeast Maya Zone: A Summary View." In *The Southeast Maya Periphery*, ed. P. A. Urban and E. M. Schortman, 168–75. Austin: University of Texas Press.

Yde, J. 1936. "A Preliminary Report of the Tulane University–Danish National Museum Expedition to Central America 1935." *Maya Research* 3: 24–37.

Yde, J. 1938. *An Archaeological Reconnaissance of Northwestern Honduras*. Middle American Research Institute, Publication 9. New Orleans: Tulane University.

10

Copán, Honduras

A Multiethnic Melting Pot during the Late Classic?

REBECCA STOREY

To talk of identity and ethnicity of past populations is to talk of something usually identified with agency, dynamism, and fluidity, which will be based here on the somewhat indirect evidence of archaeological artifacts and context. It may also be that identity and ethnicity, as studied in contemporary societies, is a modern concept that would have had little meaning to past peoples. The chapters in part 1 of this volume discuss the difficulties of defining ethnicity and identity in ethnohistoric and contemporary Maya. In fact, Restall and Gabbert warn about inferring ethnicity from material remains. Marken, Guenter, and Friedel, from the view of archaeologists, agree that it is unclear how the Classic period Maya self-identified. They do point out, as many other researchers have done, that the elite shared much material culture, texts, and cosmological ideas among the various important centers but also had their own clearly local traditions and concerns. In contrast, the various Maya populations present today clearly have ethnic identities and are only slowly accepting a pan-Maya identity (Samson, this volume).

So, in the past, did the people at least distinguish similar Maya-like peoples from non-Maya groups? Based on material remains and art, Maya are clearly differentiated from other Mesoamerican peoples in the pre-Columbian past. Also, as discussed below, there are clear examples of what we define as Maya deliberately using "foreign" identity and material elements. Of course, we know that individuals also have several potential identities besides a possible ethnic one; gender, social rank, occupation, age are all dimensions important to an identity. While some cultures

DOI: 10.5876/9781607325673.c010

may not be amenable to this kind of analysis, the pre-Columbian Maya do seem to be a candidate because of the distinctive material remains and their context recovered archaeologically, although what people called themselves and how they conceived differences are at this point unclear.

Ethnic identity is one that can be based on cultural and biological traits, often imputed by others to a group. This does not mean that people do not internalize ethnic identities, but the anthropological study has tended to concentrate on "post-Colonial situations" and "ethnogenesis," whereby peoples are active in defining and refining their identity when faced with more powerful ethnic groups (Hill 1996; Castillo Cocom, Rodriguez, and Ashenbrener, this volume). Studies of ethnic identity in the past are rarer but present (Jones 2002; Buzon 2006), although like these studies of Romanization and Ancient Egypt, they are often of situations where there is historical documentation to support a worldview that allows ethnic identification. The pre-Columbian Maya did recognize and depict "foreigners" (Demarest 2004), so a sense of Maya and non-Maya may have been present. The question of whether there were "different" ethnic Maya in the past has been little investigated before now, but as other contributions to this volume attest, there is evidence that such distinctions may have been made. The important Classic Maya center of Copán on the southeastern edge of the Maya world, at the time a frontier, may provide a good case study for the question of Maya identity.

Bioarchaeology can contribute to the study of identity and ethnicity in two ways: by biological relatedness derivable from skeletons and by the archaeological context in which the skeletons were recovered. The two sources of information are important, but they can interact in complex ways. The mortuary treatment given an individual is a strong source of identity and ethnicity, and different groups can be distinguished by their burial practices. However, some skeletal indicators can reflect genetic relatedness, so the biological information potentially informs about endogamy/exogamy and the mixing of different populations through time. Thus, the mortuary treatment could be exhibiting a uniform identity, influenced by those other dimensions of identity listed above, but the biological information could be revealing intermingling with nearby groups with different identities. The history of this particular case would then be different than one in which there was a "dominant culture" where enclaves of peoples with different ethnic identities were still present. In this latter case, the biological information could reveal that there is either a fairly strict separation of biological pools or a great deal of intermingling and relatedness within that society in spite of differing enclaves. After all, identity and ethnicity are culturally defined, and the biology will not necessarily pattern the same way.

A comparison will be made here between one of the major centers of the Late Classic Maya period, Copán, and the Formative village of K'axob, using potential skeletal indexes of relatedness and the cultural patterns of mortuary treatment. It is expected that K'axob will show more uniform identity because of its smaller size and location in the heart of the Maya lowlands, while Copán may reveal a more complex situation because of its larger size, history, and location at the Maya frontier.

COPÁN AND THE SOUTHEASTERN MAYA PERIPHERY

Copán, the great Classic period Maya center in Honduras, was on the southeastern frontier of the Maya world. While it was definitely linked culturally to the lowland Maya of Guatemala and Belize, it has long been thought that this was the result of a lowland Maya incursion into the Mesoamerican, but non-Maya, peoples living in the area (Fash 2004). Recent archaeological work and epigraphic decipherment of Maya hieroglyphs have shown that this is indeed likely what happened. Artifacts and residences from the Late Early Formative to the proto-classic (circa 1000 BC to AD 400) indicate that non-Maya peoples were living in the Copán Valley (ibid.). Then in AD 426–27, an individual named K'inich Yax K'uk Mo' (Shining Quetzal Macaw) arrived in Copán and founded a royal center and dynasty that lasted until AD 822 (Sharer et al. 2004; Stuart 2004). He had apparently received the insignia of office elsewhere (perhaps in the great city of Teotihuacan in central Mexico, the dominant place during the Classic period), at least according to the texts. He was depicted in later iconography with the trappings and insignia of Teotihuacan (ibid.), and his early constructions and ceramics are definitely Teotihuacan-inspired (Sharer et al. 2004).

This founder seems to have the isotopic signature of an individual from the Petén (perhaps Tikal) region of the lowland Maya (not a central Mexican from Teotihuacan), while his wife was local to Copán (Buikstra, Burton, and Wright 2004). The importance of this is that it represents the arrival of and colonization by Mayan-speaking peoples in the area and the clear linking of Copán with lowland Classic Maya cultural patterns. These patterns remained dominant and influential in the area until its abandonment as part of the Classic Maya collapse at the end of the Classic period. The Late Classic period (circa AD 650 to 1000) represents the apogee of Copán in terms of population size and variety and extent of residences. This period dominates the burial sample.

But what happened to the non-Maya peoples already there when the Maya arrived? Were they absorbed into the Maya world biologically as they were culturally? Or did they remain somewhat isolated and distinct within the Copán polity? Were the elite Maya the main ones who did the colonizing, in which case the commoners might represent more of the non-Maya peoples (de Montmollin 1995)? The ethnohistorically known Quiché Maya stressed their cultural distinctiveness and foreign descent through definitely different material items from those of the general populace (Henderson 1992), so it is possible that the Copáneco elite did the same. Because Copán was on the periphery of areas with other peoples, did it become a magnet for nearby non-Maya peoples as a place to settle? Certainly, Copán maintained links and trade with lowland Maya to the north and non-Maya peoples to the east, although the evidence of interchange seems stronger with the east than it is for the Petén heartland (Webster 1992). Recent research by Canuto and Bell (this volume) reveals that in a nearby valley that was part of the Copán polity, the El Paraíso center had characteristics similar to the Late Classic Maya elite at Copán, while the center of El Cafetal seemed to express a determinedly different, non-Maya identity for a time. Such are the complexities of trying to study identity in the past, especially in what was most likely a very dynamic frontier. This also makes Copán a good place to investigate whether the Maya might be viewed as multiethnic, especially during the Late Classic period.

THE FORMATIVE VILLAGE OF K'AXOB

K'axob is an agricultural community near Pulltrouser Swamp in northern Belize. Excavations were focused in the southern sector, Pyramid Plaza B, where testing found well-preserved and accessible Formative deposits under the patios of the later Classic period construction (McAnany 2004a). Plaza B was the largest construction in this area and seems to have been the focus of the sector. While very informative, the excavations were limited in areal extent and did not uncover all of each residence or the entire Formative community. Thus, what is present is only a sample, which is influenced by where the excavations were placed in the basal platforms. Although K'axob had a Classic period occupation, only the pre-Classic individuals are discussed here.

K'axob is part of the founding Maya communities in this part of the Maya lowlands. Founded in the Middle Formative (circa 800 BC) as a small settlement with generally perishable dwellings, it grew during the Late Formative and developed clear evidence of an internal social hierarchy (ibid.). However, K'axob remained a small player in the region. The local top power was Lamanai, the very long-lived Maya central place, whereas villages like K'axob were at the bottom of the power scheme (ibid.). Nevertheless, the evidence from K'axob was of a largely autonomous place where political control from outside seemed to have been unobtrusive and inhabitants had pride in their village that seemed to permeate the material remains and their context (McAnany 2004b). Although it was close to three other, larger Late Formative Maya settlements—Nohmul, San Estevan, and Cuello—K'axob nevertheless had distinct ceramics that differentiated it from other communities:

"As institutionalized power relationships began to dominate the social landscape, individual communities responded by emphasizing their own unique attributes[,] thus establishing and attesting to their place within society" (Bartlett and McAnany 2000:118). Because it was relatively small during the Formative, K'axob may have especially felt it was imperative to distinguish itself. The long, 1,000+-year history of some residences (McAnany 2004a) attests to the stability and probable close interaction among the residents of this Formative village.

The importance of K'axob is that it represents a clearly Maya village to contrast with the larger, perhaps more multiethnic people of Copán. The main possible confounding factor is the time difference between the two populations, as K'axob is from 900 years to 500 years older. However, the interest is in seeing what kind of biological variation might be present in K'axob as opposed to Copán, so the time difference is not the focus of the analysis. The results are preliminary, as not all the data that could be used as indicators of identity or biological distance have been analyzed.

METHODS FOR STUDYING BIOLOGICAL INDICATORS
OF ETHNICITY AND IDENTITY

While comparison of the DNA of individuals and populations would be the best way to determine biological relationships, such analysis is still too slow and complex to be realistic for comparing many skeletons, although the ability to recover ancient DNA is improving all the time. Thus, we must use phenotypic traits to study the possible underlying genotypes, although they are not likely to be as sensitive as DNA. Both cranial and dental metrics have been used successfully to study biological relationships and provide results comparable to genetic ones (Relethford 2002). Non-metric cranial and dental traits, sometimes called discrete traits, can also be used, but only dental metrics will be used here. The crania at Copán and K'axob were generally poorly preserved, and not enough metrics are available for biodistance analysis. The underlying thesis of this type of study is that populations that exchange mates and interact with one another are phenotypically more similar, while populations that do not exchange mates become more different. This is certainly true on an interregional basis, but biodistance analysis can also be used at the site level of analysis, even at the intra-cemetery level (Jacobi 2000). The analysis compares the similarity and amount of variation present in dental metrics, since these are partially heritable. The more they are similar, the more closely related biologically are the individuals/subsamples. The more variation present in the metrics, the more genetic heterogeneity is present, which could be a possible indication of different ethnicities in a sample.

There are a few other recent studies of biodistance for the Maya. Rhoads (2002) used dental metrics and dental non-metric morphological traits on the Copán skeletal sample to look at biological differences and the presence of non-Maya individuals in the Copán Valley. There is overlap in some of the dental measurements, but the Copán sample here is divided into different subsamples, and there is no attempt to replicate her study. Instead, the statistical methods used are different, including Bayesian discriminant analysis, discriminant functions, and principal component analysis. The results of this study will be compared with those of Rhoads, especially since morphological traits will not be used.

Jacobi (2000) also used dental measures and non-metric morphological traits to study biological relationships within the Colonial period Tipu Maya skeletal sample. His purpose was to look for families and possible Spanish presence among the individuals buried in a Catholic Church. Jacobi used discriminant function analysis as well. This method looks at how well the measures can classify individuals into particular groups. In his case, Jacobi was testing the similarity of the burials inside the church, which might have been Spaniards or a Spanish admixture, with those buried outside. Jacobi found no differences by location of burial, and all of the individuals appeared to have been Maya.

Sex of the skeletons was estimated using standard techniques (Buikstra and Ubelaker 1994). For those with enough cranial and pelvis preservation, morphology was used to estimate sex. For more fragmentary remains, discriminant function measures were calculated based on metric measurements of those sexed through morphology (considered to be of known sex). For Copán, the sex estimations are felt to be good. The K'axob individuals were more fragmentary than those at Copán, so the sex estimations are more tentative. However, individuals that could not be sexed or cases where the estimation was weak are not studied here. Only individuals sexed with clear morphological traits or where there were at least some morphological traits combined with strong discriminant functions are included in the analysis. Nine females and twenty-three males in the K'axob sample, fifteen males and fifteen females in the rural Copán sample, and sixty-five females and forty-four males in the elite 9N-8 residential compound met the criteria. These constitute the sample that will be analyzed.

The dental measurements taken were the buccolingual breadth (bl) and the mesiodistal length (md) to 0.1 millimeter, the same measurements used by Jacobi (2000), as discussed by Kieser (1990) (see figure 10.1 for an illustration of these measures). All of them were measured by the author, and most teeth were measured several times to check for intra-observer error, which was minimal and non-significant. Where slightly different measures resulted from the multiple measures, the mean of these was used for each tooth present for an individual. The main difference from the practice of Jacobi and Rhoads is that if both right and left teeth were present,

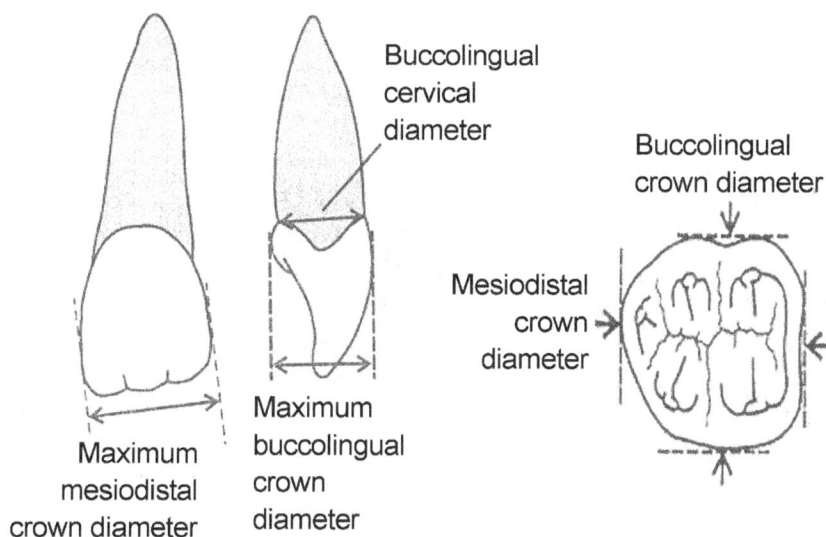

FIGURE 10.1. Dental measures taken on Maya skeletal samples (adapted from Hillson et al. 2005, used with permission)

the measurements that would result in the larger crown area were selected. The differences were usually at most two-tenths to three-tenths of a millimeter. It is felt that the measure of size differences between males and females is better calibrated when the largest teeth are used.

First, the variation in the dental metrics between males and females in each sample was compared, using both bivariate and multivariate methods (SPSS version 12 and 16). This variation has to be tested before variation between samples can be measured and interpreted. Here, both univariate and multivariate methods were used, although all analyses have the problems of small samples, which affects the ability to find statistical significance. Next, an overview of mortuary treatment was conducted to determine if any differences might indicate ethnic identities present in Late Classic Copán as opposed to K'axob. The information from both the biological relationships and the cultural patterns of mortuary treatment provides at least a preliminary indication of whether an important center of Late Classic Lowland Maya civilization was more multiethnic than most researchers have assumed.

POST-MARITAL RESIDENCE

However, more than just ethnic identity can influence possible markers of biological relationship. At an even finer level of analysis, patterns of marriage and post-marital residence are important determinants of the pattern of biological relationship. While there are always exceptions, in most societies it is expected that a newly married couple will live either near the husband's family, virilocality, or with the wife's family, uxorilocality. The result is that one sex is typically more mobile than the other, and relatives are spread out over various sites. Thus, the sex with more variability in phenotypic traits is the mobile sex, the one marrying in, while the sex with less variability is non-mobile. Members of the latter sex will be more similar because they stay among relatives. Thus, the variability between males and females needs to be studied before comparisons between K'axob and Copán can be made.

The pre-Columbian Maya are generally considered patrilineal or patrilocal, based on dynastic successions and ethnohistorical evidence, and the present-day Maya are patrilineal (McAnany 1995; Restall 1996). This means one should expect females to marry within their husbands' communities and thus be more heterogeneous, while the males of a site or residence would be more closely related. Post-marital residence is often not that simple. It could be that elites held to the pattern more strictly, while commoners tended to marry locally. In that case, males and females would be different among the elite but not as much among commoners. While K'axob is not likely to have been a totally endogamous village, mates would probably have been mostly from a restricted local area. Thus, the differences between males and females might not be very marked. There are status differences, but they are less marked than in the Late Classic, so even elite males and females here may have similar variability in phenotypic traits.

The Copán sample can be divided into several possible subsamples that might have differences. Thus, individuals from the neighborhood of Las Sepulturas, which is near the Acropolis center of the polity, might differ from the dispersed, lower-status rural people from the sustaining area. The former sample comes from an elite compound, 9N-8, the largest in Las Sepulturas. While it definitely housed an elite lineage, the compound had over 200 structures and 10 patios. With so many residents, those of the noble lineage were likely a minority, and the rest were either distant relatives or unrelated retainers. It is possible that the rural people and the retainers might have been non-Maya biologically or maybe indistinguishable and that mates were local. It is also possible that elite males and females might have come from some distance. Thus, the hypothesis here is that one could find a significant difference between males and females in some Copán subsamples as opposed to those of K'axob, where the difference is expected to be non-significant. This hypothesis reflects the likely distance of mates in the two societies. One cannot assume that males will be the less mobile sex, even though that is the patrilocal pattern.

For the univariate analysis, the between-sex variance was tested for statistical validity using the F-test for equality of variance and the Shapiro-Wilk test for normality (as suggested by Schillaci and Stojanowski 2003). Tables 10.1, 10.2, and 10.3 contain the means and standard deviations (in mm) plus the F-test results for the 9N-8 compound, rural Copán individuals, and the K'axob village. While all of the teeth could be used, the use of polar teeth (UI1, LI2, the canines, first premolars, and first molars) is often felt to be best and avoids possibly redundant information (Schillaci and Stojanowski 2003; Rhoads 2002). The comparisons of the sixteen means and SDs reveal that the 9N-8 compound had eleven measures with greater male variability, while females had five (table 10.1). Rural Copán had nine measures with greater male variability and seven in which females had more variability (table 10.2). K'axob was the same as rural Copán, with nine male and seven female measures having greater variability (table 10.3).

Although not presented in the tables, the elite 9N-8 residence had three measures that failed the normality test (males—UP1lb, UClb; females—UM1md). For rural Copán, six measures failed the normality test (males—UCmd, UI1lb, UI1md, LClb, and LCmd; females—UClb). In K'axob, only LM1md for both sexes was non-normal. These measures could not be used in testing for significant variation (defined as $p < 0.05$) between the sexes in each site. For the F-test between the sexes, there was no significant difference in K'axob. Rural Copán had only one significant difference (LI2lb) between the sexes out of ten possible comparisons, and 9N-8 had ten measures that were significantly different in variance between the sexes (see table 10.1). The difference may result from the fact that the rural and K'axob samples are small, while 9N-8 often had more than thirty in each sex for testing. Thus, as hypothesized above, the 9N-8 compound may reveal more variability in mates, as well as differences in genetic lineage (perhaps also tied to differing identities of elites and commoners). Also, as discussed, K'axob mates do seem to come from the local population.

Multivariate analysis is needed because it considers the total pattern of variability (Schillaci and Stojanowski 2003). A variety of methods have been used, but one of the basic methods is discriminant function. It is the only multivariate method used on dental metrics by Jacobi (2000) and one of the techniques used by Rhoads (2002) and Schillaci and Stojanowski (2003). Thus, it is the technique used here, pending further research. It assumes multivariate normality and equality of variance-covariance matrices of the data (Norusis 2008). Thus, the measures that are non-normal should not be used. As is usual with any statistical procedure, one should test to make sure the data meet the assumptions, which in SPSS means using Box's M (ibid.). However, the ratio of the log determinants of the variance-covariance matrices can provide a measure of which sex has more variability (Schillaci

TABLE 10.1. Copán 9N-8 Compound skeletal sample polar teeth measures

Measurement	Number	Mean	SD	F-Test p =
UM1lb–F	34	11.0	0.52	0.000
M	33	11.6	0.53	
UM1md–F	34	10.6	0.48	
M	32	11.1	0.46	
UP1lb–F	40	9.5	0.56	
M	36	9.6	0.77	
UP1md–F	40	7.4	0.42	0.136
M	36	7.7	0.50	
UClb–F	47	8.2	0.52	
M	34	8.8	0.57	
UCmd–F	47	8.1	0.46	0.007
M	32	8.4	0.57	
UI1lb–F	39	7.1	0.44	0.000
M	31	7.5	0.47	
UI1md–F	41	8.5	0.46	0.002
M	28	9.0	0.58	
LM1lb–F	40	10.6	0.51	0.007
M	29	10.9	0.57	
LM1md–F	41	11.6	0.55	0.001
M	29	12.0	0.50	
LP1lb–F	48	7.8	0.56	0.006
M	31	8.1	0.50	
LP1md–F	48	7.0	0.50	0.131
M	40	7.2	0.44	
LClb–F	52	7.5	0.49	0.000
M	34	8.1	0.56	
LCmd–F	52	7.1	0.36	0.000
M	33	7.5	0.46	
LI2lb–F	44	6.1	0.34	0.004
M	30	6.5	0.51	
LI2md–F	43	6.1	0.45	0.001
M	30	6.5	0.36	

TABLE 10.2. Copán rural skeletal sample polar teeth measures

Measurement	Number	Mean	SD	F-Test p =
UM₁lb–F	9	11.4	0.50	0.594
M	7	11.5	0.79	
UM₁md–F	9	10.7	0.73	
M	7	10.9	0.91	
UP₁lb–F	10	9.6	0.39	0.133
M	8	10.0	0.66	
UP₁md–F	10	7.5	0.76	0.555
M	8	7.7	0.54	
UClb–F	12	8.2	0.90	
M	11	8.8	0.48	
UCmd–F	12	8.2	0.53	
M	11	8.5	0.32	
UI₁lb–F	8	7.1	0.46	
M	6	7.2	0.10	
UI₁md–F	8	8.4		1.19
M	6	8.8	0.39	
LM₁lb–F	4	11.0	0.69	0.822
M	7	11.1	0.72	
LM₁md–F	4	11.8	1.09	0.901
M	5	11.7	0.78	
LP₁lb–F	11	8.0	0.45	0.562
M	8	8.2	0.78	
LP₁md–F	10	7.1	0.42	0.344
M	8	7.4	0.72	
LClb–F	11	7.5	0.61	
M	11	8.2	1.1	
LCmd–F	11	7.1	0.54	0.1
M	11	7.7	0.97	
LI₂lb–F	8	6.2	0.27	0.006
M	7	6.8	0.42	
LI₂md–F	9	6.2	0.53	0.304
M	6	6.5	0.5	

TABLE 10.3. K'axob skeletal sample polar teeth measures

Measurement	Number	Mean	SD	F-Test p =
UM1lb–F	6	11.2	1.00	0.241
M	13	11.8	0.79	
UM1md–F	6	10.3	0.47	0.894
M	14	10.7	0.54	
UP1lb–F	7	9.5	0.99	0.746
M	17	9.6	0.37	
UP1md–F	7	7.3	0.48	0.96
M	17	7.4	0.23	
UClb–F	5	8.5	0.38	0.583
M	19	8.7	0.7	
UCmd–F	6	7.9	0.7	0.636
M	19	8.3	0.43	
UI1lb–F	3	6.9	0.25	0.647
M	13	7.2	0.52	
UI1md–F	3	8.5	0.10	0.838
M	13	8.7	0.33	
LM1lb–F	3	11.2	0.51	0.333
M	13	10.8	0.85	
LM1md–F	2	11.6	0.42	
M	12	11.5	1.36	
LP1lb–F	8	7.9	0.54	0.477
M	14	8.0	0.67	
LP1md–F	8	7.1	0.50	0.189
M	14	7.2	0.48	
LClb–F	7	7.8	0.53	0.696
M	15	8.0	0.73	
LCmd–F	7	6.9	0.57	0.065
M	15	7.4	0.36	
LI2lb–F	6	5.9	0.54	0.673
M	9	6.1	0.78	
LI2md–F	7	6.3	0.40	0.306
M	10	6.3	0.32	

and Stojanowski 2003). Here, the log determinants of males and females were compared to obtain a preliminary measure of variability.

The largest sample is from 9N-8. The measures that were non-normal were not entered into a stepwise analysis, which yielded only one measure—LCmd. The Box's M was 0.702, so the variance-covariance matrices are equal. The discriminant function was only 77 percent accurate, less than the 80 percent preferred. Forty individuals were involved in determining the function, which is less than half. However, these individuals clearly displayed equality of variability, and the log determinants were 2.072 for males and 1.893 for females, indicating slightly more male variability, although not a significant amount. For all practical purposes, males and females have similar variability.

The Copán rural sample had small samples and much missing data, such that of the possible thirty sexed individuals, the maximum of twenty-three had the upper canine, which, unfortunately, is non-normal and "fails" the Levene test. Because the UI1, UC, and LC did not meet the assumptions, the other teeth were entered into a stepwise analysis, which yielded LI2lb and LM1md as the best measures. These measures resulted in a DF that is 100 percent accurate, with a Box's M that indicates assumptions are met. This means there is definitely sexual dimorphism in these measures. The log determinants for the matrices are 5.704 for males and 7.301 for the females, indicating that females are more variable, although again this difference is not significant. Only seven individuals in this sample could be analyzed this way, so the small samples here will probably make it hard to find true difference. The females seem more mobile, which fits with a patrilocal post-marital residence pattern.

For K'axob, an imbalance between the numbers of males and females, plus the missing values, made it hard to calculate a discriminant function. In fact, using only the measures that met the assumptions, there was no function because only males were available. Using a variety of combinations, the UClb and LClb could finally be used. The function had a reasonable accuracy of 83 percent. Also, the Box's M indicated met assumptions at $p = 0.798$, and the log determinants were 2.672 for males and 4.0 for females, a pattern similar to rural Copán. But again, no statistical significance in variability between males and females was found in any of the Maya samples in the multivariate analysis, as might be expected for rural Copán and K'axob. However, the univariate results for 9N-8 indicate significant differences, and males were generally more variable. Perhaps analysis between the sites will provide further evidence for that pattern.

VARIATION BETWEEN MAYA SITES

Having found at this point no difference in variability between males and females in the three samples, comparisons can be made between the sites. The sexes were combined to try to increase the sample sizes, which could be justified on the basis of there being no multivariate significance between the sexes. Again, there was only one significant difference in the sixteen tooth measures among the sites as measured by the F-test: the lower I2lb measure. Checking the post-hoc tests, which break down the F-test results into two-by-two contrasts among the sites, only rural Copán and K'axob were close to significance for this measure; actually, 9N-8 did not differ significantly from the other two samples. Thus, the tooth measures generally found that this phenotypic indication of biological relatedness shows that these sites did not show excessive variance that might indicate clear Maya/non-Maya populations.

The treatment at death also provides information on identity, as societies have traditions and rituals appropriate to the disposal of a body that differ from other ethnicities and religious traditions. For example, the Maya buried at the Tipu chapel were definitely buried in a Christian way, generally extended with head to the West, compared with prehispanic burial patterns (Jacobi 2000). The Maya, like other prehispanic Mesoamericans, buried their dead under and around residences, and the graves contained varying amounts of furnishings. Shell (both marine and freshwater) and greenstone (in the form of jadeite, fuchsite, and serpentinite) were very prestigious and valuable materials for individuals in the prehispanic world (Bartlett 2004; Isazu Aizpurúa 2004). Some recognizably Maya lowland mortuary customs have been summarized (Welsh 1988). According to Welsh, these customs include generally primary interments, flexed bodies in smaller graves and extended ones in large tombs/crypts, and differences in amount and value of grave furnishings according to social status, with rulers and elites having much more elaborate treatments. There was also a tendency to place a ceramic bowl over or under the head of the deceased. In general, males and females had similar types of grave furnishings and mortuary treatments. Some regional patterns have also been defined in which some of these customs were more prevalent, such as extended burial at some sites and flexed bodies in others (ibid.).

K'axob definitely has some of these customs but also some important differences. There were only twelve individuals around a single domestic residence from the earliest period (800–400 BC), so the larger Late Formative sample (400 BC to AD 250), sixty-five adult individuals, will be described. However, the earlier burials are in a residence that became larger and more elaborate and the center of the southern sector of K'axob (McAnany 2004b). Primary interments were more common, 63 percent, but secondary interments were also common at 37 percent. Among primary interments, extended burials were the most common (44%), but flexed (20%) and seated (36%)

positions were almost as common (this latter position was not stressed by Welsh but is found at many other Maya sites). Most notable was the number of interments with multiple individuals, some with secondary and primary interments with sequential placements or in one single episode (Storey 2004a). These multiple, secondary burials became the most common type by the end of the Late Formative among those of highest status, when ancestral shrines became more public (McAnany 2004b).

However, at all times, primary interments were common in residential structures. At K'axob, there were no stone crypts or tombs but simple earthen graves and some cists with caps. The head-covering-the-vessel pattern was also present. This is probably related to the lack of more formal grave constructions, as has been speculated: "lower class people, by contrast, were almost always buried with dirt in the face" (Haviland and Moholy-Nagy 1992:53). Thus, this treatment was probably intended to give the deceased more respect. Thirteen males, nine females, and one child had a bowl over their heads. Only four of the adults were young, probably under age thirty. Thus, this treatment was probably limited to select individuals, reinforcing the idea that it was intended for higher-status individuals. Six females and fifteen males had shell artifacts. Four females and six males had greenstone artifacts as grave furnishings.

A comparison with some of the mortuary treatment of 111 individuals during the Late Formative at the nearby larger site of Cuello shows a general similarity with K'axob (Robin 1989). The seated position (25) was the most common at Cuello, but extended (10) and flexed (15) positions were also common. There were more primary than secondary interments associated with the residential platforms. Most graves were simple earthen and cist types, but there were five crypts as well. Since K'axob is a village, it is probably not surprising that it would lack some of the more elaborate types of treatment present in Maya lowlands during this period. Nonperishable grave goods were present with 77 percent of the individuals at Cuello, which is close to the 70 percent at K'axob, indicating that providing grave furnishings was a pattern for Maya interments at this time. In contrast, 64 percent of the individuals had a ceramic vessel over the head, a higher proportion than at K'axob (27%). This Cuello pattern seems to indicate that perhaps placing a ceramic vessel over the deceased's head was a more common custom, a way to protect the head after burial.

While there are always likely to be differences between Maya sites, some dependent on differences in status, definite patterns are seen in the Late Formative: primary and secondary interments; extended, flexed, and seated positions for a primary interment; grave furnishings; and a vessel covering the skull. Burials vary by status within a site, with those of high status having more valuable grave furnishings and elaborate tombs. Burials, especially primary inhumations, still predominate in and around residences. Does the Late Classic period still have these patterns, or will there be changes because of the differences in the period? A comparison of patterns between the elite residence 9N-8 and the more modest residences of rural residents at Copán is found in table 10.4.

The pattern of residential burials and of differences according to status continues into the Classic period, although the elaboration of the highest statuses becomes more evident in the placement of shrines, pyramids, and elaborate stone tombs with valuable jadeite and shell in abundance, as is evident in many lowland Classic Maya centers (Martin and Grube 2000). At Copán, the Acropolis is the locus of several royal burials and also of other individuals characterized by elaborate mortuary treatments (Buikstra, Burton, and Wright 2004; Storey 2004b). At the large and elite residence 9N-8, however, primary interments strongly dominate for both males and females. This is an example of both continuity with and difference from Late Formative K'axob and Cuello. 9N-8 is a residence and thus has mostly primary interments, while the secondary, protracted mortuary treatments seen in K'axob and Cuello are reserved solely for the very top of the social hierarchy in the Acropolis, reflecting the greater inequality present during the Classic period.

Even most of the multiple interments at 9N-8 are primary inhumations, again a contrast with K'axob. This indicates the pattern of direct burial of individuals shortly after death and almost no disturbance of the body thereafter. Simple earthen pits are still the most common grave type, although more formal constructions are present. This is probably the case because stone is rare around K'axob but common at Copán. For body position, strong majorities of males and females are flexed, while extended and seated (only five females and five males) positions are rarer. It is more common to find individuals with no imperishable grave furnishings at 9N-8 compared with K'axob. There is, however, a statistically significant difference in the numbers of grave furnishings between the sexes, with males having more furnishings. A minority of individuals have shell and greenstone grave furnishings, but these types of artifacts are present with a larger proportion of the individuals of known sex at K'axob. The difference in greenstone items between males and females in 9N-8 is significant (Fisher's exact test). Again, this reflects the more unequal and stratified society of the Late Classic versus the Late Formative.

The Copán rural sample, which might be made up mostly of non-Maya, seems to have a very similar mortuary treatment to 9N-8, especially in the proportions of primary versus secondary interments and in body positions. There is a slight increase in the proportions that have grave constructions as opposed to simple earth graves than is the case in 9N-8. The rural males are mostly without grave furnishings, while the majority of females have them. The number of furnishings is very similar between the sexes. In 9N-8 most males do have items, but half the females do not; the differences in these proportions are not significant (Fisher's exact test p = 0.25).

TABLE 10.4. Comparison of mortuary treatment in Late Classic Copán

Sample	Primary Interments	Single Interments	Body Position	Grave Type	Grave Furnishings	Exotics
9N-8						
Males	92%	45%	63% flexed	49% earth	41% none	69% none
			18% extend	31% formal stone tombs	41% 1–17 items	31% 1–8 greenstones shell rare
			10% seated	20% cobbles		
Females	2%	73%	74% flexed	51% earth	50% none	12% 1–5 greenstones
			9% extend	12% formal stone tombs	49% 1–7 items	1 individual 123 shell beads
			8% seated	37% cobbles	1 individual 125 items	
RURAL COPÁN						
Male	75%	99%	89% flexed	33% earth	58% none	100% none
			11% extend	17% forçmal stone tombs	42% 1–4 items	
				50% cobbles		
Female	87%	99%	87% flexed	40% earth	40% none	80% none
			13% extend	50% cobbles	60% 1–4 items	20% 1–2 greenstones no shell
				1 in formal stone tomb		

The differences in the proportions of the males and females with greenstone in the rural versus the 9N-8 sample are also not statistically significant (Fisher's exact text). The smaller rural sample may be impoverished in its mortuary treatments, but the differences do not seem to be characteristic of a different mortuary tradition.

These Late Classic patterns do contrast with K'axob. When the proportion of primary versus secondary interments at K'axob is compared with each Copán sample,

Fisher's exact test is highly significant between 9N-8 and K'axob (p < .001) and very close to significance with the rural sample (Fisher's exact text p = 0.07). The pattern of flexed burials in the Late Classic is also significantly different from K'axob's extended and seated positions. The Late Classic has more stone tombs and cobblestone grave constructions, but K'axob is in an environment with little hard stone, so this difference is probably purely environmental. Shell is rare at Copán and more plentiful at K'axob, but, again, this may be an environmental difference, since K'axob is in Pulltrouser Swamp and near the coast. Greenstone artifacts in the grave furnishings are found with a minority of individuals at all samples. The other real difference with K'axob, in addition to types of interment and body positions, is the lack of individuals with ceramics over or under the head in Late Classic Copán, which Welsh (1988) identified as a general Maya mortuary custom. Might this be an indication of non-Maya influence at Copán? This might reflect the fact that most high-status individuals were in tombs, and many individuals at 9N-8 might be retainers or distant relatives or of lower status in the rural area, which would not merit the "no dirt in the face" treatment (as noted by Haviland and Moholy-Nagy 1992).

Future research will determine how different this pattern is at Copán, especially since at Dos Pilas, for example, at least one individual is depicted with an inverted bowl on the head (Wright 2006:70). However, Wright (ibid.) noted that the location of grave furnishings was not always recorded for her Pasión skeletal samples, so it was not used in her comparative analysis of mortuary treatment. At K'axob, in contrast, a Classic period skeletal sample is available, although the total numbers have not yet been determined. During the Early Classic, for example, the crania of seven out of nine interments had a head-covering vessel (Storey 2004a). In Late Classic K'axob, preliminary analysis indicates that about 58 percent of the burials had a head-covering vessel, some with clear kill holes (although preservation hampers this determination for many vessels). There also seems to be a pattern of sequential burial, with secondary interments placed with primary ones (McAnany 1997). These patterns represent continuity from the Late Formative. Also continued from earlier patterns, many burials are linked to termination/dedication rituals of buildings before new construction was begun (see Storey 2004a).

At Copán, there are a few secondary interments with primary ones, but there is less clear linkage of interments to termination or dedication rituals for buildings, as at K'axob. Individuals are often buried around buildings at Copán, with only a minority buried within structures, which means that many fewer individuals could have been involved in such rituals. Thus, there is distinctiveness to the mortuary treatments at Late Classic Copán that may be indicative of non-Maya influence among much of the population, with only individuals buried in formal tombs and crypts in the Acropolis and 9N-8 (the highest elites) having treatment similar to that at other Maya centers such as Tikal, where formal tombs and rich offerings are typical of the highest elites (Harrison 1999). These elite individuals may be the ones who identify most clearly with Maya elites at other centers, whereas other individuals in 9N-8 and the rural area seem to have formed perhaps a hybrid Maya/ local identity. This hybrid identity could have been formed over the centuries, since the arrival of the first ruler, and it may be most evident in mortuary treatment. If anything, the biological evidence of phenotype is for probable long-term intermarriage among all of the peoples present, as it shows no real difference between the 9N-8 compound and the rural skeletal sample. The evidence of Canuto and Bell (this volume) indicates that such "hybridity" of Maya and local residents seems to become present toward the end of the Late Classic in the nearby valley of Paraíso, so the Copán Valley may have been distinct throughout the Classic period. This is an interesting question that will be researched further. Additional research and comparison of the Classic period sample from K'axob may provide stronger patterns for identity than are presented here.

ACKNOWLEDGMENTS

The Copán study was done with the permission of the IHAH and received funding from the World Bank, the Fulbright Foundation, and the University of Houston. K'axob was excavated with permission of the Department of Anthropology, Belize. Funding was received from the NSF (SBR-9112310), other NSF grants, and Boston University.

REFERENCES CITED

Bartlett, Mary Jane. 2004. "Ornaments of Bone and Semiprecious Stone." In *K'axob: Ritual, Work, and Family in an Ancient Maya Village*, ed. Patricia A. McAnany, 353–64. Monumenta Archaeologica 22. Los Angeles: Cotsen Institute of Archaeology, University of California.

Bartlett, Mary Jane, and Patricia McAnany. 2000. " 'Crafting' Communities: The Materialization of Formative Maya Identities." In *The Archaeology of Communities: A New World Perspective*, ed. Marcello Canuto and Jason Yaeger, 102–22. London: Routledge.

Buikstra, Jane D., Price J. Burton, and Lori Wright. 2004. "Tombs from the Copán Acropolis: A Life History Approach." In *Understanding Early Classic Copán*, ed. Ellen Bell, Marcello Canuto, and Robert Sharer, 29–50. Philadelphia: University of Pennsylvania Museum.

Buikstra, Jane, and Douglas H. Ubelaker. 1994. *Standards for Data Collection from Human Skeletal Remains*. Arkansas Archaeological Survey Research Series 44. Fayetteville: Arkansas Archaeological Survey.

Buzon, Michele R. 2006. "Biological and Ethnic Identity in New Kingdom Nubia: A Case Study from Tombos." *Current Anthropology* 47 (4): 683–95. http://dx.doi.org/10 .1086/506288.

Demarest, Arthur. 2004. *Ancient Maya*. Cambridge: Cambridge University Press.

De Montmollin, Olivier. 1995. *Settlement and Politics in Three Classic Maya Polities*. Monographs in World Archaeology 24. Madison, WI: Prehistory.

Fash, William L. 2004. "Toward a Social History of the Copán Valley." In *Copán: The History of an Ancient Maya Kingdom*, ed. E. Wyllys Andrews and William L. Fash, 73–102. Santa Fe: School of American Research Press.

Harrison, Peter D. 1999. *The Lords of Tikal: Rulers of an Ancient Maya City*. London: Thames and Hudson.

Haviland, William A., and Hattula Moholy-Nagy. 1992. "Distinguishing the High and Mighty from the Hoi Polloi at Tikal, Guatemala." In *Mesoamerican Elites*, ed. Diane Z. Chase and Arlen Chase, 50–60. Norman: University of Oklahoma Press.

Henderson, John S. 1992. "Variations on a Theme: A Frontier View of Maya Civilization." In New Theories on the Ancient Maya, ed. Elin C. Danien and Robert J. Sharer, 161–71. University Museum Monograph 77. Philadelphia: University of Pennsylvania.

Hill, Jonathan D., ed. 1996. *History, Power, and Identity: Ethnogenesis in the Americas, 1492–1992*. Iowa City: University of Iowa Press.

Hillson, Simon, Charles Fitzgerald, and Helen Flinn. 2005. "Alternative Dental Measurements: Proposals and Relationships with Other Measurements." *American Journal of Physical Anthropology* 126 (4): 413–26. http://dx.doi.org/10.1002/ajpa.10430.

Isazu Aizpurúa, Ilean Isel. 2004. "The Art of Shell Working and the Social Uses of Shell Ornaments." In *K'axob: Ritual, Work, and Family in an Ancient Maya Village*, ed. Patricia A. McAnany, 335–51. Monumenta Archaeologica 22. Los Angeles: Cotsen Institute of Archaeology, University of California.

Jacobi, Keith P. 2000. *Last Rites for the Tipu Maya: Genetic Structuring in a Colonial Cemetery*. Tuscaloosa: University of Alabama Press.

Jones, Siân. 2002. *The Archaeology of Ethnicity*. London: Routledge.

Kieser, Jules A. 1990. *Human Adult Odontometrics*. Cambridge: Cambridge University Press. http://dx.doi.org/10.1017/CBO9780511983610.

Martin, Simon, and Nicholas Grube. 2000. *Chronicle of the Maya Kings and Queens: Deciphering the Dynasties of the Ancient Maya*. London: Thames and Hudson.

McAnany, Patricia A. 1995. *Living with the Ancestors: Kinship and Kingship in Ancient Maya Society*. Austin: University of Texas Press.

McAnany, Patricia A. 1997. "K'axob Project: Interim Report of the 1995 Field Season." Belmopan, Belize: Submitted to the Department of Archaeology, Boston University.

McAnany, Patricia A. 2004a. "Situating K'axob within Formative Period Lowland Maya Archaeology." In *K'axob: Ritual, Work, and Family in an Ancient Maya Village*, ed. Patricia A. McAnany, 1–10. Monumenta Archaeologica 22. Los Angeles: Cotsen Institute of Archaeology, University of California.

McAnany, Patricia A. 2004b. "Landscapes of K'axob in Deep and Current Time." In *K'axob: Ritual, Work, and Family in an Ancient Maya Village*, ed. Patricia A. McAnany, 11–17. Monumenta Archaeologica 22. Los Angeles: Cotsen Institute of Archaeology, University of California.

Norusis, Marija J. 2008. *SPSS 16.0 Statistical Procedures Companion*. Chicago: SPSS, Inc.

Relethford, John H. 2002. "Apportionment of Global Human Genetic Diversity Based on Craniometrics and Skin Color." *American Journal of Physical Anthropology* 118 (4): 393–98. http://dx.doi.org/10.1002/ajpa.10079.

Restall, Matthew. 1996. *Maya World: Yucatec Culture and Society, 1550–1850*. Stanford, CA: Stanford University Press.

Rhoads, Megan L. 2002. "Population Dynamics at the Southern Periphery of the Ancient Maya World: Kinship at Copán." PhD dissertation, Department of Anthropology, University of New Mexico, Albuquerque.

Robin, Cynthia. 1989. *Preclassic Maya Burials at Cuello, Belize*. BAR International Series 480. Oxford: British Archaeological Reports.

Schillaci, Michael A., and Christopher M. Stojanowski. 2003. "Postmarital Residence and Biological Variation at Pueblo Bonito." *American Journal of Physical Anthropology* 120 (1): 1–15. http://dx.doi.org/10.1002/ajpa.10147.

Sharer, Robert J., David W. Sedat, Loa P. Traxler, Julia C. Miller, and Ellen E. Bell. 2004. "Early Classic Royal Power in Copán: The Origins and Development of the Acropolis (ca. AD 250–600)." In *Copán: The History of an Ancient Maya Kingdom*, ed. E. Wyllys Andrews and William L. Fash, 139–99. Santa Fe: School of American Research Press.

Storey, Rebecca. 2004a. "Ancestors: Bioarchaeology of the Human Remains of K'axob." In *K'axob: Ritual, Work, and Family in an Ancient Maya Village*, ed. Patricia A. McAnany, 109–38. Monumenta Archaeologica 22. Los Angeles: Cotsen Institute of Archaeology, University of California.

Storey, Rebecca. 2004b. "Health and Lifestyle (before and after Death) among the Copán Elite." In *Copán: The History of an Ancient Maya Kingdom*, ed. E. Wyllys Andrews and William L. Fash, 315–43. Santa Fe: School of American Research Press.

Stuart, David. 2004. "A Foreign Past: The Writing and Representation of History on a Royal Ancestral Shrine at Copán." In *Copán: The History of an Ancient Maya Kingdom*, ed. E. Wyllys Andrews and William L. Fash, 373–94. Santa Fe: School of American Research Press.

Webster, David. 1992. "Maya Elites: The Perspective from Copán." In *Mesoamerican Elites*, ed. Diane Z. Chase and Arlen Chase, 135–56. Norman: University of Oklahoma Press.

Welsh, W. Bruce M. 1988. *An Analysis of Classic Lowland Maya Burials*. BAR International Series, vol. 409. Oxford: British Archaeological Reports.

Wright, Lori E. 2006. *Diet, Health, and Status among the Pasión Maya: A Reappraisal of the Collapse*. Vanderbilt Institute of Mesoamerican Archaeology Series, vol. 2. Nashville, TN: Vanderbilt University Press.

11

Conclusion

Identity, Networks, and Ethnicity

EDWARD SCHORTMAN

The chapters in this volume successfully challenge some deep-seated assumptions about the ways we understand: who are/were the "Maya"; how their cultures, past and present, should be studied; and what those investigations imply about those of us who call ourselves Mayanists. An additional theme, more implicitly stressed, concerns the relations that generally exist among materials, agency, and social identity. I will argue that, disagreements among the authors notwithstanding, these essays suggest very fruitful approaches to conceptualizing how we go about comprehending the human condition in general and the lives of those who inhabit(ed) Mesoamerica's southern lowlands in particular.

WHO ARE THE MAYA?

Under the culture history paradigm that dominated anthropology and archaeology through the mid-twentieth century, the Maya, like other groups, were treated as a spatially bounded entity defined by a package of traits that supposedly spread among closely related societies through diffusion and migration (Dixon 1928; Kroeber 1939; Wissler 1917; cf. Canuto and Bell, this volume). These shared materials and practices, it was argued, directly reflected values that were widely held among members of this "culture" and which emerged in the course of its unique history. The volume's contributors concur that such traditional definitions of "Mayaness" are, at best, problematic. They differ, however, on whether "Maya" still defines a

DOI: 10.5876/9781607325673.c011

useful analytical unit. Central questions here seem to revolve around whether there is such an entity as the "Maya" about which we can make generalizations and how that cultural unit relates, if at all, to living populations so categorized.

Samson, Castillo Cocom and colleagues, and Restall and Gabbert strongly argue that there was no self-conscious sense of cultural solidarity among so-called Maya people prior to the last few decades, a position Macri and Hofling bolster using linguistic data. Protracted, often hostile interactions with Colonial and post-independence governments from the sixteenth through nineteenth centuries apparently exacerbated prehispanic divisions among populations even as they reinforced indigenous allegiances to smaller units such as communities. Affiliations that transcended these identity networks, such as the pan-Maya movement of the late twentieth and early twenty-first centuries, were creative means for mobilizing segments of societies living in the southern lowlands against the incursions of agents representing state and international interests. The notion of "Maya" in the most recent of these contests is a conceptual resource adapted from academic, national, and touristic discourses that has been re-purposed to serve the needs of those it attempts to classify and control (cf. Castillo Cocom's concept of the "Indian Casino Effect"). This discussion raises important questions about the recursive relations between indigenous populations and the hegemonic discourses that seek to categorize them. Hofling's discussion of the roles linguists played in the (re)emergence of Mopan and Itza identities addresses many of the same issues.

Why, then, do the archaeologists represented in this compendium remain committed to the existence of a "Maya" culture? One key to the answer may lie in Restall and Gabbert's argument that cultural similarities can result from experiences shared among people who do not overtly recognize an ethnic connection (cf. LeCount, also Marken and colleagues' contrast between localized ethnic groupings and a macro-ethnic Maya classification). Distinctive beliefs and practices may thus arise from common approaches to dealing with recurrent factors in the physical and social environment. Consequently, whether the result of an explicitly shared affiliation or the outcome of comparable cultural strategies, "Maya" refers to a unit about which generalizations concerning modern practices and historical patterns can be legitimately made.

However "Maya" is defined, the volume's authors agree that approaches to its study must stress cultural, social, and political variation within this unit. Territorially defined entities such as society, culture, and culture area do not effectively capture the dynamism of the interpersonal dealings out of which regional differences took shape (cf. Parker 2013; Sugandhi 2013). If that is the case, how should we rethink our research programs, and does ethnicity have a role to play in such studies?

INTERACTION NETWORKS AND ETHNICITY

There seems to be a consensus among the contributors that the diverse material, linguistic, and behavioral patterns which fragment what once had been seen as a unified "Maya culture" are the results of varied decisions made by numerous individuals operating under sundry circumstances. These choices are/were enabled and constrained by the structural positions of the decision-makers and the social networks in which they participate(d). It is not surprising, therefore, that archaeologists, anthropologists, and ethnohistorians are avidly searching for ways of modeling these networks. Ethnicity is an attractive choice. As Beyyette first notes in her chapter, focusing on ethnicity draws explicit attention to sociopolitical divisions within territorial units of varying sizes, how people actively manipulate the trappings of ethnic identities to accomplish specific objectives, and the manners in which diverse assets from different sources are implicated in forging ethnic alliances and staging ethnic conflicts. Ethnic categories, groups, and communities, in short, are units of analysis that are more sensitive to the dynamic and negotiated quality of interpersonal dealings and the ways people shift among regional and local frames of reference in pursuit of goals than are such territorially rooted entities as culture, culture area, and society (e.g., Barth 1969; A. Cohen 1969, 1979; R. Cohen 1978; Despres 1975; Orser 2005; Royce 1982; Vincent 1974).

In proceeding along these lines, I recommend thinking very carefully about the appropriateness of using ethnicity in its various guises to model interpersonal interactions. As Samson, together with Restall and Gabbert, warn, the ways ethnicity is employed in studying modern populations may make its application to the analysis of past settings questionable. Ethnicity generally implies the emic acknowledgment by a group's members of a common history from which arises a perceived shared essence (e.g., Barth 1969; R. Cohen 1978; Royce 1982; Vincent 1974). These perceptions can almost never be established from archaeological data alone and are hard to document in many historical cases (Orser 2005). Hence, when imputing ethnicity to past societies, we run the risk of imposing senses of the self that the data do not warrant. In addition, confusing a specific form of affiliation—ethnicity—with all manner of identities may well obscure the wide array of social networks in which past people engaged, not all of which were ethnically defined.

The ethnicity literature is therefore a fertile source of ideas about the diverse ways people create and use social webs to define themselves and accomplish objectives. How we might use such insights in understanding the "Maya" is suggested by the volume's authors.

All of the contributors endorse the important point made by Beyyette that people deal with each other as members of social networks with which are associated specific identities, or senses of the self, acknowledged by those within and outside one's social web (Earle 1997; Galaskiewicz and Wasserman 1994:xiii; Knox, Savage, and Harvey 2006; Mann 1986; Marcus 2000:239; Ortner 1995:187, 191; Preucel 2000:59–61; papers in Brumfiel and Fox 1994). Whether defined ethnically or not, these nets are the means by which people exercise agency as they cooperate in mobilizing economic, political, and cultural resources in support of shared objectives (Schortman and Urban 2011, 2012).

As Goffman (1997:36) noted, individuals can be treated as managers of holding companies, deploying identities linked to distinct social networks strategically, in different situations, and with varying degrees of freedom to achieve diverse ends. The notion of people moving among affiliations is also captured in the concept of *ethnoexodus* offered by Castillo Cocom. Following these views fragments a society into numerous, variably well-integrated networks that people traverse with differing ease at diverse times for sundry reasons. Some of these affiliations may extend beyond a society's borders. Though the latter networks are often thought to result from elite initiatives, it is very likely that people of lower rank also forge(d) ties with their compatriots residing in different polities in pursuit of their own aims. Thus, Macri's observation that the Classic Maya "understood themselves through multiple layers of identification" could be usefully extended to their predecessors and descendants.

Canuto and Bell, Marken and his colleagues, as well as LeCount stress that these multiple social nets often emerge in the context of enduring competitions over resources. Networks, from this instrumentalist perspective, are means for marshaling efforts to secure at least a share of contested assets needed for sustenance, self-definition, social reproduction, and advancement (Barth 1969). Focusing attention on social networks, therefore, encourages appreciation for the relational processes and the assets that fund them, which operate over diverse spatial scales and out of which appear political, social, and economic structures (Orser 2005:86–87).

Thus, Restall and Gabbert argue that indigenous residents of the southern lowlands during the Colonial and early independence periods subscribed to identities that were rooted in specific places. These communities (*cahob*) were composed of people who resided together, interacted regularly, and were bound to each other by kinship and shared claims to the land's spiritual as well as economic resources. Cahob were, in turn, cross-cut by exogamous patronymic groups (*chilabob*) whose members were dispersed across numerous settlements. As Restall and Gabbert note, neither cahob nor chilabob were ethnically defined. They were, however, important touchstones of identity and formed bases for cooperative actions in pursuit of important aims.

This same integration of parochial and territorially diffuse identities is carried back into prehistory in the contributions of LeCount, Marken and colleagues, and

Canuto and Bell. On the one hand, spatially bounded polities were linked by inter-site elite affiliations that united rulers within class-based networks. On the other, identities tied to particular places joined leaders and followers through their common engagement in a wide array of practices employing objects distinguished by styles closely associated with localized social nets. These authors contend that elite power may well have depended on the abilities of potentates to participate in both parochial and dispersed social webs. By doing so, magnates could mobilize both the local and foreign assets they needed to sustain themselves and claim preeminence at home.

Balancing the potentially conflicting demands of at least these two affiliations makes for a tense and volatile situation within all complex polities (Schortman and Urban 2011, 2012; Schortman, Urban, and Ausec 2001; Yaeger 2000). One way of defusing such stresses, as Marken and colleagues and LeCount discuss, may have been by naturalizing membership claims to identity nets through participation in public rites that elevated such assertions to the sacred plane where they were beyond question (Bloch 1977). Even the most spectacular and compelling religious observances probably did not completely and permanently resolve strains born of the discordant demands made on elites by virtue of their allegiances to local and spatially extensive identity networks. Appreciation for such intra-societal tensions and their political implications is facilitated by the network perspective these authors propose.

LeCount and Canuto and Bell remind us that agents are more than capable of taking advantage of structural shifts by reorganizing social nets and redefining the symbols that materialize those affiliations (cf. Yaeger 2000). El Cafetal's rulers in the Late Classic El Paraíso basin, for example, exploited Copán's defeat by its erstwhile vassal at Quiriguá to proclaim network memberships previously denied them. These allegiances were expressed using architectural symbols formerly monopolized by representatives of the Copán state. Along similar lines, Hofling notes that Colonial policies implemented in Petén by the Spanish, such as *congregación*, established new structural conditions that discouraged some interaction strategies while encouraging others. Identity networks were reorganized as former enemies found themselves sharing the same community. Language patterns then shifted, in part to facilitate communication within the new webs.

These and other cases suggest that a recursive relation exists among social nets, the assets that travel through them, and the political, economic, and cultural structures in which these webs operate. Shifts in the movement of resources, broadly defined, across this matrix of overlapping social networks provide novel opportunities to make new choices even as they may preclude pursuit of established practices (Giddens 1984). Such choices can contribute to structural transformations through the institutionalization of novel rules by which assets needed to exercise power are acquired and deployed (ibid.; Sewell 1992). Tracing the passage of those resources and describing the varied ways they are employed by agents working in diverse social webs may be a profitable approach to understand structural change.

Reimagining the southern lowlands less as a unified culture area and more as a network of networks directs attention to how people of varied backgrounds together, if not always in harmony, create(d) cultural, political, and economic structures through their participation in social networks; the varied resources that flow(ed) through these webs and how they are/were used to underwrite political projects initiated by diverse agents; the differing spatial and temporal scales over which these nets operate(d); and the dynamism of the structures that emerge(d) as people variably cooperate(d) and compete(d) for assets across and within social nets.

This instrumentalist approach to the operation of social networks simplifies reality. Interactions are goal-oriented, with alliance networks functioning to secure resources needed to accomplish specific aims. Interpersonal dealings are not invariably calculating and competitive. It may be that such a goal-driven view of interaction is most applicable to analyses of political processes (Orser 2005:83) because efforts to secure and defend power require forging enduring alliances that link collaborators in explicit opposition to those organized along similar lines in pursuit of comparable political objectives (Hodder 1979; Knox, Savage, and Harvey 2006:125; Lightfoot and Martinez 1995:483–84). Recurrent mobilization of material and ideological resources during oft-repeated confrontations in which all parties have significant stakes reinforces a pronounced sense of self among web members who come to see each other as allies and opponents in important, life-defining transactions. Shoring up and conveying such feelings of distinctiveness often involves mobilizing physically prominent symbols of network affiliation (Goffman 1997:57–58; Hodder 1979; Lightfoot and Martinez 1995:485; Lightfoot, Martinez, and Schiff 1998:202; Schortman 1989; Spence 2005:175–76; Wiessner 1983; Wobst 1977, 1999). It is through such salient identity nets that claims to various forms of preeminence are established and legitimized.

The fact that most of the volume's chapters deal to some extent with political competition is therefore probably not accidental. Much of the ethnicity literature also relates processes of ethnogenesis to contests over political prominence. Network analysis may thus illumine competitive interactions in which securing power is at least one goal. Its relevance to describing and understanding other sorts of interpersonal dealings remains to be seen.

MATERIALITY AND SOCIAL NETWORKS

Material styles were traditionally seen as among those traits that together reflected a widespread, homogeneous, and enduring Maya identity. Ways of decorating pots, designing buildings, and organizing sites thus passively expressed widely shared assumptions and values that supposedly characterized a pan-lowland Maya culture. Recognition of considerable stylistic variation within the southern lowlands led many archaeologists in particular to question this view. Having shed old assumptions, how are we to understand the places of material styles in interpersonal interactions? The archaeologists contributing to this volume argue that distinctive motifs in diverse media were either strategically deployed to instantiate identities associated with specific social webs or arose unconsciously from the habitual practices that characterized holders of differing affiliations (this parallels Restall and Gabbert's distinction between explicit and implicit expressions of ethnicity).

How objects are implicated in social processes is not solely of interest to archaeologists. Samson, for example, references the use of painted images in ongoing contests over "Maya" identity among indigenous populations and agents of the state and tourism. More broadly, the nascent field of "materiality" is explicitly concerned with the recursive relations among agency, structure, objects, and action in all time periods (e.g., Gell 1998; Hodder 2012; Ingold 2007, 2012; Knappett 2011; Latour 2005). Debate in this domain centers especially on questions of how and to what extent objects exercise agency in their interactions with people. The archaeological case studies presented in this volume, like much of the work my colleagues and I have pursued (e.g., Schortman, Urban, and Ausec 2001), treat objects as relatively passive instruments deployed to achieve the goals of those who made and used them. Castillo Cocom's concept of *iknal* provides a provocative way of imaging a more active role for items. As a "spatial marker disembodied from the individual," a person's iknal could be indexed in part by objects intimately associated with her or him. Such associations form in the course of those interpersonal dealings in which the items figure, the objects then becoming parts of contexts that shape future interactions (cf. Gamble 1998; Orser 2005:82). Concepts such as iknal call on us to see materials as significant participants in social networks in that, once incorporated within these webs, they have the power to shape transactions in the absence of the agents the objects reference.

Rather than representations of homogeneous cultures, objects are now seen as means of expressing explicitly social affiliations that fragment and transcend territorially defined units (Allison 2008; Hart and Engelbrecht 2012; Hodder 1979; Jones 1997; Naum 2010:115; Walker and Schiffer 2006; Wobst 1977, 1999; Yaeger 2000); as instantiating, consciously or not, interpersonal connections through their exchange and use in various contexts (Chapman 2000:171; Gamble 1998; Gell

1998:83, 123; Gosden 2004:33–36; Hodder 2012:22; Hutson 2010:35, 38, 131–132; Ingold 2012:438; Latour 2005:74–75; Mauss 1967; Owoc 2005:262; Strathern 1988:164; Van Buren and Richards 2000; Walker and Schiffer 2006); and as playing active roles in shaping interpersonal dealings in which they are included (Gell 1998; Hodder 2012; Latour 2005; Wolf 1990:586). Objects are also among the assets people seek to acquire by participating in social networks (Gosden 2004:36; Schortman and Urban 2011, 2012).

As Marken and colleagues, LeCount, Canuto and Bell, and Storey note, specifying the roles materials play(ed) in these processes depends on describing the manners in which they are/were used by people operating within social nets. It is not surprising that the authors give special attention to sacred architecture and ritual paraphernalia in modeling the existence, operation, and spatial/temporal/distributions of social networks given the importance of religious observances in promoting intra-affiliation solidarity (cf. Samson, this volume). This is true whether we are considering how the Talking Cross or images of the Triad Gods figured in actions through which social webs were materialized among the cruzob in nineteenth-century Yucatán or members of different social classes at Late Classic Palenque. Storey's use of burial treatments to ferret out social affiliations elaborates on this theme, as how people are interred often speaks directly to deeply held values that are central to defining specific affiliations and their associated networks. Beyyette, LeCount, Marken and colleagues, and Canuto and Bell are careful to add that mundane objects are essential to the multiple quotidian behaviors through which people perform their senses of self in dealing with others on a daily basis.

There are clearly different approaches to modeling the ways objects ranging from pots to temples to murals are implicated in the activities through which identities are formed and social life proceeds. There is no denying, however, that it is crucial to understand the recursive relations among people and objects in the creation, maintenance, and transformation of social nets.

WHO ARE WE?

Castillo Cocom challenges us to think beyond the "Western imagery." The latter consists of such etic concepts as ethnic groups and ethnogenesis that we use to tell people who they are, how they came to be, and why they behave as they do. In keeping with the volume's theme, one might argue that this "imagery" consists of symbolic resources by which we as researchers not only understand others but enact our own social networks. The idea of a "Maya" ethnic group, in other words, defines our places in the academic firmament, positions we embody through such practices as teaching, writing, and organizing museum exhibits about the "Maya." Being a

"Mayanist" is therefore an important part of our professional identities and is integral to the strategies by which we seek employment and renown.

What are the implications of these observations? At the very least, we should acknowledge that there is a recursive relation between how we envision ourselves and the subjects of our analyses. Our senses of who we are and the manner in which we relate to others within and beyond academia are strongly conditioned by how we divide up the continuum of human cultural variation into analytical units. To be sure, as Castillo Cocom points out, power plays a large part in determining in what ways and by whom cultural variation is compartmentalized. Once created, however, these ideas have a power of their own to shape those who use them. Changing visions of the "Maya," even questioning whether such a group has ever existed, are about more than capturing and conveying the reality of indigenous behaviors and beliefs. These transformations involve a deep probing of disciplinary habitus, calling on us as investigators to reconsider seriously who we are and how we relate to the people with whom we work (Bourdieu 1977). The present volume successfully raises these disquieting issues and suggests ways we might profitably deal with them. The concept of social networks has, I believe, an important role to play in understanding and conveying the rich contingency of human lives, those we investigate, and those we ourselves pursue.

REFERENCES CITED

Allison, J. 2008. "Early Pueblo I Red Ware Exchange and Identity North of the San Juan River." In *The Social Construction of Communities: Agency, Structure, and Identity in the Prehispanic Southwest*, ed. M. Varien and J. Potter, 41–68. Lanham, MD: Altamira.

Barth, F. 1969. "Introduction." In *Ethnic Groups and Boundaries: The Social Organization of Cultural Difference*, ed. F. Barth, 9–38. Boston: Little, Brown.

Bloch, M. 1977. "The Disconnection between Power and Rank as a Process: An Outline of the Development of Kingdoms in Central Madagascar." *Archives Européennes de Sociologie* 18 (1): 107–48. http://dx.doi.org/10.1017/S0003975600003131.

Bourdieu, P. 1977. *Outline of a Theory of Practice*. Trans. R. Nice. Cambridge: Cambridge University Press. http://dx.doi.org/10.1017/CBO9780511812507.

Brumfiel, E., and J. Fox, eds. 1994. *Factional Competition and Political Development in the New World*. Cambridge: Cambridge University Press. http://dx.doi.org/10.1017/CBO9780511598401.

Chapman, J. 2000. "Tensions at Funerals: Social Practices and the Subversion of Community Structure in Later Hungarian Prehistory." In *Agency in Archaeology*, ed. M. Dobres and J. Robb, 169–95. New York: Routledge.

Cohen, A. 1969. *Custom and Politics in Urban Africa: A Study of Hausa Migrants in Yoruba Towns*. Berkeley: University of California Press.

Cohen, A. 1979. "Political Symbolism." *Annual Review of Anthropology* 8 (1): 87–113. http://dx.doi.org/10.1146/annurev.an.08.100179.000511.

Cohen, R. 1978. "Ethnicity: The Problem and Focus in Anthropology." *Annual Review of Anthropology* 7 (1): 379–403. http://dx.doi.org/10.1146/annurev.an.07.100178.002115.

Despres, L., ed. 1975. *Ethnicity and Resource Competition in Plural Societies*. The Hague: Mouton. http://dx.doi.org/10.1515/9783110898170.

Dixon, R. 1928. *The Building of Cultures*. New York: Charles Scribner's Sons.

Earle, T. 1997. *How Chiefs Come to Power: The Political Economy of Prehistory*. Stanford, CA: Stanford University Press.

Galaskiewicz, J., and S. Wasserman. 1994. "Introduction: Advances in the Social and Behavioral Sciences from Social Network Analysis." In *Advances in Social Network Analysis: Research in the Social and Behavioral Sciences*, ed. S. Wasserman and J. Galaskiewicz, xi–xvii. Thousand Oaks, CA: Sage.

Gamble, C. 1998. "Paleolithic Society and the Release from Proximity: A Network Approach to Intimate Relations." *World Archaeology* 29 (3): 426–49. http://dx.doi.org/10.1080/00438243.1998.9980389.

Gell, A. 1998. *Art and Agency: An Archaeological Theory*. Oxford: Clarendon.

Giddens, A. 1984. *The Constitution of Society: Outline of the Theory of Structuration*. Berkeley: University of California Press.

Goffman, E. 1997. *The Goffman Reader*. Ed. C. Lemert and A. Branaman. Oxford: Blackwell.

Gosden, C. 2004. *Archaeology and Colonialism: Cultural Contact from 5000 BC to the Present*. Cambridge: Cambridge University Press.

Hart, J., and W. Engelbrecht. 2012. "Northern Iroquoian Ethnic Evolution: A Social Network Analysis." *Journal of Archaeological Method and Theory* 19 (2): 322–49. http://dx.doi.org/10.1007/s10816-011-9116-1.

Hodder, I. 1979. "Economic and Social Stress and Material Culture Patterning." *American Antiquity* 44 (3): 446–54. http://dx.doi.org/10.2307/279544.

Hodder, I. 2012. *Entangled: An Archaeology of the Relationships between Humans and Things*. Oxford: Wiley-Blackwell. http://dx.doi.org/10.1002/9781118241912.

Hutson, S. 2010. *Dwelling, Identity, and the Maya: Relational Archaeology at Chunchucmil*. Lanham, MD: Altamira.

Ingold, T. 2007. "Materials against Materiality." *Archaeological Dialogues* 1: 1–16. http://dx.doi.org/10.1017/S1380203807002127.

Ingold, T. 2012. "Towards an Ecology of Materials." *Annual Review of Anthropology* 41 (1): 427–42. http://dx.doi.org/10.1146/annurev-anthro-081309-145920.

Jones, S. 1997. *The Archaeology of Ethnicity: Constructing Identities in the Past and Present*. New York: Routledge. http://dx.doi.org/10.4324/9780203438732.

Knappett, C. 2011. *An Archaeology of Interaction: Network Perspectives on Material Culture and Society*. Oxford: Oxford University Press. http://dx.doi.org/10.1093/acprof:os obl/9780199215454.001.0001.

Knox, H., M. Savage, and P. Harvey. 2006. "Social Networks and the Study of Relations: Networks as Methods, Metaphors, and Forms." *Economy and Society* 35 (1): 113–40. http://dx.doi.org/10.1080/03085140500465899.

Kroeber, A. 1939. *Cultural and Natural Areas of Native North America*. Publications in American Archaeology and Ethnology 38. Los Angeles: University of California Press.

Latour, B. 2005. *Reassembling the Social: An Introduction to Actor-Network-Theory*. Oxford: Oxford University Press.

Lightfoot, K., and A. Martinez. 1995. "Frontiers and Boundaries in Archaeological Perspective." *Annual Review of Anthropology* 24 (1): 471–92. http://dx.doi.org/10.1146/annurev.an.24.100195.002351.

Lightfoot, K., A. Martinez, and A. Schiff. 1998. "Daily Practice and Material Culture in Pluralistic Social Settings: An Archaeological Study of Culture Change and Persistence from Fort Ross, California." *American Antiquity* 63 (2): 199–222. http://dx.doi.org/10.2307/2694694.

Mann, M. 1986. *Sources of Social Power: A History of Power from the Beginning to AD 1760*, vol. 1. Cambridge: Cambridge University Press.

Marcus, J. 2000. "Toward an Archaeology of Communities." In *The Archaeology of Communities: A New World Perspective*, ed. M. Canuto and J. Yaeger, 231–42. New York: Routledge.

Mauss, M. 1967. *The Gift: Forms and Functions of Exchange in Archaic Societies*. New York: Norton.

Naum, M. 2010. "Reemerging Frontiers: Postcolonial Theory and Historical Archaeology of the Borderlands." *Journal of Archaeological Method and Theory* 17 (2): 101–31. http://dx.doi.org/10.1007/s10816-010-9077-9.

Orser, C. 2005. "Network Theory and the Archaeology of Modern History." In *Global Archaeological Theory: Contextual Voices and Contemporary Thoughts*, ed. P. Funari, A. Zarankin, and E. Stovel, 77–95. New York: Springer. http://dx.doi.org/10.1007/0-306-48652-0_7.

Ortner, S. 1995. "Resistance and the Problem of Ethnographic Refusal." *Comparative Studies in Society and History* 37 (1): 173–93. http://dx.doi.org/10.1017/S0010417500019587.

Owoc, M. 2005. "From the Ground Up: Agency, Practice, and Community in the Southwestern British Bronze Age." *Journal of Archaeological Method and Theory* 12 (4): 257–81. http://dx.doi.org/10.1007/s10816-005-8449-z.

Parker, B. 2013. "Geographies of Power: Territoriality and Empire during the Mesopotamian Iron Age." In *Territoriality in Archaeology*, ed. J. Osborn and P. Van Valkenberg, 126–44. Archaeological Papers of the American Anthropological Association, vol. 22, issue 1. New York: Wiley.

Preucel, R. 2000. "Making Pueblo Communities: Architectural Discourse at Kotyiti, New Mexico." In *The Archaeology of Communities: A New World Perspective*, ed. M. Canuto and J. Yaeger, 58–77. New York: Routledge.

Royce, A. 1982. *Ethnic Identity: Strategies of Diversity*. Bloomington: Indiana University Press.

Schortman, E. 1989. "Interregional Interaction in Prehistory: The Need for a New Perspective." *American Antiquity* 54 (1): 52–65. http://dx.doi.org/10.2307/281331.

Schortman, E., and P. Urban. 2011. *Networks of Power: Political Relations in the Late Postclassic Naco Valley, Honduras*. Boulder: University Press of Colorado.

Schortman, E., and P. Urban. 2012. "Enacting Power through Networks." *Journal of Anthropological Archaeology* 31 (4): 500–514. http://dx.doi.org/10.1016/j.jaa.2012 .04.001.

Schortman, E., P. Urban, and M. Ausec. 2001. "Politics with Style: Identity Formation in Prehispanic Southeastern Mesoamerica." *American Anthropologist* 103 (2): 312–30. http://dx.doi.org/10.1525/aa.2001.103.2.312.

Sewell, W., Jr. 1992. "A Theory of Structure: Duality, Agency, and Transformation." *American Journal of Sociology* 98 (1): 1–29. http://dx.doi.org/10.1086/229967.

Spence, M. 2005. "A Zapotec Diaspora Network in Classic Period Central Mexico." In *The Archaeology of Colonial Encounters: Comparative Perspectives*, ed. G. Stein, 173–205. Santa Fe: School of American Research.

Strathern, M. 1988. *The Gender of the Gift: Problems with Women and Problems with Society in Melanesia*. Berkeley: University of California Press. http://dx.doi.org/10.1525 /california/9780520064232.001.0001.

Sugandhi, N. 2013. "Conquests of Dharma: Network Models and the Study of Ancient Polities." In *Territoriality in Archaeology*, ed. J. Osborn and P. Van Valkenberg, 145–63. Archaeological Papers of the American Anthropological Association, vol. 22, issue 1. New York: Wiley.

Van Buren, M., and J. Richards. 2000. "Introduction: Ideology, Wealth, and the Comparative Study of Civilizations." In *Order, Legitimacy, and Wealth in Ancient States*, ed. J. Richards and M. Van Buren, 3–12. Cambridge: Cambridge University Press.

Vincent, J. 1974. "The Structuring of Ethnicity." *Human Organization* 33 (4): 375–79. http://dx.doi.org/10.17730/humo.33.4.2k10l667117p4513.

Walker, W., and M. Schiffer. 2006. "The Materiality of Social Power: The Artifact-Acquisition Perspective." *Journal of Archaeological Method and Theory* 13 (2): 67–88. http://dx.doi.org/10.1007/s10816-006-9002-4.

Wiessner, P. 1983. "Style and Social Information in Kalahari San Projectile Points." *American Antiquity* 48 (2): 253–76. http://dx.doi.org/10.2307/280450.

Wissler, C. 1917. *The American Indian*. New York: MacMurtrie.

Wobst, H. 1977. "Stylistic Behavior and Information Exchange." In *For the Director: Research Essays in Honor of James B. Griffin*, ed. C. Cleland, 317–42. Anthropological Papers 61. Ann Arbor: Museum of Anthropology, University of Michigan.

Wobst, H. 1999. "Style in Archaeology or Archaeologists in Style." In *Material Meanings: Critical Approaches to the Interpretation of Material Culture*, ed. E. Chilton, 118–32. Salt Lake City: University of Utah Press.

Wolf, E. 1990. "Distinguished Lecture: Facing Power—Old Insights, New Questions." *American Anthropologist* 92 (3): 586–96. http://dx.doi.org/10.1525/aa.1990.92.3.02 a00020.

Yaeger, J. 2000. "The Social Construction of Communities in the Classic Maya Countryside." In *Archaeology of Communities in the Ancient Americas*, ed. M. Canuto and J. Yaeger, 123–42. London: Routledge.

Contributors

McCALE ASHENBRENER, Teacher, Sage International School of Boise

ELLEN E. BELL, Associate Professor, Department of Anthropology, Geography, and Ethnic Studies, California State University, Stanislaus

BETHANY J. BEYYETTE, independent scholar

MARCELLO A. CANUTO, Associate Professor and Director, Middle American Research Institute, Anthropology, Tulane University

JUAN CASTILLO COCOM, Instructor and Researcher, Universidad Intercultural Maya de Quintana Roo, Departamento de Lenguas e Interculturalidad

DAVID A. FREIDEL, Professor, Department of Anthropology, Washington University of St. Louis

WOLFGANG GABBERT, Professor, Institute of Sociology, Leibniz Universität Hannover

STANLEY P. GUENTER, Director of Epigraphic Studies, Foundation for Archaeological Research and Environmental Studies

JONATHAN D. HILL, Professor, Department of Anthropology, Southern Illinois University, Carbondale

CHARLES ANDREW HOFLING, Professor Emeritus, Department of Anthropology, Southern Illinois University Carbondale

LISA J. LECOUNT, Associate Professor, Department of Anthropology, University of Alabama, Tuscaloosa, and Director, Actuncan Archaeological Project in Belize

MARTHA J. MACRI, Professor Emerita, Department of Native American Studies, University of California, Davis

DAMIEN B. MARKEN, Instructor, Department of Anthropology, Bloomsburg University of Pennsylvania

MATTHEW RESTALL, Professor, History, Pennsylvania State University

TIMOTEO RODRIGUEZ, Graduate Student, Anthropology Department, University of California, Berkeley

C. MATHEWS SAMSON, Associate Professor, Department of Anthropology, Davidson College

EDWARD SCHORTMAN, J. K. Smail Professor of Anthropology, Kenyon College

REBECCA STOREY, Associate Professor of Anthropology, Comparative Cultural Studies, University of Houston

Index

African arrival and immigration, 106–9
African descent, 102, 108, 110
African inferiority, 110
African slaves, 108
Afro-Yucatecans, 108–9, 223, 243, 265, 268, 271
agency, xv, 12, 35–36, 50
agricultural: community, 246; productivity, 224, 234; territory, 102
alcalde, 37
alliances, 267, 270; Chibal, 102; in Honduras, 236; between Itzas and others, 78; in Naranjo area, 175; between Xiu and Spaniards, 48
Altun Ha, 172
Amazonia, 12–13
Anasazi, 158
Appadurai, Arjun, 5
Arawak, 9, 12; language family, 13
architecture, 4–5, 9–10, 15, 151, 161, 193–98, 204, 223–24, 227, 235, 250; amalgamated, 175; city, 172; elaborate, 220; monumental, 195, 206, 221, 226; Petén, 195; religious, 162; sacred, 272; typologies, 193. *See also* house; patio; platform; structure; substructure; superstructure; sweatbaths; and temple
Aztec, 53, 166, 173, 202. *See also* Mexica
Aztlan, 202

Baking Pot, 173
ballcourt, 162
Barth, Fredrik, xiv, 5–6, 120, 157, 160–62, 166, 187–89, 191, 193, 205, 222, 230–32, 267–68
Belize, 16, 30, 73, 79, 157–76, 205, 245–47
Berdan, Frances, 12, 190, 192–93, 206
bioarchaeology, 16, 224, 243–61
blanco, 60, 111, 118
Blanton, Richard, 11, 190, 192
border, 11–12, 16, 32, 36, 63, 79, 104, 113, 160, 168, 175, 219–20, 228, 231–32, 268
Bourdieu, Pierre, 48, 50, 55–56, 163, 189, 192, 222, 273
British Industrial Revolution, 62
burial and burials, in Actuncan, 173–74; in Catholic church, 248, 256; in Copan, 245; customs and practices, 15, 151, 163–64, 173, 244, 256–57, 272; in K'axob, 256–57, 260; and osteological data, 205; in Palenque, 195; in Peten, 173; in Xunantunich, 170; in 9N8, 258, 260

cacao, 162, 169
cah, 8, 94, 97–98, 101–7, 109, 116, 118, 268
Cahal Pech, 173
Calakmul, 142–43, 162, 166, 175, 199–200

Cambodia, 201
Campeche, 42, 79, 105, 108–9, 111–12, 120–21, 123–24, 205
Cancuen, 162, 198–99
Caracol, 168, 172–73
Caribbean Sea, 169
Caribes, 79
Carrier, James, 7
Castañeda, Quetzil, 9–10, 48, 52, 91
caste, 61, 110, 114
cave, 27, 74, 79, 202
ceiba, 53–54, 67
cenote, 48, 170–71
ceramic and ceramics, 151, 205, 246, 260; bowl, 256, caches, 227; complexes, 170; economy, 228; elite, 232; fine-ware, 233; isolation, 195; jars, 227; local, 228; as mortuary offerings, 195; Palenque, 194–95; spheres, 170, 220; style, 221; Teotihuacan-inspired, 245; traditions, 194; utilitarian distribution, 206. *See also* pottery and pottery styles; vessel
ceramic assemblage, 10
Chase, Arlen, 11, 52, 170, 192, 206
Chiapas, 8, 16, 32, 36, 42, 61, 74, 77, 106–7, 133, 165, 187, 189, 194, 205
Chichén Itzá, 48, 63, 73, 77, 100, 140–41, 146–47, 150–51, 161
Chilam Balam of Chumayel, 53, 63, 73, 77, 85, 93–94, 96, 100
Chilam Balam of Maní, 99
Ch'ol, 85, 133–35, 137–38, 199
Ch'olan, 74, 77, 79–81, 85–86, 132–33, 136, 139–41, 144, 147, 149, 168, 198–99
Ch'olti', 79–80, 133, 198
Chontal, 93, 106–7, 110, 121, 123, 133, 140–41, 198–99
Ch'orti', 79–81, 133, 198–99
Christianity, 36. *See also* church
church: Catholic Church, 42, 248; church census, 108; Presbyterian church, 37; separation of church and state, 39
class, 57, 101, 163, 173, 175, 192, 206, 222, 269, 272; and dress, 112; and identity, 16, 98–99, 101–2, 114, 161, 18, 191–94, 200–201, 203–4, 221; within K'iche' society, 37; macehual, 103, 105; and marriage practice, 113, 124, 203; opposed to race, 110, 114, 119, 123; Yucatec, 98–99, 101–2, 123
class culture, 124, 191–92, 198, 204, 206, 221, 257

Classic Period, 3, 10, 15–16, 73–74, 84, 131–32, 139–42, 144, 147, 150–52, 157–59, 161–62, 164, 166–70, 172–73, 175–76, 187, 189–96, 198–99, 203–4, 206, 223–24, 228, 230–32, 234, 236, 243–46, 258, 260–61, 268
coast, 28
cobble, 228, 259–60
Cohen, Ronald, 5–7, 16, 157, 159, 222, 267
collapse, 36, 59, 105, 174, 236, 245
Colonial Period, 15, 32, 59, 85, 91–92, 100–101, 104–5, 107–8, 111, 115–16, 118, 120, 124, 198, 248
colonies, 62, 108; Spanish 59, 98, 106, 108–11; Montejos, 106; Toltec, 237
Comaroff, John, 160
commoner, 8, 11–12, 93, 98, 101–3, 116, 119, 161, 188, 192, 200, 202, 204, 206, 221, 231, 245, 250–51. *See also* elite and elites, -commoner distinctions
community of practice, 12, 159, 163, 169, 172–73
conquer, 99, 107, 234
consciousness, community, 114–15, 118–19; double-consciousness, 65; ethnic, 109, 115, 118–19; group, 166; historical, xiv–xv; race, 108; self-, 92
Copador polychrome, 228
Copán, 16, 150, 161–62, 165, 198, 219, 224–26, 228–31, 244–61, 269
Copán-style: architecture, 228, 233; ceramics, 232–33, mosaic sculpture, 226
Cordemex, 64, 149
corn, 28, 82. *See also* maize
cosmology, 30, 39–40, 191
costumbre, 34–35, 37–38
costume, 111, 113, 123, 161. *See also* dress
cotton, 112, 123, 162
covert markers of identity, 7; implied ethnicity, 104
cranial deformation, 206
cranial metrics, 247–48
cross, 28, 116–17, 119, 201–2, 206, 272
Cuello, 246, 257–58
cultural capital, 61, 192, 206
cultural politics, xiv, 9

dancer, 171
defensive works, 166
deities, 141, 158, 161, 165, 191, 194, 197, 200–203, 206

Demarest, Arthur, 11, 161–62, 220, 244
dental metrics, 247–49, 251
dental mutilation, 206
descent, 99, 111, 113, 119, 121, 202, 246; African, 102, 108; common, 5, 119, 122, 151; parallel, 9. *See also* kinship
diacritics, xiv, xv, 14, 159, 175, 222–23, 229–30, 232, 234–36
diaspora, 5, 97, 105
disease epidemics, 106
diversity, xiv, 11; cultural, 8, 14; ecological, 190; ethnic, 11–12, 106–7, 109; and identity construction, 8; of material culture, 190; social and economic, 12, 14, 159; stylistic, 175; of traditions, 8; of warriors and porters, 106
divisions: cultural, 5; ethnic, 16, 116, 188, 191, 203; geographic, 158, 200–201; language, 203; of region and class, 114, 192, 203–4; Seven Division, 167–68; social and racial, 114, 116, 267; of society, 60, 112, 266
DNA, 247
domestic economy, 11
Dos Pilas, 147, 149–50, 199–200, 260
dress, 4–5, 7–8, 37–38, 58, 111–13, 118, 120, 123, 172, 189. *See also* costume
dzul, 8, 102–3, 111, 116, 123. *See also* foreigner

Early Classic, 139, 151, 161, 223, 260
ecology, 11, 160, 167, 190
Edmonson, Munro, 77, 93–34, 100, 121–22
Egypt, 200–201, 244
El Cafetal, 225, 228–29, 231, 233–35, 237, 246, 269
El Chayal, 169. *See also* obsidian
elite and elites, 6, 12, 99, 101, 103, 113, 119; 151, 202, 233, 245; Aztec, 202; -commoner distinctions, 11, 113–14, 160, 188, 190–92, 200, 203–4, 206, 221, 231, 251, 258, 260–61, 268; and connection to deities, 194, 202; control, 6, 12, 190, 192–93, 221; in contrast to ethnicity, 198, 202; culture, 16, 36, 175, 190–92, 194–95, 206, 243, 256; dynasties, descent, and lineage, 106, 121, 150, 246, 250–51; foreign elites, 11, 99, 203; interaction, 191–93, 203–4, 206, 220, 224–26, 233–35, 260–61, 268–69; interaction with foreign groups, 190; interaction with Spaniards, 100, 103–4; isotope research on, 161–62, 251; marriages, 113, 203, 250; material culture, 10, 16, 164, 172, 191, 194–95, 200, 203, 220, 232, 235, 237, 243, 246, 256; pilgrims, 161; power,

39, 163–64, 203–4, 234, 269; prestige, 166, 233; residences and architecture, 197, 224, 226, 235, 237, 248, 250; Spaniards, 118; Spanish-speaking, 111–13, 118–19; women, 150, 161–62. *See also* burial and burials
El Paraíso, 16, 224–36
emblem glyph, 142, 158, 164–65, 173–74, 194, 200–201, 206
endogamy, 113, 122–23, 161, 244, 250
essentialism, 33, 41, 65; anti-, 31
ethnic group, 4, 6, 8–9, 11, 13–17, 32, 36, 73, 76–78, 85, 91, 110, 119, 132, 157–58, 160–62, 164–65, 175–76, 188–90, 192–93, 203, 220, 230, 233–34, 244, 266, 272
ethnicity markers, xvi
ethnicity, 3–4, 6–7, 10–17, 31, 33–36, 100, 118–20, 122, 157–58, 173, 176, 188–90, 193, 202–3, 205–6, 224, 230, 234, 236, 243–44, 266–67, 270
ethnicity definition, 3–6, 10, 13, 17, 34, 38, 104, 120, 157, 162–63, 176, 188–89, 230, 243–44, 267, 271
ethnoarchaeology, 159, 164
ethnoexodus, 4, 15, 48–51, 53–57, 63–66, 268
ethnogenesis, xiii, xiv, 4, 8–9, 11, 13–14, 30–33, 35–36, 47–53, 56, 62–66, 78, 80, 92, 100, 104–6, 115, 118–19, 131, 151, 158–62, 165–67, 169, 175–76, 222, 225, 230–34, 244, 270, 272
ethnohistoric, 7, 9, 12, 39, 42, 73, 190, 243, 245, 250
ethnohistory, 64
evangelical, 33–37, 42, 53, 63
exogamy, 77, 102, 108–9, 113, 124, 244, 268
exotic, 61, 259
exoticization, 28

factionalization, 222. *See also* ethnogenesis
Farriss, Nancy, 8, 11
Flannery, Kent, 11, 161
food, xv, 39, 163, 172, 189, 227
foreign, 11, 62, 99, 132, 142, 150, 159, 163–64, 174, 176, 190, 203, 220, 243, 246, 269
foreigner, 8, 73, 102, 110, 116, 149, 219, 237, 244
foreign speaker. *See* nun
Formative, 244–47, 256–58, 260. *See also* Preclassic
Franciscan, 59, 63, 92, 97, 100
French, 198; Enlightenment, 62; Revolution, 99, 119

frontier, 12, 15–16, 159, 161–62, 223, 225, 229, 244–46
F-Test, 251–54, 256

Garbutt Creek, 172, 175
Geertz, Clifford, 5, 35, 221
gender, 60, 62, 101, 124, 161, 164, 173, 230, 243; engendered, 116
genocide, 31
Graham, Elizabeth, 11
greenstone, 256–60

habitus, xv, 15, 50, 55–57, 63–64, 163–64, 189, 193, 195, 204, 206, 273
hacienda, 59, 112, 118
Hanks, William, 49–50, 52, 59, 63–64
hegemonic processes, 50, 159, 165–66, 169, 173–75; hegemonic discourse, 266
heterarchy, 12
heterogeneity, 9, 11, 14, 74, 116, 247, 250
hieroglyph, 10, 15, 73–74, 131–32, 140, 143, 147, 150–51, 158, 162, 165–68, 171, 173, 176, 194, 198–200, 203, 245
high culture, 191, 220
highland, 8, 10, 27–28, 31–32, 34, 40, 74, 133, 150, 158, 161–62, 169, 220
Hill, Jonathan, xiv, xvi, 9, 11, 13, 47, 78, 244
Hindu, 201
Hodder, Ian, 14, 16–17, 158–59, 162–64, 166, 172, 270–72
homogeneity, 3, 78, 92, 106, 113, 115, 151, 158, 170, 227, 271
Honduras, 16, 30, 106–7, 169, 205, 219–20, 224, 229, 236–37, 245
Hornborg, Alf, xiv, 12–13
house, xv, 139–40, 144, 146–47, 165, 169–70, 188; assemblages, 169; building technique, 164, 189–90; householder, 103; K'iche', 173; layout, 159; noble, 233; orientation, 165
Huehuetenango, 34
huipil, 173
hybridity, 142, 158–59, 162, 167, 261
hypergamy, 124

Iberian colonialism, 62
iconography, 10, 16, 28, 164, 204, 221, 236, 245
identity politics, xiii, 8, 56–59, 61, 175, 231, 234
iknal, 15, 49–51, 63–66, 271
imagined community, 3, 230

immigration, 108
incensarios, 202, 206
indígenas, 32, 51, 65, 111, 113
indigenismo, 28, 31, 38
indios, 32, 38, 56, 59, 63, 99, 111–14, 116, 118, 123–24
Inka, 166
Inomata, Takeshi, 12, 150, 161, 166–67, 194
instrumental approach to ethnicity, 5–6, 10, 13, 35, 189, 205, 221, 233, 268, 270
Itza (colonial), 73, 75, 77–79, 83, 85, 100
Itza conquest, 75, 78
Itza dialect, 106
Itzaj (language and culture), 15, 73, 75, 78–85, 133
Itzajs (people), 74, 77–79, 81, 84–85
Itzas (precontract), 73, 77–79, 85, 94, 100, 157, 176, 266
Ixtepeque, 169

Jackson, Jean, xiii, 7
jade, 162, 195, 256, 258. *See also* greenstone
Jones, Grant, 40, 73–74, 78, 83–84, 122, 167
Jones, Sian, 10, 157–59, 163, 166–67, 189, 192–93, 205–6, 244, 271
Juancy vase, 171

Kaqchikel, 30, 33–34, 37, 80, 107
Kaminaljuyu, 161
k'atun, 73, 85
K'axob, 244–51, 254–61
Kenya, 164
K'iche', 34, 36–37, 80, 107, 150, 173. *See also* Q'eqchi
kin and kin group, 122, 160, 164–65, 175, 220, 222–23
kinship, 97, 120, 176, 221, 268; and identity, 33; in relation to ethnicity, 122; structure, 11
Kowoj, 10, 73, 78, 83–85, 157
Kukulcan, 161. *See also* Quetzalcoatl

labor, 12, 52, 60, 62–64, 110, 112–13, 160, 162, 164, 167, 192–93, 235
La Florida, 232
Lakandon, 78
Lakantun, 75, 77–83, 85, 133
Landa, Diego de, 48, 92–93, 97, 109–10, 121–23
landscape, 9–10, 39, 158, 160, 170, 172; cultural, xv, 9, 159; ethnic, 4, 223–24, 234; post-Colonial, 13; religious, 34; social and political, 5, 34, 166, 174, 188, 234, 247

Late Classic, xiv, 16, 166–67, 170, 172–73, 175, 198–99, 210, 223, 225–26, 228, 233, 235, 244–46, 249–50, 257–61, 269, 272
Latin, 198
La Venta Valley, 225, 231–32
Levene test, 255
low culture, 220
lowland, 10, 27, 40, 74–75, 77, 131, 139, 142, 147, 150, 158, 161–62, 166–67, 169–73, 175, 187, 189–98, 202–3, 205–6, 233, 245–46, 249, 256–58, 265–66, 268, 270–71

Maayaj, 77, 85
macehual, 8, 103–6, 111, 114, 116, 118. *See also* commoner; masewal
maize, 58, 188, 201–2. *See also* corn
Mam, 8, 34, 37–38, 150
Marcus, George, 11
Marcus, Joyce, 11, 161, 173, 192, 206, 268
masewal, 59, 116–18. *See also* commoner; macehual
mass media, 34, 41
Maya Movement, 15, 27–42
Mayanization, 16, 42, 235–36
Mayapan, 48, 73, 77, 92–94, 97, 100–101, 105, 121, 161
Mayathan, 92–93, 103, 105, 120–21, 123
McAnany, Patricia, 11, 169–70, 189, 192, 206, 246–47, 250, 256–57, 260
Menchú, Rigoberta, 30–31, 40
Mérida, 27, 52, 58, 60, 104–6, 108–9, 112, 124
mestizaje, 38, 62
mestizo, 28, 36, 41, 59–60, 63, 105–6, 108, 111–12, 123
Mexica, 10. *See* Aztec
Mexican Revolution, 31, 60
midden, 232
military, 234; precolonial captain, 150
military conflicts, 47; precolonial, 166
missionary, Franciscan, 59
Mixtec, 107, 201–2
Mopan, 15, 73–75, 77–85, 133, 167–68, 175, 266
moreno, 108. *See also* negro
mortuary treatment, 244–45, 249, 256–61
mosaic, 226, 233, 235
Motul Dictionary, 94–95, 97, 148
mountain(s), 73, 150, 162, 174, 201
Mount Maloney, 172–73
mulato, 108–9, 116. *See also* mulatto; pardo

mulatto, 59, 103, 108, 116. *See also* mulato; pardo
multiethnic, 4–5
multilingual, 4, 30
multivariate analysis, 249, 251, 255–56
mural, 27–29, 170, 272
myth, 4, 7; and historical past, 94, 97; and identity construction, 14, 39; mythic history, 7; mythical tradition of foreign origin, 99; mythical trees, 53; mythic place, 188; mythological birth, 197, 201

Nahua, 12, 122, 144, 151; allies, 106; speakers, 37, 110, 144, 161
Nahuas, 106–7
Nahuatl, 98, 102, 144, 149
Nahualization of culture, 36
Naranjo, 143–50, 167, 171, 173, 175
narrative, xiv, 15, 28, 49, 62–64, 172, 237
Nash, June, 32
nation-states, 119; and confusion with pre-Columbian identities, 10; expansion, xvi; formation of, 60; ideology of, 60, 99; and indigenous peoples, xiii, xiv, 9, 36, 38, 249; rise of independent, xv
negro, 59, 108. *See also* moreno
nested identities, 164, 175, 205, 230
networks, 11, 42, 159, 163, 175, 236, 270; identity, 12, 66, 190–91, 266, 269–70; multi-polity, 11, 167, 236, 269; social, 13, 102, 162, 167, 204, 220, 267–73
9N-8, 248, 250–52, 255–56, 258–61
nun, 132, 147–51

Oaxaca, 106–7, 201
obsidian, 162. *See also* El Chayal; Ixtepeque
Olmec, 10, 161
Ortner, Sherry, 34–35, 268
Other, 39, 158
overt expressions of identity, 4, 7, 104–5, 115–16, 120, 266

Pacbitun, 173
Palenque, 16, 141–43, 145–47, 187, 189–90, 194–203, 206, 272
Pan-Mayanism, 9, 15, 28, 30–31, 33, 36, 58, 61, 118, 188, 202, 243, 266
pardo, 108–9. *See also* mulato; mulatto
Pasión, 143, 150, 199, 260
patio, 226, 246, 250; enclosed, 233

patronym, 8, 77–78, 83–84, 97, 100–101, 103, 112–14, 118, 121, 124, 268; Itza, 83, 100; Itzaj, 83–84; Kejach, 83; Kowoj, 83–84; Mopan, 83–84; Tipuj, 84; Yucatec, 100
Pentecost, 36–37, 42
performance, 65, 236
periphery, 3, 16, 159, 167–70, 172–73, 176, 190, 194, 219, 245–46
Peru, 159
Petén, 15–16, 73–74, 78–79, 84–85, 95, 100, 122, 142, 147, 150, 159, 162, 167–70, 172–73, 195, 199, 245–46, 269
Petén Itzá, 73, 78–79, 85, 170
Piedras Negras, 195, 197, 225
plantations, 59; and slaves, 108
plaster, 233, 235. *See also* stucco
platform, 172, 226, 228, 235; basal, 246; residential, 257. *See also* substructure
political economy, 11–12, 14
political fission, 16, 235
polity, 11, 97, 120, 160, 166–67, 172, 188–89, 192–93, 200–202, 204, 206, 221, 231–33, 236, 245–46, 250
polychrome, 195, 228
Postclassic, 10, 84, 100, 104–5, 151, 157, 161, 173, 176, 228
Portuguese, 107
pottery and pottery styles, 4, 159, 164, 172, 175, 195, 204, 206, 220, 228; and abstract motifs, 165; assemblage, 170; Classic period motifs, 172; common, 172; Copán-type, 220; costume ornaments, 161; dichotomously colored, 172; exchange, 170; fine-ware, 172, 221; international-style, 171; luxury, 170; Olmec-style, 161; Preclassic, 228. *See also* ceramic assemblage; ceramic and ceramics; Copador polychrome; Garbutt Creek; Mount Maloney; polychrome; Surlo wares; vessel
power: agentive, xv–xvi, colonial, 50, 58, 60–62, 176; communicative, xv–xvi; and construction of scientific knowledge, xvi; defense of, 270; of elites, 39, 269–70; and ethnic identity, 11, 50, 55, 57, 63, 166, 192, 271, 273; and language, 8, 34; legitimization of, 194; of nation-state, 41; powerlessness, 9; relations of, 7, 56–58, 63, 65, 204, 247; securing of, 270; shamanic, 34; and site hierarchy, 246; supernatural, 164
power struggles, 11, 59, 64, 166

practice theory, 34–36, 50, 55–57, 162–67, 175, 189, 223
Preclassic, 10–11, 139, 151, 161, 170, 172–73, 175, 220, 228, 246
prestige, 36, 132, 150–51, 161, 166, 198, 206, 220
prestige economy, 12, 161, 206, 220
Price, Barbara, 11
primordial, 163
primordialist view of ethnicity, 5–7, 13–14, 66, 157, 164, 189, 205, 220, 230, 233
processualist approach, 34, 220–21
Protestant, 33–37, 41–42
proto-classic, 245
proto-Mayan, 132, 136
Pulltrouser Swamp, 246, 260
Puuc, 27

Q'eqchi, 8, 37, 79–80, 83, 85
Quetzalcoatl, 161, 169. *See also* Kukulcan
Quetzaltenango, 33–34
Quiché, 122, 245. *See also* K'iche'
quincunx, 51, 53–54, 60, 63, 65–67
Quintana Roo, 28–29, 42, 51, 65, 118, 205
Quiriguá, 16, 219, 224–25, 229, 231, 234–37, 269

race, 47, 57–58, 108, 110–11, 119, 123–24; Indian race, 110–11; Maya race, 124; mixed, 110–11; pure, 111; and Spanish conquest, 47, 108, 110, 119; war, 114–15, 119
racial, 15, 57–60, 62, 67, 92, 99, 103–5, 108, 111, 114, 116, 119, 279
racialization, 57
raids and raiding, between indigenous peoples, 78, 116, 175; between indigenous peoples and Europeans, 116
rank, 201, 203, 206; and alliance formation, 268; and identity, 243; of settlements, 11; socioracial, 108, 110
Raxruja Viejo, 162
relational identities, 6, 189, 268
religion, 34–36, 39, 41–42, 160–61, 163. *See also* religious
religious: architecture, 162; cult, 119; groups, 6; pluralism, 42; practice, 35–39, 269, 272; landscape, 34; ties, 116; traditions, 256
repúblicas de indios, 111–13, 123
resistance, 41, 106; and Caste War, 28; Classic Maya, 167; ethnic, 28; and ethnogenesis, 230; leadership, 8

revitalization, of language, 77; movements, 80

Rice, Don, 10, 12, 73–74

Rice, Prudence, 10, 73–74, 85

ritual, 12, 14, 99, 121, 147, 164, 169, 191–92, 194, 198, 202, 205–6, 256, 260, 272; symbols, 16, 192, 204

river, 169, 236; Río Amarillo, 231; Mopan River, 79, 165, 167, 169, 175; Motagua River, 169; New River, 167–68; Pasión River, 162; Sittee River, 168; Upper Belize River, 16, 159, 167–73, 175; Usumacinta River, 147, 195, 198–99

sacrifice, 121, 175

San Bartolo, 170

Sanders, William, 11, 192

Sandstrom, Alan, 35–36

scribe, 141, 198

Schortman, Edward, xvi, 159, 161, 163–65, 189–92, 220–22, 236, 265–73

sculpture, 172, 175, 194, 202, 224–26, 233, 235

settlement, 112, 118, 165, 229, 233, 246, 268; density, 167, 169; forced, 85; hierarchy, 11, 170; patterns, 79, 165, 169–70, 205, 225–26, 228, 234; urban, 112

serpentine, 256

sexes, 120, 250–51, 256, 258

sex of skeleton, 248, 250–51, 255–56, 258

sexual dimorphism, 255

sexuality, 60, 62

shaman, 33–34, 37, 62

Shapiro-Wilk test, 251

shell, 161–62, 169, 201, 256–60

situational ethnicity, 5–7, 13–14, 66, 157, 164, 189, 205, 222

slave, 107; Atlantic slave trade, 107–8, 110; brought by Montejos, 106, importation into Mexico, 107; inter-Maya slave trade, 166

sociopolitical: complexity, 220; divisions, 267; ideology, 51; kingship system, 170; landscape, 234; world, 116, 223

South Africa, 164

Southeast Periphery, 16, 161

Spanish: alliance with Xiu, 48; arrival, 132; Caste War, 28, 47, 74, 78, 91–92, 110, 114–15, 118–20, 124; colonial accounts, 74, 92, 94, 98, 110; colonial census, 108; colonial rule, 8, 105, 109, 122, 269; conquest and invasion, 47–48, 62, 91–92, 97, 99, 105–6, 120; crown, 108, 223, 249; identity, 63; indigenous perspectives

on, 8, 98; language and terminology, 41, 78, 100–102, 104–6, 110–13, 118–19, 124; peoples, 74, 77–79, 99, 103, 106–7, 116, 122, 248; political and social strategies, 14–15, 59, 77, 92, 98, 102–4, 110, 119, 223, 269; Spanish-American colonies declare independence, 59; unity with Portuguese empire, 107–8

Staats, Susan, 7

status, 8, 15, 49–51, 54–59, 61, 64–67, 98–99, 111–14, 116, 118–19, 122, 124, 150, 158, 161–62, 166–67, 170, 175, 192, 202, 204, 221–22, 225, 230–31, 250, 256–58, 260

structure, 198; burials within, 260; funerary, 172; low, 228; monumental, 206; range, 172; residential, 222, 257; stone-faced, 226; temple, 197; vaulted, 197. See also architecture; house; patio; platform; substructure; superstructure; sweatbaths; and temple

stucco, 172, 194, 198, 226, 235; unstuccoed, 233. See also plaster

substructure, 228. See also platform

superstructure, 226, 235

Surlo wares, 228, 233

sweatbaths, 146, 196–97

symbolic capital, 31, 50, 55–57

Tabasco, 106–7, 205

temple, 187, 197, 202, 272; facades and roof-combs, 202; plans, 196; roofing style, 195

Teotihuacan, 10, 150–51, 161–62, 245

Terminal Classic, xiv, 16, 166–67, 170, 173–75

termination ritual, 175, 260. See also vessel, smashed

terrace, 165, 172, 228

territory, 49, 57, 79, 85, 102, 118, 160, 164, 173, 189, 219, 223, 233, 266–68, 271

third ethnicity, 35–36

Tikal, 143–44, 150–51, 161–62, 166, 169, 172, 175, 187, 245, 261

Tlaxcalans, 106

Toltec, 10, 161, 237

Tonina, 195

tourists, 28, 40, 63, 266

trade routes, 166, 169, 220, 224, 229, 234; communication route, 231

transactionalist approach, 221, 223, 229–30

transnational, contexts, 15, 34–35; migration, 39; space, 39

triad, 146, 170–71, 202–3, 206, 272

Tulan, 42
Tzeltal, 107, 133–39, 141–42, 187, 189
Tzotzil, 107, 133–39
tzuk, 158, 167–68

uinic, 59, 93–94, 98, 103, 121–22. *See also* winik
univariate analysis, 249, 251, 255
Usumacinta, 143, 195

vessel, 165, 172; as gifts, 172; locally made, 228; as mortuary offerings, 195, 257, 260; in Pakal's tomb, 195; prestige, 206; smashed, 175; utilitarian, 232. *See also* ceramic and ceramics; pottery and pottery styles; termination ritual
Voss, Barbara, 9, 11, 222, 230

warfare, 166, 174
Warren, Kay, xiii, 7, 31, 41

warrior, 48, 106–7, 150
water, 13, 162, 165, 167, 200, 224, 226, 256
Watanabe, John, 8, 29, 42, 60–61, 181, 190
Webster, David, 166–67, 246
winik, 78, 121, 167–68. *See also* uinic

Xiu, 27, 40, 48, 77, 85, 93–94, 99
Xunantunich, 165, 167, 169–70, 172–74

Yaxchilan, 143, 150, 195, 198, 225
Yucatán, 3, 15, 27, 31–32, 36, 42, 48, 51–52, 59–60, 63, 73, 77–79, 81, 85–86, 91–124, 132, 169, 176, 205, 219, 237, 272
Yucatec, 47–52, 58–60, 91–93, 98–111, 113, 117, 119–20, 122–23
Yukatek, 8, 15, 27–28, 73–86, 132–50, 198

Zapatista, 32, 41
Zapotec, 10, 107

www.ingramcontent.com/pod-product-compliance
Lightning Source LLC
Chambersburg PA
CBHW070911030426
42336CB00014BA/2366